ANTI-AMERICANISMS IN WORLD POLITICS

A VOLUME IN THE SERIES

Cornell Studies in Political Economy

edited by Peter J. Katzenstein

A list of titles in this series is available at www.cornellpress.cornell.edu.

ANTI-AMERICANISMS IN WORLD POLITICS

EDITED BY **Peter J. Katzenstein**
and **Robert O. Keohane**

Cornell University Press ITHACA AND LONDON

First published 2007 by Cornell University Press
First printing, Cornell Paperbacks, 2007

Printed in the United States of America

Library of Congress Cataloging-in-Publication Data

Anti-Americanisms in world politics / edited by Peter J. Katzenstein and Robert O. Keohane.
    p. cm. – (Cornell studies in political economy)
    Includes bibliographical references and index.
    ISBN-13: 978-0-8014-4517-0 (cloth : alk. paper)
    ISBN-10: 0-8014-4517-5 (cloth : alk. paper)
    ISBN-13: 978-0-8014-7351-7 (pbk. : alk. paper)
    ISBN-10: 0-8014-7351-9 (pbk. : alk. paper)
    1. Anti-Americanism.   2. United States–Foreign public opinion.   3. United States–Relations–Foreign countries.   4. United States–Foreign relations–2001–
I. Katzenstein, Peter J.   II. Keohane, Robert O. (Robert Owen), 1941–   III. Series.
    E895.A45 2006
    303.48'273–dc22   2006019347

Cornell University Press strives to use environmentally responsible suppliers and materials to the fullest extent possible in the publishing of its books. Such materials include vegetable-based, low-VOC inks and acid-free papers that are recycled, totally chlorine-free, or partly composed of nonwood fibers. For further information, visit our website at www.cornellpress.cornell.edu.

Cloth printing   10   9   8   7   6   5   4   3   2   1

Paperback printing   10   9   8   7   6   5   4   3   2   1

For the Center for Advanced Study in the Behavioral Sciences

Contents

Preface

Talking to friends and associates is an intriguing test of the interest people outside one's field of research take in a book project. Eyes often glaze over as we begin to describe the politics of small states or the procedures of international organizations, and they do so even more if we try to explain some abstractions of contemporary political science. When we started this book on anti-Americanism, however, our interlocutors, who might formerly have viewed us as harmless pedants studying abstruse subjects, suddenly took a visceral interest in our work. Americans, at least, seem to care about anti-Americanism. Even if they don't believe that "they hate us," they are both puzzled and worried by evidence that the United States, and Americans, are distrusted by many people around the world. "Why do they dislike us?" is a question that resonates in Durham, Ithaca, and Princeton.

Working on a subject of such topical interest is energizing. However, it is also risky, since people who have not studied the subject in depth often have well-formulated ideas or prejudices about it that are not easily dislodged. The very concept of "anti-Americanism" is often tinged with political opinion. We repeatedly had to interrogate ordinary language and common sense understandings of our subject. Many people, for example, vastly overestimate the incidence of anti-Americanism, forgetting that until the run-up to the Iraq War, polls consistently showed that pro-American sentiments, worldwide, dominated anti-American sentiments by a wide margin. Others associate anti-Americanism distinctively with countries such as France, occasionally mistaking opinions and sentiments of the French elite for those of the French public. Perhaps the worst misconceptions are found in universities, where academics who have not studied the subject are eager to enunciate their favored single-factor explanation for anti-Americanism—be it resentment, psychopathology, or President George W. Bush and his policies.

We, however, do not think there is one master explanation for anti-Americanism. As the title of this book indicates, we do not even think that anti-Americanism constitutes a homogeneous phenomenon that in principle could be explained in a parsimonious way. On the contrary, we distinguish several different types of anti-Americanism. Hence the title: *Anti-Americanisms in World Politics*. We insist that understanding the variety of forms anti-Americanism can take is the beginning of wisdom on this subject.

Our principal debts are to the other authors of this book. We have learned a tremendous amount from each of them. We asked some of them for numerous revisions of draft chapters that were already very strong. And we are deeply grateful for the good spirit with which they accommodated us during their normal, busy academic years, while we were on sabbatical.

For helpful conversations and trenchant comments on various drafts of this book we also thank: Rawi Abdelal, Vinod Aggarwal, Naazneen Barma, Timothy Byrnes, Lars-Erik Cederman, Kiren Chaudhry, Jeff T. Checkel, Tom Christensen, Cathy Davidson, Dale Eickelman, Philip Everts, Page Fortna, Peter A. Gourevitch, Peter Haas, Peter Hall, Ole Holsti, Donald Horowitz, John Ikenberry, Bruce Jentleson, Mary Katzenstein, Nannerl O. Keohane, Gary King, Piotr Kosicki, Stephen D. Krasner, David Lake, Jeff Legro, David Leheny, Andrei Markovits, Rose McDermott, Barak Mendelsohn, John Meyer, Helen Milner, Layna Mosley, Norman Naimark, Joseph S. Nye, Louis Pauly, Thomas Risse, John Gerard Ruggie, Robert Satloff, Gebhard Schweigler, Kathryn Sikkink, Jack Snyder, Janice Stein, Yaacov Vertzberger, Nancy Wadsworth, Steven Weber, Lisa Wedeen, and Michael Zürn.

One of the main ways we learned about the complexities of our subject was through a series of workshops for which specialists wrote memos that were enormously helpful in our conceptualization of the project. Christopher Candland, Bruce Cumings, Katharine H. S. Moon, Shelley Rigger, and Tianjian Shi taught us much about anti-Americanism in East Asia at a conference at Duke University in February 2004. We learned about anti-Americanism in the Middle East and Africa from Lisa Anderson, Kiren Chaudhry, Erik Nisbet, Farideh Farhi, Jonathan Howard, Quinn Mecham, Devra Coren Moehler, and Nic Van de Walle at a conference at Cornell University in April of that year. John Borneman, Patrick Chamorel, and Andrei Markovits wrote illuminating memos for a conference on European anti-Americanism at the Center for Advanced Study in the Behavioral Sciences, in Palo Alto, California, in November 2004.

In addition to these regional workshops, we held three other workshops at the Center for Advanced Study—in January, April, and June 2005—at which draft chapters were presented, critiqued, defended, and generally worked over.

A number of colleagues participated in either the regional workshops or the chapter-oriented workshops. We are very thankful for the insights we gained from Rick Baum, Russell Berman, Cynthia Brandt, Patrick Chamorel, Dale Eickelman, Cynthia Epstein, Matthew Evangelista, James Fearon, Peter Feaver, Christopher Gelpi, Judith Goldstein, Joseph Grieco, Charles Hirschkind, David Hollinger, Joseph Joffe, Miles Kahler, Mary F. Katzenstein, Nannerl O. Keohane, Jonathan Kirshner,

Ruud Koopmans, Stephen D. Krasner, Tod Lindberg, Barak Mendelsohn, Norman Naimark, Emerson Niou, Erik Nisbet, Mary Nolan, Suzanne Nossel, Sam Popkin, Loren Ryter, Susan Shirk, Nicole Speulda, Julia Sweig, Shibley Telhami, Michael Tomz, Chris Way, and Mayer Zald.

Our greatest debt of gratitude goes to four colleagues who have made suggestions that proved invaluable for improving our thinking about this book: Peter Gourevitch, David Laitin, Henry Nau, and Paul Sniderman.

Special thanks go to Lynn Gale of the Center for Advanced Study in the Behavioral Sciences for statistical analysis of the Global Market Insite data and to Ken Pick for making the GMI data available to us without charge. And we thank our colleagues at the Center for the innumerable personal conversations that yielded insights that may have been of more value to us than our friends ever realized.

We are also grateful to those who invited us to present our findings before audiences of graduate students, faculty members, and foreign policy experts: Vinod Aggarwal and Steve Weber of the University of California, Berkeley, who invited us for a session with graduate students on March 29, 2005; Peter D. Feaver and Bruce Jentleson, who organized a conference, including discussions of anti-Americanism, at the Woodrow Wilson International Center for Scholars, February 15, 2005; Peter A. Gourevitch of the University of California, San Diego, who invited us to present some of our findings about Europe, April 14, 2004; Tod Lindberg of the Hoover Institution, who hosted a meeting of the Princeton Project on National Security, February 17, 2005, and Suzanne Nossel of the Princeton Project, who cochaired the meeting; Louis Pauly and Janice Stein of the Munk Centre of the University of Toronto, who ran a daylong conference devoted to our book, February 3, 2006; B. Peter Rosendorff of the University of Southern California, who invited us for a presentation on April 28, 2005; Scott Sagan of the Center for International Security and Arms Control, Stanford University, who invited us for a presentation on May 26, 2005.

Kennette Benedict lent a sympathetic ear when we approached her and the John D. and Catherine T. MacArthur Foundation for financial support. We also learned a great deal from the comments of Foundation staff members at a discussion convened by the president, Jonathan Fanton, on December 2, 2004.

This book might never have materialized without the enthusiasm of the director of the Center for Advanced Study, Doug McAdam, during our planning process, between 2003 and 2005. We appreciate his unwavering intellectual, logistical, and personal support, and that of his staff and board, in making this a Center project. At our behest, he joined the project as an author, contributing what appears below as chapter 9. Our universities—Cornell University and Duke University (where Robert Keohane was on the faculty until February 1, 2005)—provided generous financial support for our workshops and a scholarly and teaching environment conducive to study and reflection.

Two anonymous readers at Cornell University Press helped all the authors with their insightful comments in preparing the final versions of their chapters. Roger Haydon proved once again that his high reputation in academic publishing is richly deserved. The team of John Raymond and Katy Meigs showed once again that copy-editing is a skill that can become an art. Karen Hwa oversaw production of the manuscript with her customary efficiency and good will. And Sarah Tarrow helped in the final coordination and meeting all the deadlines.

Once again we thank the contributors to this book for their comments and criticisms, as well as for their own contributions. They were active participants in the workshops and collaborated in ways that went beyond normal academic bounds, working to conceptualize the book as a whole.

Throughout our careers, both our work and our personal lives have been immensely enriched by our wives and partners, Mary Fainsod Katzenstein and Nannerl Overholser Keohane. Their criticisms have always been trenchant and constructive. They, unfailingly, have aimed at the center of our work. And they, unfailingly, continue to be at the center of our lives.

Finally, the Center for Advanced Study in the Behavioral Sciences is an extraordinary place with extraordinary people. We therefore dedicate this book to the Center in the hope that it will continue to stimulate creative thinking in the social sciences for many years to come.

Peter J. Katzenstein

Ithaca, New York
February 2006

Robert O. Keohane

Princeton, New Jersey
February 2006

ANTI-AMERICANISMS IN WORLD POLITICS

Introduction: The Politics of Anti-Americanisms

ROBERT O. KEOHANE

and PETER J. KATZENSTEIN

In 1941 Henry Luce spoke of the coming of "the American Century."[1] Today commentators across the political spectrum emphasize America's dominant military capabilities and economic strength. Many observers have also argued that the United States uniquely benefits from the wave of economic liberalization and democratization that followed the end of the cold war. Joseph S. Nye has coined a catchy phrase, "soft power," to suggest the importance of being admired, so that "others want what you want."[2] Nye argued that the United States has commanded a lot of soft power. Indeed, with the end of the cold war it seemed for a short while as if the United States was in a "virtuous circle," in which its success caused it to be more admired, which in turn enhanced its influence, and thus furthered its success.

Yet after sixty years of global leadership, the United States is far from universally admired worldwide. After the 9/11 attacks, there was an outpouring of grief and sympathy for the United States and Americans in many parts of the world. But little more than a year later, on February 15, 2003, the world witnessed the largest global mass demonstration in history, protesting the impending U.S. attack on Iraq. A poll by the Pew Research Center for the People and the Press of sixteen thousand people showed that in the spring of 2003 majorities in only four of the fourteen countries that were also surveyed in 1999–2000 and 2002 held favorable opinions of the United States. By contrast, in both 1999–2000 and the summer of 2002, majorities in ten of the same fourteen countries had reported favorable views of the United States.[3] A

---

1. Luce 1941.
2. Nye 2002, 8–12.
3. Pew Research Center 2005d and 2005e. See also Politi 2003, Marquis 2003, Clymer 2002. Results of the Pew polls can be found at http://www.people-press.org (accessed March 16, 2006).

series of polls taken in the winter of 2004–5 showed that in sixteen of twenty-two countries surveyed a plurality or majority of the public said that the United States had mainly a negative influence in the world, and in twenty countries a plurality or majority expressed the view that it would be a positive development for Europe to be more influential than the United States in world affairs.[4] What is commonly called "anti-Americanism"—the expression of negative attitudes toward the United States—has spread far and wide, including in parts of the world where publics showed deep sympathy with the United States after the 9/11 attacks.

The sensitivity of Americans to these expressions of dislike may say as much about America as about others' views of the United States. Alexis de Tocqueville commented on this subject in the mid-nineteenth century:

> The Americans, in their intercourse with strangers, appear impatient of the smallest censure and insatiable of praise. . . . They unceasingly harass you to extort praise, and if you resist their entreaties they fall to praising themselves. It would seem as if, doubting their own merit, they wished to have it constantly exhibited before their eyes.[5]

The undeniable upsurge in the expression of anti-American sentiment abroad since 2002 has led to anxieties among many Americans. It is not obvious, however, whether these sentiments are primarily a reaction to the Bush administration and its policies or whether they derive from more fundamental sources. As a way of distinguishing between fundamental and ephemeral sources of anti-Americanism, we begin in chapter 1 with a distinction, made by many commentators, between disliking "what America *is*" and "what America *does*." The ephemeral parts of anti-Americanism are linked to what America does, that is, American policies and the effects they have on others. The more fundamental sources of anti-Americanism refer to what America is. They include the fact that since the end of the cold war the United States has attained a position of unchallenged military power. The United States has intervened militarily throughout the world in a way that recalls empires of the past, whether it is technically an empire or not. Anti-imperial sentiments recur throughout history, as reflected in the experiences of the Chinese, Ottoman, Habsburg, British, and other European empires. Other fundamental factors include the sharp differences in public attitudes between Americans and Europeans with respect to social welfare issues, the death penalty, and the construction of binding treaties on such questions as land mines and human rights. Still other possible deep sources of anti-Americanism could include resentment of American wealth, and of America's dominant role in economic and social globalization.

Yet anti-Americanism fluctuates too much for it to be just a matter of what America is. The United States was as wealthy and powerful in the 1990s as in the years after 2002, yet as we have seen, anti-American attitudes seem to have been less widespread in the earlier years. Likewise, differences between European and

---

4. PIPA 2005.
5. Tocqueville 1994 [1835], 252, quoted in Toinet 1988, 137.

American attitudes toward such issues as the welfare state go back many decades. How much of anti-Americanism, then, is fundamental, how much ephemeral?

This book contains evidence bearing on these questions. The contributors have brought analysis, from different social science disciplines and with multiple methodologies, to bear on what is called anti-Americanism.[6] We have systematically deployed the tools of social science: examining in detail the profile of anti-American attitudes across space and time; asking questions about the conditions that shape the politics of anti-Americanism in different contexts; focusing on the dynamic changes that affect anti-Americanism; inquiring into the political effects of anti-Americanism; and bringing new evidence and interpretation to bear on different facets of this important political issue. The editors developed questions to be asked in different contexts and commissioned authors who were qualified to answer them.[7] We have done so in order to clarify the forms that anti-Americanism takes and to enable us to make more informed inferences about its sources and consequences.

Part I places anti-Americanism in the context of Americanism, by examining the concept of anti-Americanism and various types of anti-Americanisms, and by discussing the images of America held by people abroad, from 1492 onward. Chapter 1, by the editors, develops the conceptual framework for this book. We emphasize the multidimensionality and heterogeneity of anti-Americanism and the ambivalence often associated with it. We point out the importance of distinguishing among *opinion, distrust,* and *bias,* and we develop a typology of different varieties of anti-Americanism. Our emphasis on the variety of anti-Americanisms accounts for the title of the book.

But we do not focus exclusively on anti-Americanism. For a full understanding of negative views of the United States, and the politics that accompany these views, we have to place anti-Americanism within the broader context of attitudes, positive as well as negative, toward the United States. We want to know under what conditions individually held attitudes toward the United States become collectively believed views, and when anti-American discourses and policies prevail.

To understand anti-Americanism, we also need to understand "Americanism."[8] The diversity of anti-Americanisms is due to the diversity of America. As a country of settlers and immigrants, the United States represents a very broad spectrum of values, stretching from an entertainment industry that dominates key sectors of global popular culture to a publicly salient religiosity that is unique among the advanced industrial states. The heterogeneity of anti-Americanism is matched by the

6. Anti-Americanism has been the subject of many recent studies, which include Markovits 2006, Behrens, von Klimó, and Poutrus 2005, Judt and Lacorne 2005, Steinberg 2005, Levy, Pensky, and Torpey 2005, Telhami 2005, *Economist* 2005a and 2005b, Rubin and Rubin 2004, Hollander 2004b, Markovits 2004a and b, Berman 2004, Ross and Ross 2004, Ceaser 2003, Sardar and Davies 2002, Shiraev and Zubok 2000, Kaase and Kohut 1996, Granatstein 1996, Kroes and van Rossem 1986, Rubinstein and Smith 1985, Haseler 1985, Rubinstein and Smith 1985.

7. This research project extended over eighteen months and convened six workshops in which a large number of highly knowledgeable scholars commented on various drafts of the chapters in this book, which were repeatedly revised and greatly improved.

8. Hertsgaard 2002, Ceaser 1997, Rosenberg 1982, Gerbi 1973, O'Gorman 1961.

heterogeneity of Americanism. The United States is a bundle of tensions and contradictions: intensely secular and intensely religious, unilateralist and multilateralist, statist and antistatist. That is, American symbols refer simultaneously to a variety of values, which may appeal differentially to different people in different societies and, despite their contradiction, may appeal even to the same person at one time. Furthermore, as David Kennedy shows in chapter 2, from Europe's first awareness after 1492, America has been a subject of fascination and interpretation. The image of America abroad, and America's image of itself, have moved in parallel, but they have often been at odds with each other. Both anti-Americanism and pro-Americanism, as attitudes held by people outside the United States, draw on rich and varied images of America as well as on the complexity of American life and the impact of the United States on the world. Arguments about the United States by Americans are often equally intense: Americans are divided about many aspects of their own country. We need to remember that many of the conflicts in world politics that manifest different forms of anti-Americanism have strong echoes within the American polity.

When most people think about studies of anti-Americanism, they think about polling results, which are often publicized in the media. Sophisticated analysis of polling data is very important for an understanding of anti-Americanism. Part 2 is devoted to this topic. In chapter 3, Pierangelo Isernia examines European views toward the United States during the cold war and how they changed under the pressure of events. With great sophistication, he demonstrates that the European public had quite well-structured cognitions about the United States and that U.S. foreign policy, perceived cultural differences, and direct contacts with U.S. soldiers played important roles in shaping attitudes. There is no indication that anti-American views were either irrational or deeply embedded in the European public's consciousness. Indeed, Isernia shows that between 1952 and 2001 views of the United States in Europe were consistently quite favorable. They have fluctuated around a level at which more than twice as many Europeans have expressed favorable than unfavorable views of the United States. Giacomo Chiozza demonstrates in chapter 4 that the upsurge of anti-American opinion around the world since 2002 is something new. In 2002, majorities in thirty-five of forty-two countries surveyed by the Pew Research Center held favorable views of the United States.[9] In a detailed analysis of Pew's 2002 results, Chiozza demonstrates that attitudes toward the United States are multidimensional and nonideological. Very few people uniformly dislike the United States. Rather, they tend to discriminate between features of American society that they like and those they dislike. Attitudes toward the United States are overwhelmingly most negative in the Middle East. Yet even in this angry region, since attitudes are multidimensional, overall judgments vary, depending on the perceived salience of different aspects of the United States.

Polling data alone, however, do not enable us to understand the formation and activities of social movements and political organizations, the political strategies of

9. Pew Research Center 2002, 53–55.

politicians, or the policies pursued by government officials. The politics of anti-Americanism in all its richness and diversity requires a more contextual and qualitative approach. Part 3 therefore turns to intensive examinations of the views of the United States, and the politics that accompanies such views, in three important countries: France, Egypt, and China. In the case of Egypt, the focus is also on the Arab world in general, of which Egypt is a major part.[10] We asked the authors of these chapters not only to explore views of the United States in general but also to address three other sets of issues. We asked them to examine issues involving relations with the United States of particular relevance to the polity in question—issues that might be unimportant to other countries such as Taiwan for China, the Israeli-Palestinian conflict for Egypt, and Google's effort to develop library search engines for France. We also asked them to examine at least one nonpolitical issue with no apparent linkage to relationships with the United States. This permits us to explore to what extent anti-Americanism, when generated by hot-button political issues, has an impact on political views and behavior on quite separate dimensions of activity. In particular, we asked the three authors to explore reactions to the U.S.-led tsunami relief effort in the winter of 2005, which we use in chapter 1 as a way to examine the difference between negative opinion of the United States, on the one hand, and deep distrust or bias, on the other.[11]

Part 4 moves the focus away from political science toward sociology and anthropology. In chapter 8 John Bowen compares anti-Americanism in Indonesia and France, societies he knows extremely well. In both polities recent polls have shown widespread disapproval of the United States. Bowen's research yields two main findings: negative schemas help to structure these unfavorable attitudes, and these schemas are much more deep-seated in France—and not only among Muslims—than in Indonesia. Indonesian views of the United States are therefore more volatile than those in France. In chapter 9 Doug McAdam examines anti-Americanism as "contentious politics." Looking at anti-Americanism through this lens yields some surprising insights into the often unanticipated long-term consequences, or legacies, of episodes of anti-Americanism, sometimes leading to the institutionalization of distrust or bias and at other times reversing course and yielding a more pro-American orientation than one might have expected.

The chapters in parts 2 through 4 employ different methodologies, but they share a common view of the problem. Negative actions toward the United States, taken by governments, groups, or individuals, are affected by individual attitudes, especially in democracies. But actions do not follow directly from attitudes. For anti-Americanism to have a political impact, some mixture of negative opinion, distrust, and bias must be mobilized by social movements or by institutions such as political

10. Our need for coherence, and for limiting the topic sufficiently to discuss it in one book, led us to focus on Europe, East Asia, and the Middle East, and to omit analysis of anti-Americanism in Latin America, where it has a long history, and in Africa, where attitudes toward the United States remain on the whole quite positive.

11. Because it is particularly germane, the chapters on France and China also examine consumer behavior in the context of anti-Americanism, a subject that, among others, we also treat in chapter 10.

parties. Whether such mobilization occurs is likely to play a crucial role in determining whether negative views of the United States have significant political effects. Without such mobilization, it is unlikely that such effects will endure. Yet without some level of negative opinion, distrust, or bias toward the United States, there is little for political entrepreneurs to mobilize. Since both top-down organization and bottom-up shifts in attitudes are necessary for anti-Americanism to have a serious political impact, this book studies both processes.

In chapter 10 we examine the consequences of anti-Americanism. Using new empirical research, we show that specific, short-term effects of anti-Americanism, which one might expect to find, are not apparent. Indeed, there have been remarkably few negative general consequences of anti-Americanism for U.S. diplomacy relating to issues such as the war on terror, and traces of the impact of anti-American public sentiments are difficult to discover even with respect to membership in the "coalition of the willing" or responses to U.S. policies regarding the International Criminal Court (ICC). As a result of our analysis, we believe that the burden of proof has been shifted to those who argue that anti-Americanism has immediate and direct effects on world politics. There are good reasons, however, to expect that anti-American views may have indirect or delayed effects on policy. We therefore inquire into some of the conditions that may facilitate or impede such effects. A null finding on short-term, direct consequences should not be interpreted as a claim that anti-Americanism does not matter.

Expressions of anti-American sentiments vary greatly across time and space. Instead of a single anti-Americanism we find a variety of anti-Americanisms. Negative views of the United States wax and wane with political events, in different rhythms, in different parts of the world, in countries with very different kinds of politics. Anti-Americanism may lie dormant for long periods, yet sudden shifts in environmental conditions or deliberate policy can activate it, with either temporary or longer-term effects, but rarely with direct and immediate consequences for government policies.

In the concluding chapter we address the central puzzle that this book's research and interpretation has generated. Why is there such a persistence of varied anti-Americanisms? And why are the immediate effects limited? Broadly speaking, our answer to this puzzle comes back to the nature of America itself. America is "polyvalent." It combines within itself such a diversity of values and variety of ways of life that it readily serves as an object of both disapproval and approval in many different polities or in the same polity over time. Just as Americans look to the world as a mirror in which they see themselves—and wish to see themselves as better than they are—non-Americans look to the United States as a mirror that reflects their own hopes, fears, and faults.

I

ANTI-AMERICANISM AND AMERICANISM

1

Varieties of Anti-Americanism: A Framework for Analysis

PETER J. KATZENSTEIN and ROBERT O. KEOHANE

Anti-Americanism has a historical pedigree dating back to the eighteenth century. Since World War II such sentiment has waxed and waned in various parts of the world. American GIs were welcomed widely in the 1940s as liberators of a Europe occupied by Nazi Germany, and as protectors of a Europe that felt threatened by the Soviet Union in the 1950s. Yet a few years later the "ugly American" became an object of scorn and derision.[1] In the second half of the 1960s the U.S. war in Vietnam became a rallying cry for a powerful antiwar movement that fueled anti-American sentiments in Europe, Latin America, and Asia. In the early 1980s mass protests against NATO's missile deployment plans and the military buildup of the Reagan administration erupted. Between 2002 and 2006 intense expressions of anti-American sentiment—both in public opinion polls and in political demonstrations—have been evident around the globe. Anti-Americanism is again front page news, and many Americans are perplexed by its global spread.

During the course of the academic year 2004–5 we gave talks based on ideas in this book and presented earlier versions of it repeatedly at the Center for Advanced Study in the Behavioral Sciences. We thank our colleagues at the Center, and the other authors of chapters in this book, for their valuable suggestions. We also presented versions of our argument at a conference at the Woodrow Wilson International Center for Scholars, February 15, 2005; at a meeting of the Princeton Project on National Security, February 17, 2005; at Steven Weber's graduate seminar at the University of California, Berkeley, on March 23, 2005; and at the University of Southern California on April 28, 2005. Participants at all of those gatherings made cogent and useful comments. We are particularly grateful for focused oral or written comments from Doug McAdam of the Center for Advanced Study in the Behavioral Sciences, Palo Alto; Roger Haydon of Cornell University Press; Stephen Krasner of Stanford University; Vinod Aggarwal and Steven Weber of the University of California, Berkeley; and Yaacov Vertzberger of the East-West Center, University of Hawaii.

1. Lederer and Burdick 1958. The title of this book was ironic; the "ugly American" was actually a hero. But the phrase stuck while the plot of the novel was largely forgotten.

One way of beginning to think about expressions of negative attitudes is to ask whether they are based on views of "what the United States *is*"—the fundamental values and attitudes of U.S. society—or "what the United States *does*"—its policies, particularly its foreign policies. Negative views of what the United States is are less likely to change, as U.S. policy changes, than are negative views of what the United States is doing. People who are negative about the United States itself are more likely to be biased, as we define the term below, than those who are critical only of a set of American policies. It is particularly important, therefore, in an investigation of anti-Americanism, to distinguish between *is* and *does*, and between opinion and bias. Part of our task in this chapter is to explore this distinction.

This book, however, is not merely an analytical exercise in political science. We study politics because we believe that it matters for human life and happiness and because we think that understanding of politics can improve policy. It is therefore important at the outset to point out some policy implications of the findings that we will describe in detail below.

Our findings in this book suggest that the positions on anti-Americanism of both Left and Right are internally inconsistent. Broadly speaking, the American Left holds that anti-Americanism as measured by polls is what we define below as opinion rather than bias. It is largely a reaction to U.S. policy and, indeed, often a justified reaction. The Left also frequently suggests that anti-Americanism poses a serious long-term problem for U.S. diplomacy and that right-wing policies that induce it therefore need to be changed. But insofar as anti-Americanism reflects ephemeral opinion, changes in policy should be greeted enthusiastically by those who had earlier expressed negative views toward the United States. The long-term effects of· anti-Americanism should therefore be small, unless periods of intense negative opinion lead to significant social movements or enduring institutional change. Conversely, the American Right argues that anti-Americanism reflects a deep bias against the United States: people who hate freedom hate us for what we are. Yet the Right also tends to argue that anti-Americanism can be ignored: if the United States follows effective policies, views will follow. But since the essence of bias is the rejection of information inconsistent with one's prior view, broadly biased foreign publics should not be expected to change their opinions quickly in response to successes scored by a country that they fear and detest. Both Left and Right need to rethink their positions.

The Left is correct that anti-Americanism, as measured by polls, largely reflects opinion and is closely tied to U.S. policy. The Left worries that much anti-Americanism increasingly expresses a deeper form of negative attitude, which we denote as distrust. The Right overestimates resentment of American power and hatred of American values; and it overlooks the political salience of the distrust that American actions can create. If the Right were correct, anti-Americanism would have risen sharply in the 1990s, after the collapse of the Soviet Union. But as Giacomo Chiozza shows in chapter 4, except in the Middle East the United States remained broadly popular until 2002. This is not to deny that some expressions of anti-Americanism are so distrustful that they verge on bias. Such bias may be revealed by the reactions of the Greek and French publics, discussed below, to U.S. efforts at tsunami relief.

If the view of the Left on the sources of anti-Americanism seems better grounded on the whole than that of the Right, the story is different with regard to consequences. The Right is correct that the consequences of anti-American views are more difficult to detect than one would think on the basis of claims made by the Left. There is much to be said for the view (not limited to the Right) that the United States should concentrate on pursuing ethically justified and practically effective policies rather than focusing on anti-Americanism as such. Superficial manifestations of anti-Americanism seem to have few systematic effects on policy. The Right is therefore broadly on target in its claim that insofar as anti-Americanism reflects short-term and volatile opinion rather than long-term institutionalized bias, it does not pose serious problems for U.S. foreign policy.

The key question is whether negative opinion hardens into distrust or even bias, as it has among some religious fundamentalists in the Islamic world. If opinion hardens into distrust as appears to have happened in recent years in Europe, China, and in secular strata in the Arab Middle East, the political consequences for the medium and long term could be severe. If the United States becomes more associated around the world with human rights abuses at Abu Ghraib prison and Guantánamo than with the Statue of Liberty and rock music, anti-Americanism could in the future become an important impediment to a successful U.S. foreign policy. Many Mideast specialists think that this hardening of anti-American views has accelerated at an alarming rate. Episodic evidence reported in the press confirms these well-informed assessments. "For many Muslims," Somini Sengupta and Salman Masood report, "Guantánamo stands as a confirmation of the low regard in which they believe the United States holds them. For many non-Muslims, regardless of their feelings toward the United States, it has emerged as a symbol of American hypocrisy."[2] For an Indian cartoonist, lampooning the Bush administration, the simple fact is that "people suspect American intentions. It has nothing to do with being Muslim."[3] Preposterous as it may seem to most Americans, for many the world over the United States has built in Guantánamo what the French newspaper *Le Monde* has called a legal monster that undermines trust in the United States.

In this chapter we establish a framework of concepts and questions that we use throughout the book to explore the sources and consequences of anti-Americanism. Our conceptualization of anti-Americanism distinguishes among its cognitive, emotional, and normative components. We argue that anti-Americanism is heterogeneous and multidimensional. Many of the subsequent papers discuss, in different contexts, the concepts of opinion, distrust, and bias that we analyze below. Indeed, we asked the authors of the chapters on France, Egypt, and China to examine reactions to U.S. tsunami relief efforts in January 2005, so that we could compare the public discourses on U.S. tsunami relief with the comparative polling data that we

---

2. Sengupta and Masood 2005, A6.
3. Ibid.

present in this chapter. The typology of anti-Americanisms that we offer here is designed, in part, to assist the comparative analyses of France, Egypt, and China in part 3 of this book; without accepting it entirely, the authors of those three chapters all make use of it. In our typology, there are four main types, which scale from being less to more deeply experienced. There also are particularistic and historically sensitive forms of anti-Americanism. In any particular situation we expect anti-Americanism to result from different constellations of the different forms and types that "bleed" into each other in variable constellations, activated by political entrepreneurs and manipulated through political processes.

Conceptualizing Anti-Americanism

We begin with a definition of anti-Americanism since the term is used so broadly (and often loosely) in ordinary language. As our analysis continues in this chapter, we will develop a typology of anti-Americanism. In the broadest sense, we view anti-Americanism as *a psychological tendency to hold negative views of the United States and of American society in general.* Such views draw on cognitive, emotional, and normative elements. Using the language of psychology, anti-Americanism could be viewed as an *attitude.*[4] On further examination, anti-Americanism becomes much more complex than this broad definition suggests. We distinguish below among opinion, bias, and distrust, any of which could be reflected in poll results showing "unfavorable" attitudes toward the United States. Bias is the most fundamental form of anti-Americanism, which can be seen as a form of prejudice.

Although we begin by defining anti-Americanism as an attitude, taking the social-psychological literature seriously, our approach is resolutely political. Anti-American views are always contested or at least contestable. They are objects of political struggle. They are often emphasized or de-emphasized by politicians as a result of calculations about how they fit the appeals of a political party or movement and how they will resonate, at a particular time, with a particular set of potential supporters. To understand both the sources and consequences of anti-Americanism it is necessary to understand the political context that fosters or discourages negative attitudes toward the United States and that magnifies or minimizes the effects of these attitudes on policy. Our analysis of anti-Americanism thus is fundamentally about politics.

Schemas, Identities, and Norms

Anti-Americanism can have cognitive, emotional, and normative components. A schema is a *cognitive structure* that relies on specific metaphors, analogies, symbols, and

4. This formulation is indebted to Pierangelo Isernia and to personal communications with Yaacov Vertzberger. He defines an attitude "as an ideational formation having affective and cognitive dimensions that create a disposition for a particular pattern of behavior." See Vertzberger 1990, 127.

narratives of specific events and general historical developments to make sense of the world.[5] A schema performs a number of cognitive functions, including going beyond the information available to fill in missing elements and thus to form a coherent account.[6] Schemas make sense of attitudes so that they fit together. Schemas do not necessarily imply bias. Indeed they can be based on a coherent worldview based on a reasonable interpretation of available facts. When schemas are well articulated and entrenched, however, they can become hardened. As such, they create enduring distrust or become a systematic bias or prejudice that colors or systematically filters out positive or negative information. John Bowen identifies, in chapter 8, different sorts of schemas operating in France and Indonesia, which vary in their degree of hardness.

Below, we discuss the relationships we envisage among opinion, distrust, and bias. Systematic bias leads individuals or groups to expect the United States to act perniciously and to interpret the behavior of the U.S. government, corporations and organizations, or U.S. citizens in light of that expectation. But it would be a mistake to infer that unfavorable attitudes about the United States, its policies, Americans, and the American way of life are necessarily indicators of a systematic bias or prejudice against the United States that slants all new information in only a negative direction.

In our conceptualization, the *emotional component* of anti-Americanism chiefly affects the intensity with which negative assessments are held. However, our data in general do not enable us to distinguish the effect of emotion on negative assessments of the United States. We focus on the politics of anti-Americanism rather than seeking empirically to disentangle its sociopsychological components.

From a *normative standpoint*, assessments of the United States can serve as identity markers or as ways to regulate behavior. As identity markers, they are "double-edged" in that they "bind people to each other and at the same time turn people so bound against others."[7] Identities are a type of social norm that constitute the very actors whose behaviors they regulate. Identities emerge from interactions. Like nationalism, anti-Americanism contains aspects of both instrumental rationality and social construction.[8] In situations in which positive identities of "self" are hard to come by, the ready availability of a powerful, prosperous, culturally omnipresent "other" can provide a social glue that has broad appeal. Such situations are frequent, for example, in failing states, in societies divided deeply along ethnic, religious, class, or other lines, and in polities that are in the process of constructing a new collective identity. In brief, anti-Americanism can be a potent and useful stand-in for otherwise missing symbols of collective identity.

Anti-Americanism also involves norms that regulate behavior. People rationally shape their behavior to fit their expectations of what others will do. What is "normal"

5. Fiske and Taylor 1991, 98. Larson 1985, 50–57. Kunda 1999.

6. Vertzberger 1990, 157. We are very much indebted to John Bowen, who early on convinced us of the central importance of schemas for the analysis of anti-Americanism and whose intellectual lead we are following here.

7. Elias 1996, 160, quoted in Seabrooke 2006, 10.

8. Haas 1993.

is common knowledge in stable societies and therefore facilitates coordination by independent individuals. These expectations reflect behavioral regularities, which may mirror the effects of events or efforts at persuasion to interpret these events. Over time such behavioral regularities can have powerful conditioning effects that make anti-Americanism no longer open to self-reflection or reasoned dialogue. But norms also constitute the premises of action. They are regulative in prescribing socially appropriate standards of action, and they can also be evaluative in invoking moral standards.[9] During the massive demonstrations protesting the imminent U.S. attack on Iraq on February 15, 2003, it would have been socially very inappropriate to hoist and salute the American flag. Burning the flag and effigies of President Bush, on the other hand, were appropriate from the perspective of participants. The norms associated with anti-Americanism are components of political processes that generate standards of behavior.

Differentiating among schema, emotion, and norm suggests a second distinction. Anti-Americanism can be a matter of individual attitudes as revealed in public opinion polls, as analyzed by Pierangelo Isernia in chapter 3 and Giacomo Chiozza in chapter 4. But it is also a matter of collectively held beliefs with distinctive genealogies. Such beliefs can take the form of narrative collective memories analyzed in different ways by David Kennedy in chapter 2 and Bowen in chapter 8. Whether viewed as individual attitudes or collective beliefs, anti-Americanism can be experienced with varying degrees of emotional intensity.

Anti-American individual attitudes and collective beliefs are dynamic. They wax and wane over time, as people adapt their behavior to new situations. As attitudes and beliefs change, people become more or less susceptible to specific acts of persuasion, defined here as the use of argument to influence the actions of others, without using bribes or threatening force. Persuasion can occur through schemas, emotional appeals, or norms. Human beings do not carry in their heads fully developed, consistent, and articulated views of the world. As a result, how problems are "framed" is often critical for belief-driven action in politics.[10] Emotional appeals are often significant, particularly in collective settings. Finally, persuasive appeals can be made on the basis of norms—of identity, which involves "mutually constructed and evolving images of self and other," or of standards of appropriate behavior invoked by norms that regulate social or moral conduct.[11]

---

9. Barnett 1999, 15. Keck and Sikkink 1998, 223–26.

10. Tversky and Kahneman 1986. William R. Riker's (1996, 9) concept of "heresthetics" gets at the same point. Heresthetics, for Riker, is "the art of setting up situations in such a way that even those who do not wish to do so are compelled by the structure of the situation to support the heresthetician's purposes." Others refer to this strategy less elegantly as agenda setting. The key to heresthetics is the "forced choice" that the strategists create. If anti-Americanism becomes the basic frame for the analysis of action, the premise is that all forms of action and inaction represent a choice between America and what it stands for and its opponents. To the anti-American, the correct choice always has to be "oppose America." Mere belief is not sufficient, since those who may dislike America but do not act against it can be accused of weakness or hypocrisy. In his discussion of persuasion, Jeffrey Checkel (2001, 562) refers to this process as "manipulative persuasion."

11. Jepperson, Wendt, and Katzenstein 1996, 59. March and Olsen 1989.

Anti-American views can exist in politically visible form over decades, or even centuries, as in the case of France. In political settings where anti-Americanism has been part of a public discourse it operates as a collective frame that is readily deployed to mobilize people to take political actions. At other times, such views incubate for long periods out of sight, only to reappear in new forms to the surprise of everyone. At still other times, anti-American views can explode and disappear rapidly without leaving any traces. In all such situations anti-American views are often manipulated by political entrepreneurs for their own political benefits, top down. But they are also validated, bottom up, by popular conventions or memories that are not necessarily institutionalized.

We have argued that anti-Americanism is an attitude embedded in cognitive schemas, emotions, and norms. We do not go further to analyze the complex factors that make particular schemas, emotions, and norms compelling. To do so would require careful psychological analysis, applied to particular individuals and groups. What we do insist on is that anti-Americanism is not an unintelligible pathology in an otherwise intelligible world. It appears so only if we trap ourselves into projecting what appears as rational and normal in the United States onto other societies or other historical eras.

Multidimensionality and Ambivalence

The simplest way to view anti-Americanism is as a set of attitudes, as measured by results of public opinion polls or content analyses of discourses, that express negative views toward the United States or toward Americans. Three consistent and now-standard results follow.

First, until shortly before the invasion of Iraq, many more respondents worldwide had favorable opinions of the United States than unfavorable. As we noted above, in the Pew 2002 poll, pluralities in thirty-five of forty-two countries expressed favorable views. This changed dramatically in 2003 and 2004. Second, the societies most hostile to the United States, by far, are located in the Islamic Middle East, North Africa, and Pakistan. Finally, in both Islamic countries and Europe, attitudes toward Americans are more positive than attitudes toward the United States, and attitudes toward the United States are more positive than attitudes toward American foreign policy or President George W. Bush. In a 2002 Zogby poll conducted in a number of Islamic countries, the average of favorable opinions toward U.S. foreign policy across six different policies was 19 percent, compared to a 47 percent favorable rating of the American people.[12] Polls that the Pew Global Attitudes Project conducted in 2002 and 2004 show the same pattern, although some of the differences are less pronounced.

12. Zogby International 2004, 3. In a poll conducted only in Saudi Arabia rejection of al-Qaida's program and practices was almost unanimous and so was rejection of U.S. policies in Iraq and the Arab-Israeli conflict. See Zogby 2005.

In chapters 3 and 4 Isernia and Chiozza analyze these polling results in order to understand the structure and correlates of attitudes toward the United States. They also investigate two other features of attitudes that have been less emphasized, or even ignored, in both popular and scholarly discussions of this subject: multidimensionality and heterogeneity.

As is frequently noted, people seem to like and loath the United States and American society, at the same time. There is a perhaps apocryphal story about the Iranian students who participated in the holding of American hostages in 1979, asking how, after the crisis was over, they could obtain visas to the United States. "Yankee, go home—and take me with you!"

Such expressions can be interpreted either as ambivalence or as attitudinal multidimensionality. People who are ambivalent about the United States simultaneously like and dislike the same features of American society. Neil Smelser defines ambivalence as a "powerful, persistent, unresolvable, volatile, generalizable, and anxiety-provoking feature of the human condition."[13] Smelser associates ambivalence with situations in which people are dependent on a person or organization that they both respect and resent. But someone can have multidimensional attitudes without being ambivalent: that is, she could clearly like and dislike different aspects of American society without being at all uncertain about either her likes or dislikes.[14] If someone's evaluation of specific aspects of the United States involves strong elements of both attraction and repulsion, she feels ambivalent, but if she dislikes some aspects of the United States but likes others, she has multidimensional attitudes.

In practice, it is often difficult to distinguish multidimensionality from ambivalence. Yet some polling data show clearly that many people have multidimensional attitudes toward the United States, rather than being ambivalent. They positively evaluate some asoects of American society while strongly disliking others. Chiozza documents in chapter 4 that attitudes toward America differ along different dimensions. In eight Islamic countries in 2002 (before the Iraq War dramatically increased negative views of the United States), almost 82 percent of respondents held favorable opinions of U.S. science and technology. About 65 percent thought positively about U.S. education, movies and TV, and commercial products. Only 47 percent held favorable views of U.S. ideas of freedom and democracy or the American people. Those people who admired U.S. science and technology but disliked American conceptions of freedom and democracy were not ambivalent about either feature of the United States; their views were multidimensional in the sense that they evaluated differently distinct dimensions associated with the United States.

Table 1.1 compares two sets of views by respondents to the Pew Research Center's polls in 2003. Column (1) shows the difference between the percentage of respondents who expressed agreement with the statement, "People from our country who

13. Smelser 1998, 6; Jonas, Broemer, and Diehl 2000.
14. We would like to thank Paul Sniderman in particular for sharpening for us the distinction between multidimensionality and ambivalence.

Table 1.1. Views of whether emigrants to the United States have a better life contrasted with attitudes toward the United States

	(1) "better life"	(2) % favorable	(1)–(2)
Great Britain	+35 (41–6)	+24 (58–34)	11
Germany	−2 (14–16)	−31 (38–69)	29
France	+12 (24–12)	−25 (37–62)	37
Russia	+43 (53–10)	+3 (47–44)	40
Pakistan	+2 (30–28)	−50 (21–71)	52
Morocco	+20 (47–27)	−41 (27–68)	61
Turkey	+31 (50–19)	−33 (30–63)	64
Jordan	+10 (31–21)	−88 (5–93)	98

Source: Pew Global Attitudes Project 2004.

move to the U.S. have a better life there," and the percentage disagreeing with that statement. A positive number indicates that on average respondents had a favorable opinion of the United States as a place to live (relative to the home country). Column (2) records the difference between the percentage of respondents who had a favorable opinion of the United States and the percentage with an unfavorable opinion. A positive number indicates that in the aggregate, respondents had a favorable opinion of the United States. The difference between columns (1) and (2) represents the discrepancy between the net score for a given country on the question about emigrants to the United States having a better life, and the net score for the same country regarding the United States in general. That difference is always positive and in most cases remarkably large, indicating the much higher regard respondents show for the United States as a place to live than for "the United States" as an abstract entity.[15]

Table 1.1 shows that people can simultaneously say that they dislike the United States and believe that emigrants from their country to the United States generally have a better life than those who remain. These feelings can be interpreted as ambivalence toward the United States or as multidimensional views toward various aspects of it. Either way, they suggest the complexity of attitudes that are often described too simply as "anti-American."

Americans have not reciprocated the sharp decline in foreign publics' esteem of the United States. In a series of polls conducted between 1999 and 2004 Americans were asked whether a range of countries were close allies, friendly, unfriendly, or enemies.[16] The results indicate a largely positive view of other countries. Even in September 2004, in the midst of the Iraq War and an election campaign that drew attention to criticism of the United States abroad, more Americans identified twenty-

15. This analysis dovetails with the strong statistical relationship (r-square 0.78) that Isernia reports in chapter 3 between the willingness to move to the United States for a better life and more income.

16. Harris Interactive (www.harrisinteractive.com). Accessed April 12, 2005. Poll 62 (September 1, 2004); poll 52 (September 10, 2003); poll 47 (September 11, 2002); poll 54 (October 31, 2001); poll 50 (August 30, 2000); poll 51 (September 1, 1999).

Table 1.2. American attitudes toward other countries

Country	September 1, 1999		October 31, 2001		September 11, 2002		September 1, 2004	
	Close ally	Plus friend	Close ally	Plus friend	Close ally	Plus friend	Close ally	Plus friend
Canada	69	90	73	92	60	87	51	80
United Kingdom	66	83	80	93	64	86	70	84
France	38	33	51	86	28	64	15	50
Germany	32	65	39	77	29	70	19	59
Japan	23	62	26	65	28	67	33	67
China	6	28	11	40	5	32	6	32

Source: Harris Interactive (www.harrisinteractive.com). Accessed April 12, 2005. Poll 62 (September 1, 2004); poll 52 (September 10, 2003); poll 47 (September 11, 2002); poll 54 (October 31, 2001); poll 50 (August 30, 2000); poll 51 (September 1, 1999).

Note: The figures for September 2003 are very similar to those of September 2004 and are therefore omitted.

two of the twenty-five countries listed as allies or friends than as unfriendly or enemies. The only exceptions were China, Colombia, and Pakistan. Table 1.2 shows responses for six American allies over four time periods. Americans' attitudes reflect the fact that Great Britain and Japan supported the American war in Iraq and Canada, France, and Germany did not. But despite the drops in their ratings, a majority of the American public viewed these three countries in 2003 and in 2004 as allied or at least friendly to the United States.

Anti-American views are not only multidimensional but also very heterogeneous. There exists substantial and persistent cross-country variation in western European attitudes toward the United States. Between 1976 and 1997, on average, respondents in the following countries reported that they had "some trust" or "a lot of trust" in Americans: between 74 and 76 percent in Denmark, West Germany, Great Britain, and the Netherlands; between 63 to 70 percent in Portugal, Italy, Belgium, and France; but only 46 percent in Spain (1986–97) and 38 percent in Greece (1980–97).[17]

Various expressions of anti-Americanism seem to have some common elements, including resentment of the United States and charges of hypocrisy leveled against the U.S. government. There exists, however, a great deal of variation. Some expressions of antipathy are linked directly to U.S. policies or capabilities, both past and present. Others are linked to the real or imagined gap between American ideals and the actual conduct of the United States. Still others seem to reflect profound differences between the respondent's values and identity and America's. At every level, there is so much variation by country and region that it is more accurate to speak of anti-Americanisms than of anti-Americanism.

People in different countries have very different evaluations of the United States and of current U.S. policy. We conjecture that evaluations of current policy may perform a triggering function, shifting what could be pro-Americanism or

17. Chiozza 2004a and 2004b, Eurobarometer polls, various years. See also Free 1976.

neutrality to anti-Americanism, or intensifying the level of anti-Americanism. One of the important and to date unanswered questions is the extent to which opposition to U.S. foreign policy spills over into a more deep-seated antipathy toward America that generates a new kind of identity as well as institutionalized forms of bias. Such an institutionalization of bias would have serious implications for America's soft power in world politics.[18]

Opinion, Distrust, and Bias

If one probes beneath the surface it becomes clear that polling data may mask much of what is politically significant.[19] People who answer polling questions in a way that can reasonably be coded as anti-American may differ greatly both in their causal beliefs and in the intensity of their views. Cross-national public opinion polls are useful for helping us understand some basic distinctions in the political orientation of mass publics—specifically toward the United States government and its policies on the one hand and American society and values on the other. But polls risk imposing a conceptual unity on extremely diverse sets of political processes that mean different things in different contexts. Polls may even create the "attitudes" they report, since people wish to provide answers to questions that are posed.[20]

Distinguishing between opinion and bias is particularly difficult. It is also hard—but crucial for our project—to identify whether negative attitudes are accompanied by distrust. We first discuss these issues conceptually. We then describe an analysis we have conducted, seeking to identify bias in a comparative manner, using public reactions in January 2005 to the tsunami relief effort mounted by the United States in Southeast Asia.

As noted above the political Left in the United States takes comfort from analyses of public opinion polls. They seem consistent with its general view that anti-Americanism is principally a result of unpopular U.S. policies. Negative attitudes are strongest toward U.S. foreign policy rather than American society: anti-Americanism worsened during the run-up to the invasion of Iraq; anti-Americanism is highest in areas where U.S. actions are widely opposed, as in the Islamic world; most people in most countries think of the United States as a generally good place to live. For the Left, anti-Americanism is a result of "what we do," not "who we are."

But if anti-Americanism is only a matter of opinion—often transient—why care about it? The Right takes the view of Polonius: "To thine own self be true." The United States is hated by many people, but this is a mark of respect: they hate what is good about us—American values of freedom and democracy. Rather than feeling defensive, according to the Right, America should be proud of what it is and what it stands for. If the United States firmly pursues sound policies, favorable opinion

18. Nye 2004a.
19. Smelser 1998, 11.
20. Zaller 1992.

Table 1.3. Indonesian poll responses, 2003 and 2005

	2003	2005
Is suicide bombing often or sometimes justified? (% yes)	27	9
Confidence in Osama bin Laden (a lot or some—% yes)	58	23
Unfavorable toward United States (somewhat or very)	83	54
Oppose U.S. efforts to fight terrorism	72	36

Source: Terror Free Tomorrow 2005. We are indebted to Helle Dale of the Heritage Foundation for calling this poll to our attention.

will follow. For the Right, anti-Americanism is the result of "who we are" not "what we do." The Right can point to examples that support its position. For example, anti-Americanism in Japan was intense in 1960, when the Japanese police, reinforced by twenty-five thousand members of Japanese organized crime, were unable to secure the route from the airport to downtown Tokyo. President Eisenhower was thus forced to cancel a trip he had planned in order to attend the ceremonies for the extension of the U.S-Japanese security treaty. Today, however, anti-Americanism in Japan is at a low ebb. The United States stuck to its policies successfully. To take another example, anti-Americanism (as measured by polls) rose sharply in Europe during the European missile crisis of the early 1980s. In 1984 a plurality of respondents in France, Great Britain, Italy, and West Germany thought that during the past year, U.S. policies had done more to increase the risk of war than to promote peace. In 1982, between 29 and 37 percent of those polled held unfavorable opinions of the United States. Yet by 1987 the range of opinion in the same countries was down to 12 to 28 percent unfavorable.[21] The United States had not wavered from its policy of placing missiles in Europe to counter Soviet missiles aimed at Europe, even though the result was a temporary increase in anti-American opinion. After the policy had been successfully implemented, the United States once again became popular.

Polls often reflect rather transient attitudes—what is at the top of people's minds.[22] When situations change, polling results can change dramatically. A recent poll of Indonesians after the Western-led tsunami relief efforts of January 2005 illustrates this point.[23] Conducted between February 1 and 6, 2005, the poll shows a dramatic drop in support for Osama bin Laden and for such actions as suicide bombing. It also shows a sharp rise in favorable views toward the United States and U.S. efforts to fight terrorism. Table 1.3 displays a summary of differences between responses to identically worded questions in 2003 and in February 2005.

Nothing in these data suggests that the United States is very popular in Indonesia or that Indonesian attitudes toward the United States, and toward the "war on terror," will remain as positive as they were in February 2005. The point is that anti-American opinion is volatile and subject to sharp changes with new events.

21. Chiozza 2003, based on Eurobarometer polling data; British respondents were most negative.
22. Zaller 1992.
23. See Terror Free Tomorrow 2005, 5.

The problem, however, with the view that opinion does not matter is that negative shifts in opinion do not necessarily revert back to favorable or neutral views, or they may only do so after negative attitudes have contributed to actions adverse to the United States. Political practices and discourses hostile to the United States can be institutionalized at a period of high antagonism by elites, who then develop a stake in maintaining negative attitudes and poor relations with the United States. Cuba and Iran both come to mind as examples of countries that had close relationships with the United States, which turned hostile under regimes that, at times, have sought to maintain that hostility for their own purposes. In chapter 9 Doug McAdam emphasizes the possible indirect, long-term, and unanticipated impacts of anti-American opinion. We also address this question in chapter 10.

While opinion may or may not have serious consequences, distrust and bias should be of serious concern to policymakers, particularly if these negative predispositions become deeply entrenched in societies that are important to the United States. For distrust can translate easily into opposition to or lack of support of the United States. Governments of such countries are likely to demand more evidence, or more compensation, from the United States before they are willing to support U.S. policies. People who not only distrust the United States but are also biased against it will process information differently than unbiased people. For example, Indonesian and Egyptian members of focus groups list U.S. aid given to their countries erroneously in the millions, rather than as $1 billion and $7.3 billion, respectively.[24] In general, biased people are also more likely to attribute bad policies to essential features of the United States, rather than merely to specific situations. Furthermore, they will tend to discount potentially favorable information and make negative information more salient. Social psychology shows that people develop social identities easily, and that they define themselves as group members relative to other groups, responding positively to in-groups and negatively to out-groups.[25] If people define the United States as part of an out-group, they are likely to view it negatively. If anti-Americanism were to become deep and endemic it could function like a classic prejudice and become a potent marker of identity that is resistant to disconfirming evidence.

Table 1.4 suggests two distinctions, between predispositions and opinion, and, within the broad category of predispositions, between bias and distrust. The table presents these distinctions as categorical, but they can be seen as placed along a continuum involving receptivity to new information. The more predisposed someone is against the United States the less information is required to view U.S. policies negatively. The strongest predisposition—bias—implies attributing negative actions and motives to the United States as an entity, rather than to the situation in which it finds itself. Distrust, on the other hand, can reflect attribution to the essential and inherent characteristics of an actor or to the situation in which the actor finds himself or

24. Charney and Yakatan 2005, 70.
25. Tajfel 1981, Brewer and Brown 1998.

Table 1.4. Implications of negative views for predispositions, depending on openness to new information and attribution

Openness to new information	Attribution: essential	Attribution: situational
Low	Predisposition: *bias* (closed-minded)	—
Medium	Predisposition: *strong distrust* ("Show me you are good")	Predisposition: *moderate distrust* ("Show me you will behave well here")
High	—	No predisposition: *opinion*

some mixture of the two. The more distrust is based on negative evaluations of American characteristics, viewed as inherent, the deeper it is. Both bias and distrust should be distinguished from negative opinions held by people who are open to new information and who do not attribute bad practices of the United States to its essential, inherent characteristics.[26]

It is important to emphasize that opinion, distrust, and bias are found along a continuum, with distrust lying between opinion and bias. Most opinion is a mixture of reasoned assessment based on historical judgment and schemas. Bowen acknowledges in chapter 8 how difficult it can be to distinguish between these two in specific instances. Because we focus on anti-Americanism rather than pro-Americanism, we are concerned with schemas that create negative predispositions. Some of these may be so mild that they still fit within our general category of opinion. As the schemas harden, we move into the range of more or less serious distrust and, eventually, to bias.

Anti-Semitism, which is an extreme version of bias, has some links to current anti-Americanism as Bowen argues in chapter 8.[27] Earlier Nazi, Soviet, and Pan-Arab versions of anti-Semitism are feeding into contemporary Islamic anti-Semitism. The unconditional support of the United States government for Israeli policies that contradict several long-standing UN resolutions has created a strong political backlash well beyond the Middle East.[28] In the Middle East anti-Semitism and anti-Americanism often blend seamlessly into one another. This is true also in Europe, where that fusion is restricted not only to a growing Muslim population. Although European anti-Semitism and even philo-Semitism without Jews have become social facts since 1945, traditional anti-Semitism is no longer tolerated in Europe's public discourse.[29] A new anti-Semitism now focuses on Israel's military strength, religious

26. The top right cell of the table is empty because low openness to new information implies that new information about the situation in which the actor was placed would not change the subject's view. The bottom left cell of the table is empty because high openness to new information implies the relevance of situational information and, therefore, the rejection of the fundamental attribution fallacy of attributing action solely to essential characteristics of the actor.

27. Wistrich 1992, 2003; Markovits 2004a, 173–216.

28. Lieven 2004, 173–216.

29. C. Smith 2005.

vitality, strong nationalism, and predisposition toward unilateral action, all traits that, in the eyes of many Europeans, also characterize the United States.[30] By contrast, Europeans today value diplomacy, display a secular outlook, share in a diffuse national identity blending with local and European elements, and reveal an enduring commitment to the principle of multilateralism. Civilian, not military, power is the foundation for Europe's claim to great power status in world politics. Yet Israel relies on military power. Israeli policies seem therefore to be fundamentally at odds with the European experience of peacefully building a new polity on a continent for centuries divided by hatred and war. Anti-Semitism and anti-Americanism converge on the fleeting borderlines that separate serious criticism from distrust and systematic bias.

Some authors distinguish correctly between opinion and bias but then make the error of accepting polling data as "expressions of anti-Americanism."[31] Clearly we need better evidence than this before concluding that anti-Americanism, in the sense of deep distrust or bias, is widespread. Andrei S. Markovits reports some such evidence, in an analysis of nearly one thousand articles written on the United States in Britain, France, Germany, and Italy.[32] Focusing on "nonpolitical" topics such as film, theater, and sports, he found pervasive condescension and denigration toward American culture. One of his more telling examples compares European press coverage of the soccer World Cup in the United States (1994) and in Korea and Japan (2002). In the European coverage of the 1994 World Cup even unexpected events that would appear to be positive (such as sixty thousand people watching a match between Saudi Arabia and Morocco in New York on a weekday afternoon) were reported negatively. For some European commentators such a high turnout only underlined the naïveté and ignorance of the American public in attending a match between two teams unlikely to be in contention for the championship. In contrast, the South Korean and Japanese hosts received rave reviews.

Without more studies that replicate Markovits's findings in different countries and empirical domains, it is difficult to know how biased people elsewhere are toward the United States. We and our collaborators have tried in this project to figure out ways to differentiate among these types of sentiments.[33] One such effort is described below.

30. Edward H. Kaplan (Yale School of Management) and Charles A. Small (Southern Connecticut State University) are analyzing the Anti-Defamation League's 2004 European survey. Their preliminary results suggest that sharply critical views of Israel are in the single digits, much lower than one might have expected on the basis of newspaper coverage. At the same time, there is a clear statistical relationship between strong anti-Israel sentiment and anti-Semitism. We thank Kaplan and Small for sharing with us the preliminary results of their work. See Kaplan and Small 2005 and also Zick and Küpper 2005 and more generally Rabinovici, Speck, and Sznaider 2004.

31. Hollander 2004a, 15. Rubin and Rubin 2004 also make the distinction between opinion and bias.

32. Markovits 2003. See also Markovits 2004a and 2006.

33. For a particularly creative attempt, see Chiozza's chapter 4. Chapters 5–7 were designed to help answer questions about bias by focusing not only on politically salient issues but on apparently nonpolitical issues, in which bias could be more readily distinguished from strongly held political views.

Attitudes toward the United States are too multidimensional for bias to be an accurate description of most people's views, as expressed either in public opinion polls or in public discourse. Yet in countries as diverse as China, France, Egypt, and Indonesia these expressions reflect a pervasive and sometimes institutionalized distrust, which creates skepticism toward statements by the United States government and a predisposition to view U.S. policy negatively. Overall, the findings in this book indicate that attitudes toward the United States are frequently better characterized in terms of distrust than of either opinion or bias.

Tsunami Relief as a Quasi Experiment

One of the difficulties in using public opinion polls to analyze comparative levels of anti-Americanism by country is that even apparently similar questions are interpreted differently in different places. One may ask people similar questions about how favorable they feel toward the United States, yet attitudes toward the United States have different salience in different societies and people will therefore give different answers. To Germans, U.S. unilateralism in Iraq may be salient; to Egyptians, it may be U.S. support for Israel against Palestinians; to Chinese it may be the bombing of the Chinese embassy in Belgrade or the spy-plane incident of spring 2001. Different responses can thus reflect different experiences or reference groups, rather than varying degrees of bias against the United States. If one were able to design an experiment to assess bias against the United States, one would present a single, somewhat ambiguous, scenario of American behavior and ask people in different societies to react to it. The expectation would be that such a situation would be like a Rorschach test, the responses to which would reveal people's biases rather than opinion.

Paul Sniderman has conducted highly original research over the last fifteen years on prejudice, which distinguishes bias from opinion. In studying prejudice, researchers need to be aware that respondents sometimes conceal racist views, recognizing that they are not socially acceptable. Sniderman therefore devised computer-aided polling techniques that ask the same questions, except for precisely calibrated variations, to two or more experimentally controlled sets of respondents. In one such experiment, respondents are primed to express judgments on the behavior of a character in a narrative. For the treatment and control groups, everything is the same in the narrative except the ethnic affiliation of the protagonist. In another of Sniderman's experiments, subjects are given lists of things that make them angry, in such a way that they know that the investigator cannot identify which particular items they reacted to. But for the treatment group, "affirmative action" is included in addition to the items listed for the control group. By computing the mean "angry" responses, the investigator can determine what proportion of the treatment group reacted angrily to affirmative action.[34] Such an experimental

---

34. For the experiments on "treatment of various groups," see Sniderman and Piazza 2002, 186–87, and Sniderman et al. 2000. For the "list experiment" see Sniderman and Carmines 1997, 43–45.

method could be of great value in distinguishing opinion from bias in expressions of anti-Americanism.

Lacking data from such an experiment, the worldwide response to the Asian tsunami of December 26, 2004 at least provides us with a rough quasi experiment.[35] The tsunami was an enormous tragedy for millions of people, and it generated empathy and an unprecedented outpouring of generosity worldwide. President Bush's apparent initial indifference generated much critical commentary. By January 7, 2005, however, the United States government had donated $350 million—about 8 percent of the amount that had been contributed by all governments at that time— and had deployed its naval vessels in the area for a massive relief operation.[36] The U.S. relief effort was focused on Southeast Asia and was not experienced directly by people in countries outside the region. But the American response was widely publicized.

Fortunately for our analysis, between January 8 and 16, 2005 Global Market Insite (GMI) conducted a poll of 1,000 members of the urban publics in each of twenty countries, which included questions about the U.S. tsunami relief effort. By the time of the GMI poll the United States had mounted an impressive and far-reaching logistical relief operation, and the American public had proved its generosity. Since the United States response was sufficiently ambiguous to be interpretable in different ways, it approximates the conditions of a quasi experiment. That is, had we been able to run an experiment, we would have exposed subjects to an ambiguous response by the United States and asked for evaluations.

For everyone outside the affected area, and for most people in Asia as a whole, reactions to the U.S. response to the tsunami were based not on personal experience but on media reports, filtered through their own prevailing schemas about the United States. Therefore, variations in evaluations of the U.S. response are unlikely to reflect different personal experiences, particularly for publics outside of Asia. Admittedly we do not have an Archimedean standard of perfect accuracy in perception against which to judge public reactions to the American aid effort, but we can analyze these reactions comparatively. Variations in the perceptions of the U.S. effort in countries not directly affected by the tsunami or the relief efforts reflect three sorts of bias: on the part of the media, in the schemas held by individuals, and in the collective images of America prevailing in different societies. Individuals biased in favor of the United States could be expected to give positive responses when asked about the reaction of the U.S. government; those biased against the United States could be expected to give more negative responses. Even though there is no way to determine what an "unbiased answer" would be, variation in evaluations should reflect variations in the degree of bias.

The GMI poll asked the following question:

The American government has donated $350 million to aid nations impacted by the tsunami, has deployed its military to aid the region, and has called on former

35. See Cook and Campbell 1979.
36. See Mallet 2005. At that time reported figures for U.S. private donations were $200 million, over 35% of the U.S. total of $550 million.

Table 1.5. Responses by country: favorable/unfavorable to the United States and supportive or not of adequacy of the U.S. relief effort (n = 20)

Country	(1) Net favorable to United States	(2) Net supportive of U.S. relief effort	(3) Net supportive of own-country effort
United States	69 (1)	54 (1)	54 (13)
Poland	60 (2)	−19 (13)	34 (17)
India	40 (3)	11 (6)	86 (5.5)
Denmark	33 (4)	−1 (8)	88 (3.5)
Russia	25 (5)	28 (2)	67 (12)
Italy	17 (6)	−2 (9)	79 (10)
Australia	16 (7)	−36 (17)	94 (1)
China	9 (8)	13 (3.5)	86 (5.5)
Hungary	8 (9)	12 (5)	93 (2)
Malaysia	−1 (10.5)	9 (7)	84 (8)
Japan	−1 (10.5)	−11 (11)	10 (19)
Canada	−4 (12.5)	13 (3.5)	83 (9)
United Kingdom	−4 (12.5)	−9 (10)	49 (14)
Brazil	−6 (14)	−31 (16)	37 (16)
Netherlands	−8 (5)	−20 (14)	85 (7)
Mexico	−10 (16)	−13 (12)	13 (18)
Germany	−16 (17)	−21 (15)	88 (3.5)
South Korea	−21 (18)	−55 (19)	−14 (20)
France	−36 (19)	−54 (18)	44 (15)
Greece	−60 (20)	−56 (20)	71 (11)

Source: GMI 2005.

Note: Columns 1 and 2: Spearman's r: 0.68 (n = 20, p < 0.01, from exact table, 2-sided null hypothesis). Columns 2 and 3: Spearman's r: 0.27 (not significant).

President Clinton and President Bush Sr. to fundraise more money from the American people. Do you think the American government's reaction to the tsunami tragedy is adequate?[37]

The answers to this question were categorized as "agree," "disagree," and "don't know/neither." GMI also asked a fairly standard question about the United States: "Overall, how would you describe your feelings towards the United States?" The answers to this question were categorized as "positive," "negative," or "don't know/neither."

Table 1.5 arrays the data by indicating the difference between "agree" or "positive," on the one hand, and "disagree" or "negative" on the other, for each of the twenty countries surveyed on the two questions. Positive answers indicate net favorable views toward the United States or the American tsunami relief efforts. Rank orders for each question are in parentheses. The first two columns of table 1.5 seem

37. For the overall results, see http://www.worldpoll.com (accessed April 15, 2005). GMI states that the poll included representative samples of 1,000 consumers in each of twenty countries: Australia, Brazil, Canada, China, Denmark, France, Germany, Greece, Hungary, India, Italy, Japan, Malaysia, Mexico, the Netherlands, Poland, Russia, South Korea, the United Kingdom, and the United States. GMI has been extremely generous, giving us individual-level data and answering specific questions, about issues such as the precise dates of the polls, to which answers are not available on its website.

Table 1.6. Rank order of European countries in table 1.5

Country	(1) Net favorable to United States	(2) Net supportive of U.S. relief effort	(3) Net supportive of own-country effort
Poland	60 (1)	−19 (5)	34 (9)
Denmark	33 (2)	−1 (2)	88 (2.5)
Italy	17 (3)	−2 (3)	79 (5)
Hungary	11 (4)	12 (1)	93 (1)
United Kingdom	−4 (5)	−9 (4)	49 (7)
Netherlands	−8 (6)	−20 (6)	85 (4)
Germany	−16 (7)	−21 (7)	88 (2.5)
France	−36 (8)	−54 (8)	44 (8)
Greece	−60 (9)	−56 (9)	71 (6)

Source: GMI 2005.

Note: Columns 1 and 2 Spearman's r: 0.78 (n = 9, p = 0.02, from exact table, 2-sided null hypothesis). Columns 2 and 3 Spearman's r: 0.48 (not significant).

to suggest that bias—perhaps both for and against the United States—had an impact on opinions about the adequacy of American tsunami relief efforts. There is an enormous range of views regarding the U.S.-led relief effort, disregarding U.S. respondents, who were overwhelmingly favorable. Sixty-two percent of the Russian public considered U.S. efforts adequate, as compared to 34 percent who did not; at the other extreme, only 17 percent of the Greek public considered U.S. efforts adequate, as compared to 73 percent who did not. None or almost none of these respondents had any personal experience of the operation on which they had opinions; they had to be reacting to media coverage, their own schemas, and the nationally prevailing images of the American relief effort.

There exists a strong correlation between general views of the United States and views of the adequacy of American-led tsunami relief efforts, with a Spearman rank-order coefficient well under the 0.01 level of significance. Three of the five publics most favorably disposed toward the United States in general also rank among the five most favorable publics toward the U.S. relief effort, and conversely for the least favorable publics. It is particularly instructive to examine the variation in attitudes among the European countries (table 1.6) whose publics were polled by GMI. For these countries there is a wide variation in responses to the tsunami; the rank orders in the two columns are almost perfectly correlated. These correlations, for all twenty countries and only for the European ones, provide strong evidence in favor of the proposition that general attitudes toward the United States "bleed over" into attitudes toward its tsunami relief efforts, particularly for publics such as those in France and Greece with strong negative predispositions toward the United States.[38]

38. In chapter 5, Meunier argues on the basis of an analysis of the French media that the French reaction to American tsunami relief efforts should not be interpreted as reflecting anti-American bias and that the French media were also highly critical of France's reaction. But the polling data indicate that the French public was overwhelmingly supportive of France's response and even more overwhelmingly critical of that of the United States.

The third column of table 1.5 indicates clearly that, with only a few exceptions, publics rate their own country's performance highly favorably. Indeed, in about half the countries, publics are almost unanimously supportive of their own country's effort. Overall, as table 1.5 shows, there is no significant correlation between how publics view their own country's efforts and how they evaluate the American effort. It is therefore not the case that some publics are uniformly critical, others uniformly appreciative.

Publics are biased in favor of their own countries' performance. This generalization applies not only to countries such as Australia, which were generous (over $900 million in reported public and private donations by January 7), but also to countries that gave almost nothing, such as Hungary and Russia.[39] And *in every case* they rate their own country ahead of the United States, which at that time had provided $550 million in reported public and private donations.[40]

We conclude from this analysis that there is substantial variation in the bias (positive or negative) toward the United States held by different publics, and that this variation is strongly correlated with general attitudes toward the United States. Much more tentatively, we infer that significant cross-national variation in bias exists, with negative bias particularly pronounced in France and Greece.[41] The evidence is very strong that publics are positively biased toward their own countries' efforts, in a way that is consistent with widespread nationalism.

A Typology of "Anti-Americanism"

Table 1.7 sketches a typology of four types of anti-Americanism, based on the degree to which the subject identifies with the United States and its practices. The fundamental dimension along which these four types of anti-Americanism vary is the normative one of *identification*.[42] This concept refers to the degree to which individuals identify with the United States or, on the contrary, identify themselves as in opposition or even hostile to it. Liberals identify with Americans, although they may be very critical of the failure of the United States to pursue actions consistent with its professed values. Social and Christian democrats share democratic principles with the United States but define other values very differently from those of Americans, typically rejecting America's lack of an extensive welfare state and various of its social

39. Mallet 2005 reports data on donations.
40. Individual-level data analyzed by Chiozza shows that people overwhelmingly viewed their own country's performance as superior to that of the United States.
41. We note, however, that Meunier's analysis of French media coverage in chapter 5 does not support this inference of bias. Her conclusion is that the French media emphasized the unilateralism of the United States response—unilateralism to which the French take firm and reasoned objection. Whether it was bias for the media to stress features of the American reaction that the French public dislikes, rather than its humanitarian objectives, is, of course, another question.
42. In chapter 3 Isernia analyzes the multidimensionality of European views of the United States in terms of threat and mastery, involving variable degrees of in-group identification, possibly based on modal distributions of opinion in Europe, distrust in East Asia, and bias in the Middle East. They yield variable degrees of mastery over one's environment. Isernia's two dimensions are conceptually related to, though distinct from, the ones we develop here.

Table 1.7. Identification, fear, and anti-Americanism

	Degree of fear that the United States will adversely affect one's own society	
	Low	High
Identification with the United States		
Positive: subject associates herself with what she considers U.S. practices	I. Pro-Americanism	II. Critique of hypocrisy *liberal anti-Americanism*
	III. Ambivalence *latent social anti-Americanism*	IV. Severe criticism *intense social anti-Americanism*
	V. Negative feelings but not intense; unlikely to lead to action *latent sovereign-nationalist anti-Americanism*	VI. Intense negative feelings; more likely to lead to action *intense sovereign-nationalist anti-Americanism*
Negative: subject opposes what she considers U.S. practices	VII. Negative and more intense than V but less than VI and VIII due to lack of fear *latent radical anti-Americanism*	VIII. Very negative and intense; likely to lead to action, violent or nonviolent *mobilized radical anti-Americanism*

Note: This is a typology, designed as an aid to categorization and comparison. A combination of negative identification with, and fear of, the United States might cause anti-Americanism, for instance. But the reverse causal pathway is also possible: hatred of and anger toward America could lead to negative identification and fear. Even if the first causal pathway were valid, an in-depth explanation would be required to account for identification and fear.

policies, including the death penalty. Sovereign-nationalists identify with their nation, which they may or may not perceive as threatened by the United States. Radicals define themselves in opposition to the United States and the values for which it stands.

The typology is not meant to reify anti-Americanism, as if it were homogeneous within a given society even if heterogeneous worldwide. In their analyses in chapters 8 and 9, Bowen and McAdam show that dynamic processes generate and reproduce positive or negative views toward the United States in different ways in various countries and social sectors. Instead, we seek to identify components of anti-Americanism, which can combine, in some cases, with pro-Americanism, in a variety of configurations. As we have emphasized, individuals evaluate different aspects of the United States differently; and groups can be internally divided in their evaluations of the United States and the American people. Indeed, one of the key features of the four different types of anti-Americanism is that they are not mutually exclusive. On the contrary, several of them may bleed into one another, and some of the most interesting situations are those in which more than one form of anti-Americanism is at work.

Liberal Anti-Americanism

Liberal anti-Americanism seems at first to be an oxymoron, since liberals broadly share many of the ideas that are characteristic of the American creed. But the United

States is often criticized bitterly for not living up to its own ideals. A country dedicated to democracy and self-determination supported dictatorships around the world during the cold war and continued to do so in the Middle East after the cold war had ended. The war on terror has led the United States to begin supporting a variety of otherwise unattractive, even repugnant, regimes and political practices. On economic issues, the United States claims to favor freedom of trade, yet it protects its own agriculture from competition from developing countries, and seeks extensive patent and copyright protection for American drug firms and owners of intellectual property. Such behavior opens the United States to charges of hypocrisy from people who share its professed ideals but lament its actions.[43]

Liberal anti-Americanism is prevalent in the liberal societies of advanced industrialized countries, especially those colonized or influenced by Great Britain. For a long time it was prominent in the Middle East, among secular, Western-educated elites. As the influence of these groups has fallen, it has been replaced by more radical forms of anti-Americanism. No liberal anti-American ever detonated a bomb against Americans or planned an attack on the United States. The potential impact of liberal anti-Americanism would be not to generate attacks on the United States but to reduce support for U.S. policy. The more the United States is seen as a self-interested power parading under the banners of democracy and human rights, rather than a true proponent of those values, the less willing other liberals may be to defend it with words or deeds.

Because liberal anti-Americanism feeds on perceptions of hypocrisy, a less hypocritical set of U.S. policies could presumably reduce it. Hypocrisy, however, is inherent in the situation of a superpower that professes universalistic ideals. It afflicted the Soviet Union even more than the United States. But democracies display their own form of hypocrisy. When they engage in global politics, they generally find it convenient to mobilize their people by referring to higher ideals. Because states involved in power competition often find it useful to resort to measures that undercut democracy and freedom elsewhere, the potential for hypocrisy is inherent in global activism by democracies. Furthermore, a prominent feature of pluralist democracy is that its leaders find it necessary both to claim that they are acting consistently with democratic ideals while responding to groups seeking to pursue their own self-interests, usually narrowly defined. When the interests of politically strong groups imply policies that do not reflect democratic ideals, the ideals are typically compromised. Such alleged hypocrisy is criticized not only in liberal but also in non-liberal states. As Alastair Iain Johnston and Daniela Stockmann note in chapter 6, Chinese public discourse overwhelmingly associates the United States with adherence to a double standard in its foreign policy in general and in its conduct of the war on terror specifically.[44]

43. One of America's greatest secretaries of state, John Quincy Adams, was alert to the issue of hypocrisy. Arguing that the United States should not deny its hegemonic aspirations in North America, he declared that "any effort on our part to reason the world out of a belief that we are ambitious will have no other effect than to convince them that we add to our ambition hypocrisy." Quoted in Gaddis 2004, 27.

44. See Grant 1997, Shklar 1984.

Hypocrisy in U.S. foreign policy is not so much the result of the ethical failings of American leaders as it is a by-product of the role played by the United States in world politics and of democratic politics at home. It will not, therefore, be eradicated. As long as political hypocrisy persists, abundant material will be available for liberal anti-Americanism.

Social Anti-Americanism

Because democracy comes in many stripes, we are wrong to mistake the American tree for the democratic forest. During the last three decades, typologies of advanced industrial states and welfare societies, varieties of capitalism, and different types of electoral democracies have become a staple in the analysis of international political economy, comparative political economy, and comparative politics. What we denote as social anti-Americanism derives from a set of political institutions that embed liberal values in a broader set of social and political arrangements that help define market processes and outcomes that are left more autonomous in the United States. This variant of liberalism is marked by a more encompassing support for a variety of social programs than are politically feasible or socially acceptable in the United States. Social democratic welfare states in Scandinavia, Christian democratic welfare states on the European continent, and developmental industrial states in Asia, such as Japan, are prime examples. Canada is a particularly interesting case of a polity that has moved in two directions simultaneously—toward market liberalism U.S.-style under the impact of NAFTA and toward a more European-style welfare state. In this it mirrors the stance of many smaller capitalist democracies, which are market-liberal in the international economy and Social or Christian democratic in their domestic arrangements. Furthermore, judging by the experience of recent years, civil liberties in the war on terror are often better protected in Social and Christian democratic regimes (such as Continental European democracies) than in liberal ones (such as the United States).

Social anti-Americanism is based on value conflicts that reflect relevant differences in many spheres of life that touch on "life, liberty and the pursuit of happiness." In the absence of the perception of a common external threat, "American conditions" (*amerikanische Verhältnisse*) that are totally market-driven are resented by many Germans,[45] as they were in times of financial crisis by many Mexicans, Asians, and Argentineans in 1984, 1994, 1997, and 2001. Although it is not absent, hypocrisy is a smaller part of the resentment than in liberal anti-Americanism. The injustice embedded in U.S. policies that favor the rich over the poor is often decried. The sting is different here than for liberals who resent American hypocrisy. Genuine value conflicts exist on issues such as the death penalty, the desirability of generous social protections, preference for multilateral approaches over unilateral ones, and the sanctity of international treaties. Still, these value conflicts are smaller than those with radical anti-Americanism, in that social anti-Americans share broadly democratic values with the United States.

45. *Economist* 2004; Stephan 2005.

Sovereign-Nationalist Anti-Americanism

A third form of anti-Americanism focuses not on correcting domestic market outcomes but on political power. Sovereign-nationalists focus on two values: the importance of not losing control over the terms by which polities are inserted in world politics and the inherent importance and value of collective national identities. These identities often embody values that are at odds with America's. State sovereignty thus becomes a shield against unwanted intrusions from America.

The emphasis placed by different sovereign-nationalists can vary in three ways. The first is on nationalism, collective national identities that offer a source of positive identification. National identity is one of the most important political values in contemporary world politics, and there is little evidence suggesting that this is about to change. Such identities create the potential for anti-Americanism, both when they are strong (since they provide positive countervalues) and when they are weak (since anti-Americanism can become a substitute for the absence of positive values).

Second, sovereign-nationalists can emphasize sovereignty. In the many parts of Asia, the Middle East, and Africa where state sovereignty came only after hard-fought wars of national liberation, sovereignty is a much-cherished good that is to be defended. And in Latin America, with its very different history, domination by the United States has reinforced the perceived value of sovereignty. Anti-Americanism rooted in sovereignty is less common in Europe than in other parts of the world for one simple reason. European politics over the last half century has been devoted to a common project—the partial pooling of sovereignty in an emerging European polity.

Finally, through their anti-Americanism sovereign-nationalists may seek to reinforce the position of their own states as great powers. Such societies may define their own situations partly in opposition to dominant states. Some Germans came to strongly dislike Britain before World War I because they saw it as blocking what they believed to be Germany's rightful place in the sun. The British-German rivalry before World War I was particularly striking, in view of the similarities between these highly industrialized and partially democratic societies, and the fact that their royal families were related. Their political rivalry was systemic, pitting the dominant naval power of the nineteenth century against a rapidly rising land power. Rivalry bred animosity rather than vice versa.

Sovereign-nationalist anti-Americanism resonates well in polities that have strong state traditions and in which U.S. actions are perceived as detrimental to nationalism, sovereignty, or the exercise of state power. Encroachments on state sovereignty are particularly resented when the state has a tradition of directing domestic affairs. This is true in particular of the states of East Asia. The issues of "respect" and saving "face" in international politics can make anti-Americanism especially virulent, because it stirs nationalist passions in a way that social anti-Americanism rarely does.

All three elements of sovereign-nationalist anti-Americanism are present in China. The Chinese elites and public are highly nationalistic and very sensitive to threats to

Chinese sovereignty. Furthermore, China is already a great power and has aspirations to become even more powerful. Yet it is still weaker than the United States. Hence the superior military capacity of the United States, and its expressed willingness to use that capacity (for instance, against an attack by China on Taiwan) create the potential for anti-Americanism. When the United States attacks China (as it did with the bombing of the Chinese embassy in Belgrade in 1999) or seems to threaten it (as in the episode of the EC-3 spy plane in 2001), explicit anti-Americanism appears quickly.

Radical Anti-Americanism

We characterize a fourth form of anti-Americanism as radical. It is built around the belief that America's identity, as reflected in the economic and political power relations and institutional practices of the United States, ensures that its actions will be hostile to the furtherance of good values, practices, and institutions elsewhere in the world. For progress toward a better world to take place, the U.S. economy and society will have to be transformed, either from within or without.

Radical anti-Americanism was characteristic of Marxist-Leninist states such as the Soviet Union until its last few years and it is still defining Cuba and North Korea today. When Marxist revolutionary zeal was great, radical anti-Americanism was associated with violent revolution against U.S.-sponsored regimes, if not the United States itself. Its Marxist-Leninist adherents are now so weak, however, that it is mostly confined to the realm of rhetoric. For the United States to satisfy adherents of this brand of radical anti-Americanism, it would need to change the nature of its political-economic system.

Avishai Margalit and Ian Buruma, building on Werner Sombart's 1915 polemic contrasting Anglo-Saxon "merchants" with German "heroes," have labeled another contemporary variant of radical anti-Americanism as "Occidentalism."[46] The most extreme versions of Occidentalism hold that Western civilization entails values that are barbarous to the point of requiring the physical destruction of the people living in these societies. In the most extreme versions of Occidentalism the United States is the leading state of the West and therefore the central source of evil. This perceived evil may take various forms, from equality for women to public displays of the human body to belief in the superiority of Christianity. For those holding extreme versions of Occidentalist ideas the central conclusion is that the West, and the United States in particular, are so incorrigibly bad that they must be destroyed. And because the people who live in these societies refuse to follow the path of righteousness and truth, they must be attacked and exterminated.

Not all radical anti-Americans advocate violence, but as we define it radical anti-Americanism argues for the weakening, destruction, or transformation of the political and economic institutions of the United States.

46. Buruma and Margalit 2004.

It should be clear that these four different types of anti-Americanism are not simply variants of the same schema, emotions, or set of norms, with only slight variations at the margin. On the contrary, adherents of different types of anti-Americanism can express antithetical attitudes. Radical Muslims oppose a popular culture that commercializes sex and portrays women as liberated from the control of men, and they are also critical of secular-liberal values.[47] Social and Christian democratic Europeans, by contrast, may love American popular culture but criticize the United States for maintaining the death penalty and for not living up to secular values they share with liberals. Liberal anti-Americanism exists because its proponents regard the United States as failing to live up to its professed values—which are entirely opposed to those of religious radicals and are largely embraced by liberals. Secular radical anti-Americans may oppose the U.S. embrace of capitalism, but they may accept scientific rationalism, gender egalitarianism, and secularism—as Marxists have done. Anti-Americanism can be fostered by Islamic fundamentalism, idealistic liberalism, or Marxism. And it can be embraced by people who, not accepting any of these sets of beliefs, fear the practices or deplore the policies of the United States.[48]

The Role of Fear

Whether these identifications translate into anti-Americanism, or into very active anti-Americanism, depends, we conjecture, on an emotional dimension: the extent to which the United States is feared. Chiozza reports in chapter 4 that fear is stronger than hope, at least as reflected in public opinion polls. Solid majorities in four world regions thought in 2002 that the spread of American customs and ideas was negative for their countries: 78 percent in the Middle East, 72 percent in South Asia, 62 percent in Western Europe (and other industrial democracies), and 57 percent in Eastern Europe; East Asia was the only region in which a minority (49 percent) regarded the spread of American customs and ideas as negative. In general, we expect that fear can make even political liberals have negative views toward the United States, or activate and intensify the latent anti-American views of social, sovereign-nationalist, or radical individuals.[49]

In the absence of a fear of bad effects of U.S. action, liberals are pro-American (table 1.7, cell I). But if U.S. actions appear to create bad effects—as the war in Iraq

47. Chiozza, chapter 4, 118.

48. It should also be noted that, except for radical anti-Americans, people who express anti-American attitudes with respect to some aspects of the United States—such as United States foreign policy—can be quite pro-American with respect to other aspects of American society. And at other times, they may be pro-American in policy terms. When the United States acts in ways in which they approve, liberals, social democrats, and sovereign-nationalists may all be supportive of its actions.

49. Surprising to us is therefore the finding that Johnston and Stockman report in chapter 6. Chinese (specifically residents of Beijing) who have very low threat perceptions hold the most negative views of the United States, no matter what they thought of the identity difference separating Americans and Chinese. This disconfirmation of our expectations illustrates the fact that our conceptualization is very tentative and subject to revision in light of evidence.

is viewed as doing by many liberals at home and abroad—they may adopt attitudes of antipathy to U.S. policy, if not to the United States as a society (cell II). Social and Christian democrats, in the absence of fear of bad effects of the United States, may display some latent anti-Americanism—at dinner parties or when asking questions of visiting scholars from the United States—but this form of anti-Americanism is very mild, indeed passive (cell III). If the United States seems to impinge on their societies—for instance, if international competition from neoliberal societies is blamed for erosion of the welfare state at home—this anti-Americanism can become more intense (cell IV). Sovereign-nationalists may be able to ignore the United States when it does not play a major role in their region or country, or may even welcome its support against rivals. In this case (cell V) their anti-Americanism could be latent and not readily observable. But when they fear U.S. actions that could damage the interests of their polity, sovereign-nationalists respond with intense anti-Americanism, such as one has seen in China, Serbia, or Iraq (cell VI). Finally, radicals may find themselves in a situation in which they are politically supported by the United States—as is the case for parts of the Saudi elite—and therefore they have to keep their anti-Americanism latent (cell VII). In the absence of such cross-pressures, radicals are the most vociferous anti-Americans and the most antagonistic toward the United States (cell VIII).

The schemas, emotions, and norms that provide the basis for anti-American attitudes are as varied as the different types of anti-Americanism. Such attitudes and beliefs often lie dormant for long periods until events, or changes in political conditions, make them relevant and useful to political movements. We therefore need to differentiate between latent and active anti-Americanism, as McAdam does in chapter 9. Although both types of anti-Americanism will be picked up by public opinion polls, active anti-Americanism, which manifests itself as social movements, government policies, and even as violent action, is much more consequential for human welfare and for U.S. policy.

Table 1.7 is cast in terms of the attitudes of individuals. The different types of anti-Americanism can, however, also be manifested at the level of the polity in the form of collective beliefs, reflected, for example, in appropriate discourses, tropes, and acceptable rhetorical moves. Anti-Americanism can be studied also at local, regional, transnational, and global levels. Furthermore, as we have emphasized, it is often configurations of anti-Americanisms, rather than pure types, whose effects we observe. Political entrepreneurs and political organizations are very attuned to the different types of anti-Americanism, as they seek to mobilize people to whatever cause they are pursuing.

Historical Dimensions of Anti-Americanism

Table 1.7 does not take into account the particular experience of a society with the United States, which may condition the attitudes of its people. Two other forms of anti-Americanism, which do not fit within our general typology, are both historically sensitive and particularistic: elitist anti-Americanism and legacy anti-Americanism.

Elitist anti-Americanism arises in countries in which the elite has a long history of looking down on American culture, as is typically true of France.[50] As Sophie Meunier makes clear in chapter 5, France's cultural repertoire is distinctive and differs considerably in a variety of domains from that of the United States. In the words of Michèle Lamont and Laurent Thévenot, evaluations "based on market performance are much more frequent in the United States than in France, while evaluations based on civic solidarity are more salient in France."[51] French elites take great pride in such differences and their sense of cultural superiority. French intellectuals are the European epicenter of anti-Americanism, and some of their disdain spills over to the public. As tables 1.5 and 1.6 show, in 2005 the French public was particularly unfavorable toward the United States. However, polls of the French public between the 1960s and 2002 had indicated majority pro-Americanism in France, with favorable ratings that were only somewhat lower than levels observed elsewhere in Europe. And the implications of French elite coolness toward United States for policy were remarkably mild. France kept its distance from the United States during the cold war in some respects. For example, President de Gaulle withdrew France from the military arm of NATO. But France remained in NATO, and at times of crisis, such as the 1962 Cuban missile crisis, France stood strongly with the United States.

Elitist anti-Americanism has always been centered in Europe, particularly on the Continent. Indeed, discussions of anti-Americanism in Europe date back to the eighteenth century, when some European writers held that everything in the Americas was degenerate.[52] The climate was enervating; plants and animals did not grow as large as in Europe; people were uncouth. The tradition of disparaging America has continued ever since. Americans are often seen as uncultured materialists, seeking individual personal advancement without concern for the arts, music, or other finer things of life. Or they are viewed as excessively religious and, therefore, insufficiently rational.

Because elitist anti-Americanism is rooted in different identities, its adherents neither expect nor desire the United States to change its practices. On the contrary, America's continuing lack of commitment to high culture provides French elites a much-needed sense of superiority. Indeed, the character of America's system of secondary education and the all-encompassing impact of commercialized mass media ensure that cultural elites everywhere will continue to find many aspects of American society distasteful. Elitist anti-Americanism does not line up neatly in a hierarchical ordering of anti-Americanisms. Elitist anti-Americanism extracts one dimension of attitudes: the sense of superiority that an elite feels in relation to the United States. Such an elite could have any of the identities summarized in table 1.7 or a combination of them.

---

50. Chesnoff 2005; Miller and Molesky 2004; Revel 2003; Mathy 1993; Lacorne, Rupnik, and Toinet 1990; Toinet 1988; Strauss 1978.
51. Lamont and Thévenot 2000, 2.
52. Roger 2005.

Legacy anti-Americanism stems from resentment of past wrongs committed by the United States toward a respondent's society. Mexican anti-Americanism, for example, is prompted by the experience of U.S. military attacks on Mexico and various other forms of domination during the last one hundred and seventy years. The Iranian revolution of 1979, and the subsequent hostage crisis, were fueled by memories of U.S. intervention in Iranian politics, especially in the 1950s. Between the late 1960s and the end of the twentieth century, the highest levels of anti-Americanism recorded in Western Europe were in Spain and especially Greece—both countries that had experienced civil wars in which the United States had intervened on the side of the Right.[53]

If not reinforced by a continuation of the wrongs committed by the United States, by another form of anti-Americanism (as is the case in Iran), or by the institutionalization of historical memories of American wrongs, legacy anti-Americanism can be expected to decline over time. While it persists, it is likely to be restricted to specific places, taking the form of support for anti-American policies and tolerance of more radical anti-American movements, rather than being a source of direct attacks on the United States or on Americans. Legacy anti-Americanism can be explosive, but it is not unalterable. History both creates and eviscerates the roots that feed it. As McAdam shows in chapter 9, history can ameliorate or reverse negative views of the United States, as well as reinforce them.

Anti-Americanisms: Multiple Perspectives

This book is primarily an exercise in descriptive inference and comparative analysis. We aim to understand variation in what is considered "anti-Americanism," within an analytical framework that highlights the complexities of Americanism and distinguishes cognitive schema, emotions, and norms. We emphasize the multidimensionality and heterogeneity of anti-Americanism and the distinction we have drawn among opinion, distrust, and bias.

Our study spans conventional levels of analysis: individual, group, societal, domestic, transnational, and international. Selecting only one of these levels for investigation might misleadingly truncate our analysis. The various types of anti-Americanism here identified can be analyzed in different ways. Some analysts will emphasize individual attitudes and responses, relying heavily on cross-national public opinion research and experiments in the field of cultural psychology. Others may give pride of place to discourse analysis informed by theories of the public sphere or social

---

53. This is not to argue that this type of anti-Americanism is a simple linear extrapolation of the past as McAdam explores in chapter 9. We leave to future work by specialists of particular episodes of anti-Americanism comparisons and counterfactuals to probe this issue. For example, how does anti-Americanism in the Philippines and South Korea compare, as both societies were exposed to brutal Japanese occupation and both ruled in the 1970s by harsh autocratic regimes that enjoyed U.S. support? And how does the subsequent process of democratization affect the divergence in the level of expressed anti-Americanism, especially among the young?

frames. Still others may adopt a more historical-institutional approach, inquiring into the interpretation of various practices within their social and institutional context. We have asked our authors, insofar as practically feasible, to deploy several of these methods and to take several of these kinds of evidence into account. Indeed, one of the purposes of this book is to show that different perspectives on anti-Americanism can produce a richer understanding of this complex set of phenomena than the use of any single method to the exclusion of others. Methodologically, this volume is self-consciously pluralistic and eclectic.

In our analysis, we emphasize power, strategy, and legitimacy. Chapter 10 focuses specifically on the political consequences of anti-Americanism, which can only be understood in light of the strategic incentives faced by individuals and organizations. In that chapter, we interrogate conventional assumptions about the effects of anti-Americanism and search for evidence to determine whether anti-Americanism has significant effects on contemporary politics. In the conclusion, we reflect on the implications of anti-Americanism for our understanding of the United States itself and its role in world politics. We seek intellectual coherence for the whole book by focusing on the complex politics of anti-Americanisms.

2

Imagining America: The Promise and Peril of Boundlessness

DAVID M. KENNEDY

The European imagination was already groping toward a meaning for America *bien avant la lettre*. Hope and anxiety alike attended the enterprise from the outset. When Dante's Ulysses dared "to venture the uncharted distances" oceanward of the Pillars of Hercules, in search of "the uninhabited world behind the sun," was it heroism or hubris, a valorous quest to broaden the sphere of human endeavor or an insolent rebellion against the will of the gods? In Dante's account, Ulysses, after persuading his balky crew to slip the confines of the Mediterranean by sailing west of Gibraltar, roams the open ocean for five months before whirlwind-driven seas engulf his vessel. He is ever after encased in a tongue of flame deep within the eighth circle of Hell, the place of punishment for counselors of fraud.[1]

Dante's haunting allegory suggests that for medieval Europeans, the quest for lands beyond the known was sinfully treacherous. To cross the physical and imaginative boundaries of the world as then understood was to commit a transgression so grievous as to court divine ire and merciless retribution—even for a personage of such epic attributes as Ulysses. That sentiment did not wholly disappear even after the Middle Ages came to a close. In significant ways, it has colored attitudes toward America right down to the present day.

Some two centuries after the publication of Dante's tale, the liberating energies of the Renaissance began to usher Europe into the modern era. In 1492, at the Renaissance's zenith, in the decade when jubilant Roman workers excavated the classical Greek sculpture of the Apollo Belvedere, in the very year that a newly united Spanish monarchy consolidated Christendom's domains by expelling the last Jews and Muslims from the southern Iberian province of al-Andalus, a real-life mariner,

1. Dante 1964, *Hell*, 233–37.

Christopher Columbus, carved a course toward the setting sun from Palos, Spain, scarcely a hundred kilometers beyond the Mediterranean's western exit through which Dante's mythical Ulysses had fatefully voyaged. Unlike Ulysses, Columbus returned in triumph, bearing electrifying news of "innumerable people and very many islands" to the far westward in the ocean sea.[2]

Columbus's contemporary Francisco López de Gómara soon hailed his achievement as "the greatest event since the creation of the world."[3] Some three centuries later the Abbé Raynal declared that "no event has been so interesting to mankind in general, and to the inhabitants of Europe in particular, as the discovery of the new world"—though he also pointedly asked, "Has the discovery of America been useful or harmful to mankind?"[4] Adam Smith later called the discovery of America one of "the two greatest and most important events recorded in the history of mankind."[5] Columbus's discovery was unarguably momentous. No less so was the still unfinished task of making sense of it.

The staggering impact of Columbus's report on the fifteenth-century European imagination can scarcely be exaggerated. As he declared to his royal Spanish sponsors: "Your Highnesses have *an other world* here"—not merely undiscovered islands or unexplored territory or unheralded peoples, but an entire *world*, a whole sphere of existence, all of it, Columbus noted, hitherto "unknown, nor did anyone speak of it except in fables."[6] In modern parlance one might say that Columbus had uncovered something like a parallel universe, with all the challenges that such a revelation would pose to received ways of knowing and understanding.

Physically hemmed in by the Ottomans to the east, Europe now poured its energies westward, seeking to make use of America. In the first of several geopolitical tectonic shifts that the New World would occasion, the Atlantic replaced the Mediterranean as the Western world's most important sea. Andalusia, recently cleansed of both Muslims and Jews, once on Europe's far periphery, was about to become its center, at least for a season. First Spain and Portugal, then France and Britain, would seek domination in Europe on the basis of their New World possessions, until at long last an independent New World nation, the United States of America, would come to dominate the planet on a scale that earlier powers could not have envisioned.

Mentally hemmed in by the intellectual legacies of classical antiquity and Christian doctrine, Renaissance Europe sought a *meaning* for America as well. Prideful Ulysses had sinfully ruptured the boundaries of orthodoxy. Bold Columbus had daringly dilated the ambit of the known. But what Ulysses and Columbus had in common was that they had both dramatically breached the limits of their respective worlds' most cherished ideas, habits, and dreams. Ulysses and Columbus alike, in

---

2. Greenblatt 1993, 3.
3. Elliott 1970, 10.
4. Ibid., 1.
5. Smith 1981 [1776], 2:626. Smith considered the other to be the almost simultaneous opening of the route to Asia around the Cape of Good Hope.
6. Taviani et al. 1994, 59–97; Greenblatt 1993, 3–8.

short, had broken through some formidable cultural as well as geographical frontiers—a theme that would long endure in efforts to define America's significance.

By Dante's time Europeans had long since encountered Africa and the Islamic
lands—possibly even China, if one credits the account of Dante's contemporary,
Marco Polo—without feeling the need to alter substantially their understandings
of space, time, or the human condition. But in the full flush of the Renaissance,
Europe was "ready to go to school," in J. H. Elliott's phrase, to comprehend all
the geographical, cosmological, and cultural implications of Columbus's Tierra
Nueva.[7]

The inquiry continues today, more than half a millennium later, no less encumbered by ignorance and contradiction and confusion than it was five hundred years
ago, as famously registered in Columbus's historic misnomer—"Indians"—for the
indigenous peoples he took to be residents of the East Indies, his original destination. (To that end, he had traveled with an Arabic interpreter, well-marked copies of
Marco Polo's reports, and a letter from the King of Spain to the Great Khan—the
first in a long line of itinerant inquirers who were chronically ill-equipped to appreciate the American experience they actually encountered.)

The Mexican scholar Edmundo O'Gorman has suggested that fifteenth- and sixteenth-century Europeans did not so much discover America as invent it, and the
facts they found mattered less than the lenses through which they gazed. The process
of invention mingled wonder with disappointment, curiosity with skepticism, and
hope with apprehension. Columbus had sought a marine bridge to the Indies but
had instead collided with a land barrier—a continental mass athwart the ocean
highway. He came upon exotic peoples whose customs were at once quaint and repel-
lent. His reports both inspired and unsettled the European mind as it tried to take
in the enormity of what now lay revealed. Even as it expanded Europe's geographical compass, the astonishing fact of the New World strained the intellectual boundaries of a Renaissance European culture deeply in thrall to both its ancient Christian
creed and the resurrected precepts of classical Greece and Rome.

Those two sources—Christianity and antiquity—defined the principal frameworks
within which knowledge about the New World could be shaped into something comprehensible. From those traditions, fifteenth- and sixteenth-century Europeans forged
templates of understanding that have proved as long-lived as they have been inconsistent. The origins, durability, and stubbornly ambiguous character of the descriptive categories that those Renaissance-era Europeans crafted offer sobering testimony
to the staying power of inherited ways of thinking—or perhaps to the poverty of the
human intellect when confronted with the truly novel.

The twentieth-century American poet Robert Frost once wrote that "the land was
ours before we were the land's." It might similarly be said that Americans were
assigned identities before they even existed—or at least before Europe and Africa
began to send forth their children to the American continents and claim them as
their own. Well in advance of the arrival of any appreciable numbers of Europeans

7. Elliott 1970, 17.

or Africans, questions about the indigenous peoples of the Americas stimulated intense effort to define a human taxonomy into which they could be fitted. The scheme that was developed to make the native Americans comprehensible has served ever since as the basic framework for understanding all Americans.

Much was made of three observations: that the native peoples, as Columbus noted in 1493, "go about naked as their mothers bore them," and that they apparently knew neither government nor private property.[8] The nakedness of the native Americans was especially striking. It drew comment from countless commentators, from Columbus himself and the woodcut illustrators of the several versions of his reports that circulated in Europe in the 1490s to Amerigo Vespucci, the cartographer who repeatedly coasted the soon-to-be eponymously named American continents beginning in 1497, to Peter Martyr, the first great historian of the voyages of discovery, and to Juan de Sepúlveda and Bartolomé de Las Casas, who formally debated the nature of the native Americans at Valladolid, Spain, in 1550.

All of those observers sought to make sense out of the Americans by drawing on the only cultural resources available to them—the paired legacies of Christian faith and classical learning. For those who looked to the Christian tradition for guidance, the naked, propertyless, seemingly ungoverned Indians suggested a state of existence associated with prelapsarian Eden, a time of innocence, spontaneous human goodness, social equality, and uncoerced cooperation and mutuality—a golden age before the dawn of history, when mankind knew neither evil nor hierarchies of rank or status and had no need for laws or artifice, nor perhaps even for the strictures of a structured polity.

But others saw the nakedness of the Americans and recollected the distinction the ancient Greeks had made between themselves and the *barbarians*—a word whose Sanskrit root means "stammering" or a deficiency in the crucial faculty of language, the servant and medium of reason and therefore the human attribute that Aristotle considered proof of the proposition that man was destined for society. The native Americans, in this view, were barbarians who lacked the capacity for rational thought and consequently had no society worthy of the name. Being uncivilized, perhaps they were not even fully human.

Pope Paul III tried to settle this disagreement when he proclaimed in the bull *Sublimis Deus* in 1537 that the Indians were "true men" and therefore capable of receiving the Christian faith. The question remained whether they might be enslaved, which animated the confrontation between Las Casas and Sepúlveda at Valladolid some thirteen years later.

Sepúlveda invoked Aristotle in defense of the idea that since their civilized institutions made Spaniards naturally superior to the Indians, the conquistadores had a morally justifiably right to bind the New World's savage peoples to servitude. Las Casas countered by citing the traditional Christian doctrine about the command to "teach all nations" in defense of the Indians' humanity, dignity, and freedom. Las Casas is generally considered to have won the debate on its intellectual merits. The

8. Greenblatt 1993, 3–8.

enslavement of the native Americans went on nonetheless, not the last time that American reality would confound the principles of both faith and logic.

What is at issue here is not the fecklessness or hypocrisy of the conquistadores but the emergence in the immediate aftermath of Columbus's discovery of a dialogue about the American character that has recognizably endured with only slight modifications for more than five centuries. Underlying that dialogue has been a broader discourse about Nature itself. Is Nature, including especially human nature, benign or malevolent? Does it provide the standard to which all things humans should conform, or is it the implacable adversary against which all the resources of human contrivance and will must be mustered? Is Nature humankind's master or servant? Should it be given free rein or must it be tamed, bound down from mischief by laws and institutions and restrained by the coercive powers of church and state?

The debate about Nature has mapped with remarkable congruence onto the debate about America's meaning. Among other things, the discourse about Nature has arguably formed the principal conversation that has shaped the canon of American fictive literature, from James Fenimore Cooper and Washington Irving through Mark Twain and Henry James to F. Scott Fitzgerald and down to Saul Bellow and Philip Roth. Were the Americans, then and later, best understood as natural men (like Cooper's Natty Bumppo or Twain's Hank Morgan or James's Christopher Newman or Roth's Swede Lvov)—uncorrupted, innocent beings whose circumstances defined the criteria by which older civilizations should be judged? Has America therefore been a model for Europeans—indeed, for all peoples—a source of inspiration for those reformers who sought to restart history's clock and retrieve a natural order that had somehow been hijacked by priests and magistrates and monarchs? Or were the newly discovered peoples of the Americas, as well as the later immigrants to the New World, simply barbarians—savage, uncivilized, deficient in reason and understanding, and existing outside of history? And was America therefore destined, in the fullness of time, to be shepherded by more cultured and sophisticated souls (like Cooper's earnest Judge Temple or the treacherous Bellegardes in James's *The American*) onto the pathway that defined the historical trajectory of their own ancient civilization?

Among the earliest entrants in this lengthy debate was Sir Thomas More. The very title of his most famous work, *Utopia* (1516), ingeniously captured the contradictions that have plagued so many commentaries on the New World. More fashioned his title by deliberately compounding the Greek terms for "happy place" (*eu-topos*) and "no place" (*ou-topos*), and his work abounds in scholarly puns of an oxymoronic sort—the Anyder (anhydrous, or waterless) River, for example, or the name bestowed on the narrator, Raphael Hythloday, derived from the Greek for "healing nonsense."[9] Yet for all the playfully learned ambiguity of *Utopia*, on balance More took his stand with the admirers of Nature and the reformers. He built his imagi-

---

9. "More," or *morus* in Latin, itself plays on the Latin term for "folly," a verbal coincidence that More's friend Desiderius Erasmus had slyly used as a tribute to More in his classic work of 1509, *In Praise of Folly* (*Encomium Moriae* in Latin, or "In Praise of More").

nary utopia as a measuring rod with which to urge the melioration of the dysfunctional Old World.

More was a Christian humanist, deeply formed by his four years in a Carthusian monastery, a man of studious piety who fasted regularly, prayed daily, and routinely mortified his flesh with the aggravation of a hair shirt. He was also a lawyer, a trade delegate to the Continent on behalf of his London wool-merchant clients, a jurist, and a statesman. He straddled, in short, the transition from a medieval world preoccupied with devotion and subsistence to the nascent era of commercial capitalism and the rise of powerful nation-states—a transition in which Europe's engagement with America played a powerfully catalyzing role. More saw with his own eyes the promise as well as the potentially destructive power of that emerging social order, particularly in the English woolen districts convulsed by enclosure and the wholesale eviction of once-stable crofters. *Utopia* thus established the model for so many subsequent utopian theories, which typically have yearned to restore the presumed contentment and serenity of a bygone era, even while seizing the possibilities for change inherent in the disruptive present. America, as we shall see, could be used to figure both the nostalgic and the dynamic elements in that alluring compound.

Three years before *Utopia* appeared, in the land of Columbus's birth, Niccolò Machiavelli had published a trenchant attack on just the kind of imaginative speculation in which More would engage. "I have thought it proper to represent things as they are in real truth rather than as they are imagined," Machiavelli wrote in *The Prince*. "Many have dreamed up republics and principalities which have never in truth been known to exist; the gulf between how one should live and how one does live is so wide that a man who neglects what is actually done for what should be done moves towards self-destruction."[10]

Machiavelli was a realist and a pessimist. More himself was enough of an Augustinian to believe that humans could never fully escape this life's vale of tears. Yet by the time that More published *Utopia* in 1516, all Europe was throbbing with news of America, a place now undeniably seen and known to have real existence. That news inspired More to write a kind of measured rebuttal to Machiavelli's cynical counsel of resignation—an early instance of America's role as a stimulus to the reforming impulse.

Columbus's discovery helped to open the portals of More's mind, enabling him to envision a different and better world than the one he saw around him. More pointedly introduces Raphael Hythloday as someone who had "joined up with Amerigo Vespucci."[11] In Peter Martyr's *The New World* (1511), More had read that the native Americans "go naked, and they know neither weights nor measures, nor that source of all misfortunes, money; living in a golden age, without laws, without lying judges, without books, satisfied with their life, they know no difference between 'mine' and 'yours.'"[12] He ascribes similar traits to his Utopians. They wear clothing, to be sure,

10. Machiavelli 1999, 49.
11. More 1965, 38.
12. Quoted in Evans 1976, 3.

though mostly cloaks "always the same color—the natural color of wool."[13] Of far greater importance, they "have very few laws," and, as in Plato's *Republic*, they hold all property in common.[14]

Utopia, written just two decades after Columbus's news surged across Europe, was among the earliest efforts to fashion from the still-exotic knowledge of America a useful image of the New World's character. More established several perspectives and tropes that were destined, through many permutations, to persist in virtually all later appraisals of America, none more lastingly than his model of Utopia as a place where history had a different starting point, a place that held the promise of a world unburdened of its past, where the curve of time itself might be inflected anew.

In this broad sense, many of the dominant images of America were long the property of the Left, of the parties of change and progress. Countless later observers would return to this theme of America as the land whose freedom from history defined its distinctive promise as well as its metaphorical utility. For these commentators, the core of America's identity was precisely its open-ended indeterminacy. John Locke captured the point well when he wrote near the end of the seventeenth century that "in the beginning, all the world was America." Jean-Jacques Rousseau intended something similar when he said almost a century thereafter that "man is born free, but everywhere he is in chains." Perhaps most famously, Alexis de Tocqueville opened his magisterial study of democracy in America with the foundational observation that "among the novel objects that attracted my attention during my stay in the United States, nothing struck me more forcibly than the general equality of condition among the people."[15]

Equality was for Tocqueville many things: a social condition, an ideal, a value, a habit of the heart. But like More—and Locke and Rousseau—Tocqueville also dwelled on equality as a way to invoke a time before history, a time when arbitrary and invidious social distinctions had not yet taken malevolent root, a time when all things were possible, for individuals as well as for societies. Yet, unlike More, Tocqueville was not confined to imaginative extrapolation from Peter Martyr's meager knowledge of the New World. He had a real case study to examine—the recently independent and flamboyantly, raucously democratic United States. He therefore betook himself to America in May 1831 for a nine-month sojourn that furnished the basis for his classic work.

Tocqueville arrived in the United States at the height of the Jacksonian era, the moment when the new American republic perhaps most exuberantly exhibited its essential nature. The novelty of what he found and the contrasts with the Europe he knew were striking. Tocqueville made much of the fact that the French Revolution of 1789 had excited powerful counterrevolutionary forces and ultimately failed, while America's of 1776 (or 1788) had met little consequential opposition and conclusively

13. More 1965, 78.
14. Ibid., 106.
15. Locke 1980, 29; Rousseau 1997, 41; Tocqueville 1994 [1835], 3.

succeeded—an early and influential formulation of the notion that American life was best understood in terms of what was absent from it. Tocqueville noted other contrasts as well. The so-called July Revolution of 1830 had installed the dandified "citizen king" Louis-Philippe, the former Duke of Orleans, on the French throne; Andrew Jackson, the sitting president of the United States, was a semiliterate backwoods ruffian who bore two bullets in his body from frontier duels. Louis-Philippe commanded an army of some two hundred thousand men in France, which had 2.5 times the population of the United States; Jackson's numbered just 6,300. Most tellingly, more than one million voters, with no further qualification than their being adult white males, had put Jackson in the White House; the French electorate then numbered about 170,000 substantially propertied males.

Tocqueville's ambition was to trace what he called a great circle around the future—not to predict the future with precision, but to mark out an area that contained the several possible paths ahead. His premise was that democracy, for all its novelty, was inevitable. The forces that had welled up in Europe after 1789 might have been suppressed, but they had surely not been extinguished, as the mildly reformist July Revolution in France and the rising Chartist movement in Britain testified, as did the wave of Latin American revolutions in the first decades of the nineteenth century. Democratic independence movements in Mexico in 1813, Argentina in 1816, Chile in 1818, Peru and Venezuela in 1821, and Brazil in 1822 all dramatized democracy's waxing vitality. The United States, as the nation that had most fully organized itself on democratic principles, was therefore the laboratory in which the future might be beheld. Like More's Utopia, Tocqueville's America was to be an example for Europe. As Tocqueville put it: "I confess that in America I saw more than America; I sought there the image of democracy itself, with its inclinations, its character, its prejudices, and its passions, in order to learn what we have to fear or to hope from its progress."[16]

"Fear or hope"—there was the heart of the matter. In the spirit of the Abbé Raynal's question as to whether the discovery of America had been useful or harmful to mankind, Tocqueville took American democracy as a given, but maintained a studied skepticism about what would be the destiny of a society so structured and so governed.

Broadly speaking, he saw two possibilities, which might be called the centrifugal and centripetal—both of which, in turn, could be defined in relation to the master concept of Nature. In the first, equality, as the original condition and dominant value of democratic societies, might liberate the essence of the human spirit and engender a radical "individualism" (a word that Tocqueville coined to describe the unique psychology he imputed to the Americans). Individualism would unleash human ambitions and energize society; but it might also prove so corrosive of the integument that held society together that America would dissolve into anarchic chaos. With the rise of individualism, he said,

16. Tocqueville 1994 [1835], 1:14.

the bond of human affection is extended, but it is relaxed. . . . The woof of time is every instant broken, and the track of generations effaced. . . . Aristocracy had made a chain of all the members of the community, from the peasant to the king; democracy breaks that chain, and severs every link of it. . . . It throws [every man] back forever upon himself alone, and threatens in the end to confine him entirely within the solitude of his own heart.[17]

Alternatively, a radical egalitarianism might lead inexorably to a grotesque set of new social strictures—the "tyranny of the majority" that worried both Tocqueville and his celebrated friend John Stuart Mill. A society that obliterated all local loyalties to parish or lord or clan in the name of the sovereign, undifferentiated people would be at the mercy of majorities whose will would encounter no effective resistance. Thus the paradox that the "natural" circumstance of equality might ultimately generate toxically unnatural constraints on liberty and individuality.

Tocqueville, of course, found all kinds of mitigating circumstances in the America he visited that checked both of those tendencies, particularly the majoritarian despotism that was his greatest fear. Conspicuously important was the plethora of voluntary associations that sustained something quite similar to the psychological attachments that traditional societies had rooted in vassalage and serfdom and village life and religious faiths, and that served to counter the weight of the potentially tyrannical central state.

Tocqueville stands recognizably in a tradition that stretches back to Thomas More—or even to Dante. His America is a place that hearkens back to a prehistorical, natural past, even while it bears the seeds of the future. It is also, most importantly, a place whose very lack of history sets few limits on either personal striving or society's collective aspirations—at least few of the customary limits that had traditionally imparted structure to individual identity and social organization alike. Tocqueville in the end convinced himself that the Americans had managed to reconstitute the functional equivalents of those limits, but the sense of open-ended interrogation and wary skepticism that informed his inquiry broods over his pages still, defining them as the classic commentary on the several possibilities of a society whose energy, fluidity, and malleability remain as remarkable today as they were in the 1830s.

Within a generation of Tocqueville's work, another body of theory arose that did not seek simply to trace a circle around a number of possible futures. It claimed, rather, to have plotted the unique vector of all history. And in this account, however improbable it might seem from our present perspective, America proved essential to the case. "As in the eighteenth century, the American War of Independence sounded the tocsin for the European middle class," Karl Marx wrote in the preface to *Das Kapital* (1867), "so in the nineteenth century, the American Civil War sounded it for the European working class."[18] In Marx's view, victory in the Civil

17. Ibid., 2:99.
18. Marx and Engels 1992, 4.

War had eliminated the last feudal remnant—the Southern planter aristocracy—that had frustrated the agenda of the Northern industrial bourgeoisie. With that obstacle removed, the American capitalist project could go forward unchecked. The "objective conditions" that Marx believed made revolution inevitable were now established more thoroughly and unqualifiedly in the United States than anywhere else. Paradoxically, the ease with which history's burdens had been shed in the United States made it the place where history's timetable would wondrously accelerate, generating the first of the socialist revolutions that Marxist theory considered the necessary culmination of capitalist development.

Marx thus took his place in a long line of commentators who found America's distinguishing characteristic to be its freedom from the kinds of historical constraints that elsewhere encumbered the realization of an idealized future—even while America was now thought to display the properties that would first confirm the modern world's most seductive theory of history itself. A chorus of Marxists echoed the master's point as the nineteenth century approached its climax. "In European countries," Marx's collaborator Friedrich Engels wrote in the wake of the Haymarket riot in Chicago in 1886, "it took the working class years and years before they fully realized the fact that they formed a distinct and, under the existing social conditions, a permanent class of modern society; and it took years again until this class-consciousness led them to form themselves into a distinct political party. . . . On the more favored soil of America, *where no medieval ruins bar the way, where history begins* with the elements of the modern bourgeois society as evolved in the seventeenth century, the working class passed through these two stages within ten months."[19] Shortly thereafter Engels wrote to his colleague Friedrich Sorge, "History is on the move over there at last, and I must know my Americans badly if they do not astonish us all by the vastness of their movement. . . . It is a land without tradition (except for the religious) . . . , and a people full of energy as no other."[20] He remained confident in that opinion five years later, when he anticipated that the socialist revolution would go forward in America—"the advances always . . . more powerful, the setbacks less paralyzing."[21]

Engels expressed a particularly sanguine view of just how the historical speedup was expected to work in America, but his general sentiment was widely shared. Karl Kautsky, a founder of the German Social Democratic Party, declared as late as 1902 that "the United States are today unquestionably the most important and interesting of the modern cultural lands. Not England, but America shows us our future."[22]

Yet as the first years of the twentieth century unfolded, observers of the Marxist persuasion grew increasingly frustrated that the Americans were not behaving as Marxist theory so hopefully predicted. "We are waiting for you Americans to do

---

19. Engels to Weydmeyer, August 7, 1851, in Marx and Engels 1953, 25–26. Emphasis added.
20. Engels to Sorge, August 8, 1887, in Marx and Engels 1953, 190.
21. Engels to Schluter, March 30, 1892, in Marx and Engels 1953, 242–43.
22. Quoted in Moore 1970, 59.

something," the German Social Democrat August Bebel wrote to an American correspondent in 1907. "You see—your country is far ahead of Germany in industrial development. . . . You Americans will be the first to usher in a Socialist Republic. . . . The United States . . . will be the first nation to declare a Co-operative Commonwealth."[23]

That frustration soon found more formal expression in a trenchant work by a young German economist, Werner Sombart. Like Tocqueville before him, Sombart journeyed to the United States in 1904 to gauge for himself how America fitted in to the scheme of history. But unlike Tocqueville, who came to explore the several possible futures of democracy, Sombart's mission was to investigate why socialism's singular future had not yet materialized in "capitalism's land of promise," the place where, theory held, "modern socialism follows as a necessary reaction to capitalism."[24] The result was Sombart's uncommonly shrewd commentary, *Why Is There No Socialism in the United States?*

Sombart's answer constitutes a minor classic in analyses of both America and Marxism, but its details need not concern us here. What matters to this discussion is the premise of his question: something confidently predicted and eagerly anticipated had *not* come to pass in the United States, to the disappointment and even embitterment of those who had expected it. The United States that Sombart beheld had fulfilled only part of the Marxist prophecy. Industrial capitalism had triumphed, to be sure, but the socialist revolution that was presumed to be its inevitable consequence showed no sign of coming to pass. In Marxist terms, a historical force had failed to generate its expected antithesis. That failure badly confounded Marx's theory of history. Sombart's explanation for that failure rested on a venerable perception about the character of America, even as it heralded a new chapter in the long history of efforts to assess America's meaning.

Although the Marxist terminology may have been new, the basic form of Sombart's conclusion was familiar: once again America was seen as a place where any impulse, once set in motion, would tend to run its course without significant check or meaningful limitation. That much was old news. But Sombart's findings also marked some new departures in perceptions of the United States. He differed significantly from Tocqueville, who worried about the possibly self-destructive tendencies of an unbridled egalitarianism but identified several mitigating institutions and behaviors that held those tendencies in check. For Sombart, the expected countervailing forces that were supposed to contain and transform bourgeois capitalism were not in evidence. Not only did *"no medieval ruins bar the way"* but no other limiting factors took their place. America had now become quite literally the place where "anything goes"—and went on and on. As the philosopher George Santayana wrote in 1920, "America is all one prairie, swept by a universal tornado . . . there is no country in which people live under more overpowering compulsions."[25]

23. Ibid., 78–79.
24. Sombart 1976 [1906], 3, 15.
25. Ibid.

There was more. All commentators on America, up to and including Sombart and Santayana, had drawn from a conceptual inventory that was abundantly stocked even before 1492, and substantially enriched immediately thereafter. That inventory contained countless possible images—America as the land of promise or delusion, a natural Eden or a howling wilderness, home to Fortune's favorites or fools, Nature's noblemen or ignoble savages, the enlightened or the duped, just to name a few. Commentators have continued to draw on that inventory right down to the present, assigning different values to different observations according to the dictates of their own perspectives and purposes. But as the twentieth century opened, for many observers like Sombart the core conception of boundlessness, the unmatched fluidity and limitlessness and sheer uninhibitedness of American life, began to take on newly worrisome overtones.

Thomas More and John Locke and Jean-Jacques Rousseau and the Abbé Raynal and countless other imaginers of America had essentially summoned what America they willed from the wellsprings of their own intellection. Tocqueville had traced an arc of several potential fates for an American democracy still in its formative stage. The Marxists had fastened their own grand historical design onto America. All had presumed that whatever America's distinguishing characteristics were, history (or its absence) and circumstance would permit their fullest, purest, unattenuated development.

But the collapse of Marxist hopes for America that Sombart systematically explained marked America's transition from a tabula rasa, or at least an unformed youth—a historyless *object* onto which various representations, hopes, and fears could be projected—to a mature *subject* whose own actions increasingly defined its identity, and which, not merely incidentally, at the same time began seeking ways of asserting itself in the world as never before. By the opening of the twentieth century, America as a passive and protean image was giving way to America as an active and insistent reality—one that now quite literally *mattered*. Here at last the weight of history—empirical history, as distinguished from imagination or prediction or historical theorizing in the Marxist manner—was beginning to be felt.

At this point the United States could no longer serve so unqualifiedly as the repository of the hopes of the Left. Once a vessel for so many different yearnings for the future, the United States now came increasingly to be perceived as the principal agent of a single great historical process—the global capitalist project that Marx himself had described so vividly, one that "compelled all nations, on pain of extinction, to adopt the bourgeois mode of production."[26]

That transition involved more than mere representation. For more than a century after its birth, the United States had been a marginal player in the world's affairs. Absorbed in the great task of conquering and consolidating its continental domains, the United States through the nineteenth century had little interest and less influence in developments beyond North America and the Caribbean Basin. Its most assertive diplomatic pronouncement touching the wider world, the Monroe Doctrine

26. Marx and Engels 1992, 22.

of 1823, evoked only contemptuous sneers in the European chancelleries of the day. Until as late as 1893, an inward-looking United States deliberately eschewed the rank of ambassador for its representatives to foreign capitals. Many powers reciprocated, maintaining legations, rather than full-dress embassies, in Washington, D.C., where the State Department well into the 1890s managed the entirety of the nation's diplomatic business with a staff of fewer than one hundred people. The U.S. Army in the nineteenth century's last decade ranked fourteenth in size in the world, after Bulgaria's.

But as the twentieth century dawned, the presence of the United States in the world was becoming more and more difficult to ignore. The United States was by then the second-most populous Western nation, after Russia. It boasted the world's greatest rail network and the largest outputs of wheat, coal, iron, steel, and electrical energy. The Spanish-American War in 1898 and the subsequent annexation of Puerto Rico and the Philippines strongly evidenced America's capacity to project its influence abroad. By the time that President Theodore Roosevelt ostentatiously dispatched the Great White Fleet on its round-the-world show-of-strength voyage in 1907, most of the major European states had upgraded their Washington missions to embassy status and staffed them with some of their most able diplomats. The celebrated French commentator André Tardieu declared in 1908 that "Bismarck . . . called the Monroe Doctrine 'an international impertinence.' Today, the impertinence would be in mistaking its scope. . . . The United States is . . . a world power. . . . It is seated at the table where the great game is played, and it cannot leave it."[27]

That judgment was as yet premature. The Americans themselves continued to confound foreign observers in the early years of the twentieth century by their own indecision about just what kind of international role they wanted to play. They faced three choices: to reaffirm historic isolationism; to become a great power on the model of the other powers—the "realistic" course that Theodore Roosevelt urged and André Tardieu mistakenly believed was already in train; or to hearken to a new voice—Woodrow Wilson's—that would soon summon them to an idealistic crusade to remake the world in the American mold.

In a fateful inversion, the nation that the world had long bent to its own imaginative purposes now began to dream seriously of bending the world to its image of itself. And in a compound historical irony of some considerable consequence, the Americans, like the fabled public figures who come to believe their own press releases, embraced some of the oldest myths that others had long projected upon them, including the alluring idea that they were children of nature unencumbered by history, whether their own or others'.

To be sure, the transference of that attitude into the realm of foreign policy was slow to crystallize and vigorously contested. Many Americans in the early twentieth century still clung to their inherited isolationist precepts; indeed, what was arguably the high-water mark of isolationist sentiment lay in the decades just ahead, between the two world wars. And Theodore Roosevelt contemptuously dismissed idealistic

27. Roger 2005, 281; May 1961, 242.

pretensions about changing the world as so much fatuous blather. He championed a traditional great-power role for the United States, one that took the existing international order as essentially given, carefully calibrated national ambitions to national interests and national efforts to national means, and unsentimentally relied on the time-honored techniques of self-assertion and military vigor to secure the national agenda.

Yet while isolationism retained a certain vitality, Roosevelt's brand of realpolitik, with its explicit recognition of priorities and limitations, never comfortably settled in the minds and hearts of his countrymen. Even an admirer of Roosevelt like Henry Kissinger, one of the premier realists of the modern era, conceded that "neither its experience nor its values prepared America for the role assigned to it by Roosevelt," who was, Kissinger concludes, positively "un-American" in his advocacy of diplomatic realism.[28] The future—indeed, in his own mind, the past as well—belonged to Woodrow Wilson and his distinctive distillation of American experience and values into a potent foreign policy doctrine, known ever after as "Wilsonianism."

Wilson crafted that doctrine out of his own understanding of America's past. Roosevelt had urged Americans to divest themselves of the isolationist delusions that their unique history had unfortunately instilled in them. Wilson, in contrast, excavated from the peculiarities of America's historical record a vein of sentiment and belief— and an inventory of images and myths—from which he hoped to fashion a tool that would transform the world. He cast himself as the long-awaited agent who would fulfill the Revolutionary generation's promise to create a "novus ordo secolorum" (new order of the ages), abroad as well as at home. "It was of this that we dreamed at our birth," he told the Senate in July 1919, on presentation of the treaty he had just signed at Versailles.[29] Wilson believed that he was not simply selecting a foreign policy from a palette of options or inventing a new American international agenda. He believed, rather, that he was articulating the only such agenda that his countrymen would find consistent with their past, their principles, and their own self-image, if they were to have a foreign policy at all.

Wilson drew copiously from a body of Enlightenment thought that aimed to bring the social order into conformity with what were taken to be the principles of Nature—an ambition that had characteristically animated the American Founders. Wilsonianism consists principally in the notion that the world at large can be both tamed and prospered by adherence to the kinds of social and legal arrangements that had, in Wilson's judgment, served the United States so well. They included self-determination, which encompassed both anticolonialism and democratization, the twin goals of the American revolutionaries of 1776; free trade, also consistent with the antimercantilist grievances of the Founders; and a new institution, the League of Nations, intended to introduce into the international system at least the rudiments of the judicial and political apparatus that had undergirded America's own order and comity in the preceding century and a half. The independent, democratic states

28. Kissinger 1994, 39, 42, 43.
29. Link 1989, vol. 61, 436.

that were to populate Wilson's international order would respect one another's sovereignty, adhere to norms agreed on by the entire international community, energetically pursue economic development, and encourage unfettered commercial exchange.

To call those proposals transformative is accurate, but that term scarcely captures the scale of their ambition, or the peculiarly American considerations that defined and qualified them. Wilson proposed truly revolutionary changes in the very nature of international relations. But he was offering, in effect, a *contingent* internationalism for the United States, one that insisted on changing the rules and the character of the international order as a precondition for U.S. participation in it. Wilsonianism thus revealed its deep roots in notions of American exceptionalism reaching back to the time of Columbus, even while Wilson sought to break away from the isolationist diplomacy that exceptionalism had long informed.

Realists then and later gagged on these Wilsonian proposals, which they deemed nothing less than, well, utopian. Critics such as Kissinger and the diplomat and historian George F. Kennan deemed Wilsonianism to be criminally negligent of the Machiavellian principle that how we live will forever be different from how we ought to live, and hopelessly romantic in its unwarranted premise that such a thing as the "international community," understood as a body with shared values and commitments, actually exists. Tellingly, Kennan the historian charged Wilson with having "dismissed the past with contempt" and of engaging in "the colossal conceit of thinking that you could suddenly make international life over into what you believed to be your own image."[30]

Yet in Wilson's defense, it might be said that nothing could be more American than those ideas, especially the dismissal of history as a constraint on will and ambition. Perhaps more to the point, what other concepts could so powerfully inform U.S. diplomacy? On what basis other than their own experience and values can a people's foreign policy be legitimately and reliably based, especially in a democracy that rests on the consent of the governed? Here identity and policy fatefully merge, and a national identity suffused with exceptionalist thinking and joined with unprecedented capacity for action might be said to be capable of yielding nothing other than a transformative foreign policy, for better or worse.

Ever since Wilson's first formulation of his diplomatic precepts, many foreign observers have ridiculed and resisted them. French premier Georges Clemenceau in 1919 drolly sniffed at what he considered Wilson's idealistic vaporizing when he noted that despite Wilson's beliefs in the benevolence of human nature and the redeeming power of democracy, "I have lived in a world where it was good form to shoot a democrat." (An anarchist had shot and wounded Clemenceau in the midst of the Paris peace negotiations.) "God gave us his Ten Commandments," said Clemenceau, "and we broke them. Wilson gave us his Fourteen Points—we shall see."[31]

---

30. Kennan 1951, 69.
31. MacMillan 2003, 23; Bailey 1980, 608.

Wilsonianism was stillborn in 1919, its champion frustrated at Paris and eventually repudiated by his own countrymen. But a generation later, at the conclusion of another world war, the United States held near-hegemonic sway in the world—and at the conclusion of the cold war some four decades thereafter its hegemony seemed virtually complete. It then played its part with relish, and in conformity to Wilson's script, as reformulated in the Atlantic Charter of 1941. American actions were not always perfectly faithful to Wilson's principles, but on balance Franklin Roosevelt and his successors supported decolonization in Africa and Asia, encouraged democracy where they could, and, most impressively, spawned a host of new international institutions, including the United Nations, the World Bank, the International Monetary Fund, and the General Agreement on Tariffs and Trade, which transmformed into the World Trade Organization in the 1990s—by which time a new word had been coined to describe the transformed planetary order that U.S. policy had nurtured: globalization.

This was the spectacle that the world now confronted: an America that had become the chief agent of modernization in both the political and economic realms, its world-transforming agenda unchecked by any consequential opposition at home or abroad; a nation convinced that its own polity and policies were in conformity with the precepts of Nature, inhabited by a people notoriously impatient with history and keen to wield their unparalleled "hyperpower" to shape the world as they wished. Whether they liked it or not, other peoples now shared the planet with a nation that had come to embrace with gusto the idea of itself as a prairie swept by a tornado— a perception that now excited as much animosity as it did admiration.

For better or worse, America in the twenty-first century has thus *realized* many of the imaginings about its character that originated in the fifteenth century, if not before. Seen in that long perspective, both the image and the reality of modern America as an unrestrained force destined to breach all frontiers of belief and behavior seem to have a certain inevitability, whether for good or for ill. Woodrow Wilson himself acknowledged as much in his war address of 1917: "God helping her," he said of his country, "she can do no other."[32] Perhaps character is destiny after all.

32. Link 1989, vol. 41, 527.

II

PUBLIC ATTITUDES TOWARD THE UNITED STATES

3

Anti-Americanism in Europe during the Cold War

PIERANGELO ISERNIA

Anti-Americanism deservedly merits the label of an "essentially contested concept."[1] It is difficult to pinpoint precisely its nature and characteristics, since anti-Americanism in Europe has taken the form of a recurrent set of themes, some of them going back to the American Revolution,[2] that have been played out over and over again in different tunes and rhythms. Indeed, the persistence of anti-Americanism is partly explained by its very contentious nature. It serves sometimes as an instrument for delegitimizing political opponents' credentials to govern and sometimes "for mobilizing popular support and deflecting frustration away from the leadership toward a foreign, omnipresent and supposedly omnipotent protagonist."[3] Anti-Americanism has always played an important political function in the ideological clash between Left and Right both in Europe and in the United States.[4] I do not intend another reconstruction of this flow of images, an attempt typically carried on

This chapter is based partly on ideas presented at an American Institute for Contemporary German Studies workshop "The Media–Public Opinion–Policy Nexus in German-American Relations," April 22, 2005, in Berlin. I also benefited greatly from the discussion at the conference "Anti-Americanism and Its Consequences" at the Center for Advanced Study in the Behavioral Sciences in Palo Alto in June 2005. I thank the two editors and Paul Sniderman for their careful comments on a preliminary draft of this chapter. Linda Fratini conducted the bibliographic search, Davide Orsini located and collected the relevant questions on anti-Americanism, and Sara Franceschi assisted me with the statistical analyses. Teresa Ammendola helped to build the individual-level longitudinal data set covering 1952–1970 and Sara Franceschi checked it. Unless otherwise noted, analysis has been conducted using SPSS version 12.0, STATA/SE 9, and EQS.

1. Gallie (1956).
2. Schulte and Nordholt 1986, 7.
3. Rubinstein and Smith 1985, 25.
4. For Europe see Teodori 2002; for Italy Debouzy 1996; and for France Kuisel 1993. For the United States, see Hollander 1995.

at the national level, such as France, Germany, Italy or the Netherlands, and only more rarely in a comparative fashion.[5] In this chapter, however, I focus on the image of the United States held by mass publics in Western Europe during the cold war, in particular in France, Germany, Italy, and the United Kingdom, not only because of their different national cultures and the rich set of long-term survey data available but also because each has been singled out by different authors as the most anti-American country in Europe. The evidence of mass anti-Americanism during the period between 1950 and 1970, in particular, has never systematically been analyzed. I base this chapter on a secondary analysis of a very rich, systematic, and underutilized stock of surveys collected between the 1950s and the 1970s by several institutions, most prominently the United States Information Agency (USIA) and the Eurobarometer. Of course, secondary analysis is severely constrained by the kind of questions that were asked. Because of this I have chosen to utilize surveys carried out in different periods, so as to exploit the variety of indicators available, at the expense of some of the rigor offered by strict comparability over time of identically worded questions.

How Europeans Think about America

The definitions of anti-Americanism offered by the literature run the full gamut of the predispositional-situational continuum.[6] The stereotypical view of anti-Americanism—the prevalent interpretation of anti-Americanism in cultural studies—defines it as visceral and emotional, a knee-jerk reaction to anything American, rooted in personality traits similar to ethnocentrism and anti-Semitism (to which some claim it is related).[7] The cognitive view—the one prevalent in studies based on survey data—sees anti-Americanism as a reaction, situationally grounded, to U.S. foreign policies and actions.[8] In between, there are those who characterize anti-Americanism as an "ambivalent" sentiment, in which a set of different considerations are "sampled" and averaged in people's minds.[9]

In my attempt to offer an operational definition of anti-Americanism, I think it is useful to start from the more general, and neutral, concept of *image*, defined as "the organized representation of an object in an individual's cognitive system."[10] An image of a nation "constitutes the totality of attributes that a person recognizes (or imagines) when he contemplates that nation."[11] As such it is a "combinatorial con-

5. See Kuisel 1993; Roger 2005; Diner 1996; D'Attorre 1991; and Kroes and van Rossem 1986. But see Ellwood 1999 and Markovits 2004b.

6. My analysis has been based on the following texts: Crockatt 2003; D'Attorre 1991; Defleur and Defleur 2003; Diner 1996; Elwood 1999; Haseler 1985; Hollander 1995; Kroes and van Rossem 1986; Kuisel 1993; Lacorne 1986; Pells 1997; Rubinstein and Smith 1985; Spiro 1998; Strauss 1978; Teodori 2002, 2003; Toinet 1988.

7. E.g., Hollander 1995, Haseler 1985, and Markovits 2004b.

8. E.g., Smith and Wertman 1992.

9. Johnston and Ray 2004; Chiozza 2004a, but see also Chiozza, chapter 4.

10. Kelman 1966, 24.

11. Scott 1966, 72.

struct"[12] of three interrelated components: (a) cognitive, the set of attributes that the person understands as "inherent" in the object; (b) affective, representing like or dislike of the focal object; and (c) action-oriented, "consisting of a set of responses to the object that the person deems appropriate in the light of its perceived attributes."[13] This tripartite distinction, analogous to and inspired by the threefold dimensions of *attitude* prevalent in the psychological literature,[14] is helpful in disentangling three fundamentally different sets of attitudes toward the United States: *feelings*, *beliefs*, and *policy attitudes*. People can have affective or emotional feelings about the United States. They can also entertain certain beliefs about the United States. The American system has been acclaimed or assailed for several reasons, such as its capitalist nature, its democratic mission, and its being a beacon of modernity. Finally, given the powerful position of the United States in the world system, people tend to evaluate U.S. policies and actions on their own merits, possibly using standards unrelated to their beliefs and feelings about the nation. And feelings, beliefs, and attitudes can vary quite independently.

Here, I interpret anti-Americanism as a general mood of disliking America rather than negative beliefs about this or that attribute of the U.S. political, cultural, or socioeconomic system or negative attitudes toward one or another U.S. policy, decision, or behavior.[15] I therefore define anti-Americanism as the psychological tendency to systematically modulate in a negative way the assessment of the United States. Anti-Americanism is a "mood" whose main function is to act as "a primary mechanism for altering information-processing priorities and for shifting modes of information processing."[16] In other words, anti-Americanism is the "affective background" that permeates any assessment of what the United States does and is. Such a definition of anti-Americanism leaves open for empirical assessment the issue of whether its sources are rational or irrational, visceral or thoughtful. Before examining the affective nature of anti-Americanism and its relation to cognitive components in shaping attitudes toward the United States, I will briefly introduce the main indicators used to measure it in the empirical literature.

Indicators of Anti-Americanism

To measure anti-American feelings at the mass level three set of indicators have been traditionally used.[17] A first set of questions asks about the respondents' feeling toward or opinion of the United States. These questions come in two

---

12. Deutsch and Merritt 1966.

13. Scott 1966, 72.

14. Eagly and Chaiken 1993.

15. The concept of mood in psychology defines one of the many possible affective states. I found the functional definition of mood, as distinct from emotion, introduced by Davidson (1994, 51–55) useful in disentangling the prototypical characteristics of anti-Americanism. The concept of mood in psychology is related to, although it does not completely overlap, its use in public opinion research (e.g., Klingberg 1983 and Stimson 1991).

16. Davidson 1994, 52.

17. See also the discussion in Smith and Wertman 1992, 93–103.

formats.[18] The most frequent one is a standard Likert-scale question, asking the respondent's opinion of the United States on a scale ranging from very good to very bad, with an intermediate "fair" (or, alternatively, neither good nor bad) category.[19] Another way of getting at the feelings toward a country is the so-called feeling thermometer.[20] A second set of questions, also asked repeatedly over time, asks about the level of *trust* in the American *people*.[21] The third, and probably the most straight-forward way of measuring anti-American feelings, was tried in Eurobarometer 17 (April 1982) and 22 (April 1984): "How would you describe your feelings toward the United States. As strongly anti-American, somewhat anti-American, somewhat pro-American, strongly pro-American or neither pro- nor anti-American (only volunteered)."

18. The U.S. Information Agency has been asking, with slight changes, the following question for more than thirty years: "Please, use this card, to tell me your feelings about various countries. How about the United States?" The Eurobarometer series of the European Commission has been asking, in the Euro-barometer 22 (October 1984), 24 (October 1985), 27 (March–May 1987), and 28 (November 1987), a more direct version of this same question: "Do you have a very good, fairly good, neither bad nor good, rather bad or very bad opinion of the United States?" Those who answered "neither good nor bad" were probed: "On balance would you say that your feelings toward the United States are more favorable or more unfa-vorable?" In Eurobarometer 17 (April 1982), the question was, "What is your overall opinion of the United States? Do you have a very favorable, somewhat favorable, somewhat unfavorable, or very unfavorable opinion?" This wording was also used in the Pew Global Attitudes survey in 2002.

19. Between October 1952 and April 1956 the intermediate option "fair" was used. Since November 1956 the option "neither good nor bad" has been used. In November 1956 and in May 1957 the two formats were submitted to half of the sample each, to test for possible differences. Of the eight comparisons (two for each of the four countries included in the survey) in France and Italy no difference was greater than 2–3%, in Germany in one case (May 1957) the difference was 8%, and in Great Britain it was 10% in November 1956 and 13% in May 1957. In each of the three cases in which the wording of the interme-diate category makes a difference greater than 3%, the effect is an increase in those with a "good opinion" when the "neither good nor bad" category is offered in comparison to when a "fair" category is supplied. "Fair" seems to capture some of the positive feelings, while "neither good nor bad" seems more neutral. For my trend purposes, this source of difference is unproblematical, because I use the net favorability (favorable minus unfavorable).

20. An example of this question format is found in Eurobarometer 10/A: "Here is a sort of scale. You will notice that the 10 boxes on this card range from the highest position for plus 5, for something you have a very favorable opinion of, all the way down to the lowest position of minus 5, for something you have a very unfavorable opinion of. How far up or down the scale would you place [the United States]." The standard feeling thermometer scale has been tried also by the Transatlantic Trend Survey (drawing on the Chicago Council of Foreign Relations Survey for the United States) since 2002. The question is as follows: "Next I'd like you to rate your feelings toward some countries, institutions and people, with one hundred meaning a very warm, favorable feeling, zero meaning a very cold, unfavorable feeling, and fifty meaning not particularly warm or cold. You can use any number from zero to one hundred. If you have no opinion or have never heard of that country or institution, please say so."

21. Since 1970, the Eurobarometer has been irregularly asking, in different formats, a question about trust in Americans using slightly different wording: "I would like to ask you, now some questions about the trust you have in different peoples of the world. I will give you the names of different peoples; will you tell me if you have a lot of trust in them, some trust, not so much trust, or no trust at all. You can answer with the help of this card?" Or: "Now I would like to ask you about how much you would trust people from different countries. For each country please say whether, in your opinion, they are in general very trustworthy, fairly trustworthy, not particularly trustworthy, or not at all trustworthy?." This question has been asked in Eurobarometer 6, 14, 17, and 25. Eurobarometer 33 asked, "Now I would like to ask you a question about how much trust you have in people from various countries. For each, please tell me whether you have a lot of trust of them, some trust, not very much trust or no trust at all?"

Two crucial differences in the questions' content had an impact on the aggregate level of negative orientation toward the United States: the nature of the sentiments invoked (either feelings, opinions, or trust) and the referent object (either the United States or the American people).

The available evidence shows four consequences of these differences in question wording. First, respondents are able to distinguish between the people of a nation and their governments, when explicitly invited to do so, and they are more than ready to blame the latter rather than the former when asked to evaluate policies, also in situations, such as a war, in which such a distinction is less obvious and less expected. This was true of the American attitudes toward the Germans, before and during World War II; toward the Iraqis, during the first Gulf War; and of the British after World War II.[22]

Second, there is greater willingness to distinguish between the people and their government when political relations between one's country and the United States are strained.[23] In 1948 Buchanan and Cantril found that, in nine Western European countries surveyed (among which were the four considered here), "the word 'government' and 'people' . . . have been found to be *almost* synonymous."[24] In 2002, when the U.S. image was more tarnished than in 1948, Pew surveyed forty-four countries and found differences between overall feelings toward the United States and toward the American people in those countries whose relationships with the United States were more tense. In Western European countries, positive attitudes toward the American people were seven points higher than those toward the United States, and in the three Middle East countries surveyed (Egypt, Jordan, and Lebanon) there was a sixteen-point difference. In sharp contrast, no significant distinction between people and country was made by Latin American and African respondents.

Third, a generic reference to the United States seems more likely to evoke the country rather than the American people in the respondent's mind. That people are able to distinguish between governments and their subjects, when explicitly invited to do so, does not tell us whether they will always do so when this distinction is not explicitly offered to them or what is in their minds when the only reference is to "the United States." The reference to the United States has been criticized as ambiguous because "it does not refer to an explicit set of national characteristics or attributes and therefore we have no way of knowing which symbols and associations serve as referents to the respondent prior to his expression of feeling."[25] On the other hand, exactly because it is so cueless, the feeling question taps a general and basic attitude

22. Understandably, this image of the innocence of the German people deteriorated as the war went on. The percentage of those who believed the Germans were "warlike" increased from less than a fifth to approximately a third, and the percentage of those who viewed Germans were "peaceable" went down from slightly more than 40% to 25%. The prevalent image, however, remained that of a "basically peaceful but gullible" people (Merritt 1995, 37–40). For Iraq see Mueller 1994, 79. For Britain, Gallup 1947.

23. A similar conclusion is reached comparing the results of a split-half experiment run in *Fortune* magazine in 1939. More people were friendly to "all people" and unfriendly to "none" than were friendly toward "all governments" (Buchanan and Cantril 1953, 117).

24. Ibid., 40.

25. Abravanel and Hughes 1973, 113.

Table 3.1. Feelings toward Americans and the United States (in %)

	October 1958		June 2002	
	Nation	People	Nation	People
Very good/very favorable	15	15	13	14
Good/favorable	43	41	52	59
Fair	22	27	NA	NA
Bad/unfavorable	8	7	24	17
Very bad/very unfavorable	2	2	5	4
Don't know	10	8	5	6
Total	100	100	100	100
(N)	(2,475)	(2,404)	(2,516)	(2,516)

Sources: 1958: USIA XX–11; 2002: Pew Global Attitudes survey.
Note: France, Germany, Italy, and the United Kingdom pooled.

toward the referent object, an "anchoring dimension of people's images of the international environment," which is hierarchically superior to beliefs and policy attitudes, through which the respondents filter their perceptions of the international environment.[26] Table 3.1 sheds some light on the former point and table 3.2 on the latter. Table 3.1 compares what difference it makes to ask about feelings toward either a "country" or its "people," holding constant other possible sources of variation in our four countries in different periods.[27] In 1958, a split-half experiment was tried, in which people in half of the sample were asked to express their feelings about the United States and the other half about Americans. In 2002 both questions were asked of the same respondents, one after the other. In the 1958 USIA question, there is no difference in the two distributions, and in the 2002 Pew question there is only a slight difference, with the respondents being more likely to have a good opinion of the people than of the nation. The slight difference between positive attitudes toward the United States and the American people in 2002, as compared to 1958, is, I suspect, a consequence of the different degree of strain in political relations between the respondent's own country and the United States in the two periods.[28]

Table 3.2 cross-tabulates the answers given, in the four countries here considered, to two questions, respectively on favorable attitudes toward the United States and toward Americans. Eighty-five percent of those interviewed tended to either favor both or disfavor both. Among those who made a distinction, those who liked Americans and disliked the United States were far more numerous than the opposite. This

26. Ibid., 114.

27. An exact comparison between the 1958 and 2002 versions is complicated not only by what was discussed in note 21 but also because the 2002 Pew survey did not include the intermediate, stand-by category of "fair." This inflates the number of both those opposing and favoring somewhat the United States or Americans.

28. And this is even more remarkabkle because *both* questions were asked of each respondent, one after the other, creating a certain pressure toward consistency that presumably reduces the differences between people and government.

Table 3.2. Favorable toward the United States and Americans (in %)

	Favorable toward Americans		
Attitudes toward United States	Favorable	Unfavorable	Total
Favorable	66	3	69 (1,611)
Unfavorable	11	19	30 (707)
Total	77	22	100
(N)	(1,804)	(514)	(2,318)

Source: Pew Global Attitudes survey 2002.
Note: France, Germany, Italy, and United Kingdom pooled. "Don't know" responses excluded.

table seems to indicate that the question about feelings toward the United States taps a more general orientation toward the United States than the one asking about the American people.

Fourth, the different questions consistently produce similar results. In the Eurobarometer 17 of March–April 1982 three of the indicators of anti-Americanism here discussed were all included in the same questionnaire. At the beginning of the questionnaire was the question about the level of trust in Americans.[29] In the middle of the questionnaire there were questions about attitudes toward the United States[30] and about their anti-American feelings.[31] All three indicators are correlated (average interitem correlation 0.576, all correlations significant at the 0.001 level). The strength of the correlations may have been inflated by two of the items being asked in sequence. Still, the only question that was asked earlier on, in a separate section of the questionnaire (the level of trust toward Americans), shows the highest correlation with the other two items.[32]

These results corroborate the conclusion reached by Smith and Wertman more than ten years ago that the alternative ways of measuring the overall opinion of the United States produce very similar results.[33] And this is true over time and across countries. The question now becomes whether this general opinion about the United States—usually measured using a feeling question—is a valid indicator of anti-Americanism as I defined it above.[34]

29. The question was worded as follows: "Now, I would like to ask about how much you would trust people from different countries. For each country please say whether in your opinion they are in general very trustworthy, fairly trustworthy, not particularly trustworthy or not at all trustworthy."

30. The question was worded: "What is your overall opinion of the United States? Do you have a very favorable, somewhat favorable, somewhat unfavorable or very unfavorable opinion?"

31. The question was worded: "Recently, there has been some expression of anti-American feelings among West-Europeans. How would you describe your own feelings? Strongly anti-American, somewhat anti-American, somewhat pro-American or strongly pro-American?"

32. In Eurobarometer 22 (October–November 1984) the feelings toward the United States and the anti-Americanism questions were posed again. The correlation among the two is, for the four countries pooled, −0.604, significant at the 0.001 level for a two-tailed test.

33. Smith and Wertman 1992, 94.

34. Given the generally fairly positive results in terms of sympathy, trust, and respect for the United States shown in surveys, it is somewhat misleading to (continue to) use the term *anti-Americanism* for this indicator, but I will conform to the general usage here.

Anti-Americanism as a Vicarious Experience

In studying anti-Americanism it is important to keep in mind that most Europeans have an eminently vicarious and nationally framed experience of the United States and the American people. First, very few Europeans have had direct and continuous personal experience, in the United States or elsewhere, with Americans or their system of government. Only a small number (although increasing) of people from France, Germany, and Italy have traveled even once to the United States. In December 1937 (Gallup) only 8 percent of Britons had "ever traveled to America." In 1953, only 2 percent of the French had been in the United States.[35] And, according to a 2002 Pew survey, only 7 percent of Italians, 14 percent of French, and 29 percent of West Germans had ever visited the United States.[36] The United Kingdom has always been an exception. Although in July 1942 only 6 percent of Britons reported having traveled at least once to the United States, 35 percent of those interviewed knew "Americans personally." In 2002 (Pew) 40 percent of the British had "ever traveled to the United States." Fewer, presumably, have spent time in the United States for more than a short period of tourism or business.

In addition, the image of the American way of life and politics is, for most of the Western European population, mediated and framed by *national* sources, such as music, movies, sports, and, in countries like Italy, by immigrants to the United States. Messages coming from the United States are not apprehended directly, in the same sense in which a person who is fluent in English might appreciate a novel by Saul Bellow. On the contrary, they are channeled through a framework made by opinion leaders, intellectuals, and an assorted set of pundits in each national culture. Their task is "translating," not only literally but also metaphorically, the object in a different national context, making it understandable to people used to a different discourse context. As a 1960 USIA survey shows, only 3 percent of the respondents in these four countries read American newspapers and 7 percent read American magazines (in Great Britain this percentage was doubled). Also books, radio, and the new medium of television were prevalently national sources of information on America (with the exception of Great Britain, where 33 percent mentioned American TV programs). The only widespread somewhat direct vehicle of information about American society is the movie. In 1960, American movies were an important source of information for 26 percent of the public in these four countries (in Italy it was 32 percent, the highest percentage of the four).

There is, however, an important difference between the experience Europeans had of the United States during the cold war and the experience they had of other countries, such as the Soviet Union or China. Americans had a unique opportunity to make themselves personally known to Western Europeans as a result of World War II and its immediate aftermath, including U.S. military presence in several of these countries. It might sound paradoxical that the war, the liberation, and the American occupation of much of Western Europe helped create a positive image of the United

---

35. *Sondages* quoted in Kuisel 1993, 29.
36. Pew Global Attitudes survey 2002.

States, but this is the impression one gets from the scattered data available on this matter.

Once large numbers of U.S. troops began to leave Europe and the physical presence of the U.S. government began to fade away, along with the direct or indirect benefits of the Marshall Plan, the image of the United States came to be conveyed primarily by the national mass media.

Beliefs about America and Anti-Americanism during the Cold War

Given the indirect and vicarious nature of the experience of America by most of the public in Western Europe, the question immediately arises as to what extent this image is grounded in reality. I have concluded that given how little the public is credited with knowing about politics, the image of the United States at the mass level is remarkably well rooted in empirical facts. Furthermore, people's beliefs about the United States have a quite differentiated and, overall, modest impact on general feelings about the United States.

To examine the role of mass public beliefs about the United States as a source of anti-Americanism one has to assume a linkage between the attitude object, that is, the United States, the relevant belief about it, and the final evaluative judgment. First, people must be able to give meaning to specific political attributes, such as democracy, capitalism, or socialism. Second, they must be able to attach a positive or negative evaluative judgment to each attribute. Third, they must be able to recognize that the United States is endowed with specific attributes, such as being capitalist or democratic. Fourth, this negative (or positive) judgment about the attribute has to bring about a more general negative (or positive) sentiment about the United States. The issue here is that people who hold anti-American views not only see the United States as inherently, or strictly, associated with attributes (such as being capitalist or modern) that they dislike, but also that this critical evaluation generalizes into an overall anti-American mood that shapes other perceptions and biases information.

To reconstruct such a four-step movement at the mass level is not an easy task, considering that one must rely only on a scattered set of secondary data of the late 1950s and early 1960s, which were not designed with this purpose in mind. In fact, the available survey data allow us to explore only the role of one set of beliefs, those about capitalism. This is an important test, however, if, as stated by Hollander, "much of the criticism directed at American society is part of a general critique of capitalism of which the United States is not only the pre-eminent example but also the global defender."[37]

37. Hollander 1995, 54–55. The attack on the United States as the epitome of capitalism has traditionally moved, in Europe, from both Right and Left in different periods. In the 1930s the European Right stressed the perceived negative social consequences of capitalism: individualism, consumerism, anomie, political alienation, and, more generally, the destruction of traditional social bonds and the texture of society. After the World War II, it was the Left that pointed out the negative worldwide consequences of capitalism as an inherently aggressive, exploitative, and neocolonialist system (Teodori 2002, 71–97).

Let us first examine what opinion the public of our four European countries had of capitalism in the 1950s and early 1960s. The survey data show that bad feelings toward capitalism were quite widespread. Anticapitalist feelings were found among the French public (40% and 48% respectively for 1956 and 1962), followed by the Italians (37% in 1962), the British (32% in 1956 and 30% in 1962), and the Germans (29% in 1962). Most of the mass public in these four countries preferred a combination of socialist and capitalist elements, with a plurality in all four countries preferring an economic system approximately in-between a socialist and a capitalist one. Asked, in June 1962, to locate their preferred economic system on an 11-point scale ranging from completely socialist to completely capitalist, 44 percent of the French, 36 percent of the British, 30 percent of the Italians, and 28 percent of the Germans positioned themselves exactly in the median category.[38] The sympathy for socialism (more popular than capitalism among the European public) in part springs from the way the public thinks of it.[39] Requested, in June 1962 by the USIA, to choose between two different meanings of socialism—either ownership of "all the major industries" or responsibility "for social welfare measures (like health and old age assistance and unemployment benefits)"—68 percent of the sample in the four European countries answered that socialism meant to them the latter rather than the former.

Second, granted that most of those interviewed had an idea of what they were talking about, could they also locate the United States on a hypothetical scale from fully capitalist to completely socialist? A question, in June 1962, invited the respondent to locate both his or her own national economic system and the U.S. system on a socialist-capitalist continuum, ranging from completely socialistic to completely capitalist. Table 3.3 reports where, on average, the respondents located their preferred economic system, their national economic system, and the United States on a 1–11 scale.[40] This table illustrates three things. First, as previously stated, people preferred an economic system that combined elements of both capitalism and socialism. Second, their own country's economic system was always seen as *more* capitalist than they would prefer. Third, and more important, the United States was located at the capitalist extreme of this continuum, with an average of ten points out of

38. The question, which was asked of only half of the sample, was: "Suppose we go back to the ladder again and lay it on its side. Let's think of one end as a completely socialistic economy, the other as a completely capitalistic economy [Show Card C]. Thinking of the kind of economic system you in general like best, about where would you place this system along the ladder—at the completely socialistic end, the completely capitalistic end, or some mixture of the two? What step?" This choice probably hides a share of pure guessers (Brady and Sniderman 1985) that prudently locate themselves in the middle. The level of education has no significant impact on the distribution, however, with the modal category for both education groups in the middle and some polarization at both extremes. The better educated are more likely to be procapitalist and the lesser educated are more likely to be prosocialist. These might both be signs that the amount of guessing is quite limited.

39. 56% of those interviewed in 1962 in these four countries who had an opinion had a good or very good opinion of socialism, while only 22% had a favorable opinion of capitalism.

40. The exact wording of the question was: "About where along the ladder would you place the present economic system in the following countries—at the completely socialistic end, the completely capitalistic end, or some mixture of the two? First, what step for the economic system in [Sweden, Great Britain, West Germany, France, Italy, United States]? And . . . ?"

Table 3.3. Assessment of the preferred, national, and U.S. economic system

	Preferred	National	U.S.
France	5.2	6.8	10.0
Italy	5.3	6.7	10.2
Great Britain	5.6	7.2	9.8
Germany	5.6	7.7	10.0
Average	5.4	7.1	10.0

Source: USIA XX–14 form A, June 1962.
Note: Average score. Range: 1 (completely socialistic) to 11 (completely capitalistic).

eleven, while their own country was located, on average, three steps below (and approximately 1.6 steps above their preferred mix). There is no doubt then that the United States was perceived as *the* truly capitalist system in the world, a perception, by the way, shared by many experts and observers.

The ability of the public to accurately perceive a difference between the U.S. economic system and their own national economic system is confirmed by the results of another question, asked by USIA in April 1956. This question invited the respondents to explicitly compare their national economic system with that of the United States. On average, no more than 9 percent of the public in France, Germany, and the United Kingdom answered that the two systems were "very similar," ranging from 13 percent of the Germans to 12 percent of the British to only 1 percent of the French. On this basis, one can conclude that the Europeans at that time were not only able to express their preferred economic system—a "mixed economy"—but they could also locate the United States as very close to what might be considered the pure capitalist economic system.

Third, it is necessary to establish whether this belief about American capitalism makes any difference in the public's evaluation of the United States. Is the capitalist nature of the U.S. economic system a reason to harbor bad feelings toward the nation? Before examining this question in the context of different beliefs about America, let me provide two pieces of evidence that can help answer this question. The first is a quasi-experimental question built into the USIA XX–14 survey of June 1962. In that survey, half of the respondents were given a question about their "opinion in general of the American economic system," while the other half was asked, "What is your opinion in general about capitalism in the United States." Table 3.4 reports the distribution for the two versions, broken down by country. It shows a statistically significant negative impact of the reference to capitalism in regard to the American economic system.[41] When the question asks for an opinion

---

41. The impact of the experimental factor remains significant in all four countries' samples using both a t-value test and a one-way ANOVA F-ratio.

Table 3.4. Opinion of U.S. economic system and U.S. capitalism (split-half sample, June 1962)

	Germany		France		Great Britain		Italy	
	U.S. economic system	U.S. capitalism	U.S. economic system	U.S. capitalism	U.S. economic system	U.S. capitalism	U.S. economic system	U.S. capitalism
Very good	14	5	5	2	7	4	26	8
Good	49	29	33	15	30	19	32	27
Neither	17	37	27	33	25	29	11	25
Bad	3	7	9	14	9	11	3	5
Very bad	2	1	3	7	2	4	1	6
Don't know	15	21	24	29	27	34	26	29
Total	100	100	100	100	100	100	100	100
N	614	620	692	615	614	647	672	672

Source: USIA XX–14.

Note: The difference of the means for the two split-half groups, in the pooled sample, has a t-value = –16.25, significant at the 0.001 level. Pearson Chi-square = 283.45, significant at the 0.001 level. One-way ANOVA F-ratio = 264.04, significant at level 0.001.

"in general on the American economic system," 63 percent of the Germans, 38 percent of the French, 37 percent of the British, and 58 percent of the Italians give a favorable one. If the reference to "U.S. capitalism" is included, the percentage of those having a favorable opinion drops to 34 percent for the Germans, 17 percent for the French, 23 percent for the British, and 35 percent for the Italians. However, the major effect of priming capitalism in the question is to increase the number of bystanders, those who choose the "neither" option, rather than the number of those explicitly opposed. On average, across the four countries, introducing a reference to capitalism increases by 11 points the percentage of those choosing the intermediate option, while it increases by only 3 points the percentage of those with a negative opinion.

These results do not yet in themselves imply that the negative impact of an explicit reference to capitalism is also translated into a general negative affective orientation toward the United States. Both questions made reference only to the American economic system." A second piece of evidence bears more directly on this latter point. Cross-tabulating attitudes toward capitalism (on a good-bad scale) with anti-Americanism (as measured by a feelings question on a good-bad scale) produces a quite clear relationship between the two variables and shows that attitudes toward capitalism had some impact on anti-American feelings in general. Pro-American sentiments decline from 79 percent to 58 percent when we move from those with a positive orientation toward capitalism to those with a negative one, a drop of 19 points. However, the decline of pro-American feelings does not automatically increase the number of those who are anti-American, but rather of those who are indifferent. The percentage of those with a "fair" feeling toward the United States moves up from 18 percent to 32 percent as one goes from the pro- to the anticapitalists, an increase of 14 points, while those with negative feelings toward the United States rise from 3 to 10 percent, a 7 point increase. These results seem to indicate that feelings about America are in general positive, even when, as in this case, feelings about capitalism are quite negative. Although orientation toward capitalism is prevalently negative in all four countries, this does not necessarily make people anti-American, but, if anything, just more tepid about the United States.

The United States is not only viewed as a capitalist country. It is also seen as a symbol of modernity, a beacon of democracy, and a superpower whose foreign policy can be perceived either as arrogant and imperialistic or progressive and forthcoming against external threats. Examining the role economic considerations play alongside beliefs about the democratic nature of the United States, its modernity, and its hegemonic role in the international system will shed some light on the possible nature of anti-Americanism and its determinants. A survey carried out in October 1958 (USIA XX–11, form B) in France, Germany, Italy, and the United Kingdom allows such a comparative analysis of the impact of three sets of beliefs—economic, political, and cultural—on anti-Americanism.

To measure the economic beliefs, I use two indicators. The first is a summative index of economic attitudes based on two items, one asking whether it was true that "the U.S. economic system does not benefit only a few but the most" and a second asking whether "their economic system brings regularly economic crises."[42] The second is a question asking the respondent's opinion about "business" in the United States (on a 5-point scale ranging from a very good opinion to a very bad opinion, with an intermediate category), used as a proxy, although imperfect, of anticapitalist attitudes. Two questions were used to measure political beliefs. One asked for an opinion about "political life" in the United States, again on a 5-point Likert scale. The other asked for an overall impression of U.S. foreign policy on a 4-point scale, ranging from very favorable to very unfavorable, with no intermediate category. To measure cultural beliefs, a question asking the respondent's "opinion of cultural life in [the United States]—that is, art, music, literature, and the like"—was used. The answers ranged from 1 to 5 on a good-bad Likert scale with an intermediate category.

Besides this set of beliefs, I also include a measure of pro-Sovietism, or sympathy toward the Soviet Union, especially in countries with strong Communist parties such as in France and Italy, which are a driving force behind anti-Americanism. The question measuring opinion toward the Soviet Union allows us to test whether anti-Americanism was negatively correlated with pro-Sovietism. The control variables were gender, age (in categories), party preference (arranged on a left-center-right continuum), and education (elementary school, high school, and university). All these measures were regressed on anti-Americanism, as measured by the feeling question. Table 3.5 reports the regression coefficients of an ordinary least squares (OLS) estimate.

Two results stand out. The first is that all these beliefs together do not account for a higher proportion of variance in anti-Americanism. The quite low variance explained by the model leads one to think that beliefs alone do not explain variation in anti-Americanism. There are other sources of anti-Americanism. The second noteworthy feature is that these beliefs play a differentiated role in explaining anti-Americanism. All economic, social, cultural, and political beliefs have a significant impact in the expected direction. The relative weight of these beliefs for anti-Americanism, however, is different in the different countries. In 1958 cultural and foreign policy beliefs about the United States were preeminent in determining anti-Americanism. Political considerations, admiration for the American domestic political system, was also important, although less so than the other two considerations. Economic considerations are much less important. The orientation toward business is not significant (with one exception) and the opinion of the U.S. economy, once compared to other predictors, dwindles. This is, in part, also due to the imperfect indicator of anticapitalist beliefs I was compelled to use. As we have seen, beliefs about the U.S. economic system are sensitive to priming "capitalism" in the question. This means that this model probably underestimates the impact of the capitalist orientation on anti-Americanism. With this limit in mind, however, this model

---

42. Those who answered "No, it is not true" to the first statement and "Yes, it is true" to the second were coded as having a negative economic orientation toward the U.S. economic system. Those who thought the opposite—that the U.S. economic system did not create recurrent economic crises and did benefit most people—were coded as having a positive economic opinion of the United States. All other possible combinations were coded as mixed.

Table 3.5. Determinants of general feelings toward the United States (OLS estimate)

	b	Beta	Standard error
Constant	0.896***		0.248
U.S. international policy	0.221***	0.240***	0.037
U.S. cultural life	0.267***	0.273***	0.035
U.S. domestic politics	0.132**	0.144**	0.041
Economic attitudes	−0.103*	−0.080*	0.046
U.S. business	0.051	0.052	0.038
Pro-Soviet	−0.063*	−0.076*	0.030
Germany	0.105	0.050	0.078
France	0.191*	0.071*	0.096
Italy	−0.046	−0.022	0.080
R's sex	0.038	0.020	0.061
R's age	0.021	0.020	0.033
Education recoded	0.008	0.035	0.008
Party preference recoded	−0.020	−0.019	0.037
Adj. R^2	0.387		
SEE	0.726		
N	634		

Source: USIA XX–11, 1958.

Note: Dependent variable: feelings toward Americans (1, very good opinion—5, very bad opinion).

Baseline: United Kingdom.

Independent variables: opinion U.S. foreign policy (1, very favorable—4, very unfavorable); opinion U.S. cultural life (1, very good—5, very bad); opinion U.S. domestic politics (1, very good—5, very bad); opinion U.S. business life (1, very good—5, very bad); U.S. economy attitudes (0, negative; 1, mixed; 2, positive).

Control variables: sex, age, education, and party preference.

* p significant < .05.   ** p significant < .01.   *** p significant < .001.

works quite well comparatively. Only the French national dummy variable remains significant, once all predictors are included. Looking at the national differences in detail, one finds that the most important country differences are the economic index in France and anti-Sovietism in Italy.[43] In France, the index combining different beliefs about the economic nature of the U.S. system is the most important predictor of anti-Americanism. In Italy, anti-Sovietism plays a greater role than in the other countries, ranking second in importance, after attitudes toward U.S. foreign policy, in explaining anti-Americanism. In the other countries this variable is not significant (although the sign is in the expected direction in two out of the three). These results point in the same direction as Smith and Wertman's claim about the (lack of) attraction of the Soviet model.[44] The national analyses confirm what the general model tells us. In all countries cultural beliefs stand out as significant (this coefficient is the

43. The table is not reported here, but it is available on request from the author.

44. Smith and Wertman 1993, 92. In general, the model performs much better in Italy than in the other three countries. The variance explained by this model in Italy is twice as good as the adjusted R^2 in the other countries.

most important one in Germany and the second most important in the other three countries). Also relevant, in relative terms, in all countries except France is the general attitude toward U.S. foreign policy. In Italy and Great Britain this is the most important predictor of anti-Americanism. In conclusion, of the several different beliefs about the United States, cultural and political ones appear to be the major sources of anti-Americanism. Anticapitalism, at least at the mass level, is much less relevant, although this conclusion is still tentative, pending a better way to measure this set of beliefs.

The Affective Dimension of Anti-Americanism

As discussed earlier, anti-Americanism is seen here as the affective or evaluative dimension of the image of the United States. This image is firmly grounded in beliefs about the U.S. system, but cognitive beliefs have a quite differentiated impact, and alone they are not able to explain the totality of anti-Americanism. The affective and cognitive components, although they both concur in shaping attitudes toward the United States, work in a partially independent way. In this section I examine in more detail the affective nature of anti-American opinions. After a very brief review of different ways of measuring the affective component of attitudes I will test, in a preliminary way, a "circumplex model" of anti-Americanism, drawing on the work of Marcus and others on the role of emotion in politics.[45]

Since the 1990s, political science has thoroughly reevaluated the role of affect and emotion, both theoretically and methodologically. Although the "primacy of affect in generating the particular contents of image" was acknowledged in the 1950s, only in the 1990s was the role of feelings in shaping our evaluations of political figures set at the center stage of research.[46] With it, the role of passions in politics has been reevaluated.[47] I do not intend to enter into a discussion of the role of feelings and affect in politics nor to take a stand on the relationship between cognition and affect in shaping attitudes.[48] My task is simpler and more preliminary: to evaluate the dimensional nature of anti-Americanism as an affective state. The structure of affect that usually underlies the concept of anti-Americanism is typically assumed to be unidimensional, with respondents locating themselves on a point of a continuum ranging from negative to positive. All indicators of anti-Americanism discussed so far assume this structure. Recent developments in the study of emotion posit a more complex dimensionality.[49] Two competing structures have been suggested. One model assumes a "discrete" structure of emotions, in which different fundamental emotions are aroused, depending on the context and motivations. A second structural model, one that Marcus calls "circumplex," posits a fundamentally bidimensional structure of emotions, rooted in different neuropsychological

---

45. Marcus 1988, 2002; Marcus et al. 2000.
46. Scott 1966, 82.
47. Marcus 1991.
48. For two different viewpoints on this, see Zajonc 1982 and Lazarus 1984.
49. See Marcus 1988, 1991, and 2000.

Table 3.6. Emotional mood reactions to the United States (% respondents)

	West Germany		France		Great Britain		Italy
	1955	1961	1955	1961	1955	1961	1955
Peaceloving	40	59	45	50	44	33	55
Aggressive	3	4	20	10	12	9	6
Imperialistic	10	11	31	25	6	5	19
Materialistic	30	30	39	34	22	28	5
Cultured	37	55	38	33	15	11	26
Immature	2	3	17	17	10	18	7
Trustworthy	31	54	27	38	24	25	33
Domineering	12	8	36	31	25	31	9
Reckless	7	6	11	11	19	19	9
Democratic	54	73	58	46	42	43	65
Religious	23	38	32	48	18	16	21
Cooperative	67	68	49	27	28	24	NA

Source: USIA 1955 and 1961.

structures.[50] A first dimension, which he calls "mastery," is characterized by positive emotionality, while a second, called "threat," "monitors the environment for signs of evident danger."[51]

To explore the dimensional nature of affective orientation in relation to anti-Americanism, seen as an emotional assessment of the United States, I will avail myself of a survey carried out in August 1955 in the four countries here examined. In this survey, respondents were asked which of a list of words best described the United States. Table 3.6 reports the percentage of respondents choosing each word in the list in 1955 and 1961 in our four countries (with the exception of Italy in 1961).

In all four countries, with varying national patterns, positive terms were more likely to be chosen than negative ones. Adjectives such as "democratic," "cooperative," and "peace-loving" were most likely to be associated with the United States. The most frequently mentioned negative word was "materialistic," chosen by 39 percent of the French and 30 percent of the Germans. To explore the dimensional nature of the structure of emotional arousal of anti-Americanism, a factor analysis of these items was carried out. As figure 1 plots, three fundamental dimensions emerge from this exploratory analysis.[52] One dimension, with the highest eigenvalue, clusters those words that can be described as "positive." The second dimension captures the "negative" image of the United States, while the third factor is probably a consequence of the imperfect measurement of the variables and therefore due to error. These results disconfirm the prevalent assumption of anti-Americanism as a simple

50. Marcus 1988.
51. Marcus 1988, 742.
52. The analysis presented in figure 1 reports the results for only three countries: France, Germany, and the United Kingdom. In Italy one of the options—"cooperative"—was not presented. Including Italy (i.e., excluding the cooperative item) does not change the results.

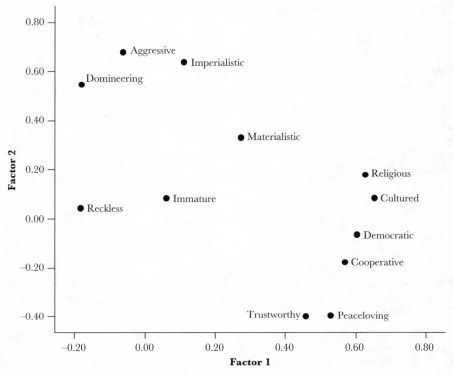

Figure 1. Emotional reactions to the United States on 12 mood items. *Source:* USIA XX–5, August 1955 (France, Germany, United Kingdom pooled).

undimensional evaluative dimension and point to the fact that people can entertain *both* positive *and* negative affects toward the same object.

To further explore the dimensional nature of anti-Americanism I carried out a confirmatory factor analysis (CFA) of the 1955 data, postulating a two-dimensional model of emotions. I assume that the underlying structure of anti-Americanism is made of two dimensions, one positive and the other negative. The CFA allows us to evaluate how well our model fits with the data. The nine items describing the United States are used as indicators of the two latent structures to which we add the feeling indicator, as a synthetic measure of anti-Americanism. My intent here is to see whether overall feelings toward the United States are driven by this bidimensional emotional structure. The first dimension—the "mastery" or positive one—is defined by the indicators peace-loving, cultured, trustworthy, democratic, and religious. The second dimension—the "threat" or negative one—is construed by the indicators aggressive, imperialistic, materialistic, immature, domineering, and reckless. The feeling opinion is measured by the 5-point Likert scale. The variables are all dichotomous, except the feeling question.

The two-dimensional model fits the data well. This analysis shows that anti-American feelings, as usually measured by the simple unidimensional traditional Likert scale indicator, are actually accounted for by two independent dimensions, one referring to a positive orientation toward the United States and the other to a negative one. The positive sign between the two latent factors seems to corroborate the hypothesis that the overall image can be thought of as being made up of *both* positive and negative judgments about a political object. As such, the general feelings indicator is a combination of the two factors, with the positive one more important than the negative one in determining the overall sentiment toward the United States.

This bidimensional nature of sentiments helps explain the fluctuating nature of anti-Americanism, clarifying under which conditions anti-Americanism is more likely to be activated. When the perceived threat coming from the environment becomes strong enough this dimension will become more salient. On the contrary, when the scanned environment does not produce ominous signs, the mastery dimension is more relevant, as was the case in 1955.

Cycles of Anti-American Mood during the Cold War

There are two good reasons why a long-term perspective is particularly useful in studying the determinants of anti-Americanism, as here defined. The first is that if anti-Americanism is driven, as we have seen, as much from the foreign policy of the United States as from beliefs in what the American system is, only an analysis of the impact of events on general attitudes can help to capture this dynamic. Second, in light of the intense debate about the resurgence and intensity of contemporary anti-Americanism, only a long-term analysis allows us to assess the degree to which the present period is different from previous ones. Figure 3 shows, for our four countries, the evolution of net general feelings toward the United States between 1948 and 2004, obtained by subtracting the number of those with a negative opinion from those with a favorable one. The figure points to three main results. First, in all four countries sentiments toward the United States have been mainly positive over time. This long-term view confirms once again what other authors have stressed, that "anti-Americanism has been the view of only a limited minority in most Western European countries throughout the postwar period."[53] Second, although substantially positive, the aggregate level of anti-American feelings varies across countries. The French are systematically more anti-American, while Germans and Italians are less so than the overall average. Great Britain is in the middle. The net average feeling toward the United States in the period 1952–2004 in France was 20 points, while in Germany and Italy it was respectively 50 and 48, with Britain slightly lower at 43 points. This confirms the popular image of the French public as generally less pro-American than the other European countries. Third, the figure shows some fluctuation over time in the net level of anti-Americanism.

53. Smith and Wertman 1992, 101.

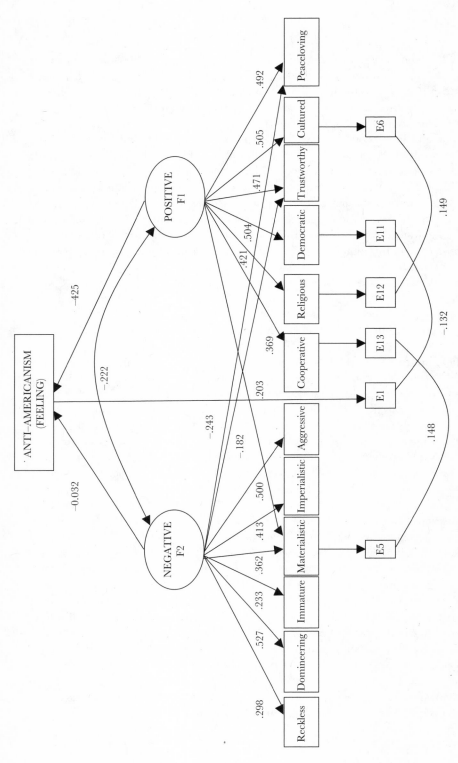

Figure 2. Model of feelings toward the United States. *Note:* Standardized scores. Chi-square = 321.573 (57 Dgf), significant at the 0.001 level. Comparative fit index (Cfi) = 0.934. *Source:* USIA XX–5, August 1955 (France, Germany, United Kingdom pooled).

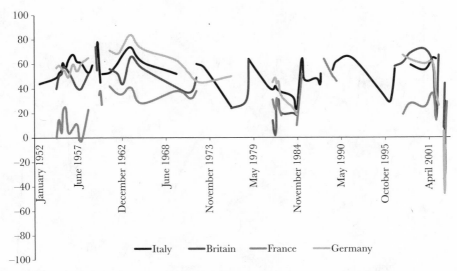

Figure 3. Trend in net attitudes toward the United States. *Note:* The vertical line reports the net favorable toward the United States, measured by subtracting those who have had a bad opinion from those with a good opinion. A positive number means that the percentage of those having a positive opinion is higher than that of those having a bad opinion, and a negative sign the opposite. *Sources:* USIA XX series 1952–67, Eurobarometer series 1970–2000, Pew Global Attitudes survey 2002, and Transatlantic Trend Survey 2002–4.

To give a clearer view of these fluctuations of anti-Americanism over time, I smoothed the four trend lines, using a procedure Stimson developed to measure mood.[54] In plotting and evaluating the general movement of anti-Americanism over time, the differences between countries can be ignored. In fact, the four series move quite in parallel, with an average correlation between pairs of 0.617, with only the British-French pair less than 0.5 (at 0.377) and one higher than 0.8 (Italy-Germany, at 0.865). Forced to vary around the same average and range of variation, the series flattens a bit and shows the starker picture in figure 4.

This figure gives us a fourth piece of information: the fluctuating nature of anti-Americanism after World War II shows no clear trend, either up or down. Contrary to what has been recently argued, over a long period of time anti-Americanism is not on the rise. The data rather indicate a cyclical nature of anti-American mood, around the (definitely positive) mean. We have waves of anti-Americanism, with some fluctuations, whose amplitude, interestingly enough, increases over time. Each downward movement is very quickly followed by a reversal of the trend line toward the mean.

54. Stimson 1991, 36–39. I first normalized the four series starting from the raw data in figure 2 and then converted them into an index computed as 100 plus the percentage of those in favor of the United States minus the percentage of those opposed to the United States. I then standardized each score, using the mean average and standard deviation across the four series. These calculations were done for all the four series.

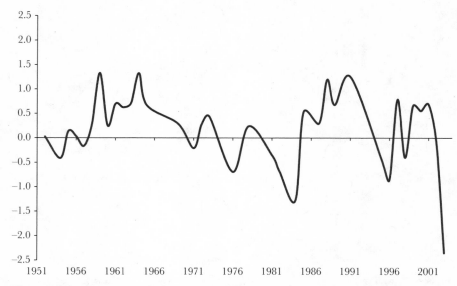

Figure 4. Trend in net attitudes toward the United States (normalized average, yearly base). *Sources:* USIA XX series 1952–67, Eurobarometer series 1970–2000, Pew Global Attitudes survey 2002, and Transatlantic Trend Survey 2002–4.

These fluctuations in anti-Americanism, as measured by the net favorability indicator, furthermore seem related to the evolution of the international political environment. The increases in anti-Americanism (as measured by dips in net favor) all seem related to crises in transatlantic relations. The first spike in anti-Americanism recorded by the available data was in October 1954, exclusively due to the French data point, following the French National Assembly's failure to ratify the European Defense Community. A second spike, in the second half of the 1950s, came after the Suez crisis and lasted until November 1957. The 1960s were a period of steadily declining anti-Americanism, as shown by the net favorable attitude. The third surge in anti-Americanism materialized between 1971 and 1976, a likely consequence of the controversies over the Vietnam War, the monetary crisis over the termination of dollar convertibility, and the economic drift brought about by the Arab oil embargo. The next display of anti-Americanism manifested itself in the early 1980s, in connection with the collapse of détente, the controversial NATO Euromissiles decision, and the acrimonious debate over Reagan's foreign policy toward the Soviet Union. Things started to get better again in 1985 with the arrival of Mikhail Gorbachev and the policy changes he introduced. The first spike in anti-Americanism after the end of the cold war occurred in 1994–95, but it should be interpreted with caution, since it is based on only one data point, that of Italy. It probably occurred as a consequence of the reluctance of the United States to be embroiled in the war in Bosnia and the uncertainty over the American willingness to intervene there in support of

European troops on the ground. Eventually, the deepest crisis, since survey data are available and as far as anti-Americanism is concerned, took place in 2003. In 2003, net favorable opinion in these four countries not only reached the lowest level ever, but for the first time net opinion became negative (i.e., there were more who had a negative opinion than who had a positive one) in Germany and Italy and reached the bottom lowest +8 points for Great Britain. However, as in the past, sympathy toward the United States was quick to recover.[55] Already in July 2003, positive feelings in France outmatched negative ones by 29 percent. This upward swing in positive feeling is quite characteristic of attitudes toward the United States overall for the entire fifty-year period.

Figure 4 also emphasizes a second dynamic in the trend of anti-Americanism. Although fluctuations are characteristic of anti-American sentiments, the range of variation becomes wider and wider over time. In other words, anti-American sentiments remain a minority view, but they are less and less stable as time goes by. The end of the cold war (although this trend seems to start earlier, in the early 1980s) has made it easier to express anti-American feelings when international events put the United States at odds with their European partners.

Now that the general pattern of anti-Americanism over time is made clear, it is possible to explore the sources of anti-Americanism in the cold war period between the early 1950s and 1970.

Attitudes toward America during the Cold War, 1952–1970

World War II and the cold war that quickly ensued in Europe and elsewhere contributed to frame a new image of the United States as both powerful and benign, and of its role in the foreign policy of the Western European countries. This image was largely built by national European elites for their own domestic purposes, taking into account the realities and constraints of the external environment. The way the image of the United States was created for the public—largely by and through elite discourse—after the war was shaped by several forces, among which the "shared experiences" of the war and the domestic exigencies of political elites both played a role. In turn, this image, once created, persisted over time, producing a "path-dependent" set of beliefs about and attitudes toward the United States.[56] An image, created in a certain period, persists over time until a set of events or policy changes produces a change in it. In this connection, one might point to the 1970s (with the Vietnam War and the Watergate scandal) or the 1990s (with the end of the cold war and the creation of a European polity) as possible critical junctures for changes in the image of the United States.

---

55. In figure 2 the 2003 data overlook that this recovery is a yearly average of different surveys, but that it is there can be seen from the raw data in figure 1. Positive feelings go from a net average feeling of 47 down to −7 in February 2003, to the all-time low of −31 in March 2003 (the start of the Iraq War) and then rise again and become positive by April 2003.

56. Pierson 2000.

To understand what role the United States—or, more properly, Americanism—came to play in the public political discourse of Western Europe we have to consider both the domestic and international problems that elites had to face and the way Americanism (or, its opposite, anti-Americanism) played in their strategy. The end of World War II left a world in which U.S. presence was hegemonic and therefore impossible to ignore, a situation quite similar to the U.S. presence in the Middle East since 1991 (see Lynch, chapter 7). European polities were either destroyed or severely tested by the war. With the end of the war, all four countries had to cope, to varying degrees, with a dire economic situation paired with a crisis of legitimacy, which in countries such as Germany and Italy verged on a crisis of national identity. This twofold challenge of rebuilding both state and nation required the creation of political legitimacy around a brand-new set of political institutions in countries emerging from a deeply divisive war and lacking all or most of the needed material resources. The contrast with the power and strength of the United States was striking. The positions different European governments took vis-à-vis the United States's omnipresent power were indeed agonizing. These positions did not depend exclusively on domestic constraints and debates. As a consequence of the rapid deterioration in relationships between the Soviet bloc and the American bloc, the emergence of a bipolar world, and the modalities through which the American "empire" became established in Western Europe, U.S. presence and policies were high up in the minds of both the political elites and their electorates.[57] The Marshall Plan, the Atlantic Alliance, and the beginning of the European integration movement were important events in which the United States acted, and appeared to act, as the real driving force in Western Europe. This combination of overwhelming political presence, of being the carrier of the seeds of economic and social modernization and of cultural challenge to established traditions, made the United States, at the end of the war, a focal point for both its European admirers and critics. This historical moment offers a unique vantage point for studying the way anti-Americanism emerged and evolved in Western Europe.

In studying the determinants of anti-Americanism during the cold war at the mass level in these four countries four factors seem to be particularly important: (a) the direct experience with U.S. military forces during the war (the first truly mass "shared experience" of America for most Europeans); (b) the policies of the U.S. government after the war; (c) the prospects of the cold war, with particular reference to the Soviet threat and the risks of war; and (d) the dire economic situation in all of the four Europeans countries here considered that helped to create high expectations—often more imagined (see Kennedy, chapter 2) than realistic—of the United States as a place where one could live the good life. I will discuss what role each of these factors might have played in shaping anti-Americanism in Western Europe, and how I measured them with existing data in order to explore their relative importance.

57. Lundestad 1998.

Memory of the War

The Second World War, much more than the First World War, fostered Europeans' first real mass encounter with America. American GIs with their physical appearance, tastes, and habits spread all over Western Europe, bringing European and American cultures and habits into direct contact at the mass level. The consequences of these encounters were already present during the early stage of the cold war, and they affected elite debates about how to frame the interaction with the United States. They may have exerted an impact on the mass public's image of the United States that is still with us.

Available evidence indicates that the war experience, and especially the American military occupation, contributed greatly to a *positive* image of the United States and its people in the eyes of the mass populace. This is true in Germany and Italy, the two defeated countries, as well as France, liberated in 1944 from Nazi Germany's occupation. In contrast to other Allied contingents (e.g., the British), American soldiers during 1943–45 left a remarkably good impression among Italians, French, and, to an extent, even the Germans. In October 1946, Doxa (an Italian statistical research and public opinion analysis organization) asked a sample of 5,013 Italians the following question: "Of all Allied soldiers that you have seen in Italy in the last years, which made the best [worst] impression on you?" Sixty-two percent said that the Americans left the best impression, and only 2 percent said they left the worst.[58] Only 12 percent of the respondents mentioned the British (and Scottish) as among those who left the best impression, while 10 percent said that the British (and Scottish) left the worst impression. In March 1945, Gallup asked a French sample "Do you think American soldiers behave well?" Seven percent answered "always" and 55 percent "generally." Only 16 percent answered "rarely" and 3 percent "never" (19 percent had no opinion). In Germany, where 41 percent of German respondents in the AMZON (American Zone) had in December 1949 a chance to see U.S. troops during "an average day," opinions about U.S. troops were good or very good for a majority of the population, and they had been improving since 1948.[59] Overall, the United States came out of the immediate aftermath of World War II more popular than any other country. How lasting this impression has been the available data cannot tell us, but it is clear that political and cultural elites have been playing on these memories constantly since then.

My hypothesis is that this socializing experience had a positive impact on people's attitudes toward the United States. I will use age as an admittedly imperfect indicator of this experience. Those who had this contact with the United States on a more personal level at that time lived in France, Germany, Italy, and the U.K. As time went by, and as the remembrance of the war experience receded, only members of that cohort still remembered. This difference should show up in the cooler sentiments in

58. Luzzato Fegiz 1956, 781–82.
59. HICOG Report 6, March 6, 1950, quoted in Merritt and Merritt 1980, 58.

subsequent decades by the youngest cohort, who were not personally affected by this vivid image of the United States.

The Policies of the United States

America's image was also shaped by what the United States did *after* the war. The immediate postwar policies of the United States played an important role in shaping positive feelings, reinforcing attitudes formed during the war and its immediate aftermath. In Italy, for example, a first test came with the peace treaty, a source of heated discussion among political parties well after the treaty was signed. In October 1946, ten months after the beginning of discussions about the peace treaty with Italy and in the middle of the conference of Paris in which the final decision was taken, Doxa asked, first, which among the four great powers (France, Great Britain, the Soviet Union, and the United States) was best disposed toward Italy and, second, which of the four left the respondents disappointed with the outcome of the peace conference. To the first question, 76 percent thought the United States was best disposed, 9 percent the Soviet Union, and France only 2 percent and Great Britain 5 percent. On the other hand, only 6 percent were disappointed by the United States, whereas 32 percent were disappointed by the Soviet Union, 21 percent by France, and 27 percent by Great Britain.[60]

What is probably the most important (and best known) policy decision that left an enduring impact on the image of the United States after the war was the Marshall Plan and its implementation through the European Recovery Program.[61] Solid majorities in all four countries were in favor of it, left-wing parties' opposition in three of the countries notwithstanding. In January 1948, 65 percent, 60 percent, and 60 percent of Italians, French, and British respectively were in favor of it (while 14 percent of Italians, 13 percent of French, and 20 percent of British were opposed, and between 20 and 27 percent in these three countries did not have an opinion).[62] In November 1949, in response to a Gallup question in France asking whether the Marshall Plan was good or bad for France, 45 percent answered that it was good (25 percent very good) and 23 percent that it was bad (15 percent bad and 8 percent rather bad). Thirty-two percent had no opinion.

However, U.S. foreign policy has not always been evaluated in a positive way in the different European countries. Since the end of the war, relationships with the United States have been marred by crises and resentments. During the 1950s the most important crisis in Euro-American relations, whose impact on anti-Americanism we can observe with the available data, was probably the Suez crisis

---

60. Luzzato Fegiz 1956, 668 and 670.

61. In January 1948, 78% of Italians, 91% of French (versus 72% in August and November 1947, according to Gallup) and 89% of British (40% in July 1947) respondents had heard or read about the Marshall Plan. In a survey carried out April–May 1948 by Elmo Roper for *Time* magazine, 74% of Italians, 80% of British, and 90% of French respondents had heard of the Marshall Plan, while 55%, 50%, and 61%, respectively, had heard of the Western European Union (Vielemeier 1991, 589–90).

62. Luzzato Fegiz 1956, 700–701.

in the autumn of 1956. In its divisive effect on transatlantic relations, in particular in France and the United Kingdom, the Suez crisis can be compared only to the Iraq War crisis of 2003. After having attacked Egypt without consulting with their American ally, and confronting a possible Soviet nuclear threat, France and Britain were then confronted by the Eisenhower administration with the stark alternative of either withdrawing from Suez or losing all U.S. support (including withdrawal of U.S. backing of the British pound). Both countries stopped the operation and withdrew in good order. This crisis allows us to explore the impact on sentiments toward the United States of U.S. policy that undercuts the interests of European states.

To examine this dynamic I will use time, creating a dummy for each year, as an imperfect proxy for the international climate. The way the international climate might affect anti-Americanism can also be seen by looking at the state of East-West relationships during the cold war.

The Soviet Threat and Pro-Sovietism

The positive image of the United States was without doubt boosted, at least among some, by the start of the cold war. Few among the European public had doubts about the real hegemonic intentions of the United States. The crucial difference from the Soviet Union was that U.S. hegemony was seen as more benevolent, such as to appropriately deserve being called an "empire by integration."[63] At the same time, suspicion about Communism and the Soviet Union was widespread among the populace of these four countries, well before the outbreak of the cold war. Anticommunism was a strong propellant of pro-American sentiments, as the United States was widely viewed as the only bulwark against the Soviet threat, both domestically and internationally. I hypothesize that strong anticommunist sentiments should be correlated positively with pro-American views, and vice versa.

A second indicator of the international climate is the fear of war, measured on a thermometer scale in which a low value means the subjective probability estimate of a world war is high and a high value that this probability is estimated to be low. The underlying hypothesis here is that as the level of tension increases, so do feelings of closeness to the United States.

A Country Where One Can Live the Good Life

A last, important factor is the appeal the United States had as a country where one could live the good life that was not possible in the dire European economic postwar conditions. Figure 5 reports a scattergram of the percentage of those in nine countries surveyed by UNESCO who thought the United States provided the "best chance of leading the kind of life you would like to lead" along with the 1949 per capita income in U.S. dollars as reported by the Statistical Office of the United

63. Lundestad 1998.

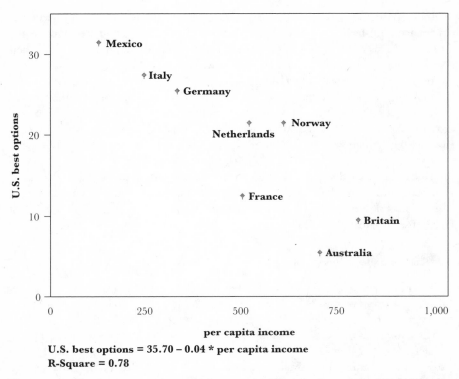

U.S. best options = 35.70 – 0.04 * per capita income
R-Square = 0.78

Figure 5. Relation between 1949 per capita income and willingness to move to the United States for a better life. *Source:* Buchanan and Cantril 1953.

Nations.[64] The results show a clear and strong correlation between the level of economic hardship and the choice of the United States as a country where one can live a better life, which presages similar data reported in the present period (see Katzenstein and Keohane, chapter 1).

These data confirm what some commentators have claimed, that anti-Americanism in Western Europe is mostly an elite phenomenon, while mass publics are predominantly pro-American.[65] If this hypothesis is true, we should expect that the better off should be less likely to be pro-American than the poorer sectors of society. To explore this, I used two indicators, subjectively perceived socioeconomic status and level of education (as a proxy of the respondent's socioeconomic condition).

In conclusion, I suggest that during the cold war there were four possible sources of feelings about the United States: the memory of the war and its aftermath, the perception of the policies carried out by the United States, the degree to which the

64. Buchanan and Cantril 1953, 34, table 4.
65. E.g., Spiro 1988, Markovits 2004b.

Table 3.7. Surveys available for the analysis of anti-Americanism (sample size, including "don't know" responses)

Study number	Date	Germany	France	Great Britain	Italy
XX–1 (218)	09/52				1,505
XX–2	10/54	836	847	832	
XX–3	02/55	820	899	805	
XX–4	06/55	857	790	790	810
XX–5	08/55	864	790	788	792
XX–6	11/55	813	803	814	
XX–7	04/56	863		799	
XX–8	11/56	1,138	1,206	1,188	1,188
XX–9	05/57	1,106	1,156	1,231	1,267
XX–10	11/57	783	779		
XX–11	10/58	904	626	610	635
XX–12	02/60	1,222	1,228	1,221	· 1,170
XX–12.5	05/60	1,010			
XX–13	06/61	1,145	1,330	1,283	
XX–14	06/62	1,234	1,307	1,261	1,344
XX–15	01/63	1,176	378	1,195	
XX–16	02/64	1,200	1,215	1,055	1,175
XX–17	05/65	1,199	1,228	1,178	1,164
XX–18	10/69	1,703	1,208	1,159	1,202
EUB-70	07/70	2,014	2,046		1,806
Total		20,587	17,836	16,209	14,058

United States is seen as a country in which people would like to live, and the perception of threat from the Soviet Union.

Besides these variables another important factor is the traditional left-right divide in each of these countries. Attitudes toward the United States have been critical on both the right and the left. The cold war, however, by adding an anticommunist dimension to the traditional political cleavages, helped to shape anti-Americanism as a typical left-wing leitmotif. This was particularly so in France and Italy, where strong Communist parties influenced mass attitudes toward the United States and framed the perceptions of large sectors of society. We should therefore expect to find that, in general, left-wing parties are more anti-American than right-wing parties, and in France and Italy even more so than in Germany and Great Britain.

To assess the relative weight of these determinants in explaining anti-Americanism during the cold war at the mass level, I use a set of surveys carried out in France, Germany, Italy, and the United Kingdom between 1952 and 1970. Table 3.7 reports all surveys I was able to locate in which a question on anti-Americanism was asked. Out of seventy surveys carried out in the four countries, at twenty-five different occasions between 1952 and 1970, sixty-one had at least one question on anti-Americanism. In ten cases, identical surveys were carried out during the same period in all four countries, for a total of forty surveys.

My analysis is based on two partially overlapping sets of data. The first set comprises the forty surveys that were carried out simultaneously in all four countries. This analysis covers 1955 to 1969.[66] A second set of analyses, covering a longer period, is based on all surveys in which the anti-Americanism question was asked in each country. The time span varies across countries, ranging from 1952 to 1970 in Italy, from 1954 to 1969 in Britain, and from 1955 to 1970 in Germany and France.[67] All results are based on an ordinary least squares estimate. I also conducted an ordinal logit regression. Since the two methods do not produce dramatically different results, for the sake of clarity only the OLS estimates are discussed.

The dependent variable is obtained using three different indicators of anti-Americanism. They have all been transformed into an ordinal variable with three categories, where 1 means a good opinion of the United States, 3 means a mixed feeling, and 5 means a negative opinion. As the value of this variable increases, anti-Americanism also increases.[68]

Models and Results

Using a cross-section time series analysis of repeated surveys over time, that is, of surveys asking the same questions to different samples of the reference population,[69] I tested what influence this set of factors has had on anti-Americanism and whether they changed over time, using a "changing-parameter model."[70] The rationale is that, given the fluctuating evolution of anti-Americanism, its determinants have been changing as well, depending on the international climate. To test this general hypothesis, I modeled the changing-parameter model through a set of interaction terms, each for every year in which the survey was carried out.[71]

To assess the changing parameter model I used four main sets of interaction-terms: threat perception, anti-Sovietism, age, and party preference. In the discussion, I will present the general model (model 1 in table 3.8) as a reference point. It includes all variables and covers the shortest period (1956, 1957, 1958, and 1960), with 1960 and Great Britain as baselines. I then compare the effects of further refinements introduced either by the changing parameter models or by country-specific analyses.

66. The analysis including the threat variables covers the 1956–1960 period, because the question was never asked after that date. Excluding the threat variables for the four cases covers the 1955–1969 period. If we exclude Great Britain, the analysis moves on to 1970.

67. Altogether, 68,690 persons were asked about their anti-American feelings during this time span.

68. The mean value, across all cases and time points, is 1.84 (on a 1–5 range), with a standard deviation of 1.28 points (and a mode of 1).

69. Firebaugh 1997, Duncan and Kalton 1987.

70. Firebaugh 1997.

71. See Firebaugh 1997, 42–63. In vector form, the model is the following: $E(Y) = \alpha + X\beta + \gamma D_{yr} + \delta (X D_{yr}) + \varepsilon$. In this model D_{yr} is a dummy variable assuming value 1 for each year, X is a vector of all the independent variables excluding the dummy variables and the interaction terms, and $(X D_{yr})$ is a subset of relevant interaction terms. In the general model, unless otherwise indicated, I set 1955 as the baseline year and α is the intercept for that year; ε is the error term. The β coefficients are the time-invariant impact of each regressor on the dependent variable and the δ coefficients are the change in the impact of each regressor on the dependent variable in each specific interval between 1955 and the specific year. Therefore we included as many dummies D_{yr} as the years minus one. Also for the interaction terms we used 1955 as a baseline and the other years as interactive terms set to 1 when relevant. In this model, the interaction terms are the indicators of whether each independent variable has changed its impact over time.

Gender, education, and age are all in the expected direction. Males are more likely to be anti-American than are females. This is true in all countries and in all models. The coefficient is always significant, except in the British case. Age has mixed effects. In model 1 it is in the expected direction: older cohorts are more likely to be anti-American than younger ones. This, I surmise, is the result of their different socializing experiences. The younger cohort experienced the (positive) American presence, while the older one reflected the anti-American climate of the 1930s and the war. However, the baseline model 1 hides some interesting country differences. The age coefficient is in the expected direction and is significant only in Germany (where the coefficient is always significant) and in Great Britain. In Italy and France the coefficients are often insignificant and in the opposite direction, that is, the older generations are less anti-American than the younger ones. This sign reversal might be a consequence of the fact that the left-wing (especially Communist) voters, traditionally more anti-American, are also younger. There is no time-dependent change in the age coefficient, either in the general model or in the country models. I therefore did not include any change-parameter interaction term for age in the subsequent analyses. As for education, the better educated are less anti-American than the less educated.[72] Assuming that this is an indicator of the respondent's position in the social structure, an assumption based on the limited access to higher education for lower classes in Europe during that period, the relationship runs against what has been hypothesized by some scholars and reported above: that anti-Americanism in Europe is an elite phenomenon.[73] This is always true across countries. The social elites of the country—in this admittedly loose definition—are more pro-American than the general populace (with one exception, Germany, where the coefficient is in the opposite direction, but it is not significant).

Taking now into account the time and country dummies, these are all strong in the predicted direction and significant. France is more anti-American and Italy and Germany less so than Great Britain (the baseline). Time, a proxy for the general world climate—in model 1, which covers only the period 1956–60 (with 1960 as baseline)—is in the expected direction: positively correlated with anti-Americanism and decreasingly so. The greatest positive impact on anti-Americanism was, as expected, in 1956, the year of the Suez crisis and Hungarian revolt, contributing to an increase in anti-American feelings. The time effect then remains positive, but its impact declines over time. With a longer time perspective (as in model 2, which covers the period 1955–1969) time has a curvilinear impact on anti-Americanism. It is positive, increasingly anti-American in the late 1950s, and then becoming negative in the 1960s. This is clearly related to the level of East-West tension and the general climate of the cold war. To test more precisely this effect, I also used the level of U.S.-Soviet tension, as measured by the Conflict and Peace Data Bank (COPDAB) East-West

---

72. The results using subjective SES (Socio-Economic Status) as an indicator are not shown but they are always in the expected direction. To increase the sample size—the SES indicator has been used less regularly than education—all subsequent analyses report only education.

73. E.g., Spiro 1988 and Markovits 2004b.

Table 3.8. OLS estimate of determinants of anti-Americanism

	Model 1 (1956–60)		Model 2 (1955–69)		Model 3 (1956–60)	
	b	Beta	b	Beta	b	Beta
Constant	1.998***		2.244***		1.651***	
	(0.079)		(0.040)		(0.101)	
Sex (0 = female, 1 = male)	.067*	.025	.077***	.030	.073**	.027
	(0.027)		(0.013)		(0.027)	
Age in four categories	.032*	.021	.006	.004	.034*	.023
(<29, 30–44, 45–64, >65)	(0.015)		(0.008)		(0.015)	
Education (1 no school–4	−.043*	−.026	−.019*	−.013	−.038	−.022
University)	(0.017)		(0.008)		(0.017)	
Attitudes toward Soviet	−.128***	−.132	−.080***	−.093	−.056**	−.057
Union (1 good–5 bad)	(0.010)		(0.005)		(0.019)	
Danger of war thermometer	−.001	−.003	—	—	.025*	.060
(1 = 100 war–11 = 0 war)	(0.005)				(0.012)	
Right (1 = right-wing party)	−.087*	−.026	−.155***	−.049	−.085	−.025
	(0.039)		(0.019)		(0.039)	
Left (1 = left-wing party)	.326***	.111	.281***	.099	.310***	.105
	(0.033)		(0.017)		(0.033)	
Germany	−.242***	−.083	−.289***	−.102	−.262***	−.090
	(0.041)		(0.019)		(0.041)	
France	.774***	.256	.387***	.123	.746***	.247
	(0.044)		(0.021)		(0.044)	
Italy	−.168***	−.049	−.313***	−.106	−.205***	−.060
	(0.046)		(0.020)		(0.046)	
Dummy 56	.402***	.119	.072**	.018	.974***	.289
	(0.049)		(0.026)		(0.182)	
Dummy 57	.346***	.124	.060*	.015	.720***	.257
	(0.038)		(0.026)		(0.114)	
Dummy 58	.246***	.073	−.012	−.002	1.197***	.357
	(0.048)		(0.032)		(0.146)	
Dummy 60		—	−.215***	−.054	—	—
			(0.026)			
Dummy 62		—	−.188***	−.045	—	—
			(0.027)			
Dummy 64		—	−.416***	−.106	—	—
			(0.026)			
Dummy 65		—	−.275***	−.060	—	—
			(0.029)			
Dummy 69		—	−.028	−.007	—	—
			(0.026)			
Threat 56	—	—	—	—	−.058***	−.134
					(0.016)	
Threat 57	—	—	—	—	.009	.016
					(0.015)	
Threat 58	—	—	—	—	−.086***	−.218
					(0.017)	
Soviet 56	—	—	—	—	−.073*	−.102
					(0.035)	
Soviet 57	—	—	—	—	−.144***	−.185
					(0.025)	
Soviet 58	—	—	—	—	−.107***	−.135
					(0.027)	
Adjusted R^2	0.155		0.096		0.162	
SEE	1.204		1.217		1.247	
N	8,688		33,670		8,688	

Note: Standard error among parentheses. 1960 and United Kingdom as baselines.
* Significant of the level 0.05.   ** Significant of the level 0.01.   *** Significant of the level 0.001.

conflict indicator.[74] The relationship is confirmed. When tension is high, anti-Americanism increases, and when it is low, it declines.

Moving now to the attitudinal variables, table 3.8 shows that anti-Soviet and pro-American sentiments are strongly related during this stage of the cold war. This variable is significant and in the expected direction in all countries. Its impact is strongest in Italy (confirming what was found in table 3.5). The threat of war is not significantly related to anti-Americanism in model 1. The sign shows that those less likely to believe a war will break out are more anti-American. In other words, the more one was frightened by the possibility of a war, the more he or she was pro-American. Also, not surprisingly, the right-left cleavage significantly affects anti-Americanism. Right-wing voters were more likely to be pro-American than left-wing voters. This general result, however, hides some interesting national differences. In Italy, *both* the Right and the Left are more anti-American than the Center. In Germany and Great Britain, right-wing voters were less likely to be anti-American, while being on the left did not move voters further toward the anti-American camp. France is the country in which the relationship found in the general model holds: those on the left are significantly more anti-American, while those on the right are significantly less anti-American. These results qualify the different national impacts the right-left cleavage has on anti-Americanism.

In examining how the impact of some of our parameters changed over time, I focus on two variables: the threat of war and anti-Sovietism. The first is relevant to our earlier discussion of the dimensions of anti-Americanism and the second because of the argument previously made that anti-Sovietism did not always play a crucial role in explaining anti-Americanism. A dynamic perspective throws more light on these issues.

Model 3 (table 3.8) examines both these effects between 1956 and 1960. This period offers a quasi-experimental situation for studying the complex impact of events and attitudes on anti-Americanism. To model this impact, I estimated the interactive effect of the 1956 events on both the image of the Soviet Union and the perception of threat on anti-Americanism. Here we can see that the 1956 crises had the effect of making both threat perception and anti-Sovietism more salient, with a differentiated impact on anti-Americanism.

Because the interactive impact of attitudes toward the Soviet Union on anti-Americanism can be seen over a longer time perspective (see discussion below on table 3.9), I first assess the impact of threat perception. Models 1 and 2 have already shown that the perception of threat has either no impact or a slightly negative one on anti-Americanism. Overall, the more one perceives that there is a threat of war the less likely one is to be anti-American. This is in line with the hypothesis that anti-Americanism has different dimensions, mastery and threat, that can be differently relevant for different people. Those who are worried about war during a relatively quiet political period are more likely to be driven in their assessment by the threat dimension and see in the United States a way to cope with their worries. However,

74. Azar et al. 1972.

things seem to change when the international climate worsens. When the level of international tension increases, the perception of threat not only becomes statistically significant but also it reverses its sign. It moves from negative to positive: those who are afraid of a war become more anti-American. This is coherent with our description of anti-Americanism as a feeling based on two main dimensions, one positive and another negative, related to the ability of the United States to exert its leadership in a responsible way. When the threat of war increases, the threat dimension of anti-Americanism becomes more important for some people than the mastery dimension. This contributes to an increase in the level of anti-Americanism. When the threat of war decreases, threat perception has either no impact or a negative one on anti-Americanism. In other words, in times of détente, those more worried about a war were also more sympathetic toward the United States. On the contrary, in time of tension, those who were more worried about a war tended to be less sympathetic toward the United States.

Anti-Soviet attitudes interact with anti-American attitudes in complex ways, in both the country and the time period. To model this third-order effect, I recorded (in table 3.9) the interaction terms of country and time period. Looking first at the general pattern, in all four countries the impact of anti-Sovietism on anti-Americanism is negative: those more anti-Soviet are also more pro-American and vice versa. Moreover, in all countries this relationship becomes less and less important in shaping attitudes toward the United States as time goes by. Finally, this general pattern shows some important national differences that interact with the degree of East-West tension. Discussing the impact of tension first, we can see that the impact is always in the same direction, but it is of different strengths. In France, the impact of tension on anti-Sovietism was absent or negligible in shaping anti-Americanism. In Italy, Germany, and Great Britain, in this order, political tension strengthened the negative relationship found at the general level. Even more interesting is the dynamic when the level of tension is low. In this case, the strength of anti-Sovietism in shaping anti-Americanism declines. Again, there are important national differences. In Italy the relationship remains negative, but less strong than during periods of tension. In Germany and Great Britain the relationship almost disappears. In France, the direction of the relationship changes: those who are anti-American become *also* anti-Soviet and vice versa. The data point to the intriguing result that in a climate of bipolar détente, both anti-Americanism and anti-Sovietism ran parallel. This seems to have been the case in Germany as well. The major difference between these two countries was that in Germany it occurred later than in France. These results seem to validate a pattern that we found in the recent Iraq crisis as well: the major source of anti-Americanism in France and, to a lesser extent in Germany, was related to the "hyperpuissance" of the United States in a unipolar world, rather than to more deeply entrenched beliefs. During the cold war, it was the possibility of the Soviet Union and the United States to gang up against Europe to worry the French and, to a lesser extent, the Germans. These results seem to suggest that the pattern we observed between 2002 and 2004 during the invasion of Iraq has its roots in attitudes shaped during the cold war, well before recent events.

Table 3.9. Impact of attitudes toward the Soviet Union on anti-Americanism and change over time

	France		Germany		Italy		United Kingdom	
	b	Beta	b	Beta	b	Beta	b	Beta
Attitudes toward USSR (1 good–5 bad)	−.063*** (0.012)	−.074	−.063*** (0.012)	−.074	−.063*** (0.012)	−.074	−.063*** (0.012)	−.074
1956	.019 (0.023)	.011	−.151*** (0.022)	−.094	−.233*** (0.023)	−.141	−.109*** (0.023)	−.070
1957	−.011 (0.022)	−.006	−.113*** (0.020)	−.069	−.223*** (0.021)	−.131	−.124*** (0.021)	−.073
1958	.007 (0.025)	.003	−.100*** (0.024)	−.043	−.191*** (0.025)	−.073	−.113*** (0.026)	−.043
1960	.076*** (0.021)	.035	.004 (0.018)	.002	−.060*** (0.020)	−.028	−.022 (0.021)	−.011
1962	.019 (0.023)	.007	−.012 (0.019)	−.008	−.085*** (0.021)	−.044	−.014 (0.021)	−.007
1964	.145*** (0.022)	.067	.023 (0.018)	.014	−.035 (0.020)	−.017	.025 (0.021)	.012
1965	NA	NA	.043* (0.020)	.025	−.011 (0.022)	−.005	.063** (0.023)	.029
1969	.035 (0.022)	.015	.048** (0.018)	.031	−.013 (0.020)	−.006	.057** (0.021)	.028

Note: Other regressors as in model 2 in table 3.8. Adjusted $R^2 = 0.113$, standard error of estimate = 1.205, N = 33.670. Standard error in parentheses.
  * Significant of the level 0.05.   ** Significant of the level 0.01.   *** Significant of the level 0.001.

In the Eyes of the Beholder

In this chapter I have tried to convey a twofold message. The first message stems from the controversial nature of anti-Americanism, a concept looking for an empirical referent, rather than the opposite. To link one to the other, I narrowed its scope. I postulated, with the comfort of the indicators commonly used to measure it, that anti-Americanism is a psychological, emotional mood that helps us frame a set of phenomena and behaviors attributed to the United States. I have provided two main sets of evidence. The first shows that ordinary people, busy as they are in their own personal activities, still can entertain a differentiated and complex set of attitudes, beliefs, and feelings about the United States, its people, institutions, and policies. These beliefs, attitudes, and feelings neither produce a coherent syndrome—of the kind Hollander has in mind when speaking of anti-Americanism—nor disappear in a set of undifferentiated nonattitudes, of the kind Converse suggested people's minds on political issues are made. Beliefs, attitudes, and feelings are knitted together, but not so tightly. Sometimes they are loose because the connections are not where we expect them to be. Other times people are abler than we think to elicit differences where in fact those differences are.

The second set of evidence is the multidimensional—or more precisely bidimensional—nature of Europeans' feelings toward the United States. When people have attitudes about a political object as complex and multifarious as the United States, they can entertain several feelings at the same time. This does not necessarily mean that people balance their considerations out or that they are ambivalent, but, put more simply, that different dimensions are important to different degrees for different people at the same time and that their relative importance in shaping general feelings toward the United States can change. The main engine behind this change is events. The interaction terms captured by time and perception of threat reported in table 3.8 sheds some light on why anti-Americanism spikes and bounces back quite quickly.

By implication, my second message is that anti-Americanism is mostly driven by our assessment of what Americans—or more appropriately the American government—do or what we think they do. And here, I would like to stress "we think." The longitudinal analysis shows that, no matter how important events are, they only play a role to the extent that they interact with other attitudes and beliefs, and in this way they shape our feelings toward America. These attitudes are somehow an individual constellation of experiences, beliefs, and sentiments, which lead us to orient one way or the other. As shown, anti-Soviet attitudes and level of tension interacted in producing an impact on anti-Americanism. It is different if we hate (or love, for that matter) the Soviet Union in a period of tension or in time of détente. But this is not the whole story. A lot of variance can be explained by purely national factors, as the significance of our country dummies testify. Anti-Americanism, like beauty, is often in the eyes of the beholders.

4

Disaggregating Anti-Americanism: An Analysis of Individual Attitudes toward the United States

GIACOMO CHIOZZA

In the wake of the terrorist attacks on the United States, anti-Americanism—the opposition to America, its name, its ideals, and its actions—has become a central feature of public discourse in the United States and the world over. That anti-Americanism is spreading and deepening is taken as a matter-of-fact statement that does not deserve any further empirical validation. Charles Krauthammer, the influential *Washington Post* columnist, popularized this notion with harrowing words: "It is pure fiction that this pro-American sentiment was either squandered after Sept. 11 or lost under the Bush Administration. It never existed. Envy for America, resentment of our power, hatred of our success has been a staple for decades, but most particularly since victory in the cold war left us the only superpower."[1]

In this scathing indictment of the "Opinions of Mankind," the views of European, Arab, and Muslim publics are usually singled out as the most rabidly opposed to the United States and the most deserving of ridicule and dismissal. For Daniel Pipes and Russell Berman, the negative view of the United States in the Islamic world and Europe is primarily a reaction to the perception of the weakness of the United States that only unadulterated shows of power could redress by inspiring awe

I thank Carol Atkinson, John Bowen, Miles Kahler, Peter Katzenstein, Bob Keohane, Doug McAdam, Henry Nau, Abe Newman, Samuel Popkin, and Paul Sniderman for comments and suggestions. I also thank Joe Grieco, Hein Goemans, Chris Gelpi, and John Aldrich for their support and guidance. This chapter was written when I was a fellow at the Olin Institute for Strategic Studies at Harvard University. I thank the Olin director, Stephen Peter Rosen, for his support during my year there. An appendix containing tables with the full details of the regression models and additional information about the survey items, including a list of all countries in the survey, is available on request from the author and the editors. Mistakes, omissions, and other assorted infelicities are my own responsibility.

1. Krauthammer 2003, 156.

and respect.[2] For Barry and Judith Rubin, criticism of the United States is a persistent psychological device that societies resort to—and have been resorting to ever since America appeared on the world scene—in order to compensate for their own failures, because America epitomizes the notion of success and symbolizes the realization of a better world.[3] Fouad Ajami summarized the state of America's standing worldwide with no equivocation:

> If Germans wish to use anti-Americanism to absolve themselves and their parents of the great crimes of World War II, they will do it regardless of what the United States says and does. If Muslims truly believe that their long winter of decline is the fault of the United States, no campaign of public diplomacy shall deliver them from that incoherence.[4]

But concerns over the diffusion of anti-American sentiment are not the exclusive preserve of the conservative intellectuals who have defined the theoretical foundations of U.S. foreign policy during the reign of President George W. Bush. The editorial page of the *New York Times* laments that "if there is such a thing as the European street, anti-American feeling is strong and universal."[5] Scholars of the realpolitik school are no less inclined to pass judgment on the strategic choices and policy stances of the United States in terms of their alleged impact on the rise of anti-Americanism. Thus, to take a least likely example, John Mearsheimer bemoans the reliance of American grand strategy on military force as a factor that would contribute to increasing popular hostility toward the United States and, instead, invokes winning the "hearts and minds" of Islamic publics as the blueprint for improving America's security.[6]

In this chapter I take these expressions of concern to task and investigate whether anti-Americanism has indeed become the dominant frame through which foreign publics relate to the United States. The empirical analyses that I pursue in this chapter offer an overview of the attitudes toward the United States as they are portrayed in mass surveys. Thus, in this chapter I place the phenomenon of anti-Americanism at the mass popular level and identify the patterns of evaluative reactions that the United States elicits among ordinary people in the post–cold war, post–September 11 world. In its descriptive emphasis, this chapter reformulates the fundamental question that underlies the discussions on the status of America's popular standing worldwide: not "Why do they hate us?"—the question that explicitly or subconsciously Americans strive to answer whenever they reflect on anti-Americanism—but "Do they?" and "Who exactly are they?"[7]

---

2. Pipes 2002, Berman 2004a.
3. Rubin and Rubin 2004.
4. Ajami 2003, 61.
5. See *New York Times* 2005.
6. Mearsheimer 2002.
7. Among the books and articles that asked "Why do they hate us?" are D'Souza 2002, Friedman 2003a, Gilpin 2005, Rubin and Rubin 2004, Sardar and Davies 2002.

Thus, before elaborating any explanatory account of anti-Americanism, we should delineate the empirical features of this phenomenon. How do foreign publics view the United States? To what extent do they perceive the United States as a benevolent hegemon that contributes to the stability and prosperity of the international system? And to what extent do they believe that the diffusion of American ideals and institutions is a welcome development for their own societies and their own standard of living?

The investigation begins with an analysis of the status of America's image in 2002 in five regions of the world: East Asia, South Asia, eastern Europe, the Middle East, and the advanced industrial democracies of western Europe and Canada. This investigation relies on the extensive survey data of the Global Attitudes Project of the Pew Research Center. Given the pervasiveness of the anti-American rhetoric, it might come as a surprise that the prevalent opinion of the United States was mostly positive. However, the survey data from the Pew project also show that beneath a veneer of warm feelings toward the United States there is a more nuanced image that is composed of alternative and sometimes contradictory evaluations of different features of the United States. This finding no doubt will reassure all those who have fallen for the dire descriptions of anti-American hatred taking hold of the world's imagination. But not everything about the United States, and not under all circumstances, is always liked by ordinary people the world over.

Finally, I offer a brief illustration of how the image of the United States has changed since 2002 in the Middle East and among Islamic publics. The comparison of the attitudes about the United States in two different periods serves as an additional point of reference to evaluate what is persistent and what is more volatile in people's perceptions of the United States. Interest in the phenomenon of popular anti-Americanism is heightened in times of crisis, as was the case in the late 1960s or the mid-1980s when people took to the streets to protest against the Vietnam War and nuclear missile deployments in western Europe.[8] A comparison of samples of responses taken in 2002 against responses taken in 2003 or 2004 would still be an analysis of the image of the United States in *times of crisis*, as the prelude to the Iraq War and the war itself indeed were. But, given that we would be hard pressed to think of a year that would serve as a representative benchmark of the ordinary life of an exceptional country, a comparison of different moments of crisis is all we can practically pursue.

The main finding of this chapter is that a systematic negative classification of any referents associated with the United States was more of an exception than the rule among the respondents to the 2002 Global Attitudes Survey. With the exception of Middle Eastern publics, opposition to the United States was not unidimensional, but rather the result of a confluence and cumulation of factors. But even in the Middle East, where positive sentiments toward the United States were rare, opposition to the United States was framed by *both* policy and polity, not just simply by either, as is

---

8. Free 1976, Smith and Wertman 1992.

usually maintained in the political debate.[9] Elsewhere, the collective imagination of the mass publics was still inspired by the polyvalent nature of American society and culture.

Patterns of Opinion about the United States in 2002

In 2002, when the Pew Research Center asked more than thirty thousand people in forty-two countries their opinion of the United States, their response was predomi-nantly positive: of all those who expressed an opinion (91 percent of the interview-ees), 43.3 percent expressed a "somewhat favorable" opinion and 21.3 percent expressed a "very favorable" opinion, thus revealing that anti-American sentiment was a minority view in most of the world.[10] Anti-American views were rare in Ghana, Guatemala, Honduras, Nigeria, the Philippines, Poland, Uzbekistan, and Venezuela, all countries where fewer than 15 percent of the respondents had an unfavorable opinion of the United States. France and Germany, which so much epitomize the vanguard of the anti-American front in the American mind, displayed solid majori-ties with pro-American sentiments: 64.6 percent of the respondents in France and 61.1 percent of those in Germany declared that they had at least a somewhat favor-able opinion of the United States. But the presence of pro-American feelings was not uniform across the sample of countries in the Pew Research Center survey: in six countries—Argentina, Egypt, Lebanon, Jordan, Pakistan, and Turkey—the per-centage of respondents who held an unfavorable opinion of the United States crossed the threshold of 50 percent, and abundantly so in the Middle Eastern countries where about three in four respondents had at least a somewhat unfavorable opinion of the United States.

An analogous, if not rosier, picture emerges from the analysis of the attitudes toward Americans as a people. Those who thought highly of the United States tended to think highly of its people as well, and, conversely, those fewer respondents who did not hold a high opinion of the United States as a country did not hold a high opinion of its people either. The high levels of congruence in the way respon-dents assessed the United States vis-à-vis the American people again underscores the widespread popularity of the United States among the general public in 2002. Any discrepancy to this pattern had a pro–American people connotation: in the Middle Eastern countries, in particular, about 31.3 percent of the respondents who expressed an opinion had more positive views toward the people than toward the

9. Lynch, in chapter 7, connects the attitudes toward U.S. policies and polity to the schemas Arab people use to interpret political processes. For a characterization of the views of the Right and the Left on anti-Americanism, see Katzenstein and Keohane, chapter 1.

10. The 2002 Pew Global Attitudes Project survey included forty-four countries. The two countries excluded from this count are the United States itself and China, where questions about the United States were not asked. The surveys were conducted either through face-to-face interviews or through tele-phone interviews, mostly between July and August 2002. The interviews were conducted between Sep-tember and October 2002 in Egypt, Ghana, India, Ivory Coast, Jordan, Lebanon, Mali, Nigeria, Senegal, and Uganda.

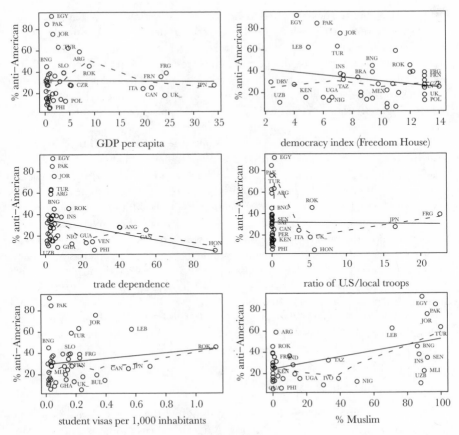

Figure 6. Correlates of anti-Americanism in 2002. *Note*: Data analysis is based on the Pew Global Attitudes survey.

country, which sets the overall percentage of people with an unfavorable view of the American people at 58.3 percent.[11]

In sum, if we had any apprehensions of finding the specter of anti-Americanism spreading over the world, such dire expectations were mostly exaggerated. The voice of the people in 2002 predominantly had a pro-American accent. With one major exception: the Middle Eastern countries along with Pakistan, where popular dislike of the United States was ripe and rampant.

Among the forty-two countries analyzed in the Pew 2002 Global Attitudes Survey, the presence of large Muslim populations is the single most powerful predictor of the presence of anti-American sentiment. No other factor, from domestic political institutions to economic conditions, from military relations to cultural connections,

11. The distinction between people and government in people's assessment of the United States is also analyzed by Isernia in chapter 3 and Johnston and Stockmann in chapter 6.

is substantially or statistically related to anti-American sentiment.[12] In figure 6, measures of gross domestic product (GDP) per capita, democratic institutions, trade dependence, presence of U.S. military personnel, and number of student visas granted were plotted against the percentage of respondents with somewhat favorable or very unfavorable opinions of the United States.[13] The lack of a relationship between anti-American sentiment and macro-level structural conditions that the panels in figure 6 portray indicates how anti-American sentiment can be found in a large variety of political and economic circumstances.

Given these findings, our first task is to analyze what lies behind these patterns: first, by analyzing how ordinary people assessed different features of the United States and whether they formed coherent opinions of those different features; second, by analyzing whether the apparent good standing of the United States in people's opinions was more a reflection of a reluctance to display dislike of a country as a whole or whether it was a genuine feeling of empathy with the United States; third, by eliciting from the patterns of responses across different attitudinal dimensions an empirical profile of the anti-American respondents. The analysis focuses on twenty-four countries in five regions: (1) a group of advanced industrial democracies, which includes Britain, Canada, France, Germany, and Italy; (2) eastern Europe, which includes Bulgaria, the Czech Republic, Poland, Russia, Slovakia, Ukraine, and Uzbekistan; (3) the Middle East, which includes Egypt, Jordan, Lebanon, and Turkey; (4) South Asia, which includes Bangladesh, India, Indonesia, and Pakistan; and (5) East Asia, which includes Japan, the Philippines, South Korea, and Vietnam.

Dimensions of Anti-Americanism

It is undoubtedly an egregious platitude to say that the United States cannot be easily summarized by any single definition. But as is the case with platitudes, it captures an important point that is often missed in the current discussions about anti-Americanism: namely that when people think of the United States, a large number of characteristics, events, and symbols are evoked in their minds. If we just contemplate in dismay the litany of statements that depict the United States as degenerate, immoral, hypocritical, and domineering, we may very well ponder how far the anti-American mind might go.[14] But we would miss out on the fact that the name "America" acquired a positive valence in the collective imagination of intellectuals and ordinary people from its inception on the world scene.[15]

The theme of America as the *New World* is the precursor to the theme of the *American Dream*, "the dream of human possibility, of a society in which all persons may be encouraged to do their best, to achieve their most, and to have the reward of a

---

12. Chiozza 2004b.

13. All the measures for the explanatory variables are averages computed over a five-year period, from 1997 to 2001.

14. For a tour de force covering two centuries of anti-American discourse, see Rubin and Rubin 2004.

15. For an insightful analysis of the myth of America through time, see Kennedy, chapter 2.

comfortable life," as Immanuel Wallerstein eloquently defined it.[16] The political implications of this unique feature of America have been summarized by Joseph Nye under the concept of "soft power": the ability to lead that the United States derives from its ability to attract.[17]

Given that the anti-American tropes evoked by Rubin and Rubin and the tropes of the American Dream coexist in the public discourse about America, it is important to go beyond summary statements of like and dislike, such as those we have discussed so far, and identify what characteristics feature prominently in people's mental frame of America.[18] As Nye points out, soft power is more likely to be operative and effective whenever there are "willing interpreters and receivers," that is, whenever there is a cultural and ideational context that is shared and commonly understood.[19] I will focus on more specific dimensions of the United States in order to clarify what about America attracts or repels foreign publics and to investigate whether the attitudes toward the United States form coherent patterns across dimensions.

As soon as we start analyzing the responses given to more focused inquiries, we can notice how individuals are less effusive about the United States. Beneath the surface of widespread support of the United States and its people lies a more nuanced image of America abroad. Positive attitudes toward the United States coexist with negative appraisals of fundamental features of the U.S. polity and society. As we can observe in table 4.1, when asked to state their opinion about American ideas about democracy, a substantial number of people—41.4 percent—responded that they disliked such ideas. The regional variation in the attitudes toward American democracy is also revealing: this percentage was lower in East Asia and in eastern Europe, but less so in Russia where the American style of democracy was seen in a negative light by as many as 46.3 percent of the respondents. It is also noticeable that weak enthusiasm for American ideas about democracy can be found in the Middle East, a region where democracy is not flourishing, as well as in the consolidated democracies of Canada and western Europe.

If these findings do not portray any overwhelming appreciation of a central feature of America's soft power, a marginal variation on a similar theme, namely the attitudes toward the spreading of American ideas and customs, elicited even more negative reactions. Solid majorities in four regions declared that the spreading of American customs and ideas was a negative development for their countries. A partial exception to this pattern is found in East Asia, where those concerned about the spreading of American ideas and customs was 49.1 percent on average, and as low as 36.9 percent and 34.6 percent in Japan and the Philippines, respectively.

Less politically charged aspects of the United States, on the other hand, revealed more favorable views. Admiration for U.S. scientific and technological achievements was universally widespread: only 20.4 percent of respondents expressed a negative evaluation of the United States on this count. American popular culture, in the form

16. Wallerstein 2003, 2.
17. Nye 2004a.
18. Rubin and Rubin 2004.
19. Nye 2004a, 16.

Table 4.1. Dimensions of anti-Americanism

	U.S. democracy		U.S. customs		U.S. popular culture		U.S. science	
	%	NA	%	NA	%	NA	%	NA
Industrial democracies	43.50	10.31	61.17	8.39	25.73	5.27	25.03	4.44
Eastern Europe	33.33	16.70	57.21	12.95	38.16	6.83	28.04	8.37
Middle East	54.41	8.79	77.75	8.11	50.90	6.37	28.27	6.84
South Asia	43.77	23.25	71.72	12.00	61.57	12.30	11.14	16.92
East Asia	29.47	7.50	49.08	9.30	35.26	6.22	12.37	3.87
Total	41.41	15.40	65.03	10.49	45.34	8.03	20.38	9.35

	U.S. business		War on terror		Different values		Balancing	
	%	NA	%	NA	%	NA	%	NA
Industrial democracies	55.31	12.04	24.20	6.37	37.70	6.30	27.95	11.24
Eastern Europe	26.52	20.61	14.56	6.85	41.91	10.77	32.04	19.54
Middle East	46.37	11.35	69.39	8.98	35.84	11.95	33.42	12.42
South Asia	36.41	24.06	39.41	18.26	27.55	27.21	35.08	18.02
East Asia	30.21	11.20	37.50	5.77	38.44	6.26	28.17	6.88
Total	38.27	17.13	37.63	10.42	35.32	14.54	32.04	14.59

Source: Data analysis based on the Pew Global Attitudes survey.
Note: Percentage of individuals selecting a response with an anti-American valence on eight items. "NA" stands for "don't know or refused to answer."

of movies, music, and television, was very much liked in western Europe and Canada, in eastern Europe, and East Asia—regions where at most 38.2 percent of the respondents did not like the primary products of the American entertainment industry—but it was less appreciated in the Middle East and South Asia, where such percentages reached 50.9 percent and 61.6 percent, respectively. Similarly, American ways of doing business were very much appreciated, with the exception of the countries in the advanced industrial democracies, and in France in particular where 72.6 percent declared that they disliked such ways.

The final three items in table 4.1 move us closer to the types of actions the United States pursues in the international arena. Respondents were asked to evaluate the actions taken by the United States in the "war on terror," the relative importance of values and policies in accounting for any differences between the respondents' countries and the United States, and the extent to which they believed that a military counterweight to the United States would make the world more secure. The most remarkable of these three items is the one investigating attitudes toward the American-led efforts to fight terrorism. In the summer of 2002, a majority of respondents in the industrial democracies of western Europe and Canada, in eastern Europe, in South Asia, and in East Asia said that they favored such efforts.

On the other hand, there might be reasons to discount respondents' inclination to downplay the existence of clashing values when they were explicitly asked, a response selected by 35 percent of the respondents overall. In particular, the skepticism about the spreading of American customs and ideas would suggest a values incompatibility more pronounced than that conveyed in the answers to the specific item tapping into the values versus policies divide. But for all the United States might do in the international arena, few people would welcome the emergence of another power balancing the United States: only 32 percent of the respondents believed that the emergence of another country as powerful as the United States would make the world a safer place.

In sum, these patterns of responses indicate how individuals make distinctions between different features of the United States. Even what might appear as a slight variation on the same fundamental aspect of the U.S. polity—American customs and ideas vis-à-vis American ideas on democracy—induces different evaluative reactions whereby American ideas about democracy elicit more widespread support. These findings, therefore, indicate that the status of the United States in the belief systems of ordinary people is multifaceted and fluid.

This character of America popular standing is also underscored by the fact that only 912 individuals in a sample of about twenty thousand from five world regions disliked everything about America, from its democracy to its customs, from its popular culture to its technology, from its approach to business to its actions in the war on terror. If we add the respondents who also attributed to different values any differences between their countries and the United States, and those who thought that balancing against the United States would make the world safer, the head count drops to 109. For all the other respondents there was something about America to appreciate. With so many distinctions and so much nuance among so many individuals, stereotyping, demonizing, and the attribution of evil intentions—three defining features of anti-Americanism as a cultural syndrome, as Josef Joffe so eloquently argued—were hardly part of the mind frame of the mass publics in the summer of 2002.[20]

Multifaceted Opinions of America   But how do all these distinctions between different aspects of the United States compare with the overall favorable view that ordinary people have of the United States? In other words, what factors feature prominently in the minds of those who are well disposed toward the United States? And what, on the other hand, turns ordinary people against America?

The plots in figure 7 show how many respondents endorsed the democratic ideas and the customs that America embodies, and how many rejected them, at each level of overall opinion toward the United States using fourfold displays.[21] Starting from the top left panel, we can observe that there was substantial agreement about the positive character of American ideas about democracy and American customs among those who had a very favorable opinion of the United States. Analogously, those who held the United States in very low esteem (in the lower right panel) largely

20. Joffe 2004.
21. In these graphs the number of respondents in each cell is represented by a quarter circle whose radius is proportional to the cell count. For an introduction to this technique to represent categorical data organized in 2 × 2 × k tables, see Friendly 1999.

concurred that customs and democratic ideas that emanate from America were to be viewed with suspicion. But more interestingly, these patterns of consistent attitudes did not emerge from the responses of those who had a somewhat favorable opinion of the United States. Among those mildly supportive of the United States, we find about as many individuals who said they liked American ideas about democracy and favored the diffusion of American customs and ideas as we find individuals who were opposed to both or individuals who liked American ideas about democracy but were opposed to the diffusion of American customs and ideas. In other words, a recording of a somewhat favorable opinion of the United States might coexist with more skeptical attitudes about what America stands for. Indeed, what is especially remarkable about figure 7 is how conflicting opinions about American customs and democratic ideals permeate the thought processes of the individuals who harbor good feelings toward the United States.

But if we can so easily find individuals who disparage fundamental features of the U.S. polity while still liking America, what else could come into their minds to compensate for the negative connotations associated with American customs and democratic ideas? A possible conjecture is that the discrepancy between the overall approval of the United States and the criticisms of the fundamental features of the U.S. polity and society follow from the existence of an implicit association between the United States and the widespread appeal of its popular culture. When the Marxist historian Eric Hobsbawm wrote that "in the field of popular culture the world was American or it was provincial," he established a connection between America and the emergence of a worldwide mass culture as a defining feature of the twentieth century.[22] Movies and television are arguably the two main venues that have defined the United States as a popular icon. Therefore, we could expect to observe a tighter congruence between overall expressions of pro-American attitudes, on the one hand, and the evaluations of American popular culture, on the other. We should also expect that admiration of American science and technology should feature prominently in the attitudinal outlook of those who expressed favorable opinions of the United States, given the widespread approval received by U.S. technological and scientific advances.

Indeed, when we analyze the pattern of responses in figure 8, we notice how the admiration of American science and technology was widespread even among detractors of the United States in general, and it was nearly unanimous among those who had a very favorable opinion of the United States. What is more striking, however, is the dislike of American popular culture among those individuals who had a favorable opinion of the United States: about 38.2 percent of the people who were mildly supportive of the United States disliked its music, movies, and television, and about 29.5 percent of those with a very high opinion of the United States thought likewise of its popular culture.

Many individuals, therefore, hold opposing affective orientations toward the United States. Likes and dislikes extensively coexist in people's minds as they

22. Hobsbawm 1994, 198.

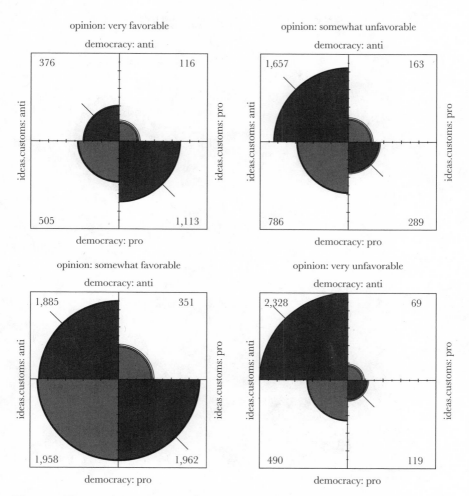

Figure 7. The spread of American ideas and democratic ideals. *Note:* The charts show the frequency of respondents who were either supportive or opposed to the spread of American ideas and customs and American ideas about democracy, given their overall opinion of the United States. The survey item asking about attitudes toward American ideas about democracy was not asked in Egypt and Vietnam. *Source:* Data analysis is based on the Pew Global Attitudes survey.

evaluate the multifaceted nature of America. But such evaluations need not generate any syndrome of ambivalence, the sense of anxiety and tension that apparently irreconcilable feelings generate.[23] There is nothing inherently contradictory in the simultaneous appreciation of American democratic ideals and concern over the excesses of its popular culture. Nor is there any underlying conflict over competing

23. For a theoretical and empirical investigation of ambivalence in people's attitudes, see Alvarez and Brehm 2002 and Smelser 1998.

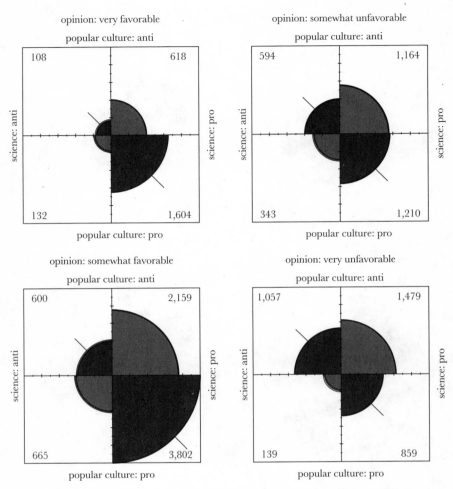

Figure 8. Admiration of American scientific achievements and of popular culture. *Note:* The charts show the frequency of respondents who expressed admiration of American technological and scientific advances and who expressed appreciation of American popular culture in terms of music, movies, and television, given their overall opinion of the United States. *Source:* Data analysis is based on the Pew Global Attitudes survey.

core values, as individuals express their admiration for American technology while disapproving of American business practices.

But as much as individuals make distinctions between the different aspects of the United States as a country and as a symbol, they also aggregate them into overall assessments of approval and disapproval. Such mental processes of aggregation reflect the different salience of each feature of the United States and, as a consequence, offer an indication of the balance that respondents strike across different dimensions. In table 4.2, I empirically investigate that balance by identifying the

Table 4.2. The effect of opposing specific U.S. features on overall opinion of the United States (in %)

	Industrial democracies	Eastern Europe	Middle East	South Asia	East Asia
No dimension	4.01	6.28	20.73	11.16	8.19
U.S. democracy	7.72	10.27	42.06	19.58	11.03
U.S. customs	8.98	10.70	40.11	19.45	16.00
U.S. popular culture	6.49	8.24	26.43	18.35	8.94
U.S. technology	6.11	10.96	20.57	21.61	7.54
U.S. business	7.38	12.07	20.18	21.37	13.46
U.S. war on terror	11.65	14.77	45.00	22.79	22.99
U.S. values	5.19	6.37	16.67	10.73	9.04
U.S. supremacy	5.57	6.94	20.29	8.66	6.67
U.S. democracy and war on terror	20.90	22.84	69.43	36.39	29.33
U.S. customs and war on terror	23.76	23.67	67.70	36.20	38.93
U.S. democracy and customs and war on terror	38.45	34.63	85.33	52.37	46.99
All dimensions	85.16	75.14	85.07	87.10	58.20

Source: Data analysis based on the Pew Global Attitudes survey.

Note: Entries measure the probability that a respondent holds a somewhat unfavorable or very unfavorable opinion of the United States. Estimated probabilities are obtained from an ordinal logistic model. Contact the author for more information on regression coefficients and the significance tests.

different weights that the eight attitudinal items from the Global Attitudes Survey receive in people's aggregate evaluations of the United States.[24]

Thus, for the individuals who answered in a pro-American fashion all the items, the probability of holding anti-American opinions was within single digits in the advanced industrial democracies of western Europe and Canada, in eastern Europe, and in East Asia, where it ranged between 4 percent and 8 percent. It was 11.2 percent in South Asia, and it reached an already sizeable 21 percent in the Middle Eastern countries. That is to say, the image of America was tarnished enough in the Middle East that one in five respondents expressed an overall negative opinion of the United States despite their positive assessment of what America did and stood for on eight different counts.

At the opposite end of the spectrum we have all the respondents who selected the answer with anti-American valence on all of the items: as we might expect, the probabilities of holding negative opinions of the United States substantially increased, reaching levels well above 80 percent in the advanced industrial democracies, the Middle East, and South Asia but not in the countries of East Asia, where the prob-

24. These probabilities are computed from the estimates of ordered logit models that regressed overall attitudes about the United States on each of the eight dichotomous components listed in table 4.1. Missing values were imputed by generating ten simulated data sets with a semi-parametric model and summarizing coefficients and estimate uncertainty using Rubin's rules. The imputation model relies on the "approximate Bayesian bootstrap" to approximate the process of drawing predicted values from a full Bayesian predictive distribution. It first fits a flexible additive model to predict all of the original missing and nonmissing values for the target variable and then uses predictive mean matching to impute the missing values. This procedure is implemented using Frank Harrell's `aregImpute` function in R.

ability of expressing an overall negative assessment of the United States was at most 58.2 percent. For East Asian publics, in other words, the United States had a positive valence that went well beyond any of the specific characteristics of the U.S. polity and American society.

Of all the eight items that disaggregate the United States into a series of political and societal components, the one that was most closely associated with negative views of the United States was that measuring attitudes about the war on terror. Opposition to the American-led war on terror engendered the largest shift in the probability of disliking the United States in all the five regions. Substantively, this effect amounts to an increase in the probability of holding negative opinions of the United States between 7.6 and 24.3 percentage points when we compare the respondents who had no objections on any of the eight dimensions with those who only opposed the U.S. war on terror.

The effect of the opposition to the war on terror is particularly noticeable in the Middle East, where the likelihood that a respondent that opposed U.S. actions to combat terrorism would have cold feelings toward the United States was as high as 45 percent. But, for the Middle Eastern publics, similarly large effects were also associated with the disenchantment with American democracy and with the spreading of American customs, as the probabilities of expressing unfavorable views of the United States increased to 42.1 percent and 40.1 percent for such respondents. While policy considerations were a factor of primary relevance in the formation of people's attitudes toward the United States, two fundamental features of the U.S. polity were nearly as important in the region where opposition to America was most diffused. In other words, two dimensions associated with "what America stands for" and not just with "what America does" carried a predominant weight in the formation of an overall negative stance toward the United States.

This empirical result marks a major difference between the sources of negative attitudes toward the United States in the Middle East and in all the other regions. It is not just that for Middle Eastern respondents both policy and polity, what America does to combat terrorism and what America is in terms of its political values, were the strongest determinants of their negative assessments. But it is also true that in regions other than the Middle East we do not find a major issue framing the overall orientation toward the United States. Instead, outside the critical area of the Middle East, opposition to the United States is the resultant of a cumulation of factors. It emerges whenever we come across respondents who were critical of several aspects of America.

For example, respondents who were concerned about the spreading of American customs and opposed the American war on terror would be likely to hold a negative opinion of the United States with a probability as low as 23.7 percent if they lived in an advanced industrial democracy or in eastern Europe; between 36 percent and 39 percent in South Asia or in East Asia; but as high as 67.7 percent in the Middle East. Criticism of American ideas about democracy increases those probabilities to a staggering 85.3 percent in the Middle East and pushes them close to the 50 percent threshold in South and East Asia (52.4 percent and 47 percent, respectively), while leaving them well below 40 percent in eastern Europe and in the advanced industrial democracies (34.6 percent and 38.5 percent, respectively).

In other words, for the Middle Eastern respondents who had grown disenchanted with American democracy and American antiterrorist policy, none of the other factors that they might still appreciate about the United States had enough psychological leverage to keep them from forming a negative opinion of the United States. Elsewhere, and in particular in eastern Europe and in the advanced industrial democracies, the United States still enjoyed a reservoir of good feelings generated by the multifaceted nature of its society and culture.

By emphasizing the multifaceted nature of attitudes toward the United States, these results give validation to the prosaic perspective on anti-Americanism that Bruce Russett advocated long ago: "One must be extremely careful to specify the content of the attitudes in question when using broad labels like 'anti-American.'"[25] Large portions of the general public are willing to entertain simultaneously positive and negative opinions of the United States on its multiple dimensions, while a systematically negative classification of any referents associated with the United States is more of an exception. That multifaceted evaluation of the United States also helped temper the formation of negative views about the United States, given that popular dissatisfaction with the United States emerged when respondents systematically felt at odds with feature after feature of the United States.

But for all the reassurance this finding might provide, such a reluctance was no longer operative among the Middle Eastern respondents who disregarded the multifaceted nature of the United States and primarily based their negative assessment of the United States on their negative opinions of U.S. polity and its antiterrorist policy. This finding, therefore, points to a qualitative difference in the popular standing of the United States in the Middle East. It shows that America's "polyvalence" was not serving as an asset for the popularity of the United States in the Middle East.[26]

Are People Just Trying to Be Polite?

The patterns of responses we have uncovered so far paint a more encouraging picture of popular attitudes toward the United States. With the exception of the respondents in the Middle Eastern countries and Pakistan, ordinary people tend to like the United States overall. If the simple answer "I have a somewhat favorable opinion of the United States" is the resultant of a process of aggregation of multiple considerations, then we can conjecture that positive factors overwhelm negative factors in people's minds. Any question that makes a reference to the United States in general cues the respondents to abstract from any specific societal or political or cultural element. What is then evoked in people's minds is an image of the United States that is larger and more encompassing than the sum of any single component.

25. Russett 1963, 213.
26. See also Katzenstein and Keohane, conclusion.

Can we conclude, then, that the case of the conservative critics who have been denouncing the rise of popular anti-Americanism has been disconfirmed? If we take survey results as a fair representation of the status of public opinion, we might be inclined to answer affirmatively. Indeed, it is remarkable to see the extent to which pro-American views color the attitudes of the mass publics on issue after issue, when the conservative critics' case was predicting otherwise.

But a less flattering interpretation of these findings can also be formulated. Rather than representing the deep-seated predispositions that preordain respondents' judgment, the survey responses recorded in the Global Attitudes Survey could be discounted as a bowdlerized version of the popular feelings about the United States. Under this interpretation, the responses to the question "What is your opinion of the United States?" would not reveal the "true" appreciation of the United States but would overstate the levels of pro-American support because subjects might deem it inappropriate to display a wholesale rejection of a country publicly, thus hiding the predispositions that truly condition their political behavior.

Scholars of public opinion would recognize in this alternative conjecture another instance of the broader phenomenon of "preference falsification," to use Timur Kuran's label.[27] The behavioral manifestation of attitudes and preferences, whether it occurs in public rallies or survey questions, Kuran argues, should not be taken at face value but should be seen as the outcome of a strategic calculus of individuals who assess the consequences that might follow from telling the truth. Adam Berinsky, while eschewing the concept of preference falsification, raises an analogous point when he argues that "opinion surveys may fail to measure accurately the conscious will of individuals who are uncomfortable expressing opinions that are socially undesirable."[28]

We can call the tendency to report favorable assessments of the United States as the expression of a "politeness norm," that is, the norm to keep to oneself the dislike of a country. But for the conservative commentators, from Krauthammer to Ajami, these results would just reflect the mendacity of large portions of the mass publics who would say positive things while being convinced of the opposite. Fouad Ajami did not mince any words when he urged to dismiss the more conciliatory conclusions on anti-Americanism emanating from survey results: "There is no need to go so far away from home only to count the cats in Zanzibar."[29]

Although thicker descriptions of individual attitudes might be necessary to get at the heart of this conundrum, it is nonetheless possible to clarify some of its empirical implications using the survey items collected in the 2002 Global Attitudes Survey. To do so, we can conjecture that the view expressed in the response to the question "What do you think of the United States?" consists of two elements: the first element is the "true" feelings about the United States and the second element is the adher-

27. Kuran 1995.
28. Berinsky 2004, 19.
29. Ajami 2003, 54.

ence to the "politeness norm." The goal would be to analyze answers that have been purged of the effects of the desire to give polite answers.

If we assume that adherence to the "politeness norm" is an individual feature of each respondent, we can get additional leverage on the attitudes toward the United States by establishing a pair comparison between how a person assesses the United States and how that person assesses some other country. We might expect high degrees of congruence in how people rate countries, given that such ratings would respond to the same ideological outlook of each person and to an analogous set of social norms. The discrepancies in people's evaluations, however, open an additional window into individual attitudes toward the United States.

In particular we can distinguish four different types of subjects:

1. the *contrarians*: those who dislike the United States as well as other countries;
2. the *politically correct*: those who like the United States as well as other countries;
3. the *anti-Americans*: those who dislike the United States but like other countries;
4. the *pro-Americans*: those who like the United States but dislike other countries.

The subjects in the first two categories—the *contrarians* and the *politically correct*—are the ones whose attitudes are more impervious to categorization, because their attitudes can be generated by alternative but observationally undistinguishable mechanisms. In those two groups we can indeed find people who bear deep-seated, and even visceral, grievances against the United States and other countries, on the one hand, and people who feel a sense of shared communality with the United States and other countries. But in the same groups we can also find people whose response style is to say always positive things of the United States and other countries or to say always negative things. And, we can also find people who find the expression of negative opinions inappropriate or shameful and who prefer hiding behind the mask of a "somewhat favorable" opinion. In other words, congruent responses are less informative.

In the third and fourth category, on the other hand, we find respondents who might feel the pressure to conform to the norm of politeness but who decide to make a distinction nonetheless. The use of the labels *pro-American* and *anti-American* should be seen as a way to characterize the higher level of deliberation that is inherent in the responses of the people who make a distinction between the United States and other countries. Given that the desire to be polite is constant across the evaluations of two countries, the discrepancies that we observe can be imputed to different predispositions toward the United States.

The survey items in the Pew Research Center's Global Attitudes Project allow for an analysis of the empirical relevance of these four categories. Along with the questions asking their opinion of the United States, respondents were asked to state their opinion of another country, namely the country that the Pew researchers deemed the "dominant" country in a given region. Under this category, we can find a vast array of countries: for example, Japanese respondents were asked what they thought of China; Egyptians were asked what they thought of Turkey; Pakistanis were asked

Table 4.3. Opinion of the United States and opinion of a referent country

Opinion of United States	Opinion of other country							
	All regions				Industrial democracies			
	Positive	Negative	NA	Total	Positive	Negative	NA	Total
Positive	37.81	11.56	2.56	51.94	55.50	6.70	4.18	66.38
Negative	9.94	16.74	1.76	28.43	21.02	5.84	1.92	28.78
NA	4.34	0.94	14.35	19.63	0.99	0.13	3.71	4.84
Total	52.09	29.24	18.67	100.00	77.52	12.67	9.81	100.00
	Eastern Europe				Middle East			
Positive	64.30	5.93	1.07	71.30	12.92	8.46	2.66	24.04
Negative	14.44	7.69	0.90	23.03	11.52	46.37	6.17	64.06
NA	1.78	0.36	3.53	5.67	0.57	0.52	10.80	11.90
Total	80.53	13.97	5.50	100.00	25.01	55.35	19.64	100.00
	South Asia				East Asia			
Positive	17.78	25.80	0.66	44.24	53.34	16.11	1.18	70.62
Negative	6.24	38.43	0.37	45.05	12.69	13.58	0.55	26.82
NA	0.62	3.54	6.55	10.71	0.38	0.28	1.90	2.56
Total	24.65	67.77	7.58	100.00	66.40	29.97	3.63	100.00

Source: Data analysis based on the Pew Global Attitudes survey.
Note: Entries show the percentage of respondents holding a given opinion of the United States and of another country. "Positive" combines the response categories of "somewhat favorable" and "very favorable"; "negative" combines the response categories of "somewhat unfavorable" and "very unfavorable." "NA" stands for "don't know or refused to answer."

what they thought of India; and the French were asked what they thought of Germany. The question we should ask is whether the attitudes toward the United States are any different from those toward the "dominant" country.

As a general pattern, we find again that it is not very common to state an unfavorable opinion of a country: 52.1 percent of all respondents had a very favorable or a somewhat favorable opinion, a distribution that closely resembles the one we find for the United States. Not only the United States, therefore, but any other country is usually seen in a positive light, which would indicate an overall reluctance to state unfavorable opinions of a country. But to detect the impact of the "politeness norm" on survey responses, we should analyze the joint distribution of the attitudes toward the United States and the respondents' opinion of the "dominant" country in table 4.3.

Overall, we find that in this classification scheme the most common attitudinal stance was that of the *politically correct*, and the least common was that of the *anti-Americans*, 37.8 percent and 9.9 percent respectively. In other words, the dislike of America in conjunction with appreciation of some other country, which we take as manifestation of anti-American predispositions, pertained to a minority of respondents.

As we could expect from these aggregate results, there was a high level of congruence of opinion: 72.6 percent of all the respondents who thought highly of the referent country also thought highly of the United States, and, analogously, 72.8 percent of those who thought highly of the United States also thought highly of the other country they were asked to evaluate.[30] Conversely, those respondents who had a negative opinion of the referent country—and did not have any qualms about letting their opinions be known—were less inclined to think likewise about the United States. Indeed, a sizeable 40 percent of those who disliked other countries had fonder dispositions toward the United States. Thus, if there are any discrepancies in the respondents' assessments, those discrepancies had overall a pro-American slant.

But as much as the aggregate findings describe the existence of a bedrock of genuine good feelings toward the United States, the regional patterns reveal that the image of America was not admired all over the world. The bleaker state of America's popular status in the Middle East transpires through these patterns of data: with 64.1 percent of the Middle Eastern respondents holding a negative opinion of the United States, America was clearly not much loved. But such a negative outlook was also extended to other foreign countries that play a geopolitical role in the area, not exclusively to the United States. Indeed, nearly half the Middle Eastern respondents could be labeled as *contrarians*.

It was, instead, in the advanced industrial democracies that an anti-American sentiment could be detected. About three out of four respondents with a negative opinion of the United States had a positive opinion of their referent country. Given how rare it was to find respondents willing to openly bad-mouth other countries among the respondents from the advanced industrial democracies, the findings in table 4.3 show that the lack of appreciation for the United States was strong enough to displace the countervailing effect of the desire to state an "appropriate" opinion. But still, such a negative sentiment pertained to a minority of respondents, 21 percent of them, not to hordes of effete barbarians lacking any common purpose but their disdain of America, as we so often read in commentaries and editorials during the diplomatic crisis over the war in Iraq.[31]

Individual Profiles of Anti-American Attitudes

The third step in the investigation of popular attitudes toward the United States in five world regions in 2002 is to elaborate an empirical profile of the individuals who are more likely to express anti-American opinions. Using a series of regression models, I evaluate several propositions about the demographic and attitudinal characteristics of the individuals who expressed anti-American views. Identity markers,

30. To compute these figures from table 4.3, we should divide the cell percentage by the appropriate marginal percentage: for example, the relative percentage of respondents with a positive opinion of the United States in the group of respondents with a positive opinion of the other country is equal to $37.81/52.09 = 72.59\%$.

31. For an overview see Pond 2004. The most vivid intellectual catalyst of the debate over the European perceptions of the United States is Kagan 2003.

such as gender, age, levels of education, religious affiliation, and occupational status are examined along with indicators that distinguish the ideological outlooks and the broader belief systems of the respondents.

Typologies, such as the one developed by Peter Katzenstein and Robert Keohane in chapter 1, distinguish alternative motivations that animate popular opposition to the United States and elaborate conjectures about the mechanisms that would induce the emergence of beliefs with an anti-American valence.[32] Along such lines, we could speculate that the differential impact of generational experiences may very well be reflected in the presence of clusters of similar opinions about the United States in each age group. Such generational similarities might be seen as instances of what Katzenstein and Keohane call *legacy* anti-Americanism, a form of anti-Americanism that originates in the resentment of past wrongs perpetrated by the United States.[33] But to specify *ex-ante* what those generational experiences would be and how they might translate into opinion patterns goes beyond the theoretical frames so far elaborated about anti-Americanism. Anything from the bombing of the Chinese embassy in Belgrade to the downing of an Iranian airliner by the USS *Vincennes*, from the killing of two Korean girls by a U.S. Army vehicle in Seoul to the scandal at the Abu Ghraib prison in Baghdad could potentially serve as the focal point for the emergence of resentment against the United States for entire generations of people in a country.[34]

But beyond the description of the distribution of anti-American attitudes across different subpopulations defined by the explanatory variables in the models, the regression models of anti-American attitudes allow for the testing of a series of conjectures about the connections between popular belief systems and the presence of anti-American attitudes. In particular, I consider four conjectures: (1) the information-and-contacts hypothesis; (2) the traditional worldview hypothesis; (3) the anti-market worldview hypothesis; (4) the scapegoating hypothesis. These conjectures differ from the descriptive analysis regarding age groups or gender effects because they elaborate specific causal mechanisms that would lead people holding specific worldviews to be more likely to adopt anti-American beliefs. These hypotheses can, therefore, be engaged in a confrontation with the empirical record.

The first conjecture—*the information-and-contacts hypothesis*—subsumes the claim that people who have closer contacts and better information about the United States are less likely to hold negative views of it. This perspective undergirds the argument advanced by Joseph Nye, who claims that social interactions with the United States foster socialization into the values and goals of America, and for that reason, he advocates cultural exchange programs as a way to promote and sustain the image of the United States.[35] In a model of opportunistic politicians with no qualms about spreading hatred for political purposes, Edward Glaeser also shows that hostility

32. Katzenstein and Keohane, chapter 1.
33. Ibid.
34. In chapter 9, McAdam analyzes the dynamic processes through which both negative and positive legacies emerge, and clarifies how contingent and idiosyncratic those processes might be.
35. Nye 2004a, 2004b.

toward a social group—be it an ethnic minority or the population of a country— declines as the incentives to dismiss the false stories manufactured by the "entrepreneurs of hate" increase.[36] In his theoretical formulation, increased economic interactions serve as the mechanism that would make believing in hate-creating stories counterproductive. The lack of social interactions is explicitly selected by Glaeser as a key causal factor accounting for the low status of the United States in the Middle East: "This combination of America's relevance (which creates the incentives for supply) and the absence of interactions (which ensures that there is little desire to know the truth) fosters the spread of hatred in this region."[37]

Two measures are employed to test whether the information-and-contacts hypothesis is reflected in the patterns of responses toward America recorded in the Pew Global Attitudes Project Survey. The first measure is an indicator that identifies the respondents who declared that they watched an international news channel such as the BBC or CNN. People who did so were arguably interested in expanding their sources of information beyond their domestic channels. In this respect, watching an international news channel might be seen as a proxy for the incentive to "learn the truth" about an out-group emphasized in Glaeser's model. The potential drawback for this measure is that watching international news channels might very well be a consequence, rather than a cause, of attitudes toward America.[38] Therefore, I primarily consider a second indicator that is less likely to be endogenous to the attitudinal stances toward the United States, namely whether the respondents had friends or relatives living in the United States whom they visited regularly or with whom they corresponded regularly in writing or by telephone. The risk of endogeneity associated with this second indicator is lower, given that the bonds of kinship and friendship drive the desire to keep contacts with friends and relatives living in the United States. This second measure has also an additional advantage because it offers an individual level measure of the mechanism that underlies Joseph Nye's proposal to foster cultural exchanges with the United States.[39]

The *traditional worldview* and the *antimarket worldview hypotheses* place the origins of popular opposition to the United States in the perception of a gap between individual normative and ideological predispositions and the implications that the societal and political model of the United States entails for those predispositions. These two hypotheses share a common logic insofar as they derive from the perception of a values gap. They differ, however, with respect to the content of the values they emphasize. In the *traditional worldview hypothesis*, popular anti-Americanism stems from a reaction to the challenges that the individualistic and egalitarian ethos of the United States mounts to the forms of traditional authority and the subordinate position of women in society. This argument has been advanced with respect to a values gap that allegedly distinguishes Western and Islamic societies. In challenging Samuel

36. Glaeser 2005.
37. Ibid., 79.
38. On this point see also Gentzkow and Shapiro 2004.
39. Nye 2004b.

Huntington's thesis in the *Clash of Civilizations*, for example, Pippa Norris and Ronald Inglehart show that the cultural cleavage existing between Western and Islamic civilizations pertains to the social beliefs about gender equality and sexual liberalization and not to the appreciation of democratic values and ideals.[40] At the macro level, a similar argument has been elaborated by Steven Fish, who places the causal roots of authoritarianism in Islamic societies in the repression of women's rights permitted by authoritarian institutions.[41]

Three indicators are used to identify the respondents who embrace a traditional worldview: the first distinguishes the respondents who declared that "they liked the pace of modern life" from those who did not; the second identifies the respondents who declared that a marriage where "the husband provides for the family and the wife takes care of the house and children" entailed a more satisfying way of life than "a marriage where husband and wife both have jobs and both take care of the house and children"; the third indicator identifies the respondents who agreed that "their way of life needs to be protected from foreign influences."

The third conjecture—*the antimarket hypothesis*—is primarily inspired by what Katzenstein and Keohane call *social* anti-Americanism.[42] Under this label, they summarize the position of that part of the mass public who is concerned about the societal consequences of unfettered market competition. The allegation is that the model of the U.S. political economy is based on unregulated labor markets and gives premium to efficiency and making profits at the expense of social protections for the lower and middle classes. As Katzenstein and Keohane point out, underlying this welfarist type of anti-Americanism is a disagreement about the balance between efficiency and equity, and about the importance of the welfare state as an institution that mediates between market and social outcomes.

But a second element pervades the opposition to the United States summarized in the antimarket hypothesis. This element pertains to the beliefs held with respect to the broader forces that drive success in life. It is often emphasized how the American way of life values individual achievement over ascriptive status to determine one's position in society. The American creed is premised on the belief that individuals are arbiters of their own success in life and that a competitive marketplace is the institutional setting in which individuals can see their talents thrive.

This belief is often invoked to account for differences in political preferences over a large variety of social and economic issues. In an original investigation of the sources of happiness in the United States and Europe, Alesina, Di Tella, and MacCulloch, for example, attribute the differences in the effects of inequality on happiness among the rich and the poor to the different degrees of social mobility on the two sides of the Atlantic.[43] What accounts for that aversion to inequality embodied in the European social model is not simply a matter of different "taste," but— Alesina, Di Tella, and MacCulloch conclude—it is a reflection of the fact that

---

40. Huntington 1996, Norris and Inglehart 2004.
41. Fish 2002.
42. Katzenstein and Keohane, chapter 1.
43. Alesina, Di Tella, and MacCulloch 2004.

"opportunities for mobility are (or are perceived to be) higher in the US than in Europe."[44]

By extension, the logic of this argument implies that a *social* or welfarist type of anti-Americanism should be more likely among those individuals who are disillusioned with the opportunities they have to improve their own and their families' position through effort and talent. This is because these are the people whose happiness and well-being would be more negatively affected by the income disparities generated in a competitive market economy and who, as a consequence, would be less likely to see America as the beacon of a better life.

Two indicators are used to distinguish the individuals who embraced the worldviews implicit in the antimarket hypothesis: the first identifies all the respondents who asserted that they disagreed with the statement that "most people are better off in a free market economy, even though some people are rich and some are poor"; the second indicator identifies the respondents who declared that they believed that "success in life is pretty much determined by sources outside their control."

The final conjecture—the *scapegoat hypothesis*—claims that the origins of popular anti-Americanism are to be found in a psychological mechanism that induces individuals to transfer dissatisfaction with the state of affairs in their countries onto the United States. This conjecture is a staple feature in the rhetorical repertoire of the *anti*-anti-Americans, the cadre of pugnacious intellectuals who denounce any form of criticism of the United States, be it mild or preposterous.[45] It would be difficult to match the scorn that Jean-François Revel bestows on all those who express negative views of America to deflect any shortcomings of their own: "Here we see how the Americans are useful to us: to console us for our own failures, serving the myth that they do worse than they do, and that what goes badly with us is their fault."[46]

The converse of the scapegoat conjecture is that people who are satisfied with their countries are less compelled to blame the United States in all its manifestations and actions because they do not feel the need to project their inadequacies onto the United States. To assess the extent to which this conjecture is reflected in the survey responses, I rely on an indicator in the Pew survey that directly taps into the sense of dissatisfaction with the state of affairs in their country. By extension, I also analyze whether concerns about "how things were going in the world" were related to the patterns of responses individuals gave when they were asked about the United States.

The Findings Who then are the individuals who expressed negative views of the United States? The results from the regression models are summarized in tables 4.4 and 4.5 for six different attitudinal items. The "+" sign indicates that a factor was significantly associated with higher propensities to offer responses with anti-American content; the "−" sign indicates that a factor was significantly associated

44. Ibid., 2036.
45. See, for example, Berman 2004a, Joffe 2004, Revel 2003, Rubin and Rubin 2004. For a sophisticated analysis of French *anti*-anti-Americanism see Gopnik 2003.
46. Revel 2003, 170.

Table 4.4. Effects of individual factors on anti-Americanism (part 1)

	Opinion					U.S. democracy					U.S. customs				
	ID	EE	ME	SA	EA	ID	EE	ME	SA	EA	ID	EE	ME	SA	EA
Male	ns	+	ns	+	ns	−	−	ns	ns	−	ns	ns	ns	ns	ns
Age	ns	ns	ns	ns	ns	ns	+	+	ns	ns	+	+	+	ns	+
Education	+	ns	ns	−	ns	−	−	−	−	ns	+	ns	ns	ns	ns
Catholic	ns	ns	ns			+	ns	+			ns	ns			
Atheist	+	ns	ns		+	+	ns	ns	+	ns	+	ns	ns		+
Muslim	+	ns	+	+		+	ns		+		ns	ns	+	+	
Orthodox		ns					ns					ns			
Hindu				+					ns					ns	
Buddhist					ns					ns					ns
Other religion	ns	ns	+	ns	+	ns	ns	ns	ns	ns	ns	ns	+	ns	ns
Unemployed	ns	ns	ns	+	+	ns	ns	ns	ns	ns	−	ns	ns	ns	+

	Popular culture					Science/technology					War on terror				
	ID	EE	ME	SA	EA	ID	EE	ME	SA	EA	ID	EE	ME	SA	EA
Male	ns	−	ns	−	−	ns	ns	−	ns	ns	−	−	ns	+	−
Age	+	+	+	+	+	ns	ns	ns	ns	ns	ns	−	ns	ns	−
Education	ns	+	−	−	−	ns	ns	−	−	−	+	+	ns	−	−
Catholic	ns	ns				ns	ns				+	ns			
Atheist	ns	ns	ns		ns	+	ns	+	ns	ns	+	ns	ns		ns
Muslim	ns	ns	+	+		ns	ns	+			+	ns	+	+	
Orthodox		ns					ns					ns			
Hindu				+					ns					ns	
Buddhist					ns					ns					ns
Other religion	ns	ns	ns	+	ns	ns	ns	ns	ns	ns	ns	ns	+	ns	ns
Unemployed	ns	ns	ns	ns	ns	−	ns	ns	−	ns	ns	ns	ns	+	ns

Source: Data analysis based on the Pew Global Attitudes survey.

Note: ID = Advanced industrial democracies; EE = Eastern Europe; ME = Middle East; SA = South Asia; EA = East Asia. The + sign indicates a positive and significant effect; the − sign indicates a negative and significant effect; "ns" stands for not significant relationship.

with lower propensities to offer responses with anti-American content; the "ns" abbreviation identifies the factors that were not significantly associated with individual attitudes toward the United States.[47]

We first consider the results on five factors with a primarily descriptive content, namely gender, age, levels of education, religious affiliation, and employment status. Starting with gender, the patterns of responses of males and females is mostly undistinguishable, and whenever gender differences emerge, they do not seem to follow any systematic pattern. Thus, for example, males in eastern Europe were more likely to have less favorable opinions of the United States, but at the same time eastern European males were also less likely to hold negative views of American ideas about democracy or of U.S. policies for combating terrorism.

More evidence, on the other hand, is found with respect to the presence of generational effects. The age of the respondents was coded by distinguishing five ten-year age cohorts and by selecting the youngest cohort (18–25 years old) as the reference category.[48] The effects of age are clear and substantial when we consider attitudes toward American popular culture: there we observe that in all five regions the young generations were the ones most enthralled with all the glamour of Hollywood stars and starlets. Older generations became less enchanted with American popular culture in a nearly linear fashion: the size of the coefficients progressively increases as we move up the age ladder. A similar pattern characterizes attitudes toward the spread of American customs and ideas: the younger generations were again the most supportive, and markedly so in the Middle East and in eastern Europe.

The marked generational effect associated with appreciation of American popular culture, however, does not translate into keener appreciation of America's political ideals, or its national security policies. For example, people of older generations in eastern Europe manifested a less favorable opinion of American democracy and American customs—which may indicate the lingering effects of a *legacy* type of anti-Americanism. But such a legacy does not affect their evaluations of U.S. policy against terrorism, which attracted more approval from those older than thirty-five, that is, from those who came of age *before* the end of the cold war, rather than by the young kids who love Madonna and her replicas.

Of all the variables in this analysis, level of education shows the least consistent pattern of effects. Respondents with higher levels of education made greater distinctions among the multifaceted aspects of America. They appreciated American ideas about democracy in all regions but East Asia, a sentiment that was not extended to the spreading of American customs and ideas. The educated class was the least

47. The findings about the individual profiles of anti-American attitudes were obtained by running a series of regression models (ordered logit or binary logit models depending on how the variables measuring the attitudes toward the United States were coded). Missing values were imputed using the approach described in note 24. (Tables with regression coefficients, standard errors, and significance tests of the coefficients are presented in full detail in the appendix available from the author or the editors.)

48. Table 4.4 lists the overall effects of age as they are conveyed through five regression coefficients associated with the age groups and lists the significant findings obtained using Wald tests of joint significance on the five coefficients.

inclined to express overall positive opinions of the United States in the advanced industrial democracies, but they were the most keen on doing so in South Asia. Educated people were more likely to reject U.S. antiterrorism actions in the advanced industrial democracies and in eastern Europe, a finding that foreshadowed the deep controversies over the Iraq War in Europe. On the other hand, education was negatively correlated with disapproval in South and East Asia of the American-led war on terror.

All this shows that the relationship between education and anti-American beliefs varies across regions and across attitudinal dimensions. The lack of a uniform connection underscores the circumstantial character of the phenomenon of anti-Americanism and its multifarious nature. At different levels of educational attainment, different people in different regions reach different conclusions about what they like and dislike about the United States.[49] As a consequence, ideological opposition cannot be the causal venue that substantiates the connection between education and extremist political beliefs and violence that Krueger and Malečková have uncovered.[50]

Religious beliefs are yet another factor that is systematically associated with attitudes toward the United States. The models included several indicators of religious affiliation and offer comparative evaluations of the average propensity to express negative attitudes toward the United States. The baseline category is Protestants in the advanced industrial democracies and in eastern Europe; and Christians in the Middle East, South Asia, and East Asia. Thus, compared to Protestants, individuals from the Muslim minority in the advanced industrial democracies had more negative attitudes toward the United States. But so did Hindus and atheists. Catholics, on the other hand, were usually as keen on America as their Protestant brethren. Muslim respondents in the advanced industrial democracies, in the Middle East, and in South Asia were particularly opposed to the antiterrorist policies of the United States. No other religious group expressed such strong disapproval of the U.S.-led war on terror.

Thus, the quest for the anti-American version of the "soccer moms" and the "NASCAR dads" that so much intrigue the readers of opinion polls inside the Beltway leaves us with a paltry catch. The anti-American respondent can be either male or female, is more likely to be older and of Muslim religion, but can have reached low or high levels of educational attainment, all depending on what feature of America is relevant. This finding gives additional empirical substance to the overall pattern of popular anti-Americanism as a multifaceted phenomenon, too loose to be a well-knit ideology, too differentiated to be a cultural syndrome. In the introduction, Keohane and Katzenstein refer to the "polyvalent" symbolism of America, and write that "American symbols refer simultaneously to a variety of

---

49. In chapter 6, Johnston and Stockmann find a more consistent relationship in their analysis of Beijing respondents whereby higher levels of education are systematically associated with higher levels of amity toward the United States and with lower levels of identity differentiation.

50. Krueger and Malečková 2003. For a brilliant solution to Krueger and Malečková's puzzle, see Bueno de Mesquita 2005.

values, which may appeal differentially to different people in different societies, and despite their contradiction may appeal even to the same person at one time."[51] The empirical findings from the analysis of the 2002 Pew Global Attitudes Survey validate that claim.

Findings on the Four Conjectures   Earlier, we discussed four causal conjectures linking specific attitudinal and ideational orientations of the respondents with their attitudes toward the United States. The findings are summarized in table 4.5.

Starting from the information-and-contacts hypothesis, which claims that higher levels of information about the United States lead to more pro-American opinions, we observe that the data reveal widespread support for such a conjecture across attitudinal dimensions and world regions. The indicator measuring whether the respondents watched news on international channels and the indicator identifying the respondents who had friends and relatives in the United States are significantly associated with more pro-American views in the assessment of the United States in general, of American ideas about democracy, and the spreading of American customs. It is noteworthy that the Middle Eastern, South Asian, and East Asian respondents who communicated with friends and relatives residing in the United States had more favorable views of American popular culture. Such a favorable assessment also extended to the evaluation of the war on terror for the respondents in the Middle East and in East Asia.[52]

These findings on the information-and-contacts hypothesis place the lack of connection between the aggregate levels of anti-Americanism and the number of student visas granted to a country—as was shown in figure 6—under a different light. The relevant comparison is not across countries, where we saw no relationship between the number of student visas granted and popular anti-Americanism, but within each country between the individuals that are directly affected by the flow of information that they receive from their friends and relatives. It appears that the claims Nye and Glaeser made from different theoretical perspectives about the importance of information in fostering friendlier relations among countries and groups receive empirical support.[53] The "American uncle," that common fixture in popular folklore, does not just bequeath a rich inheritance to his dispossessed nephews overseas, but contributes to the diffusion of the good name of America and the American dream.

The evidence associated with the traditional worldview hypothesis is less clear cut. On the one hand, we observe that respondents that had a positive view of modernity were usually more inclined to positive attitudes toward the United States. The connection between appreciation of the "pace of modern life" and "pro-Americanism" obtains across regions and across attitudinal dimensions. On the other

51. Keohane and Katzenstein, introduction.

52. Similarly, Johnston and Stockmann in chapter 6 find that, among Beijing respondents, those who follow international news and those who have traveled abroad have higher levels of amity toward the United States.

53. Nye 2004a, 2004b; Glaeser 2005.

Table 4.5. Effects of individual factors on anti-Americanism (part 2)

	Opinion					U.S. democracy					U.S. customs				
	ID	EE	ME	SA	EA	ID	EE	ME	SA	EA	ID	EE	ME	SA	EA
Information-and-contacts hypothesis															
Contacts in United States	–	ns	–	–	–	–	ns	–	–	–	–	ns	–	+	–
Watch international news	–	–	ns	ns	–	ns	–	ns	ns	–	–	ns	ns	+	ns
Traditional worldview hypothesis															
Protect culture	ns	+	ns	ns	ns	ns	+	ns	ns	ns	+	+	ns	+	ns
Modernity OK	–	–	–	–	–	–	–	–	–	–	–	–	–	–	ns
Traditional marriage roles	ns	ns	ns	ns	ns	–	ns	ns	+	ns	ns	ns	ns	+	ns
Antimarket worldview hypothesis															
Market outcomes OK	–	–	–	–	ns	–	ns	–	ns	–	–	–	–	–	–
Fatalist	ns	ns	ns	+	–	ns	ns	ns	ns	–	ns	ns	ns	ns	–
Scapegoating hypothesis															
Country OK	–	–	ns	ns	ns	–	–		ns	ns	–	ns	–	–	–
World OK	–	–	–	–	–	ns	–		–	ns	–	–	–	–	–

	Popular culture					Science/technology					War on terror				
	ID	EE	ME	SA	EA	ID	EE	ME	SA	EA	ID	EE	ME	SA	EA
Information-and-contacts hypothesis															
Contacts in United States	ns	ns	–	–	–	ns	ns	ns	ns	–	ns	ns	–	ns	–
Watch international news	–	–	–	ns	–	ns	ns	–	–	ns	ns	ns	ns	ns	–
Traditional worldview hypothesis															
Protect culture	ns	+	ns	ns	ns	–	ns	ns	–	ns	–	+	ns	ns	ns
Modernity OK	–	–	–	–	ns	–	–	+	–	–	ns	–	ns	–	ns
Traditional marriage roles	+	ns	+	+	+	ns	ns	+	ns	+	ns	ns	+	ns	ns
Antimarket worldview hypothesis															
Market outcomes OK	ns	–	–	ns	–	–	–	ns	ns	ns	–	–	–	ns	ns
Fatalist	ns	ns	–	ns	ns	ns	–	ns	ns	ns	ns	ns	ns	ns	ns
Scapegoating hypothesis															
Country OK	–	+	–	–	ns	ns	–	–	ns	ns	–	ns	–	ns	ns
World OK	ns	–	–	ns	ns	ns	ns	–	–	ns	–	–	–	–	–

Source. Data analysis based on the Pew Global Attitudes survey.

Note. ID = Advanced industrial democracies; EE = Eastern Europe; ME = Middle East; SA = South Asia; EA = East Asia. The + sign indicates a positive and significant effect; the – sign indicates a negative and significant effect; "ns" stands for not significant relationship. The survey item "country OK" was not asked in Egypt.

hand, the evidence associated with the other two indicators relating to this hypothesis is much scantier. The beliefs of those who would like their culture to be protected from foreign influences did not have a systematic impact on attitudes toward America in all the regions, with the exception of eastern Europe. East European respondents with protectionist feelings about their way of life were more likely to hold less favorable views of the United States, its democratic polity, its customs, its popular culture, and its antiterrorism policies.

In general, respondents wary of the empowerment of women in modern society did not manifest colder attitudes toward the United States than the respondents supportive of gender equality in the household and in the workplace. The only instance in which belief that "women should stay home and raise children while husbands provide for the family" was systematically related to anti-American views was in the case of the evaluation of American popular culture. Dislike of American movies, television, and music—the three fundamental expressions of American popular culture—was significantly higher among the respondents with traditional views about the place of women in society in all regions but eastern Europe, where no relationship was found. It also emerged as a factor accounting for greater aversion to American ideas about democracy and the spreading of American customs and ideas in South Asia and for greater aversion to American science and technology and American antiterrorism policies in the Middle East. Otherwise no relationship was found in the patterns of responses.[54]

As is the case in Norris and Inglehart's account of the divergences in norms and cultural values in different civilizational settings, the findings summarized in table 4.5 show that political institutions and democratic values are not singled out as incompatible or unacceptable by respondents who come from different cultural traditions and who espouse traditional ideas about gender roles. What riles those who would like to keep women in traditional roles is not American democratic values or the United States in general but a popular culture that portrays the liberation of women and the commercialization of sex.

The third hypothesis posits a connection between antimarket views and anti-American attitudes. Of the two indicators selected to identify respondents holding such beliefs, only the one measuring acceptance of market outcomes even in face of income disparities is systematically associated with the popular dispositions toward America. As is implied in the social-welfarist type of anti-Americanism, people who expressed a preference for equity over efficiency, by disagreeing that the market makes people better off in general despite the inequalities it engenders, tended to be more inclined to distance themselves from the United States. In particular, this result obtains in all five regions in the models explaining attitudes toward the spreading of American customs and ideas, which was a sore point in the belief systems of large portions of the respondents, as we have seen in table 4.1. In other words, the

---

54. In their chapter 6 analysis of Beijing residents, Johnston and Stockmann find a contingent, and nonlinear, relationship between the perception of a cultural threat and the levels of amity toward the United States.

spreading of American customs and ideas is opposed because of the belief that it would have a negative effect on income distribution and social stratification in their societies. On the other hand, the second indicator for an antimarket worldview—the survey item measuring a fatalist outlook on life—is usually uncorrelated with anti-Americanism.

Finally, we also find evidence for the scapegoating hypothesis. We expected respondents unsatisfied with the state of affairs in their countries or in the world to be more likely to transfer that dissatisfaction onto the United States. This syndrome holds rather uniformly across dimensions and regions with respect to dissatisfaction about the state of world affairs, but less conclusively with respect to the dissatisfaction about the state of affairs in the respondents' countries. A consistent pattern of anti-American opposition existed among those dissatisfied with their countries in the industrial democracies, but not in the other four regions where only some aspects of the United States were affected by the dynamics of scapegoating.[55]

The Image of America among Islamic Publics beyond 2002

From 2002 to 2005, from Afghanistan to Iraq, from President Bush's "Axis of Evil" speech to "preemption" in action, so much has taken place on the world scene that it is worth investigating how the image of America has fared among ordinary people. Here, I briefly focus on how the mass publics in a group of countries with predominantly Muslim populations assessed the United States, its polity, and society. By looking at the reactions of Muslim publics over a brief time span encompassing a pre- and post–Iraq War period, we can find some indication of whether the perceptions of the United States respond to different political dynamics.

Figure 9 tracks the pattern of attitudes toward the United States and the American people in Indonesia, Jordan, Lebanon, Morocco, Pakistan, and Turkey using data from four waves of the Pew Global Attitudes Survey taken each year from 2002 to 2005. Each of these four data points captures different political circumstances—the effects of the September 11 terrorist attacks in the 2002 wave, the war in Iraq in the 2003 wave, the transformation of Iraq amid the insurgency, the first steps of an electoral process, and the risks of fragmentation in the 2004 and 2005 waves—as well as conditions that are more specific to any of those countries, such as the consequences of the tsunami tragedy and the U.S. relief efforts in Indonesia.

Overall, the popularity of the United States and its people reached its minimal levels in 2003 and 2004, in the immediate aftermath of the Iraq War, but had nearly

---

55. Unfortunately, the data from the Global Attitudes Survey do not allow for a full evaluation of the scapegoating hypothesis in the Middle Eastern countries, because the survey item measuring whether respondents were satisfied with the state of affairs in their country was not asked in Egypt. The analyses conducted on a reduced sample consisting of Jordan, Lebanon, and Turkey found no relationship with respect to overall attitudes toward the United States, the spreading of American customs, and the war on terror. The analyses also found that respondents satisfied with their country situations were more likely to oppose American ideas about democracy, American popular culture, and American technology.

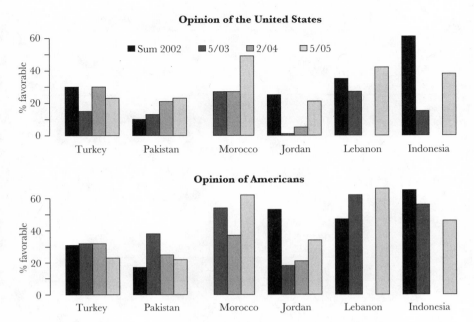

Figure 9. Opinion of the United States and Americans, 2002–2005. *Source:* Pew Global Attitudes survey.

recovered its prewar levels in 2005. Of the six countries listed in figure 9, Lebanon, with its higher approval of the United States among its Christian population, and Morocco showed rates of favorable responses above the 50 percent threshold with respect to the American people, and just below 50 percent with respect to the United States in 2005, while the pro-American voices were still the minority in the other four countries, as was also the case before the Iraq War.[56]

In table 4.6, I broaden this overview to include responses given to six survey questions that tapped into different features of the United States in Egypt, Lebanon, Saudi Arabia, and the United Arab Emirates. These data come from two surveys conducted in March and April 2002 and in June 2004 by Zogby International, which again allows for a prewar-postwar comparison. Respondents were asked to express their "overall impressions" of American science and technology, American freedom and democracy, the American people, American movies and television, American-made products, and American education. In 2002, in line with the patterns discovered in the Pew Global Attitudes Survey, the mass publics expressed their

56. The 2005 wave of the Pew Global Attitudes Survey was conducted in May 2005, as allegations about the desecration of the Koran at Guantánamo Bay were reported worldwide. The Pew researchers analyzed the responses given before and after May 11, 2005—the day the story broke—and found that the percentage of favorable responses dropped from 30% to 16% in Pakistan and increased from 9% to 26% in Jordan, and were unable to make comparisons in the remaining countries. See Pew Global Attitudes Project 2005b, 13.

Table 4.6. Attitudes toward U.S. culture and society in the Middle East, 2002–2004

Country	Science and technology	Freedom and democracy	People	Movies and TV	Products	Education
		2002				
Egypt						
% Favorable	77.86	52.71	34.71	53.29	50.14	67.57
% Don't know	11.57	9.14	18.57	7.14	4.57	15.14
Lebanon						
% Favorable	82.40	58.40	63.00	63.60	72.40	81.00
% Don't know	2.00	2.00	4.00	1.00	2.20	3.20
Saudi Arabia						
% Favorable	71.14	52.14	42.57	54.29	52.86	57.71
% Don't know	3.14	3.71	6.71	3.71	3.14	7.57
United Arab Emirates						
% Favorable	80.60	49.60	42.80	63.80	68.00	79.00
% Don't know	5.40	6.00	14.80	4.60	5.00	4.60
		2004				
Egypt						
% Favorable	71.06	57.18	61.06	37.88	47.18	35.06
% Don't know	11.29	3.18	11.18	3.18	7.65	42.12
Lebanon						
% Favorable	51.50	42.00	39.50	28.75	38.75	38.00
% Don't know	1.50	2.25	3.25	4.50	4.75	7.75
Saudi Arabia						
% Favorable	48.29	38.57	28.14	34.86	36.57	12.43
% Don't know	0.43	1.29	7.71	4.86	4.29	14.00
United Arab Emirates						
% Favorable	82.64	38.60	45.34	52.33	60.88	62.44
% Don't know	5.96	9.07	20.47	6.74	5.96	14.51

Sources: Data are taken from Zogby International, Ten Nation Impression of America survey (2002) and the Impressions of America survey (2004).

Note: % favorable corresponds to the sum of "somewhat favorable" and "very favorable" responses.

appreciation of several features of the United States. A majority of respondents had somewhat favorable or very favorable impressions of American science and technology, of American movies, and of American products. But even more politically charged aspects of America were receiving the endorsement of substantial numbers of respondents: about 50 percent approved of American freedom and democracy and American education.

Two years later, the general publics were less inclined to manifest their appreciation of the societal and cultural features of America. Percentages of approval dropped in many, but not all, instances, and substantially so in a few of them, such as the dramatic decrease in the appreciation of American education among Saudi respondents. It is remarkable that even American science and technology, the dimension of American society that most elicited favorable responses before the war, was no longer seen in such a favorable light after the war. When interviewed about their evaluations of U.S. policies in the Middle East, however, the same respondents were strongly critical, and hardly any manifested approval, again as was the case before the Iraq War.

If we were afraid of witnessing a complete collapse in the popularity of the United States, such an expectation does not receive empirical validation. If we cast aside those catastrophic predictions, however, these figures are nonetheless reason for concern. On the one hand, we observe a slow return to the rates of approval that the United States enjoyed before the war. The dramatic plunge in the percentage of people willing to express a favorable opinion of the United States in 2003 appears to be a momentary reaction to the exceptional circumstances of the Iraq War rather than a structural shift in the popular perceptions of the United States. On the other hand, several aspects of American culture and society attracted substantially less approval. These data seem to indicate that the negative assessment of the policy stance of the United States toward Muslim countries has seeped into the evaluations of the cultural and societal features of the United States to a much greater degree than was the case before the Iraq War.

Multiple Perceptions of America among Ordinary People

At the end of this investigation of the image of America in 2002, we find that there is not an all-encompassing element that subsumes popular perceptions of the United States in the post–cold war, post–September 11 world. Multiple perceptions are the main theme that underlies the way America features in the belief systems of ordinary people. And plenty of good feelings pervade ordinary people's attitudes. Although not all about America is always liked by all people, very few reject the United States altogether. Although some aspects of America are disliked, many more are appreciated. The wholesale rejection of America was not the common stance among twenty thousand respondents the world over in 2002.

Variation in the appreciation of the United States exists across regions. In the Middle East, among Muslim respondents, we find greater propensity to express critical views of the United States. However, it is not just a quantitative difference that distinguishes the popular standing of the United States among Middle Eastern respondents, but a qualitative one. Not only are Middle Eastern publics more inclined to manifest negative attitudes toward the United States but they are also likely to make negative assessments about America, even if they only disagree with American policies and question American democratic ideals. In other words, Middle Eastern respondents were less inclined to revise their evaluations of the United States as they processed "new" and additional information associated with each feature of American society and culture. In the language of Katzenstein and Keohane's analytic framework, the attitudes of Middle Eastern respondents are closer to the category of distrust, in the middle position on the continuum measuring receptivity to new information, but still far from the hardened closure associated with bias.[57]

In all other regions, opposition to the United States appears to be the state of mind of those who dislike America on issue after issue, not just a few topical dimensions. Outside the Middle East, appreciation for one of America's features tempers the opposition and disagreement generated by some other aspects. Multidimensionality—that incommensurable asset of America—seems to have lost its psychological appeal among Middle Eastern respondents.

The war in Iraq, the intense controversies that flared up in the months before the war, the uncertainties that surround the future of Iraq, and the denouement of the false assumptions underlying the case for war are all focal elements that likely direct the attention of the mass publics to the military might of the United States, its determination and self-assuredness, and away from all the symbols of America that define the collective imagination of the young and the old alike: the lights in the City, the bottle of Coca-Cola, the majesty of the Grand Canyon, the Statue of Liberty. The torture scandals at Abu Ghraib and Guantánamo that have tormented the collective soul of the United States as the beacon of liberty might indeed become the tragic shock that will shatter the polyvalent symbolism of America. If ever such a scenario came to fruition, it would mark the end of the myth of America. But, for now, as Chou En-lai would say, it is too early to tell.

57. See table 1.4 in Katzenstein and Keohane, chapter 1.

ANTI-AMERICANISM IN DIFFERENT SOCIETIES

5

The Distinctiveness of French Anti-Americanism

SOPHIE MEUNIER

"The French president has no rivals as global spokesman on anti-Americanism," the *Economist* recently wrote.[1] Between taking the lead in the anti-globalization movement in the late 1990s and in the movement against a war in Iraq in 2003, France confirmed its image as the "oldest enemy" among America's friends.[2] After all, even before the days of Chirac and de Gaulle, France had always seemed to be at the forefront of animosity toward the United States—from eighteenth-century theories about the degeneration of species in the New World to twentieth-century denunciations of the Coca-Colonization of the Old World.[3]

In recent years, in a context of international public opinion highly critical of U.S. involvement in Iraq, the French surprisingly did not stand out from other Europeans in their overall feelings toward the United States.[4] Whether assessing American Middle East policy, the big threats facing their respective societies, or even American culture, French public opinion was very much in line with German, Spanish,

This chapter greatly benefited from the comments by participants in the workshops on anti-Americanism organized by Peter J. Katzenstein and Robert O. Keohane at the Center for Advanced Study in the Behavioral Sciences, Palo Alto, in November 2004, January 2005, and June 2005; the Duke University Globalization and Equity Seminar, March 8, 2005; the Brown University Department of French seminar, April 18, 2005; and the University of Chicago Program in International Security Policy seminar, April 26, 2005. I thank Rawi Abdelal, Nicolas Barreyre, John Bowen, Patrick Chamorel, Bernard Chazelle, Marion Fourcade-Gourinchas, Peter Gourevitch, Miles Kahler, Peter Katzenstein, Judith Kelley, Robert Keohane, Richard Kuisel, John Mearsheimer, and Mary Nolan for their thoughtful comments and suggestions. Thanks also to Carolina Ardila Zurek and Cleosie Kirkland for research assistance.

1. *Economist* 2005d.
2. Miller and Molesky 2004.
3. Kuisel 1993.
4. See chapter 4 by Chiozza. For recent polls, see Pew Global Attitudes Project 2005a and 2005d; PIPA 2005; German Marshall Fund 2004.

Dutch, and even British opinion. But polling data confirms that over time the French have been systematically more critical of the United States than most other European publics. As shown by Isernia in chapter 3, even though French sentiments toward the United States have been prevalently positive over time, only Spain and Greece in western Europe have consistently manifested stronger hostility toward the United States than France. In particular, the French public, along with French politicians, became extremely critical of the perceived trend toward U.S. unilateralism in world affairs throughout the 1990s, many years before their European counterparts. It is also during this period that French politicians and intellectuals articulated the concept of "managed globalization"—a series of multilateral regulations and initiatives designed to shield Europe from the negative effects of the global law of the market.[5] Is the lesser French enthusiasm for the United States over time evidence that France is anti-American, as common wisdom usually assumes? What makes French anti-Americanism a singular phenomenon? The introduction to this book defines anti-Americanism as a very heterogeneous set of attitudes, resting on different sets of beliefs and cognitive schemas. In chapter 1 on the varieties of anti-Americanism, Katzenstein and Keohane show that one must distinguish opinion from distrust from bias, although it is often difficult to do so. What is often portrayed in shorthand as anti-Americanism may actually be reasoned criticism, and what is passed off as reasoned criticism may mask real prejudices. In this chapter I explore the distinctive dynamics of French anti-Americanism, by first demonstrating that France harbors an enduring distrust of America centered in the past decade on the related issues of unilateralism and globalization. I then explain why French distrust of the United States is so deeply institutionalized, arguing that the deep reservoir of anti-American arguments that have accumulated over the centuries and the simultaneous coexistence of all types of anti-Americanism have made anti-American rhetoric a tool that can be used at no cost for political benefit. Finally, I focus on the potential consequences of French anti-Americanism for economic relations and the war on terror.

Is French Opposition to the United States Driven by Anti-Americanism?

France exhibits an enduring distrust of the United States, which sometimes shades into bias, especially among the elites. But contrary to the assertions of many American French-bashers who have made a cottage-industry of denouncing innate French biases, the most important source of French distrust of the United States is the deep national opposition to unilateralism and American-style globalization.[6] The deterioration of the image of the United States in France preceded the Franco-American clash over Iraq—even though it skyrocketed after 2002.[7] That France was less prone

5. Gordon and Meunier 2001, Kuisel 2004, Abdelal 2006.
6. Chesnoff 2005, Boyles 2005, Miller and Molesky 2004.
7. Kuisel 2004.

to anti-American demonstrations at the height of the Euromissiles crisis in the 1980s than it was to criticism of the United States in the late 1990s suggests that unregulated globalization has been at least as big a trigger of negative reactions than U.S. military bullying.[8] The dominant French anti-American critique that emerged during the 1990s centered on the increasingly unilateral actions of the United States, whose international power was now unchecked as a result of the end of the cold war. The image of the United States became one of a domineering ally, unbearable to France because it was increasingly acting as a triumphant, self-centered, hegemonic "hyperpower"—in everything from trade to the environment, from culture to foreign policy.[9] In France the denunciation of these hypocritical, unilateral U.S. actions became enmeshed in a virulent French critique of the globalization that is often equated with Americanization.[10]

I analyze the content of French discussions in three examples that are most likely cases of anti-Americanism at work. As in the chapters on the Arab world by Lynch and on China by Johnston and Stockmann, these examples have been chosen, in consultation with the editors, to range from foreign policy to apparently less political areas of activity. In all three cases, however, negative French opinions of the United States can be explained more by heightened concerns about unilateralism than by anti-American bias.

Iraq

The Iraq conflict is often presented as a poster child of French anti-Americanism in action, with French leaders bowing to public opinion, which has been stirred up by the media, and acting more out of genuine subversion than legitimate dissent.[11] Most likely, however, the anti-war position of France was motivated by a rational assessment of its interests in the post–cold war, post-9/11 geopolitical environment, as well as by a distrust of unconstrained unilateralism.

For anti-American bias to be the cause of French actions, one would have to establish a correlation between levels of anti-Americanism and adoption of French policies in direct conflict with the interests of the United States. Opinion polls suggest that negative French views of U.S. unilateralism were steadily rising throughout the late 1990s and early years of the George W. Bush presidency.[12] But if anti-

8. Kuisel notes that in 1984 more French citizens (44%) than Germans or British declared themselves pro-American. In a 1988 survey, the French men and women polled rated "power," "dynamism," "wealth," and "liberty" as the words they most commonly associated with the United States. The majority thought that America set a good example for political institutions, the media, and free enterprise. By 1996, however, the French polled said that "violence," "power," "inequalities," and "racism" first came to their mind when describing America. Kuisel 2004.

9. The term was coined by French foreign minister Hubert Védrine, even though the French word "hyperpuissance" does not have the pejorative connotations associated with "hyper" in English—"hyper" in French means only the next size up from "super." Védrine and Moisi 2001. See also Mélandri and Vaisse 2001.

10. Meunier 2000, Gordon and Meunier 2001, Abdelal 2006.

11. See, for instance, Chesnoff 2005, Miller and Molesky 2004, Timmerman 2004, Friedman 2003b.

12. Kuisel 2004.

Americanism is a primary driver of French foreign policy, French actions should have been as opposed to the United States at that time as they were later in regard to Iraq. Instead, France enthusiastically backed the United States in Afghanistan and was the only country whose fighter pilots joined U.S. forces and struck targets in Afghanistan during Operation Anaconda in March 2002.[13]

French policy on Iraq was motivated primarily by a very different understanding of the threats facing the world, as well as of France's interests in the world. First, France had long disagreed with the United States over the threat posed by Saddam Hussein and over what to do about it, seeing him as dangerous primarily to his own people.[14] Moreover, France had expressed strong reservations and concerns over the new American doctrine of preemption if not supported by the United Nations. Finally, for French foreign policy, the only legitimate objective in Iraq was to destroy any existing weapons of mass destruction, which would be done through inspections and, if they failed, through the use of force mandated by the UN. The consistent strands of this policy reflect distrust of U.S. unilateralist temptations and support for multilateralism rather than bias and hatred directed at U.S. policy.

French foreign policy is also shaped by the specificities of French history and experience. French intelligence was convinced that the Iraqi regime and al-Qaida had had no significant contact. Moreover, the lessons learned by France in fighting Islamic terrorism since the 1980s suggested that the war proposed by the United States was not the right approach. Most important, many French analyses of the Iraq situation, including those of President Chirac, were informed by their own experiences in Algeria, the main prism through which they understood what might happen in Iraq, and they predicted more frustration, anger, and bitterness in the Arab and Muslim world if Iraq was invaded.[15]

Rather than being the cause of the Franco-American crisis over Iraq, anti-Americanism may instead have been a by-product of the crisis. In the aftermath of 9/11, French public opinion had initially given the benefit of the doubt to the U.S. strategy. But the deeper the rift between the French and American positions became, the stronger were the anti-American prejudices that appeared in the French media, and the stronger the stereotypical French-bashing that surged in the United States. The French even gave mixed signals about whether they really wanted the United States to succeed in Iraq, so much so that French prime minister Jean-Pierre Raffarin had to remind public opinion that "the Americans are not the enemies. Our camp is the camp of democracy."[16]

Anti-Americanism was also used during the crisis as a political tool. To justify his positions, it was useful for Chirac to showcase the overwhelming support he had at home. Like Bush, whose first election had been tainted by the ballot mishaps, Chirac's legitimacy suffered from the conditions under which he had been elected in 2002: the 80 percent of the votes he received in the second round of the election,

13. Starobin 2003, Gordon and Shapiro 2004.
14. *New York Times* 2002.
15. Howorth 2003, Starobin 2003.
16. Timmerman 2004.

in defense against National Front candidate Jean-Marie Le Pen, hardly masked the paltry 19 percent he had received in the first one. Stirring up anti-American sentiment during the Franco-American clash over Iraq was a way for Chirac to increase his political legitimacy, both domestically and internationally. Indeed, whereas Prime Minister Raffarin reminded the French population that Saddam Hussein, not the United States, was the enemy, Chirac did no such thing.

Anti-Americanism was certainly not the primary cause of France's initial decision to refuse to give a blank check to U.S. foreign policy in Iraq. Viewing the invasion of Iraq as a major error is not a reflection of a prejudicial bias against the United States. In most other European countries public opinion was deeply opposed to the American war in Iraq, and their media was as outraged at the United States as was France's. And some in the United States had words as harsh for their own administration, if not harsher, than those of the French. What happened in France is that the escalating war of words with the United States triggered atavistic reflexes of distrust. Even if French hostility was initially motivated by a fundamental opposition to the policy, it quickly turned to age-old anti-American clichés—and in the process shifted from reasoned opinion to gut bias. But, as I have shown, even this poster-child case is not as clear-cut as it initially seems in proving France a European outcast in its anti-Americanism.

The Google Print Project

Cultural policy is the other area, along with foreign affairs, in which French behavior is often interpreted as being motivated by anti-Americanism. Examples of actions to protect French culture from American invasion abound over the years, from the fight to preserve the French language from Anglicisms to proactive policies subsidizing French movie production to resist the onslaught of Hollywood. Culture is an area particularly susceptible to anti-Americanism. First, this is so because anti-American arguments in France have mostly been developed by intellectuals, who have a vested interest in preserving their cultural turf. Second, Americanization has truly disrupted traditional national cultural patterns. The stronger the disruption, the more intense the resistance and the suspicions about American intentions. Yet, even in the case of culture, the course of action taken is not motivated by a willingness to hurt the United States but rather by a desire to shield France from the perverse effects of unregulated globalization.[17]

The latest instance in the "culture wars" between France and the United States concerns the search-engine company Google's December 2004 decision to scan fifteen million books in the next ten years and make them available online. The California-based company made agreements with five major "Anglo-Saxon" (U.S. and British) libraries to digitize all or part of their collections: Stanford, the University of Michigan, Harvard, Oxford, and the New York Public Library. Google's project

---

17. Gordon and Meunier 2001, Abdelal 2006.

barely made the news at first, either in the United States or in France, where initial reactions were rather positive.[18]

Nevertheless, the controversy soon arose with a roar. In January 2005, Jean-Noel Jeanneney, a noted historian and head of the French National Library (BNF), wrote a long op-ed in *Le Monde* titled "When Google Challenges Europe." He argued that Google's plans to digitize books and make their contents available on the Internet were a threat to France because this would, in the long run, create a unipolar world-view with a strong bias toward English works and American culture. Although this project was portrayed in the United States as a fulfillment of the long dream of humankind to have a universal library, in France it was presented as "omni-googlization"—"a crushing domination by America on future generations' understanding of the world."[19] In particular, Jeanneney emphasized the problem of history seen through English and American eyes by giving the example of the French Revolution, where English historiography typically focuses on the plight of the aristocrats and the guillotine and the Terror, rather than on the Declaration of the Rights of Man and the institutional innovations of the Convention. In response, Jeanneney proposed that the European Union counterbalance the American project by creating its own digitization program to make European literature available on the Internet, build a super-European library, and create a new search engine with its own way of controlling the page rankings of responses to searches.

President Chirac took up the fight with dispatch. He ordered the culture minister, Renaud Donnedieu de Vabres, to find the quickest way to put French and European library collections online. He also mounted a campaign to persuade other European countries to join France in a $128-million project to counteract the dominance of Google as a search engine. For Chirac, Europe must play a determining role in the large digitization program for the sake of humankind, and in this project France should be the central player, in part because of its special responsibility toward the Francophone world. In April 2005, at the initiative of France and supported by nineteen national libraries in Europe, six European countries (France, Poland, Germany, Italy, Spain, and Hungary) asked the European Union to launch a "European digital library" to coordinate the digitization actions of national libraries.[20] This library is now taking shape, and the European commission expects 2 million books to be accessible through its portal by 2008.

The U.S. and British media presented this as more evidence of French anti-Americanism, and they often derided the French as being paranoid. As Stephen Castle wrote in the *Independent*, "France has identified a new enemy in its battle to protect the language of Molière: the search engine Google, which French critics say is bent on an act of Anglophone cultural imperialism."[21] Many commentators brushed off Jeanneney's comments as those of an incorrigible anti-American, as

18. Saint-Martin 2005.
19. Jeanneney 2005.
20. *Libération* 2005.
21. Castle 2005.

reflecting the national mood. "Clearly, Paris sees Google as a cultural aggressor whose advance must be checked," a Canadian journalist wrote. "Washington, by contrast, will be hard-pressed to understand the commotion and, at most, will shrug off Mr. Jeanneney as an anti-American pest."[22]

It is possible to see French actions as motivated by hints of anti-Americanism. The line of argument followed by Jeanneney and his numerous supporters is that the English language is one of the levers through which the United States dominates the world and that Google's initiative will enhance the hyperpower of the United States by giving English works primacy. This could lead to world brainwashing, especially if Google (read: America) is left alone to make unilateral choices about what becomes part of the collective cultural heritage of humankind. Therefore it needs to be checked or counterbalanced. It could be objected that English is more than the language of the British and Americans: it is the new lingua franca of the world. The French cannot see this reality because they are blinded by their prejudices and resentment of the United States. Jeanneney's call to arms to the Europeans to build a parallel system is further evidence that France cannot simply admire a great American initiative (emanating from a private company, not the U.S. government). Another country concerned about the project might have asked to join the Google bandwagon and volunteer its own libraries. But the prism of anti-Americanism that colors the views of many French intellectuals favors instead the creation of an alternative project. This impression is reinforced by Jeanneney's various writings and interviews, which suggest that he likes the project very much, but resents that it is being done by an American company: "I have nothing in particular against Google. I simply note that this commercial company is the expression of the American system, in which the law of the market is king."[23]

The French see Google Print as propagating the globalization they dislike: unilateral, unconstrained, unregulated, a natural outcome of the market and of a non-hierarchical democracy. But this is not a clear-cut case of anti-American bias. The French reaction to Google was primarily motivated by a legitimate desire to fight for French cultural interests, already adversely affected by globalization, that has been institutionalized in the EU-wide policy of "cultural exception," which preserves homegrown culture that is unable to compete with Hollywood. If the Google project is successful, it will strengthen English even further as the dominant world language and American thought as the dominant cultural influence. If works in English are the only ones searchable this way, they will become more influential and this might lead to the overwhelming world preponderance of a single culture, with the power to unilaterally set the global cultural agenda.[24] As Jeanneney, custodian of thirteen million titles in the French National Library, said in an interview about the controversy: "I am not anti-American, far from it. But what I don't want is everything

---

22. Kipling 2005.

23. *Economist* 2005c.

24. "The worry is that the 'Google Print' project would rank sources in order of popularity, thereby giving prominence to Anglophone texts above those written in other languages." Castle 2005.

reflected in an American mirror. When it comes to presenting digitized books on the Web, we want to make our choice with our own criteria."[25]

Moreover, Jeanneney's attack was directed as much at France's lackluster effort to digitize French books as it was at Google and the evil Americans. His criticisms were probably intended as a fund-raising effort and a wake-up call to the French government to invest more in the digitization of books timidly started with the Gallica project, which then had a budget for digitization of $1.35 million (versus $200 million for Google).

Finally, the various French critics of the Google project raised a legitimate question, which can be asked without holding an anti-American bias: Should a multinational company control the digital literary heritage of humankind? As a French journalist asked, "Can we accept Stendhal standing side by side with commercials for anything and everything?"[26] France has long argued in multilateral trade negotiations that culture is not merchandise and that therefore it cannot be left to the laws of the market. To assuage French fears, Google officials declared that page rankings on Google Print will be defined by public demand and not by political, cultural, or monetary variables. "We never planned only to scan English books," a spokesman said. "Google users can look forward to finding non-English speaking literature as well. . . . But it is only logical that we would start the scanning project with English-language books. We are, after all, an American firm."[27] Maybe French fears about Google are not unfounded, after all.

The Tsunami Relief Effort

French responses to the U.S. tsunami relief effort, especially when compared to the Chinese responses studied by Johnston and Stockmann in chapter 6 and the Arab ones reported by Lynch in chapter 7, provide an opportunity to analyze whether anti-Americanism "bleeds" from highly political to less political arenas. The disaster of December 2004 occurred amid still-tense Franco-American relations and against a backdrop of highly negative French public opinion of the United States, especially after the reelection of President Bush. Katzenstein and Keohane find in their analysis of the tsunami survey data that French public opinion was biased against the U.S. performance, with a large majority (73%) finding the U.S. response to the tragedy inadequate.[28] Yet a content analysis of the French media during the period following the disaster suggests that even though the French singularly emphasized American unilateralism, their criticisms of the U.S. tsunami relief effort reflected distrust more than bias.

The first French criticism was about the initial inaction of the United States. The French media reported that President Bush, who stayed at his Texas ranch to con-

25. Riding 2005.
26. Roussel 2005.
27. Tiesenhausen Cave 2005.
28. Katzenstein and Keohane, chapter 1.

tinue his Christmas vacation even after the disaster had struck, was being insensitive to a humanitarian catastrophe of epic proportions and communicated, through his words and deeds, a lack of urgency.[29] But the French press was only echoing the fierce criticisms of editorials in the U.S. press, above all the *New York Times*, the *Washington Post*, and the *Los Angeles Times*, including their comparison of the tsunami relief aid promised by the United States and the budget for the festivities at the second Bush inauguration.[30]

The main controversy over the U.S. tsunami relief effort was initiated by the United Nations. Jan Egeland, the UN emergency relief coordinator, called Western nations "stingy" in their foreign aid—a comment particularly addressed to the United States, which had promised only $35 million for tsunami relief.[31] Interestingly, France did not use the anti-Americanism potentially raised by the tsunami relief effort for political purposes, but the United States resorted to France-bashing to deflect criticism of its own (in)action. A few days after the Egeland comment about stinginess, which had sent the American press into a frenzy, Andrew Natsios, the head of the U.S. Agency for International Development, said in a Fox television interview about the U.S. tsunami relief effort that "the aid program in France is not that big" and that the French "do not tend to be dominant figures in aid."[32] This blame-shifting to France led the French ambassador to the United States, Jean-David Levitte, to question the reasons for "misguidedly impugning France" and to show that French development aid exceeded that of any of the G8 countries as a proportion of a country's economic output.[33] According to the Organisation for Economic Co-operation and Development (OECD), France allotted 0.41 percent of its gross national income to development aid in 2003, compared to 0.15 percent in the United States, 0.28 percent in Germany, and 0.34 percent in Great Britain.[34] Following the Natsios comments about French generosity, France doubled its aid pledge for tsunami victims on December 30, 2004—thereby briefly claiming the role as leading donor nation (before Britain quickly surpassed France). France also conducted extensive relief operations in Indonesia, Sri Lanka, and the Maldives—sending warships, a helicopter carrier, teams of doctors, and about a thousand soldiers to clear debris and rebuild schools.[35]

The second criticism focused on possible ulterior motives of U.S. aid. The French press commented at length on the statement by U.S. Secretary of State Condoleezza Rice, in her Senate confirmation hearings, that the tsunami had provided a "wonderful opportunity" for the United States to reap "great dividends" in the region.[36] Critics said that Washington was seizing on the disaster to advance its

---

29. For instance, Agence France Presse 2005a, Sabatier 2005.
30. Harris and Wright 2004, *New York Times* 2004, Efron 2004.
31. See, for instance, Efron 2004, *New York Times* 2004.
32. Leicester 2004.
33. Knowlton 2005. The G8 (Group of Eight) is made up of Canada, France, Germany, Italy, Japan, the United Kingdom, the United States, and the Russian Federation.
34. Leicester 2004.
35. Casey 2005.
36. See, for instance, Amalric 2005a and 2005b.

strategic interests, in particular by improving ties with the Indonesian military and repairing its image, which was damaged in Indonesia by the U.S. invasion of Iraq. Some in the French military criticized the U.S. relief effort: "How can you really boast of doing something from this tragedy? People were saying, 'They are doing it again. They are showing off.'"[37] Yet it is difficult to interpret this criticism as evidence of anti-American bias. First, because the French press looked at the ulterior motives of all the countries engaged in the tsunami relief competition, including Japan, China, India, and, yes, France.[38] Second, because the U.S. press was similarly dissecting which type of relief effort would best serve U.S. foreign policy interests. And third, because many French analysts commented that the ultimate motives for providing aid do not matter as long as aid is given.[39] The French media reported on the generosity of private donations in the United States.[40] And Bernard Kouchner, the most respected French political figure, the former health minister and founder of Doctors without Borders, said publicly that the competition between donors was healthy.[41]

It is the third criticism of the tsunami relief effort, about the U.S. approach to the management of the crisis, that seems distinctly French. The United States announced in the early days after the disaster that it would form a separate aid coalition with Australia, Japan, and India. This decision, including the use of the word "coalition," reminded France of the controversial international alliance that the United States had assembled in order to invade Iraq without the approval of the United Nations. French diplomacy was concerned that the U.S tsunami aid operation had deliberately sidestepped traditional UN channels and was trying to compete with the international organization.[42]

President Chirac was reportedly increasingly concerned about the unilateral tone of U.S. aid efforts. The *Frankfurter Allgemeine Zeitung* wrote that Chirac, without openly criticizing the Bush administration, feared "that Washington is deliberately circumventing the United Nations and wants to compete with the international organization." The report also said that "President Chirac wants to hinder America from using its ad hoc–organized aid operation to set a precedent that will lastingly weaken the role of the United Nations" and quoted him as having said publicly that the tsunami had provided proof that the fate of all people "cannot be separated from that of our planet" and that global organizations like the United Nations must therefore be strengthened.[43]

37. Casey 2005.

38. Sabatier 2004, Dupont 2005, Amalric 2005a and 2005b, Leser 2005, Delhommais and Le Boucher 2005.

39. Sabatier 2005.

40. *Le Monde* 2005a.

41. Nathan 2004.

42. Knowlton 2005. On January 6, 2005, U.S. Secretary of State Colin Powell announced that this coalition would be disbanded and its assets put under UN direction. *Economist* 2005e.

43. Cited in Knowlton 2005.

Several members of the European Union discussed ways to improve future intra-European disaster cooperation. France took the lead by suggesting the creation of a rapid-response civil defense group in the European Union, in reaction to the non-cooperative tone taken by the United States in the early days after the catastrophe.[44] But this distrust of the unilateralist tendencies of the United States is not evidence of hard-core anti-Americanism. This suggestion was based less on prejudice and stereotypes than on the practical realization that France, if it wished to continue to play a role in world affairs, had better organize with its neighbors and European partners first. It was also highly consistent with the multilateralist, "managed globalization" line of French foreign policy in the past decade.

Overall, there is little evidence that anti-Americanism determined either French foreign policy or French interpretations of the tsunami relief effort. The mainstream French press was critical of the United States in the days following the catastrophe, but it was very critical of France as well and was, overall, quite restrained in analyzing the U.S. effort. Anti-Americanism may have "bled" into public opinion, explaining the overwhelming view that the U.S. relief effort was inadequate, as highlighted by Katzenstein and Keohane in chapter 1, but when asked the more specific question of whether it was appropriate to deploy the U.S. military to help in the relief effort, 77 percent of the French agreed—one of the highest percentages in Europe. Once again, the tsunami example shows that a detailed examination of bias versus distrust and opinion tempers claims of anti-Americanism as suggested by opinion polls.

The analysis of these three cases where one might expect to find anti-Americanism, from the most to the least political, in precisely the policy areas always highlighted by those who accuse France of rampant, insidious anti-American prejudices, shows that the French actions were accounted for by alternative explanations—whether geopolitical interests, economic interests, or cultural competition. There is pronounced French opposition, supported by considerable distrust of the United States, but it is on the whole better explained by French policy principles, overall wariness of unilateralism, and by a defense of French culture in the face of globalization, than by anti-American bias.

Explaining French Distrust of the United States

Specific historical and institutional conditions can explain the sometimes latent, sometimes salient distrust of the United States in France. Three related factors account for the institutionalization of this distrust: the deep reservoir of anti-American arguments accumulated by French intellectuals over the centuries; the simultaneous coexistence of all types of anti-Americanisms in the collective national background; and the low cost to French politicians and elites of using anti-Americanism for political benefit. I will explore all three factors in turn.

44. Quatremer 2005.

The Reservoir of Accumulated Intellectual Arguments

France has the deepest reservoir of intellectual argumentation against America of any country in Europe. French distrust of America is as old as, if not older than, the United States itself, since it began as an extension of the centuries-old antagonism between France and England. Its long genealogy has been well documented over the years, most clearly by Philippe Roger, who argues that its building blocks were constructed long before Gaullism.[45] Anti-Americanism in France seems to have proceeded in cycles that have been triggered, though not exclusively, by conflicts in the Franco-American relationship. Each period in this long relationship saw the development of a new set of anti-American arguments, which over time accumulated into a vast repertoire, often based on the belief that France and the United States represented two competing universalisms. As a result, each time there has been an occasion for criticizing the United States, French opinion makers could use these arguments and adapt them to the current situation.

French animosity and contempt toward America (where degenerate dogs supposedly did not bark) first built up in the eighteenth century when France was also an American power.[46] In spite of the mythology of Lafayette, American passiveness during the French Revolution and the 1798–1800 Quasi-War confirmed this image of a self-serving, hypocritical American nation. The victory of the North in the Civil War and the end of France's Mexican adventure contributed to the next layer of anti-Americanism, composed of accusations of materialism and resentment of the nascent formidable power of the United States. A major layer of French anti-Americanism was added after World War I, in a period of disappointment over postwar U.S. isolationism and perceived biased indifference to France in the matter of war debts and reparations from Germany, when French intellectuals first reported that America's consumer and profit-oriented culture threatened to spread to France and affect its own traditions negatively.[47] The word "anti-Americanism" entered the French language in the late 1940s, when opposite sides of the political spectrum—Left Bank, Communist intellectuals, and General de Gaulle and his followers—focused on the need to counter the domineering presence of the United States.[48] The Vietnam War further reinforced this image of the United States as an imperialistic, expansionist, out-of-control superpower that represented a threat to world order.

By the end of the cold war, therefore, French rhetoric had accumulated a variety of anti-American arguments, some building on arguments articulated in an earlier historical period, others rooted in previous discourse but adapted to modern conditions. These arguments triumphantly resurfaced in the denunciation of American hyperpower associated with the onslaught of globalization in the 1990s, a time when France was undergoing a more profound overhaul of its society than most of its

---

45. Roger 2005. See also Mathy 1993 and Lacorne, Rupnik, and Toinet 1990.
46. Duroselle 1978, Roger 2005. See also Kennedy, chapter 2.
47. Duhamel and Thompson 1931, Kuisel 1993.
48. Roger 2005.

European partners.[49] Growing fears in France of U.S. unilateralism were confirmed when the new Bush administration rejected the Kyoto Treaty. After initial sympathy expressed to the American people after September 11 and the decision to support the United States in Afghanistan, France started to drift rapidly apart from the Bush administration on the issue of Iraq, especially after the passage of UN Resolution 1441 in November 2002, the collapse of French efforts to avoid the war in early 2003, and the simultaneous outpouring of Francophobia in the United States.[50]

France has had one of the longest sustained relationships with the United States of any nation, and the length of the interaction partly explains why the French have been able to build up such a vast repertoire of anti-American arguments. But other countries, such as Spain and England, also have a shared American history that predates the independence of the United States, without as deep a reservoir of negative stereotypes. What makes France unique is not so much the length and depth of its historical relationship with the United States but the consistency with which its intellectuals have developed anti-American arguments that have become part of national, collective references. The most plausible explanation for this is the thesis of the two universalisms, developed among others by Pierre Bourdieu and Stanley Hoffmann.[51] Their contemporaneous revolutions lent legitimacy to the universalist claims of both the United States and France. The legitimacy of U.S. political universalism came from its constitution and its plural political system, and today its cultural universalism comes as much from Hollywood as it does from its most prestigious universities. The legitimacy of French political universalism came from its Declaration of the Rights of Man and of the Citizen, and its cultural universalism from its long monopoly over style and good taste, which it tried to export through the "civilizing mission" of its colonial enterprise.[52] The perceived competition between these two universalisms led many French intellectuals to fashion anti-American arguments, especially when French imperialism was on the wane and American "imperialism" was on the rise. In this sense, anti-Americanism is as much a statement about France as it is about America—a resentful longing for a power that France no longer has. French efforts to constrain globalization through multilateral rules in the past decade, of which the French position on Iraq was the logical consequence, are a way to curb U.S. hegemony.

These entrenched arguments have been mostly developed and used by French intellectual elites. This explains what seems to be France's peculiar focus on cultural issues in its negative stereotyping of the United States. This also explains why there often seems to be a disconnection between the harsh tone of the public critique and the generally more positive view of America expressed by the French public. Indeed, this repertoire of anti-Americanisms has relatively little impact on the French public, which is only slightly more negative toward the United States than publics elsewhere in Europe, as shown by Chiozza and Isernia in this book. However, in times of crises

49. Schmidt 1996, Gordon and Meunier 2001, Abdelal 2006.
50. Vaïsse 2003.
51. Bourdieu 1992, Hoffmann 2000. See also Mathy 1993.
52. Bourdieu 1992.

the tropes bleed from the intellectual to the general public, as they are readily available in the "background" of the national consciousness.

Breadth of Types of Anti-Americanism

This deep reservoir of anti-American arguments accumulated by French intellectuals over the centuries has resulted in the simultaneous coexistence of many varieties of anti-Americanism, thereby giving the impression that the whole country is anti-American. But anti-Americanism is not a unitary phenomenon, and French anti-Americanisms are quite heterogeneous.[53] And, yes, the list of French grievances toward the United States is long and varied. But these grievances are not simultaneously shared by all French men and women, which explains some paradoxes, such as individuals disliking some aspects of American society while aspiring to others at the same time. Following the typology developed by Katzenstein and Keohane in chapter 1, I distinguish seven types of anti-Americanism(s) found in contemporary France and explore briefly their behavioral implications. These types are not mutually exclusive, as one individual or group may draw his or her anti-Americanism from several sources simultaneously. Neither do they suggest that an individual who puts forward one type of anti-American argument can necessarily be classified as "anti-American."

Liberal Anti-Americanism   Like many other Europeans, who share America's ideals but do not support its actions, the French offer a "liberal" critique of America as not living up to its principles. The charge is one of hypocrisy: the hypocrisy of demanding of others virtues that it does not uphold itself (in the case of Abu Ghraib or Guantánamo, for instance),[54] and the hypocrisy of displaying selective outrage (in the case of Middle East policy, for instance). As a result of this hypocrisy, the United States becomes a danger to the very cause it pretends to be promoting. For instance, the United States posits itself as a champion of free trade, but it does not hesitate to impose tariffs on steel or provide tax loopholes to U.S. companies to give them a competitive edge. Similarly, the United States preaches environmental conservation and aid to international development, but its international policies speak otherwise. U.S. intervention brought down Saddam Hussein's regime, while other dictators and nuclear powers go unchallenged, and successive U.S. administrations have turned a blind eye to the human rights violations of many of its allies in the Middle East. Another example of American hypocrisy, often advanced in Europe, especially by the Left, is U.S. unconditional support for Israel to the detriment of the Palestinian people, the U.S. media's unbalanced representation of the pain and suffering of Israelis and Palestinians, and the U.S.'s biased insistence on respecting some United Nations resolutions and not others—charges leveled with increasing frequency at the Bush administration. The main behavioral implication of this type of anti-

53. In the same way, Lynch, in chapter 7, argues for the existence of Arab anti-Americanisms.
54. Agence France Presse 2005b.

Americanism is that the United States is not considered to have the high moral ground. If the United States does not do what it preaches, then it should either be held accountable or else not be trusted. Note that this is the anti-American critique that leads many U.S. observers to judge France as incorrigibly anti-Semitic.

Social Anti-Americanism   One of the most widespread denunciations of America in France focuses on the social order in the United States—a critique widely shared by other European countries. This social critique has three main components, each reflecting deep national differences over the definition of a good society—equal and protective for the French, offering opportunity and risk for the Americans. First, the United States is often portrayed as a fundamentally unequal society. For Europeans, the absence of universal health care, the weak social protections, the lack of good public education, and the numerous policies favoring the rich over the poor are evidence of the inferiority of the American capitalist system and the superiority of the European system. Second, the French like to indict the United States as a violent and hypocritical society—one where abortion is a highly divisive issue while guns and crime are rampant and the state condones the violence of the death penalty. Finally, many in Europe disapprove of the excessive religiosity and the bigotry of American society. This is particularly true in France, which observes a strict separation between government and religion—and where an overwhelming majority claim that it is not necessary to believe in God to be moral.[55] The popularity of creationist theories in the United States is simply mind-boggling to the French. The main behavioral result of this type of anti-Americanism is domestic support for public policies that contrast with the U.S. model. Interestingly, all of these social indictments of the United States come more from an idealized vision of what France should be (just, equal, caring, free from prejudice) than from what it really is.

"Sovereignist" Anti-Americanism   A frequent French critique of the United States focuses on its power in the international system and is often associated with Gaullism ("souverainisme" is a French term coined to designate those concerned with the primacy of national sovereignty, although it is typically used in reference to European integration). The foreign policy of General de Gaulle had a lasting effect on France, as indicated by many surveys showing that the French have often led the rest of Europe in disapproving of U.S. foreign policy. Many politicians on both the right and the left, have insisted on the importance of not losing control over the country's sovereignty and destiny, even if this means getting in the way of the United States. This anti-Americanism is rooted in a sensitive national ego and in a national bitterness over the loss of great power status. In fact, this critique of the United States as a domineering, self-interested nation that uses its immense power to establish global hegemony may stem as much from genuine concern about world peace as from envy

---

55. The French stood out dramatically from other Europeans in a survey question asking about America's religiosity, with 61% responding that Americans were "too religious" (versus 39% of the British and the Germans). Pew Global Attitudes Project 2005a.

and resentment. The result is a predisposition to fear U.S. power, which has been reinforced by the series of unilateral actions the United States has taken since the end of the cold war. This has led to a series of foreign policy actions designed to quell the excessive power of the United States—from insistence on building a common foreign and security policy in Europe to an open challenge to U.S. policy at the United Nations.

Radical Muslim Anti-Americanism   A more recent type of anti-Americanism in France comes from some Muslims who subscribe to the "clash of civilizations" idea. Over the years, some disenfranchised youths of North African origin who have not been "integrated" in French society have become religiously radicalized. They consider the United States to be the Great Satan, whose goal is to lead the Jews and the Western world in destroying Islam; they believe in jihad to weaken or even eliminate this nation that is involved in a crusade against Muslims in Afghanistan, Iraq, and Palestine.[56] Of all the anti-Americanisms found in France, this is the only one that calls for violence against the United States and the American people. It is also the only one directly linked to anti-Semitism.

Elitist Anti-Americanism   Driven mostly by cultural arguments, rather than policy actions, the most stereotypical form of anti-Americanism in France has been a patronizing elitist critique of the United States. This is the anti-Americanism with the longest history and greatest virulence in France. In the eighteenth century haughty French intellectuals looked down on the New World for its paucity of historical richness and tradition and the lack of education and taste of its citizens. Survey data, as well as consumption patterns, suggest a large discrepancy in attitudes in contemporary France between elites and the rest of the nation in relation to American culture, from fast food to Hollywood blockbusters. The same differences between elites and masses are found, to a lesser extent, in other western European countries. What distinguishes France is the particular role of intellectuals in society. As a result, this chronic elitist contempt for American culture bleeds into the popular psyche; the feeling of French superiority over the United States is well ingrained, even in those who have wholeheartedly adopted American popular culture. The main consequence is a constant bashing of American culture (with the exception of the American counterculture, which is highly lauded) without any lessening in the consumption of American culture.

Legacy Anti-Americanism   A related type of anti-Americanism comes from the legacy of a sometimes tense Franco-American history. Resentment of the United States, built up over decades if not centuries, breaks out episodically in critiques of the self-centeredness of America. The individuals articulating this critique focus on the half-empty glass of Franco-American relations and the bad memories left from instances of U.S. involvement or noninvolvement in French affairs: U.S. isolationism

56. Kepel 2004, Roy 2004.

during World War II until Pearl Harbor; a U.S. administration that recognized Vichy France until 1942; the heavy bombardments that accompanied the Normandy invasion and the liberation of France from the Nazis; the American "treason" at Dien Bien Phu and later Suez; the U.S. involvement in Vietnam, despite French pleas against it; and so forth. A particularly vivid legacy of anti-Americanism comes from the cold war period, whose ideological divisions left a lasting imprint on French views of the United States. In the countries where Communist parties were a nonnegligible political force (such as France and Italy), the United States was often presented as the embodiment of what the Left was against: an imperialistic, capitalist, profit-oriented society. From the execution of the Rosenbergs to the invasion of the Bay of Pigs, from McCarthyism to the Vietnam War, the United States provided its critics with plenty of ammunition. Even though the cold war ended over fifteen years ago and Communism has lost its appeal in France, the repertoire of anti-American thought developed over the decades of cold war politics has become ingrained in the vocabulary and the mind-set of many French intellectuals. Some of those who were active during the cold war period are still alive and active today. Whether coming from the Left or the Right, "legacy anti-Americanism" manifests itself as a predisposition toward believing that what the United States did in the past, as well as what it does today, means that it is a partner that cannot be trusted. Such a predisposition suggests that even if U.S. policy changes, attitudes will not change as quickly because bad feelings linger. The main behavioral implication of this predisposition is that France needs to take its national security into its own hands instead of being at the mercy of the vagaries of U.S. foreign policy—meaning, for instance, building an independent European security policy and promoting potentially balancing alliances.

Nostalgic Anti-Americanism The six types of anti-Americanisms highlighted by Katzenstein and Keohane do not entirely capture the French experience, which has developed in addition a "nostalgic" kind, caused by a longing for times past and a resistance to change. Unlike elitist anti-Americanism, the negative sentiments about American culture and society are, in this case, shared by individuals from all walks of life, united in their belief that their country used to be a better place before the United States (and its contemporary fig leaf, globalization) transformed it, dehumanized it, and cut it off from its traditional roots. The complaints in France about how McDonald's has eliminated traditional bistros recall complaints in the 1950s about how Coca-Colonization hurt traditional French wines; and those complaints were reminiscent of earlier complaints about the deleterious effects of U.S. mass production of goods.[57] These complaints are not particular to France—Belgian, Dutch, and Austrian politicians, for instance, have tried, sometimes successfully, to mobilize support by claiming that national traditions were under attack by the joint forces of modernization, globalization, and Americanization. Nevertheless, nostalgic anti-Americanism has particular resonance in France where it also feeds on a reluctance

57. Kuisel 1993.

to accept the international decline of the French language in favor of English as the global lingua franca. This is a defensive anti-Americanism, one that calls for protectionist actions and proactive policies, from the EU-wide policy of "cultural exception" to preserve homegrown culture to rules about preserving the French language from the invasion of American words and the worldwide promotion of "Francophonie."

The distinctiveness of French anti-Americanism in Europe appears to be its breadth: all seven types are present simultaneously, even if few individuals harbor all of them at once. Some of these types may indeed be mutually exclusive, for example, "radical Muslim anti-Americanism," which is at loggerheads with "liberal anti-Americanism," which is itself mostly incompatible with "social anti-Americanism." Other types might be compatible, however, and may even "bleed" into each other, notably through political processes. Overall, the vast repertoire of anti-American arguments and their broad variety have contributed to creating a collective national "background" of distrust of the United States, which has become institutionalized through the political process.

Costless Use of Anti-Americanism in the Political Process

The third reason French anti-Americanism stands out in Europe is political. Anti-Americanism has been embedded in the French political discourse in a singular way. It has been able to endure and propagate in France because it has been exploited politically and because the costs associated with using anti-American rhetoric in France have been far smaller than the benefits derived from it, which is not the case in most other European countries. French politicians have few incentives to defend the United States or criticize anti-American pronouncements. At the same time, anti-Americanism can be mobilized as a political resource to support many different policy agendas. Indeed, the absence of pro-American voices can serve as a proxy measure of the strength of the anti-American message in France.

Over time, anti-Americanism seems to have fulfilled a structural role by helping to create a national and supranational identity. A negative discourse against the United States has been at various times a rhetoric produced in order to positively construct French identity. To some extent, the United States has replaced England as the inimical friend against whom to forge a French national identity; the two have often blended in the frequently used French concept "Anglo-Saxon." Anti-Americanism has served a useful purpose by redefining national identity in contrast to the perceived American model—what John Bowen in chapter 8 refers to as the "diacritic use" of anti-American schemas. For instance, at a time that France is challenged by the reality of the Muslim component of its identity and struggles to update its guiding principles over the separation of church and state, the French critique of the failures and hypocrisies of American multiculturalism reflects back on the idealized French republican model based on assimilation, integration, and equality. The same can be said of the economic and social model: policies such as the thirty-five-hour workweek have been elaborated against widely criticized American practices, partly to reinforce the distinctiveness of the French identity against the backdrop of a globalized, converging, capitalist world.

The demonized (and idealized) American model is also used as a mirror to define European identity—something that has been an elusive concept for many centuries. It is in this sense that anti-Americanism has such an important role to play in the contemporary period: it can create, by negative refraction, a European identity where little previously existed. This is not to say that a European identity can only construct itself against an American foil. Many prominent European thinkers and politicians, from Jacques Derrida and Jürgen Habermas to Joschka Fischer and Hubert Védrine, have explored how to build a new Europe whose collective identity would be more in contrast to the old days of European nationalism than to threats represented by Americanism.[58] Yet at a time that Europe hardly seems to be a cohesive entity, anti-Americanism can easily serve as one of the glues that can bind together very disparate entities.

Anti-Americanism can also play an important role by legitimizing (and delegitimizing) specific policies. Political entrepreneurs are particularly apt to resort to anti-Americanism as a way to lend legitimacy to status quo policies. To ensure the absence of reform, politicians can highlight the similarities between the proposed reformist policy and the American model, in the hope that anti-American sentiments will trigger opposition to the reform. For instance, when French politicians discuss implementing affirmative action (anathema to the French model of integration and equality) or rules on sexual harassment (a far cry from the flirtatious, libertine national culture), opponents of the reform invoke the American model to ensure rejection of the new policy. Another example can be found in the realm of economic reform where, according to Jean-François Revel, one of the few openly anti-anti-American intellectuals in France, "the principal function of anti-Americanism has always been, and still is, to discredit liberalism by discrediting its supreme incarnation."[59]

Conversely, another political role of anti-Americanism is to enable national politicians to scapegoat the United States. In borrowing from the background repertoire of anti-American arguments, French politicians can undertake unpopular policies by blaming them on the United States. This scapegoating shifts the blame and exonerates them of wrongdoing. Globalization was used in a similar way in the late 1990s as a readily available bogeyman that was to blame for unpopular structural reforms.[60] The United States (often seen as synonymous with American multinational corporations) becomes the villain that forces unpopular industrial restructuring, outsourcing, and the whittling down of the state.

Finally, political entrepreneurs can mobilize anti-Americanism as a focal point around which to rally their troops. When domestic support is failing, an appeal to anti-American sentiments can reinvigorate support, since anti-Americanism is one of the few things that can unite people across the political spectrum. One can

58. Derrida and Habermas 2003, Levy et al. 2005.
59. Revel 2003.
60. Gordon and Meunier 2001, Meunier 2003.

interpret the firm stance taken by President Chirac on Iraq in early 2003 as an ironic attempt to "wag the dog" and take the public focus away from domestic trouble by mobilizing on this consensual issue.[61] The same can be said of President Chirac's performance on French national television in April 2005 in order to arouse support for the French referendum on the European Constitution and reinvigorate his discontented political base. When pressed for arguments in favor of European integration, he kept playing the anti-American card, arguing that only by being part of a united European Union could France have a chance to stand up to the United States and that only a united Europe could protect France from the "Anglo-Saxon" socioeconomic model.[62]

Nevertheless, even though anti-Americanism can be and has been exploited for clear domestic purposes, there are limits to its use for political gain. In contemporary France, the image of the United States is not really a divisive element. On the contrary, it is used more for establishing consensus than for fostering divisions and controversies, which explains why it is costless. A well-timed, well-delivered anti-American critique can rally support for anyone's agenda. But because of its consensual nature and the fact that citizens across the political spectrum hold some type of anti-American views (though not necessarily the same type), it is difficult for political leaders to exploit popular concern about America for domestic political gain relative to their opponents. And it does not even always work. Chirac's appeal to anti-Americanism to rescue the European referendum was hardly a success. In a televised interview two weeks after that address, he tried out many different arguments in favor of the referendum, this time not one of them related to the United States.[63]

The four uses of anti-Americanism I have analyzed do exist in other countries, and politicians elsewhere in Europe have resorted to anti-American appeals with more or less success. What distinguishes France is the seeming lack of costs associated with using anti-Americanism for political purposes. This is because France possesses singular characteristics, both internally and internationally. Internally, anti-Americanism has often been exploited because its benefits have typically far outweighed its costs: it spreads all across the French political spectrum, including the moderate Right, which in most other European countries has traditionally been pro-American.[64] Externally, one specific feature that explains why French politicians have incurred so few costs in using anti-Americanism was the particular geopolitical situation of France in the twentieth century. During the cold war, France was not subject to the same geopolitical constraints as Germany, for instance. Because it was less dependent on the United States for its security and economic well-being, because it was a nuclear power, and because of the status of France in the United Nations,

---

61. Chirac's strategy seemed different from that of Gerhard Schröder in Germany, who appealed more to pacifism than to anti-Americanism to win his election.

62. Lorentzsen 2005.

63. Gurrey 2005.

64. A few intellectuals are known for their pro-American views (such as Pascal Bruckner, Bernard-Henri Lévy, Alain Minc, Guy Sorman, and the late Jean-François Revel). But there is so far no institutionalized pro-American grouping of any real stature in French politics, although this may change in the future as the generation of Nicolas Sarkozy reaches the helm of the old Gaullist party.

French policymakers were able to use anti-American arguments without too much fear of retribution. Similarly, the end of the cold war had a different impact on France than on other European countries, leading it to look for a new niche in international politics, which it found partly in the anti-globalization movement and in the insistence on the recourse to multilateral institutions. This geopolitical situation also explains another peculiarity of France—its distinctive, obsessive focus on culture: unlike the countries defeated in World War II, such as Germany and Japan, France was not afraid to claim cultural superiority in the postwar period. And unlike Great Britain, France had a national language to defend from the assaults of English.

Consequences of French Anti-Americanism

A French analyst recently remarked that "anti-Americanism barks more than it bites."[65] Is it indeed a gratuitous discourse on the part of frustrated elites in search of legitimacy or a worrisome political force that affects individual and collective actions? Background anti-Americanism has less of an influence on French foreign policy than is usually portrayed in the American media. As the Iraq example showed, anti-Americanism is secondary to self-interest in guiding French foreign policy, and only a fraction of French actions in the past decade appear confrontational. France was a major member of the U.S.-led coalition in the Gulf War. In 1999 France sent more military aircraft to bomb Yugoslavia than any European nation and placed them under U.S. command. The French government strongly supported the 2001 operation in Afghanistan, and French troops were still present in 2006. And France and the United States have cooperated on the Syrian-Lebanese question in the wake of Rafik Hariri's assassination in 2005. Even France's 2005 proposal to lift its arms embargo on China, which was interpreted in many Washington circles as a blatant case of a French policy motivated by anti-Americanism, may be more about commercial greed than grand geopolitical ambitions.[66] There are two areas in which institutionalized French distrust of the United States might indeed be more consequential and prejudicial than in foreign policy: consumer behavior and intelligence cooperation.

Consumer Boycotts

Before the Franco-American rift over Iraq, the main perceived impact of French anti-Americanism was on consumer behavior. After all, France is the country where José Bové, a sheep farmer who organized the destruction of a McDonald's restaurant, became a national hero and *Le Monde*'s man of the year in 1999.[67] Beyond anecdotes, however, there is no hard evidence that French people prejudiced against the

65. Chazelle 2004.
66. Bernstein 2005, Peel 2005, Weisman 2005.
67. Meunier 2000.

United States stop consuming American products as a way to demonstrate their hostility. This confirms Keohane and Katzenstein's findings in chapter 10. Many French individuals declare that they will boycott American products as a form of symbolic politics, but in fact they do not, and so far the declaratory grandstanding has failed to affect sales of American products in France.[68] Indeed, a 2004 Harvard Business School study concluded:

> It simply didn't matter to consumers whether the global brands they bought were American. To be sure, many people *said* they cared. A French panelist called American brands "imperialistic threats that undermine French culture." A German told us that Americans "want to impose their way on everybody." But the rhetoric belied the reality. When we measured the extent to which consumers' purchase decisions were influenced by products' American roots, we discovered that the impact was negligible.[69]

On the contrary, American businesses seem to be flourishing in France. There are twelve GAP stores in Paris, the capital of fashion, and thirty-five throughout France (with none in Germany or Italy). In this culture of cafés, Starbucks opened its first coffeehouse in September 2003, at the height of the clash between France and the United States over Iraq, while the United States Congress was renaming french fries "freedom fries" in its cafeteria menu. By January 2006, the Seattle-based chain had seventeen outlets in the Paris area. As for cinema, the number-one box office attraction in 2003, the year of the Iraq invasion, was *Finding Nemo*, and seven out of the top-ten movies were from the United States, in a country known for its protection of homegrown film production.[70] In 2004, three out of the five top-grossing movies were American.[71] In 2005, nine out of the ten top grossing movies were produced in the United States.[72] If there is a consumer boycott, it is a negligible one.

With respect to McDonald's, the paradox is the greatest. Of all the European countries, it is in France that McDonald's has been performing best for the past three

68. A Global Market Insite poll, taken in early 2005 after the tsunami relief effort, found that the three countries with the highest percentage of consumers who intended to boycott iconic American brands as a way of displaying their discontent over recent American foreign policies and military action are South Korea 45%, Greece 40%, and France 25%. See http://www.gmipoll.com (accessed August 11, 2005).

69. Holt, Quelch, and Taylor 2004.

70. The top ten movies of 2003 were, in order, (1) *Finding Nemo* (U.S.); (2) *Taxi 3* (France); (3) *Matrix Reloaded* (U.S.); (4) *Lord of the Rings: The Return of the King* (New Zealand); (5) *Chouchou* (France); (6) *Pirates of the Caribbean* (U.S.); (7) *Catch Me if You Can* (U.S.); (8) *The Jungle Book 2* (U.S.); (9) *Matrix Revolutions* (U.S.); (10) *Terminator 3* (U.S.). Source: Centre National de la Cinématographie, http://www.cnc.fr/d_stat/fr_d.htm (accessed August 11, 2005). Note that France subsidizes the production of national movies, not their distribution—unlike on television, where at least 40% of the broadcast must be in French, and on the radio, where at least 40% of pop music broadcast must be in French.

71. The top five movies of 2004 were, in order, (1) *Les Choristes* (France); (2) *Shrek 2* (U.S.); (3) *Harry Potter and the Prisoner of Azkaban* (U.K.); (4) *Spiderman 2* (U.S.); (5) *The Incredibles* (U.S.). Source: Centre National de la Cinématographie, http://www.cnc.fr/d_stat/bilan2004/pdf/1-filmsensalles.pdf (accessed August 11, 2005).

72. In 2005, the top five movies were: (1) Harry Potter and the Goblet of Fire (U.S.); (2) Star Wars Episode 3 (U.S.); (3) The Chronicle of Narnia (U.S.); (4) Brice de Nice (France); (5) Charlie and the Chocolate Factory (U.S.). Source: http://www.cbo-boxoffice.com (accessed March 14, 2006).

years. In 2004, the sales growth of McDonald's France was 5.5 percent, among the best recorded worldwide, achieved against a background of a 3 percent decline in the French fast food market.[73] The number of McDonald's restaurants in France doubled between 1996 and 2004, with 1,035 in December 2004 (out of about sixty-two hundred in Europe), and the company was planning thirty-five more openings in 2005. Present in 750 French cities, McDonald's France serves on average more than one million customers daily. In spite of José Bové and the Franco-American falling out over Iraq, McDonald's France has been doing so well that in 2004 its president, Denis Hennequin, was named McDonald's vice president for all of Europe, in the hope that he could turn around the slumping markets of England and Germany.

The paradoxical state of the Franco-American economic relationship is not limited to consumer behavior. There is no evidence of the "bleeding" of political tensions into the investment side either. In 2003, the year of the falling out between France and the United States, corporate France invested $4.2 billion in the U.S. economy, confirming the place of France as one of the largest investors and largest foreign sources of jobs in the United States.[74] Why is the trade and investment relationship robust in spite of political tensions? Why is there no anti-American backlash in purchasing decisions? There are a host of reasons that consumption has been insulated, so far at least, from the contagion of political sentiments. Individuals are contradictory: they are willing to condemn something in one situation and then consume it in another, especially when self-interest prevails. For most consumers, getting quality products at good prices trumps political prejudices. Moreover, boycotting is often seen as futile when U.S. brands are so ubiquitous.[75] And the very concept of an "American" or a "European" company is becoming increasingly out of date with globalization (except for the iconic American brands, which are often made in China and other countries ironically).[76]

Yet the negligible impact of anti-Americanism on consumer behavior in France does not mean that anti-Americanism will never have an impact.[77] As Keith Reinhard, founder of the group Business for Diplomatic Action, explains, "Research across much of the globe shows that consumers are cooling toward American culture and American brands, but there is still no hard evidence showing direct impact on bottom lines. In marketing, we know that attitude precedes behavior, and the warning signs are there."[78] The "bleeding" may not have occurred yet because of the time lag between attitudes and behaviors, but it may (or not) happen in the future, depending on how long anti-Americanism is sustained by current events and on the availability of non-American alternatives. It should also be noted that even if U.S. firms

73. *Le Monde* 2005a, Palierse 2005.
74. Quinlan and Hamilton 2004.
75. Woodnutt and Burnside 2004.
76. Gordon 2005.
77. Even though Fourcade and Schofer (2004) show why consumer boycotts are not a form of protest widely used in France.
78. *Corporate Citizen* 2004. See also http://www.businessfordiplomaticaction.org/index.php.

have not suffered overall from boycotts, specific sectors and specific companies can suffer from the political strains more than the economy as a whole.

The War on Terror

French anti-Americanism could also have consequences for the United States by affecting the war on terror. First, the anti-American prejudices embedded in the French collective discourse could provide a fertile ground for the emergence of terrorist acts directed against U.S. interests. After all, the constant pounding in the press and elsewhere with negative comments about the United States might prompt some to organize and act. Indeed, the actions of José Bové and other antiglobalization activists against McDonald's and genetically modified crops have been interpreted by some as acts of economic terrorism. Some analysts have suggested that members of the antiglobalization movement may organize into Red Brigade–like "groupuscules." But it would be a major intellectual leap to equate their actions with the type of terrorism that is really trying to hurt the United States. Most of these actions have not been directed at the United States per se but at globalization as an alienating, homogenizing, destructive force related to, but distinct from, the United States. Moreover, the French antiglobalization movement has been careful, so far, not to hurt individuals on purpose through its protest actions.

Even if France does not produce anti-American Red Brigade–type activists intent on hurting Americans, anti-Americanism may still provide a fertile breeding ground for another type of terrorism—radical Islamist. France has a very large Muslim community, with some individuals less integrated into mainstream French society than the majority. Several Islamist terrorists with a hatred of the United States have come from France—from 9/11 suspect Zacarias Moussaoui to French citizens arrested in Iraq among the insurgents, which led to the discovery and breakup of a network in France that was attempting to funnel French citizens to Iraq.[79] But this does not answer positively the question of whether background French anti-Americanism has a mobilizing effect, motivating these individuals to act against American interests. First, the hatred that underlies these acts is not solely turned against the United States. Some deadly acts of Islamist terrorism were committed in France prior to 9/11, such as the 1986 Paris bombings, the 1994 hijacking of an Air France plane, and the 1995 multiple Paris bombings. It is more a hatred of Western civilization and religions than a hatred of the United States. And second, this hatred of Muslim extremists is qualitatively and quantitatively different from the mainstream anti-American discourse of French politicians. Moreover, these extremists typically have weak links to French society and are not well integrated into the local culture, so the chances that their actions are motivated by the musings of Left Bank intellectuals are pretty slim while the chances that they are motivated by broader currents of Islamic radicalism are very great.[80]

79. Agence France Presse 2005a, Sciolino 2005a.
80. Roy 2004, Kepel 2004, Kepel 1997.

Second, the ambient French distrust of the United States could potentially jeopardize Franco-American cooperation on intelligence. France has long cooperated very effectively with the United States in counterterrorism efforts—a matter the French think they understand better than the Americans. For instance, it is thanks to French intelligence that the "millennium bomber" was arrested in Seattle in December 1999 with a truck full of explosives intended for attacks in the United States.[81] Can the anti-American sentiments currently channeled through the media and the political process hinder the efforts of the French government in organizing joint actions with the United States to combat terrorism?

As long as it is in the self-interest of France to cooperate with the United States, it will do so, no matter the international political climate or domestic political pressures. For the past two decades, France has been among the European nations most affected by terrorism. Counterterrorism is one of its top policy priorities. In this domain, its interests seem to be converging with those of the United States. Al-Qaida has also attacked France since 9/11, even if these events have made few headlines in the U.S. media; there was, for instance, the suicide bombing that killed French naval construction workers in Karachi in June 2002, the attack against the French oil tanker *Limbourg* in Yemen in October 2002, and the kidnapping of French journalists in Iraq in 2004 and 2005. Cooperation at the official level should not be affected drastically by anti-American rhetoric, as long as the interests of the two countries converge. It also helps that a lot of this cooperation takes place out of the limelight.

Indeed, according to many directly involved, the degree of cooperation between France and the United States on counterterrorism is better than ever, insulated from French anti-Americanism and American Francophobia.[82] A good example is the December 2003 cancellation of six Air France flights during the busy holiday season at the request of the U.S. government. American intelligence had gathered information that al-Qaida might be using flights between Paris and Los Angeles on Christmas Day or New Year's Eve to commit terrorist acts in the United States.[83] Heeding the warnings of American intelligence, Prime Minister Raffarin ordered Air France to cancel these flights. This was critically portrayed in the French media as France acceding to American paranoia and ridiculed in the next few days when the press revealed that the CIA had mistaken infants and old ladies for members of al-Qaida with similar-sounding names. What is remarkable is that France did it anyway, and the criticisms did not prevent Air France, following orders from the French government, from grounding flights again on January 31, 2004, acting on information provided by U.S. intelligence that al-Qaida might use the planes for a terrorist attack.[84]

A July 3, 2005, *Washington Post* article disclosed that Franco-American cooperation in counterterrorism had even become institutionalized, notwithstanding the political

81. Bruguière 2003.

82. Interview with Robert Hutchings, chairman of the National Intelligence Council, 2002–4, May 16, 2005. See also Bruguière 2003, Priest 2005.

83. Locy et al. 2004, Savage 2003.

84. Lichtblau 2004.

acrimony between the two countries.[85] Since 2002, the CIA and the French secret services (DGSE) have operated jointly a top-secret center in Paris, code-named Alliance Base, that is headed by a French general. This multinational center has already planned twelve special operations.

Anti-Americanism may affect intelligence cooperation, though, if the domestic costs of cooperating on intelligence get higher because of domestic political pressure, and if the costs of cooperating become higher than the costs of not cooperating. One can think of instances in which public pressure (in addition to French law) would be strongly for not cooperating, especially in a case that would include some of the arguments used to feed anti-Americanism, for instance, the extradition of a French prisoner to the United States where he might be subjected to abuse or incur the death penalty. Another serious potential impact of French anti-Americanism on intelligence cooperation could be in information gathering. The large Muslim population in France makes it a particularly valuable asset in that respect. So far French intelligence has been able to infiltrate terrorist networks and gather useful tips. To continue to play this counterterrorism role, France must be confident that its population will be willing to come forward with tips, instead of holding on to information because of anti-American sentiment—and so must the United States.

Overall, background French anti-Americanism has not produced openly confrontational policies, contrary to what is commonly believed in the United States. Nevertheless, it could still affect the United States, because it could lead to stronger demands for global governance. The more prevalent anti-Americanism is in Europe, the more likely European leaders—the French chief among them—are to ask for a world system governed by a multitude of rules in order to curb the almightiness of the United States, whether in the United Nations or in functional institutions such as the World Trade Organization and the International Monetary Fund.[86] Distrust of the United States could also shift French policy toward increased European integration and a stronger Europe, able to assert its independence from the United States. Indeed, in the years preceding the Iraq conflict, Europeans engaged in a series of joint defense initiatives and committed the European Union, though the ambitious Lisbon process, to becoming the world's most competitive and dynamic economic area by 2010. However, the consequences of anti-Americanism on the future of European integration depend on which type of anti-Americanism is at play. Parties with sovereignist anti-Americanist tendencies desire a stronger Europe able to counter the overwhelming domination of their U.S. ally. This is why Chirac supported the creation of the European single currency, justifying the euro as a means to curb the power of the dollar. This is also why he is now proposing a stronger European foreign policy, independent of the United States. Indeed, this policy finds great resonance with French public opinion. By 2003, the French overwhelmingly (91%) said they wanted the European Union to become a "superpower like the US"—a much greater

85. Priest 2005.
86. Gordon and Meunier 2001, Abdelal 2006.

percentage than the Italians, Germans, Dutch, British, and Poles surveyed.[87] A size-able French minority even hoped that the European Union would compete with, or counterbalance, the United States.[88] Parties with social anti-Americanist tendencies also desire a stronger Europe, but one that will offer an alternative social and economic model on a continental scale. Overall, the case seems pretty clear that if France is to play a counterweight role to the United States, it must be through Europe. Nevertheless, as the divisive French debate on the referendum over the EU Constitution showed, anti-Americanism does not seem to be weighing heavily on people's minds—otherwise they would have voted massively yes in May 2005.

If French distrust of the United States does not generate defiant public policies or individual behaviors, it can still raise the costs of U.S. foreign policy in the long run. It remains to be seen how French and European anti-Americanism affects the course of U.S. foreign policy, whether anti-Americanism promotes greater support in the United States for isolationist positions or, on the contrary, greater international involvement, and whether it strengthens domestically those who promote greater unilateralism or multilateralism.

"We Are All Anti-American"

Anti-Americanism spans the whole political spectrum in France, from the far left Trotskyist parties to the far right National Front. Yet in spite of its long history and the existence of a vast reservoir of anti-American arguments, it would be unfair to characterize France as an anti-American nation. To be sure, an irreducible fraction of French public opinion is viscerally anti-American and exhibits a dispositional bias that negatively interprets the actions of the United States irrespective of reality. These are the people whose hatred of the United States made a bestseller out of Thierry Meyssan's *L'effroyable imposture*, a book that argued that it was an American missile that crashed on purpose into the Pentagon on 9/11 and that the September 11 attacks were carried out by the U.S. government.[89] The prejudice such people display is referred to in French as "anti-américanisme primaire" (primal anti-Americanism).

Nevertheless, public opinion polls show that most French people have consistently been no more anti-American than Spaniards and Greeks and only marginally more so than Germans and other western Europeans, and there is little evidence that French policy opposition to the United States is motivated by bias rather than by policy disagreements or a clash of interests. French anti-Americanism stands out because over the years intellectuals and politicians have developed a common corpus

---

87. According to the 2005 Pew Global Attitudes Project, 73% of the French (by far the highest number in Europe) want Europe to be more independent from the United States in its security and diplomatic affairs. Pew Global Attitudes Project 2005a.

88. Kuisel 2004.

89. Meyssan 2002.

of biases against the United States, which have become embedded in the national policy discourse and have been exploited politically. Anti-Americanism often takes the form of institutionalized distrust, at times bordering on bias, but these biases hardly affect the behavior of most French citizens, even if they periodically affect their attitudes.

This common corpus is made up of at least seven types of anti-American arguments. That French society would nurture simultaneously these seven types, however, does not imply that, to paraphrase *Le Monde*'s Jean-Marie Colombani, "we are all anti-Americans."[90] For all these manifestations of anti-Americanism, there are also daily manifestations of pro-Americanism, even if not in daily newspaper columns: in the world of business (which admires and imports many American methods of management); in the world of higher education (which envies and aspires to American-style universities); in the world of entertainment (which emulates some aspects of American popular culture and lionizes many American cultural figures); and even in the world of food (where French chefs admire the working conditions of their American counterparts, whose professional teams consistently win international competitions).[91] In a way, the French "are all Americans," that is, they have integrated America into their daily lives, from television to food, from business practices to rap music. This Americanization is taken for granted and does not make the headlines, but it explains the complexities and contradictions of French views of the United States.

Perhaps the United States grants too much importance to the negative perceptions of the French. And perhaps this stems from a misunderstanding of French national political culture, which prides itself on its rebellious nature and counts as one of its heroes the fictitious indomitable little Gaul Asterix, who was able to resist the powerful Roman Empire. The United States is not the exclusive object of French antagonism. If there is anything like a collective national psyche, in France it would be a rebellious, grumpy character, and a high propensity for opposition—no matter whether the object in question is the United States, the European Constitution, or domestic policy reforms. Indeed, surveys such as the World Values Survey consistently show that the French are very distrustful in general—of each other, of their government, of politicians, of America, and so on.[92] The French just like to be "anti," especially when the disruption of French society created by the phenomenon in question is strong. Maybe anti-Americanism, or at least what is perceived as anti-Americanism on the U.S. side of the Atlantic, is nothing personal.

90. "We Are All Americans" was the title of *Le Monde*'s front-page editorial on September 12, 2001.

91. When asked in a multination survey to assess the positive characteristics of Americans, the French were at the top or close to the top in judging Americans as "hardworking," "inventive," and "honest." Pew Global Attitudes Project 2005a.

92. See http://www.worldvaluessurvey.org/ (accessed August 11, 2005).

6

Chinese Attitudes toward the United States and Americans

ALASTAIR IAIN JOHNSTON
and DANIELA STOCKMANN

The conventional wisdom in the United States is that anti-Americanism is on the rise in China, particularly among Chinese youth, as the state fosters nationalism to replace Marxism-Leninism as the basis of its legitimacy.[1] This particular conventional wisdom about China has not been subject to careful empirical analysis.[2] Part

The authors thank the following for their assistance, insights, comments, and criticisms: Joe Fewsmith, Shen Mingming, Yang Ming, Chas Freeman, Don Keyser, Nico Howson, Robert Kapp, Charlie Martin, Susan Shirk, Ken Lieberthal, Ken Pick, Will Lowe, Pat Powers, Doug McAdam, Chris Murck, Andy Conn, David Shambaugh, Traci Smith, Scott Kronick, Stephen Turner, Chen Changfeng, Fan Shiming, Jin Canrong, Zhao Mei, Xiao Ming, Liu Zhiming, Li Xiaogang, Lu Bin, Wang Yuhua, Shu Chunyan, and the participants at the Duke and Stanford workshops on anti-Americanism. Our thanks as well go to the University of Maryland, Global Market Insite, IMI Information Market Research Institute, and Horizon for their cooperation in providing data or data reports. Thanks as well to Alex Noonan, Marusia Musac-chio, He Yewen, and Zhang Yunqing for research assistance. Finally, we are grateful for the detailed and incisive comments on earlier drafts from Rick Baum, Peter Katzenstein, and Bob Keohane.

1. In the media and pundit world, see, for instance, Waldron 2003, 41; CNN, May 10, 1999; *National Interest* (Winter 2000–2001); CNN, April 3, 2001; *Newsweek*, April 16, 2001; Al Hunt on CNN, April 21, 2001; *Newsweek*, May 7, 2001, to list a few sources. In the academic world, see Shambaugh 2001; Fewsmith and Rosen 2001; Xu 1997, 208–26; and Zhao 1998. Media analyses suggest, however, that ordinary Chinese are not being bombarded with a steady stream of exclusively hostile or biased messages about the United States. The topics covered in these media are quite diverse (ranging from entertainment and sports to economics and politics), and the tone of the reporting is not uniformly negative. See Zhai 2002 and the University of Maryland 2002.

2. A high-profile U.S. poll of global attitudes toward the United States, the Pew Research Center's Global Attitudes Project 2002, included questions about assessments of the United States, U.S. power, and the degree of threat from American values, but did not ask these questions of Chinese respondents. Chinese polling results appear to question some of the U.S. conventional wisdom. Although levels of dislike can be relatively high, when questions did not refer directly to politics most respondents gave answers that suggest a positive image of the United States. Respondents tended to perceive the United States as a potential threat, pursuing a one-sided policy aimed at preserving its hegemonic status in the world and containing China. Still in some polls a majority seemed to be quite satisfied with Sino-U.S. relations and did

of the problem is that the conventional wisdom has come from three sources that are methodologically problematic: anecdotal evidence based on U.S. media reporting, selective attention to certain popular publications in China, and conversations with a relatively small group of Chinese scholars and officials. For instance, the sources used by the U.S. media to draw inferences about public opinion are biased (in a sampling sense), relying mostly on nonrandom interviews with students and young urbanites.

As for Chinese publications, often analysts examine only those writings that support the rising anti-Americanism and nationalism trope (such as the 1996 screed *China Can Say No*). As far as we are aware, no one has taken publications that lie along a spectrum of positive to negative views of the United States and looked at their relative number, readership, or impact.

And as for interaction between American and Chinese scholars and officials one might very well expect Chinese interlocutors to have a better sense of Chinese opinion than Americans. Still, elites can often be wrong about popular opinion, as the debate over casualty aversion and isolationist views in the U.S. public attests. Moreover, the number of scholars with whom U.S. specialists on Chinese politics and foreign policy interact is exceedingly small and likely to be unrepresentative of popular attitudes.

In short, no one has provided a threshold or baseline against which to observe whether anti-Americanism is rising, declining, or remaining stable. In this chapter we examine Chinese attitudes toward the United States across time, issue area, and socioeconomic, demographic, and ideological contexts. There are still considerable political and logistical obstacles to the systematic collection of information about Chinese views of the United States in different issue areas. We use language analysis, interviews, content analysis, and survey data to examine Chinese attitudes from multiple angles.

We first discuss the Chinese discourse about U.S. external policies and internal politics, focusing on the concept of *hegemony* in foreign policy and on assessments of the attractiveness of the U.S. political system as a model. The hegemony discourse frames much of the discourse about the nature of U.S. power and its role in international relations. The reason for examining the attractiveness of American political values and institutions is that these values are core to U.S. identity, and core to what Americans believe the United States "stands for" abroad. The status of these values in the eyes of Chinese should tap into the degree to which "Americanism" is seen as a positive or negative identity trait.

We then look at elite and mass attitudes toward Americans as people and the United States as a state. Here we rely mainly on the Beijing Area Study (BAS), a ran-

---

not perceive the United States as an enemy (see China Mainland Marketing Research Company 1998; Institute of American Studies from the Chinese Academy of Social Sciences 2004; PORI 1997; Horizon 2003, 2004; Renmin Wang 2005b). But it is hard to assess the reliability and validity of many of these results: sampling procedures are often unclear; question wording can be leading. None of these studies provides time-series data; few report standard socioeconomic and demographic controls. For a more detailed analysis of the knowledge base for understanding attitudes toward the United States see our longer online paper, Johnston and Stockmann 2005.

domly sampled time-series survey. The question we added to this survey enable us to examine general levels of amity toward the United States, and the degree of identity difference that Chinese respondents believe exists between Chinese and Americans and between China and the United States as a state.

In parallel with the chapters by Sophie Meunier on France and Marc Lynch on the Arab world, we then focus on four domains of analysis to determine the degree to which negative perceptions of the United States and of Americans spill over into specific issue areas. To the extent that they do not, this suggests that there are attitudinal firewalls between issue areas.[3]

The first domain, the Taiwan question, is one where the U.S. and Chinese governments have a sharp conflict of interest. This domain should give us a rough baseline of relatively fixed negative views of the United States at both the elite and nonelite levels.

The second domain covers issues where Sino-U.S. interests as their leaders have defined them do not collide dramatically; there is either substantial reason for collaboration or at least little reason for conflict. Here we look at Chinese views of the United States through the prism of the war on terror.

For similar reasons, and for the sake of comparability with the chapters on France and the Arab world, we examine a third domain—Chinese analyses of the U.S. response to the South Asian tsunami disaster of December 2004. In principle, tsunami relief is an area where we might expect states to play up their own roles and denigrate the contributions of adversaries. This domain ought to reveal a great deal about how extensive and intensive any baseline views of these other states are.

The final domain concerns attitudes toward U.S. consumer products in China. We ask whether negative attitudes toward the United States are "active," that is, whether they have any concrete impact on the day-to-day behavior of ordinary Chinese. At the moment, U.S. economic relations with China seem to have an anchoring effect for the fragile political relationship. The effect or noneffect of views of the United States on consumer habits could be important for forecasting the political relationship.

Chinese officials, elites, and the general public generally differentiate between the American people and the U.S. government, viewing the latter more negatively than the former. The degree of amity for the United States has declined over the past few years, beginning with the 1999 bombing of the Chinese embassy in Belgrade, but it has dropped off fairly substantially since about 2003. In addition, after years of little change, within 2004 there has been a noticeable increase in the perceived identity difference between Chinese and Americans. Using categories of analysis developed by the editors in chapter 1, we find a great deal of distrust (as well as anger), but very little hatred or systematic denigrating bias—in contrast to attitudes toward Japan and the Japanese, where such attitudes are prevalent.

There are differences in the degree of negative attitudes across the different domains. The most consistently negative views of the United States concern its

---

3. Markovits 2004b.

overall strategy of "hegemony" and its specific application to the relationship with Taiwan. Attitudes toward U.S. counterterrorism strategy are more mixed, with an element of empathy for the United States. There is not much evidence of direct bias in coverage of the U.S. tsunami relief efforts. Rather, officials and the media tended to stress the altruistic nature of China's assistance while ignoring or downplaying U.S. assistance. Finally, images of American material and cultural products are relatively positive, and for the most part consumption is cushioned from the vagaries of the political relationship.

The Hegemony Discourse and the Declining Appeal of U.S. Political Values

The overall framework that official and nonofficial China uses to understand U.S. behavior has two components—understandings of the basic nature of U.S. foreign policy, and understandings of the basic institutions and values of U.S. domestic politics.

In foreign policy, the framework can be summarized by the term "hegemonism." This term and its variants infuse the discourse about the nature of the United States and its role in the world. According to one Chinese survey, when students were asked what term first came to mind when the United States was mentioned the most common answer was "world hegemon."[4]

What, then, does the term commonly mean? In modern Chinese usage "hegemonism" (*baquanzhuyi*) derives from the ancient concept of the "way of the hegemon" (*badao*). Over time this term came to refer to tyrannical, bullying, overbearing, often violent, and certainly illegitimate behavior by the powerful, with no regard for the well-being of the less powerful.[5] Thus a reference to the United States as hegemon means the United States is the unjust and overbearing dominant state in the system.[6] The existence of a hegemon constitutes nonhegemonic states as innocent victims, blameless for the consequences of hegemonic practice.

These basic meanings show up in surveys and interviews. According to one series of surveys of Chinese university students, respondents tend to identify three features of hegemonism. First, the United States always wants to interfere in issues around the world as the global cop. Second, U.S. hegemonism is hypocritical—the reasons given for interference in the affairs of other states (for example, to defend human rights, promote democracy, or maintain peace) are not the real reasons behind U.S. actions. Rather the United States only wants to promote its own interests.[7] Third, the means to these ends are often coercive. Commonly cited examples of U.S. hege-

---

4. Cited in Chen 2002a, 8.

5. In its original meaning it referred to the intermediary state between the Son of Heaven and less powerful feudal states. See Shambaugh 1991, 81–83.

6. For a smart analysis of U.S. and Chinese uses of the term *hegemon*, see Wang 2003.

7. Not all students view U.S. justifications as obscuring true motivations. As one interviewee said, the United States is quite direct and blunt in foreign affairs and usually does what it says is in its interests. Chen 2002b, 8.

monism include the 1999 intervention in Kosovo, U.S. policy in the Middle East, arms sales to Taiwan, opposition to China's Olympics bids, alleged obstruction of China's entrance into the World Trade Organization, the 1999 bombing of the Belgrade embassy, and the EP-3 incident.[8]

Two general components of the hegemony discourse can cue sharply negative feelings in Chinese respondents—*containment* and *double standards*. First, the mainstream view is that a major component, if not the essence, of U.S. strategy toward China is containment. It is commonly believed that the United States wants to weaken China and obstruct its economic and military development. The Chinese term for containment, *e'zhi*, connotes holding back, controlling, manipulating, suppressing, and causing defeat. And those who refer to U.S. strategy in more mixed terms—as "engagement plus containment," for example—contend that engagement is the means, containment is the end.[9]

Second, the Chinese discourse often claims that U.S. foreign policy is characterized by "double standards" (*shuangchong biaozhun*).[10] The United States is accused of a double standard in the promotion of democracy abroad (where the United States supports nondemocratic actors and behavior),[11] the war on terror, and the critique of other countries' human rights conditions.[12] When searching online the *Peoples' Daily*, the *Peoples' Liberation Army Daily*, and Google (in Chinese) for the term "double standard" and then for the keywords "double standard" and "United States," the percentage of hits with both terms were 64.1 percent, 71.2 percent, and 68.9 percent, respectively. In other words, in Chinese discourses about international relations, the United States is strongly associated with behaving according to a double standard.

In short, the hegemony discourse provides the dominant frame through which Chinese officialdom, intellectuals, and nonelites analyze U.S. power and its role in the world. The question is whether this frame affects attitudes across the different domains in Sino-American interaction.

The critique of U.S. foreign policy as hegemonic has been less debated in China than the critique of U.S. domestic political institutions and values. In the 1980s, there were discussions within the Chinese Communist Party (CCP) about the potential advantages of certain features of the U.S. system—the division of powers, for instance. But in the wake of Tiananmen and the sudden downturn in Sino-U.S.

8. See Chen 2002a, 2. During the EP-3 incident in April 2001 a U.S. surveillance plane collided with a Chinese F-8 fighter, which resulted in the loss of the Chinese jet and the death of its pilot. The damaged American plane made an emergency landing on Hainan island. Beijing blamed the United States for the collision and demanded that the United States end surveillance flights near its coast and apologize for the loss of its aircraft and pilot. Washington blamed the incident, which occurred in international airspace over the South China Sea, on the Chinese pilot and demanded the return of its plane and crew. After the American crew was released negotiations continued until a deal was struck about the specifics of the American aircraft's return to the United States in June 2001. See, for example, Agence France Presse, April 13, 2001, and June 3, 2001.

9. See Yang 2001, 4, and Deng 2003, 75–77. This description parallels somewhat how some American analysts describe or prescribe U.S. strategy—one of hedging or "congagement."

10. Da 2005.

11. See Zhang 2004, 49, and Tang 2004.

12. See, for example, *People's Daily* 2005b and Renmin Wang 2005a.

relations, the CCP has had very little positive to say about U.S. democracy. The most authoritative statements against the U.S. political system—in particular about the notion of independent branches and checks and balances—come from Deng Xiaoping. In his view, the "system of a three-sided division of powers" is in fact a system of "three governments": "We cannot adopt this solution."[13] Presumably, then, the notion of three independent branches is considered a threat to the CCP's monopoly on power.[14]

That said, there has been a vigorous three-cornered debate among intellectuals over the relative value of American (and more broadly "liberal") political values from the 1980s on. In one corner is the state orthodoxy—preserve the dominant role of the CCP, implement incremental measures to increase legitimacy (e.g., village-level elections), and increase to some degree inner-party democracy and pluralism. In another corner is a big-tent category that includes neoconservative nationalists and social democratic–oriented reformers.[15] In the third corner are liberals—supporters of small government, marketization, an independent judiciary, and the rule of law, or constitutionalism.[16] It is, of course, the liberals who have most admired U.S. political institutions and values. They draw on thinkers such as James Madison, Isaiah Berlin, Milton Friedman, Karl Popper, and Friedrich Hayek, among others.[17]

According to Joseph Fewsmith, the debate between these groups over the past twenty-five years has been less about the ends of reform and more about the process—how best to preserve stability as marketization proceeds. In the 1980s the liberal position was vigorous, new, and relatively popular among intellectuals. But by the 1990s the liberals were on the defensive, both in the appeal of their ideas and the party's reaction to them. This was a function of three developments. One was the violence of Tiananmen in 1989: the crackdown did much to undermine the appeal of liberal (seen as "radical" political reform) ideas. Radical change was seen as too provocative, leading to outcomes that were counterproductive.[18]

Another source of this disillusionment with liberalism came from the critique of U.S. foreign policy—the perception that the United States was trying to block China's emergence as a strong power.[19] This perception emerged early in the 1990s, initially in response to the U.S. decision in 1992 to sell 150 F-16s to Taiwan, simultaneously with the beginning of a "China threat" discourse in the United States. The Chinese responded by developing their own counterdiscourse, claiming that the China threat was created to justify a policy of opposing China's economic development and national unification.[20]

---

13. Deng Xiaoping 1986. See also Jiang Zemin 2001.
14. See Tang 2004.
15. See Fewsmith 2001, 80–87, 94, 97, 109–20; Guo 2004, 23–43; and Gao 2004, 44–62.
16. For a summary of liberal views see Killion 2003, 11–12, and Fewsmith 2001.
17. Fewsmith 2001, 128. See Guo 2004, 27.
18. Fewsmith 2001, 92, 123.
19. Zhao 2001, 18; Fewsmith 2001, 106.
20. On the Chinese response to the "China threat" see Deng 2006.

The Belgrade embassy bombing in 1999 helped consolidate this claim. For many, the bombing was another source of disillusionment with the United States and its political values. According to one of Chen Shengluo's university student informants:

> When we heard the news about the bombing of the embassy we did indeed cry; it was hard to bear. Why did the United States do this? Were they not pushing us to hate them? In fact, before, when it came to values we were very much oriented toward theirs [Americans']; to a large degree the education we received was similar to theirs. They became the goal of our study. But this slap in the face, it hurt in our hearts.[21]

Finally, over the 1980s and 1990s many scholars and analysts came to believe that individual states cannot provide particularly good models for political reform in an era of globalization. In the early 1980s reformers looked at the experiences of more liberal Eastern European polities, such as Hungary and Yugoslavia. But by the 1990s many had concluded that one country or group of countries could not provide adequate answers to some of the unique challenges China faced in an era of globalization—massive income gaps, a growing middle class, demands for stronger legal institutions.[22]

Whichever of these factors is more important, the decline of liberal thought or values among intellectuals has not been merely an epiphenomenon of growing tensions in Sino-U.S. relations or solely the result of a state crackdown on "pro-American" thought in intellectual circles in the 1990s.[23] The problems faced by liberal thinkers have a lot to do with a genuine debate about ideas, and the context of that debate post-Tiananmen helped swing it toward those who argued for stability first and democracy second. But as the appeal of *American* political values has diminished so too has an ideational backstop to further distrust of the United States and its identity.

Attitudes toward Americans and the United States

There seems to be a consensus in the secondary literature that Chinese today hold sharply bifurcated views of the United States. These split views are similar to those among Arab publics.[24] On the one hand, the United States is admired for its level

21. Cited in Chen 2002b, 9. Note the similarity to the Egyptian university student's quote in an article by the *Washington Post* (cited in Lynch, chapter 7): "We were in awe of America, and now, we are bitter, confused. The admiration is gone."

22. Interview with Wang Yizhou, deputy director of the Institute of World Economics and Politics (IWEP), January 2005.

23. The Chinese government has put more constraints on public *expression* of liberal ideas, which has helped reduce the appeal of liberalism, but *access* to liberal ideas has not been cut off. One can buy the works of major foreign liberal thinkers in Chinese bookstores. On the publication of liberal works in the last few years, see Guo 2004, 24–25.

24. Lynch, chapter 7.

of development, openness, social individualism, opportunities for economic advancement, and the efficiency of its bureaucracies. The United States often is the unspoken comparison against which China's backwardness is measured. On the other hand, many of the same people see it is as hegemonistic, aggressive, and arrogant on the foreign policy side.[25] In addition, there is usually a distinction made between people and state, with the latter (or its leaders) being the object of criticism rather than former. Although the short-term reaction of Chinese students and netizens[26] to 9/11 tended to blur this distinction, their discourse was still mainly about the attacks being revenge against U.S. state policy, not the punishment of Americans for being Americans.[27]

In general, then, much of the Chinese secondary literature concludes that current views of the United States are more nuanced than they were in the past. The Chinese people, it is claimed, understand the variety and complexity of U.S. society better.[28] This more complicated perception of the United States is found in media coverage as well. A University of Maryland study found that in the three short periods they studied, media coverage was relatively diverse and balanced, except when there was political tension between the United States and China.[29]

The complexity of Chinese perceptions is underscored by our analysis of the only extant time series on Chinese views of the United States, the Beijing Area Study, an annual randomly sampled survey of Beijing residents from 1998 to 2004. The two main variables of interest in the study are amity and identity difference. Amity toward the United States is measured on a standard 1–100 degree feeling thermometer.[30] The identity variable tries to tap into the degree to which respondents perceived Chinese as different from Americans and Japanese. Social identity theory suggests that the construction of in-group identity generally leads to the construction of different, often devalued and conflictual notions of out-group identity. Higher levels of perceived identity difference, ceteris paribus, can lead to more devaluation, and this, in turn, is associated with more competitive or threatened views of the out-group.[31] To capture the degree to which respondents believed Chinese and Americans differed in their inherent characteristics, we constructed an identity difference measure. Respondents were asked where they thought Chinese and Americans as people were on a 1–7 peaceful-to-warlike scale and a 1–7 moral-to-immoral scale. The scales were combined, and the Chinese means were subtracted from the

25. See Zhao Min's summary of these bifurcations in surveys and in secondary literature in Zhao 2001, 3–12. This characterization of Chinese views is also shared by Rosen 2004, 99.

26. "A portmanteau of *Internet* and *citizen* . . . A person actively involved in online communities" (Wikipedia.com).

27. Chen 2004, Wang 2004.

28. Yuan 2001, 19–20; Chen 2002a, 6; Yang 1997. One Peking University professor claims that Yang's book is seen as a particularly authoritative description and explanation of Chinese views of the United States.

29. See University of Maryland 2002, Johnston and Stockmann 2005.

30. See Johnston and Stockmann 2005 for details on question wording, measurement, and survey sampling methods.

31. On social identity theory see Tajfel 1982, Turner 1987, and Abrams and Hogg 1990.

American means, yielding an identity difference score that ran from −6 to +6. The greater the distance from zero, the greater the perceived identity difference.[32]

We use various socioeconomic and demographic control variables to do some descriptive "brush clearing" about which factors appear to matter in accounting for variations in attitudes toward the United States. Due to the lack of ideational control variables in the portion of the BAS data that we used, we do not try to develop a multivariate explanatory model of respondents' attitudes. Instead, we look mainly at bivariate relationships.

Our first control variable is *income*. One should expect those with higher incomes to demonstrate relatively lower levels of anti-Americanism than those from lower-income groups. This might be a reflection of their respective positions vis-à-vis benefits from integration with the outside world.[33] *Education* is our second variable. One should expect that higher levels of education are related to lower levels of anti-Americanism, as exposure to more information about the outside and to more sophisticated modes of analysis and thought contribute to a more critical or nuanced view of one's own group.[34] We also consider *political generation*. This variable tests the common impression in the United States that the post-1989 generation has, in particular, been successfully targeted by a state effort to whip up nationalism and anti-Americanism in an effort to repair the damaged legitimacy of the CCP.[35] We also use age as of the year in which the respondent is interviewed. A fourth factor is *gender*. There are no definitive findings about gender and foreign policy preferences in the international relations literature. There is conflicting evidence about whether women tend to adopt somewhat more "liberal" and "internationalist" attitudes toward international-conflict issues. So we make no definite predictions about the relationship between gender and the view of the United States in China. We also consider *foreign travel* to be an important control variable. One should expect that those who have gone abroad will tend to express lower levels of anti-Americanism than those who have not been abroad. This might reflect a higher income or education level (in other words, those going abroad are a self-selected group). Or it might reflect a more critical eye toward one's own nation and a more empathetic eye toward others as a result of travel. The final variable is *interest in international news*. This variable should tap into levels of awareness of the outside world, and possibly levels of negativity toward the United States. A low interest in international news should correlate with lower levels of amity.

Turning now to the first variable of interest, amity toward the United States has been relatively volatile compared to other states, except for Japan.[36] In 1998 the mean

32. A positive sign indicates that Americans are perceived more positively than Chinese, a negative sign that Americans are viewed more negatively than Chinese. See Johnston and Stockmann 2005 for more details.

33. For a discussion of hypotheses about the foreign policy preferences of high-income groups, and for the reasoning behind our coding rules for income groups, see Johnston 2004b.

34. Brown 1986.

35. Zhao 1998; Xu 1998; Hollander 1992, 341.

36. Indeed, there is a very high positive correlation between change in amity for the United States and for Japan (Pearson's r = .9).

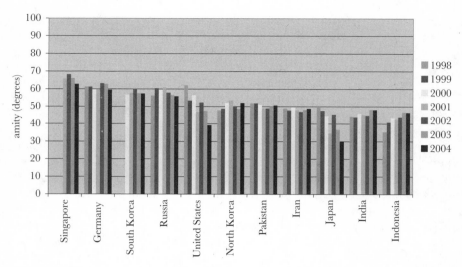

Figure 10. Levels of amity (degrees) for various countries, 1998–2004.

temperature on the 100-degree feeling thermometer was highest for the United States, and the mean was significantly greater than the mean for all states (see figure 10). The levels of amity dropped substantially in 1999 and 2001, possibly due to the Belgrade embassy bombing and the EP-3 incident. From 2001 to 2002 it climbed again, dropping in 2003 and 2004. The general trend, therefore, was a zigzag decline until the last two years. The United States has gone from a country with one of the highest levels of amity as late as 1998 to a level that is now below that of Indonesia, India, and North Korea. Indeed the 2004 BAS shows amity at levels that Japan "enjoyed" for most of this period. Beijing residents, at least, now show considerably lower levels of amity toward the United States than do Europeans, according to the recent German Marshall Fund Transatlantic Trends 2004 poll of European nations.[37] Indicative of this shift is the distribution of amity levels in the 1998 and 2004 data. They are, in essence, mirror images (see figure 11).

What then are the relationships between the level of amity expressed toward the United States and the various socioeconomic and demographic control variables listed above? Concerning income levels, the BAS data indicate that the middle class (in fact, the wealthiest income group in Beijing) has held consistently higher levels of amity toward the United States than others.[38] As for education, those with more

---

37. The lowest is Spain at 42 degrees on a 100 degree feeling thermometer. Most of the other countries polled were in the 60s. See German Marshall Fund 2004 poll, 22.

38. This group had mean temperatures steadily above average, the association (chi square) between income level and amity was only statistically significant at the $p = 0.05$ level in 2000 and 2003.

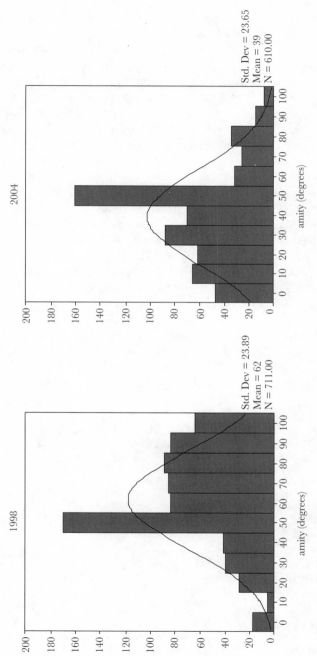

Figure 11. Distribution of levels of amity (degrees) toward the United States, 1998 and 2004.

education have expressed warmer feelings toward the United States.[39] Concerning political generation, it is not clear whether younger respondents dislike the U.S. more than older ones: the findings vary depending on the coding of the variable.[40] As for gender, there do not seem to be any clear trends. In 1999, 2001, 2003, and 2004 women showed a lower level of amity than men, but the difference was significant only in 2001 and 2004 ($p = 0.03$ and $p = 0.099$, respectively). In all other years gender differences were virtually nonexistent.[41] Foreign travel, however, was always consistently associated with high levels of amity.[42] Finally, with regard to interest in international news, in the two years this question was asked (1998 and 2000) those who followed international affairs closely had higher degrees of amity than those who did not. In both years these differences were statistically significant.[43] This suggests that, on average, those who were better informed about the outside world felt warmer toward the United States than those who were less well informed.[44]

In summary, in many of these years the wealthier, better educated, better traveled, younger, and better informed (or those more interested in the external world) have had more positive feelings toward the United States. In 2004, however, the relationships between these variables weakened. We are unclear which factors that we did not observe in our survey might be at work. But the trend bears watching. If it continues it might suggest that, as in attitudes toward Japan, a societal consensus around lower levels of amity toward the United States may be emerging.

Do these patterns hold up in perceptions of identity difference? Beijing respondents clearly believed that Chinese and Americans differ considerably. BAS respondents perceived Chinese to be much more peaceful and moral by nature than Americans (and Japanese) (see figure 12).[45] Still, until the BAS survey was conducted in 2004 one might have been cautiously optimistic in that the identity difference scores appeared relatively stable, reflecting perhaps somewhat deeply rooted

---

39. In three of the five years the overall relationship was statistically significant at or below the $p = 0.05$ level. This relationship holds if one uses years of education or a more detailed breakdown of graduation level. In 1998, 2002, and 2003 the Tukey Honestly Significant Differences (HSD) indicates that the numerical difference between those with some secondary and some university education was not statistically significant. In 2004 the relationship was not statistically significant.

40. Using ANOVA to test the difference of means across political generations shows that except for two years (2000 and 2001) there was no statistical relationship between political generation and amity. Using ordinary least squares regression and a dummy variable (1) for those born between 1951 and 1967 and (0) for those born before and after shows that youth like the United States less. See Johnston and Stockmann 2005 for more details.

41. This is consistent with Chiozza's finding (chapter 4) about the nonrelationship between gender and anti-Americanism in the Pew data.

42. In 1998 and 2004 this relationship was not statistically significant, but in 2001, 2002, and 2003 it was significant ($p = 0.02$, $p = 0.017$, and $p = 0.00$, respectively).

43. In 1998 the difference in mean temperature was statistically significant at the $p = 0.1$ level, with the main significant difference being between those who were very interested and those who were hardly interested (Tukey HSD $p = 0.08$). In 2000 the overall difference was statistically significant at the $p = 0.05$ level.

44. This result is consistent with Chiozza's findings (chapter 4) that those who show higher levels of political knowledge about the outside world have more pro-American attitudes.

45. The difference between Japanese and American scores is statistically significant in all years (using a paired difference of means t-test).

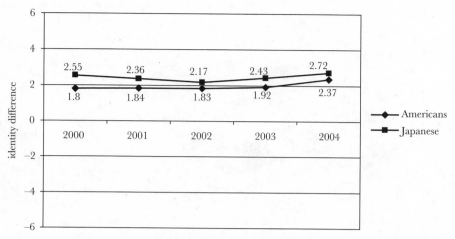

Figure 12. Identity difference scores for Americans and Japanese, 2000–2004. *Source:* Beijing Area Study.

assumptions about the other, regardless of specific ups and downs in political relationships. The 2004 data, however, indicate a substantial increase in the perceptions of difference.

Turning to the control variables, as expected, high-income respondents perceived lower levels of identity difference between Chinese and Americans.[46] Education was also clearly related to perceived differences between Chinese and Americans with regard to peacefulness and morality traits. Those with at least some university education perceived a lower degree of difference than those with less education.[47] The data also show that those who had traveled abroad consistently perceived fewer differences between Chinese and Americans.[48] And when it comes to gender differences BAS data show that women perceived greater levels of identity difference between Chinese and Americans than men. The gender difference was statistically significant for all years except 2004. Political generation was not significant, however. In almost all years there was no significant difference in the perceptions of how different

46. The ANOVA shows that the differences in these means were statistically significant in 2000, 2002, 2003, and 2004.

47. The ANOVA indicates that these differences were statistically significant across all years except 2001 and 2004. The relationship is consistent with Chiozza's preliminary finding (chapter 4) that educated elites in developing countries tend to be more pro-American than educated elites in industrial countries.

48. The ANOVA statistic shows that these differences were significant at the $p = 0.01$ level in all four years in which the question was asked, including 2004. It is unclear, of course, what the causal direction might be here. Are those who travel abroad more likely to have a priori a lower perception of difference (due perhaps to wealth or education qualifications that enable travel in the first place), or does travel abroad help create a less black-and-white perception of the other? We cannot explore these questions here, but most likely the relationship is endogenous. A panel study might help settle the question.

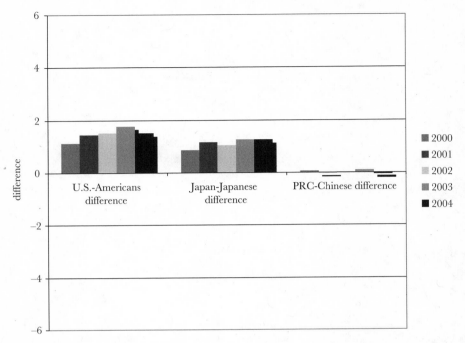

Figure 13. Difference in identity scores of the United States as a major power and Americans as people, 2000–2004. *Note:* The state identity score is the average of two trait scales, a 1–7 peaceful-warlike scale and a 1–7 constructive-unconstructive scale. Recall that the identity score for people is the average of two trait scales, a 1–7 peaceful-warlike scale and a 1–7 moral-immoral scale. *Source:* Beijing Area Study 2000–2004.

Americans and Chinese are across generations including the post-Tiananmen one.[49] These last findings are interesting because they run counter to the strong assumption in U.S. policy and punditry discourse that younger Chinese are more anti-American than older Chinese.

Overall, our findings do not confirm the view that negative sentiments toward the United States cut across socioeconomic and demographic groups, as much of the conventional wisdom in the United States implies. The BAS data do confirm the findings of the Chinese secondary literature that, like Arabs, for instance, most Chinese differentiate between the United States as a state and Americans as people.[50] From 2000 through 2004 the identity difference score for the United States as a major power is consistently higher than the score for Americans as people (see figure 13). It is also higher than the perceived difference between Japan and China. Thus,

49. These results hold for different coding schemes of the generation variable (pre- and post-1989 as well as the generation socialized between 1971 and 1988). See Johnston and Stockmann 2005.
50. Lynch, chapter 7.

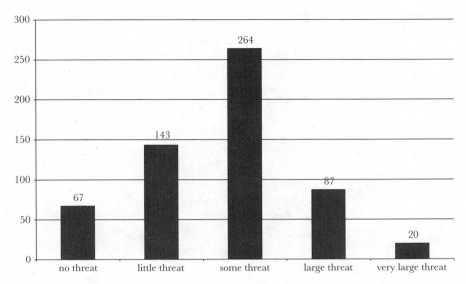

Figure 14. Distribution of responses to the question, "How much of a threat is American culture to China's own culture?" *Source:* Beijing Area Study 2004.

despite the decline over time in amity toward the United States, Chinese respondents continue to differentiate between state and people.[51]

In order to examine where Chinese urban residents fit in the cells of the Katzenstein-Keohane matrix (chapter 1) that conceptualizes how attitudes toward the United States might vary across states, we added a question to the BAS 2004 survey designed to measure beliefs that American values will adversely affect Chinese society. Respondents were asked how much of a threat American culture posed to China's own culture: a plurality of respondents chose "somewhat" (see figure 14).[52]

With our identity difference variable as the first dimension (Y axis) and the cultural threat variable as the second dimension (X axis) we were then able to describe respondents' views in the terms laid out in the matrix in chapter 1.[53] Based on much of the conventional wisdom in the United States about rising anti-Americanism in China, we would expect most respondents to hold what Keohane and Katzenstein

51. The GMI Internet polls (wave 6, November 2004) asked its elite respondents if they trusted the United States government—56.1% said no. When asked if they trusted the American people only 9% said no.

52. For exact question wording see Johnston and Stockmann 2005. We were unable to ask specifically about "U.S. values"; the survey administrators judged this to be too sensitive. Those who selected "somewhat" did *not* continuously choose "no response" or medium categories of other questions.

53. When we correlated cultural threat with perceived identity difference, we found that those two variables were not correlated (−0.05). Similarly, cultural threat and amity, the latter of which was correlated with identity differences, were not correlated (0.05). We can therefore be quite confident that the two variables constitute two separate dimensions.

Table 6.1. Matrix of perceptions of cultural threat and identity difference

Identity Difference	Cultural Threat				Keohane and Katzenstein matrix[b]
	no threat	little/some threat[a]	large/very large threat	Total	
Americans rated more positively than Chinese *OR*					
Americans and Chinese rated the same (no identity difference)	2.25% (13)	10.4% (60)	2.1% (12)	14.7%	Cells 1 and 2
Americans rated a bit more negatively than Chinese	3.3% (19)	**25.9%** **(150)**	5.7% (33)	34.9%	Cells 3 and 4
Americans rated more negatively than Chinese	3.3% (19)	**19.3%** **(112)**	5.2% (30)	27.8%	Cells 5 and 6
Americans rated much more negatively than Chinese (large identity difference)	2.8% (16)	**14.5%** **(84)**	5.4% (31)	22.6%	Cells 7 and 8
Total	11.6%	70.1%	18.3%		
Keohane and Katzenstein matrix	Cells 1, 3, 5, and 6		Cells 2, 4, 6, and 8		
N of respondents is in parentheses.					

[a] The reason for this categorization is that in Chinese "a little" and "some" are closer together conceptually than "none" and "a little." Furthermore, when comparing amity levels of those subgroups, the people who responded "some" and "little" behave more similarly to each other than those who responded "no threat" or "little threat" (see also Johnston and Stockmann 2005).

[b] Table 1.1. Matrix of perceptions of cultural threat and identity difference.

call "sovereign-nationalist" or "radical anti-American views." That is, they should cluster in cells 5 through 8 in the original matrix. The conventional U.S. characterizations of Chinese anti-Americanism would even suggest that a considerable portion has intense as opposed to latent beliefs (e.g., cells 6 and 8 in the original matrix).

The BAS data, however, suggest that the picture is more complex (see table 6.1). By disaggregating the cultural threat variable into three response categories it is clear that most respondents perceived low or no cultural threat from the United States and thus can be said to hold "latent beliefs" (cells 3, 5, and 7 in the original matrix).[54] Only a very small minority of respondents (5.4 percent) could be classified in what Keohane and Katzenstein call the radicalized and mobilized cells in their matrix (cell 8). Furthermore, although about 50 percent of respondents held either "sovereign-nationalist" or "radical" beliefs (cells 5 to 7 in the original matrix), about one-third held ambivalent or highly critical but not intense, active, or radically negative views (cells 3 and 4 in the original matrix).[55]

54. This contrasts with the Arab public's perception of the American cultural threat, according to Lynch, chapter 7.

55. We consider those with "no," "little," and "some" threat perceptions to fit into cells 1, 3, 5, and 7 of the original matrix. Those with "large" and "very large" threat perceptions fit into cells 2, 4, 6, and 8.

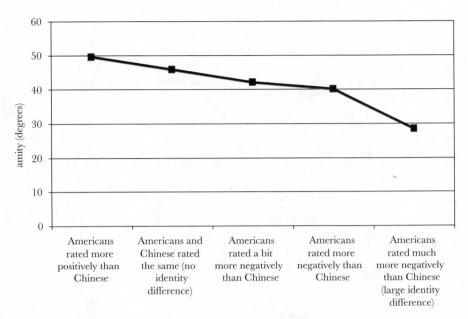

Figure 15. Mean of amity by level of perceived identity difference. *Source:* Beijing Area Study 2004.

Do the people in these cells in our revised Katzenstein-Keohane matrix have the views that the intuition behind the matrix suggests? Yes and no. It is certainly true that identity difference is related to amity; those who perceived Chinese traits to be "better" also liked the United States less. Figure 15 shows the mean amity scores toward Americans by perceived identity difference.[56]

However, the relationship between cultural threat perceptions and amity is non-linear. We found a shallow U-shaped relationship between cultural threat and amity (see figure 16).[57] Those who thought that American culture posed no threat to Chinese culture and those who thought it posed a very large threat had higher than average levels of amity.

It stands to reason that those who see no cultural threat (indeed, who may embrace U.S. culture) show higher levels of amity than average. But why would those who believe there is a very high cultural threat also express relatively higher levels of amity? A full explanation requires more space than we have here. It is possible that a portion of those who see a very large cultural threat nonetheless may not view the

56. For results of t-tests see Johnston and Stockmann 2005.

57. Differences between subgroups are larger when looking at amity levels by cultural threat perceptions *and* identity difference. When we analyzed how cultural threat perceptions and perceptions of identity difference interacted with mean levels of amity toward Americans, those with very low threat perceptions held the most negative views, no matter how different they thought Americans were from Chinese. For results see Johnston and Stockmann 2005.

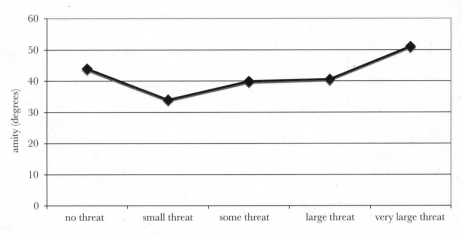

Figure 16. Mean of amity by perceived cultural threat. *Source:* Beijing Area Study 2004.

United States with too much enmity when taking into account other facets of the United States, for example, its economic relationship with China. They also may differentiate between Americans and the United States, holding higher levels of amity toward Americans as people while worrying about the cultural threat from the United States as a state.[58] Finally, nationalists may differ in their perceptions of threat: some could be dismissive (our culture is superior and dynamic, it can withstand assault from inferior cultures) while others might be hypervigilant about an external cultural threat. Regardless of which BAS 2004 question was used to tap into nationalism, strong nationalists had different views about the degree of cultural threat (see figure 17). However, a plurality of strong nationalists located themselves at the medium position (some threat). These results leave open the possibility for any hypotheses stated above to be accurate.

In a final step, we investigated whether the people in the cells of the Keohane-Katzenstein matrix differed with respect to their perceptions of Americans' sincerity or hypocrisy. In principle, charges of hypocrisy against an actor add elements of emotion and a sense of moral opprobrium to the criticisms. The BAS data suggest that cultural threat perceptions were unrelated to whether or not Beijingers regarded Americans as sincere or hypocritical (figure 18), but that identity difference *was* strongly related to views of Americans as hypocritical. As perceived American traits were more devalued, so too were Americans perceived to be more hypocritical (see figure 19).

In summarizing the data it is important to make three comparisons: across time, across socioeconomic and demographic contexts, and across countries.

58. Respondents could have interpreted the two survey questions in different ways due to question order and question wording.

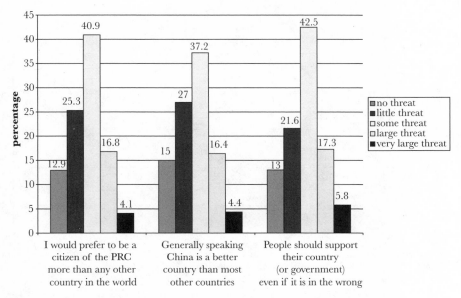

Figure 17. Cultural threat beliefs of strong nationalists. *Source:* Beijing Area Study 2004.

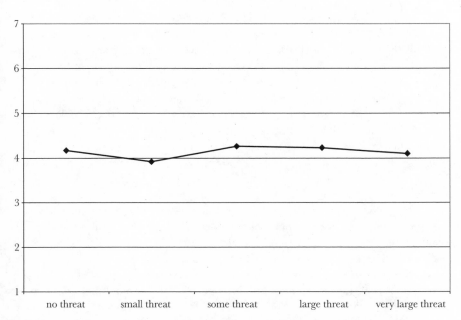

Figure 18. Cultural threat and perceptions of Americans on a 1–7 sincere-to-hypocritical scale. *Source:* Beijing Area Study 1994.

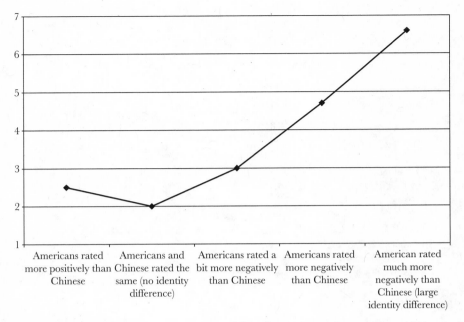

Figure 19. Identity difference and perceptions of Americans on a 1–7 sincere-to-hypocritical scale. *Source:* Beijing Area Study 1994.

Across time there has clearly been a decline in levels of amity. In the first few years the pattern of decline matched the effects of major crises in the Sino-U.S. relationship—the 1999 embassy bombing and the 2001 EP-3 incident. But in 2003 and 2004 the decline has been steady and substantial. Although we do not have the space to look at any hypotheses in detail, our hunch is that this reflects the cumulative and probably interactive effect of distress at the application of U.S. power in Iraq and closer strategic ties between the United States and Taiwan. As for perceived identity difference, this remained constant from 2000 to 2003, but increased in 2004. Again, this might reflect the cumulative effects of several years of the exercise of U.S. power after 9/11 in ways and in contexts that the Chinese do not approve.

As for cross-socioeconomic and demographic variables, the decline in amity cuts across socioeconomic and demographic groups in relative terms. Still, those who are wealthier, better educated, have traveled abroad, and are better informed about the outside world have tended to express higher levels of amity toward the United States and/or to perceive lower levels of identity difference. In many cases the signs of these differences across socioeconomic and demographic background are in the right direction, but statistical significance is inconsistent across time. It is safe to say, however, that there is still a fair amount of diversity in views of the United States and Americans.

Regarding cross-national comparisons, in the case of China the largest proportion of respondents fall into what Katzenstein and Keohane call a sovereign-nationalist category of anti-Americanism. Only a small number are radically or actively anti-American in their beliefs. Whatever level of anti-Americanism the Chinese express, they reserve their harshest, most essentializing views for Japan and the Japanese.[59] The socioeconomic and demographic differences that show up in attitudes toward the United States (at least prior to BAS 2004) disappear when it comes to Japan. This suggests that an early warning indicator of rising anti-Americanism in China would be the difference in attitudes toward the United States and Japan, assuming the latter is a relatively stable baseline for highly negative attitudes.

We turn now to see to what degree negative views of the United States seep into other domains.

Domains of Analysis

Views of U.S. Strategy on the Taiwan Question

Chinese understandings of the U.S. approach to the Taiwan issue are framed by the hegemony discourse[60] and by historical memory of the "century of humiliation."[61]

The impact of the hegemony discourse on understandings of the Taiwan issue is affected by two themes, both of which give a certain emotional edge or sharpness to Chinese views. One is the *violation of agreements* and another is *hurting feelings.*

The Chinese believe that the United States has violated its fundamental agreements with China—embodied in particular in the normalization agreement of 1979—about the status of Taiwan.[62] The Chinese and English versions of the communiqué differ in their descriptions of the U.S. views on China's ownership of the island of Taiwan. The Chinese version is much more unequivocal, claiming, basically, that the United States diplomatically endorses the PRC's view that Taiwan is a part of the PRC. So for most Chinese, the United States is violating its commitments to China by knowingly selling arms to, and politically supporting, a part of the PRC against the rest of the PRC. U.S. hegemonism is therefore not to be trusted; and in this case, it encourages separatists in Taiwan to believe they have the backing of the United States.

In addition, official China often claims that U.S. actions "hurt the feelings of the Chinese people" (*shanghai zhongguo ren de ganqing*). This sounds bizarre to most Americans: How would a dictatorship know what the feelings of the Chinese people were? The meaning of "hurting feelings" is more complex than a literal translation sug-

---

59. There are some parallels here to Lynch's finding in chapter 7 of the differences in Arab opinion toward the United States and toward Israel.

60. Wu 2004, 19.

61. See Katzenstein and Keohane, chapter 1, and McAdam, chapter 9, on the continuing impact of historical legacies on views of the United States.

62. See Zhang and Xu 2003, 263.

gests. There are at least two dimensions to hurt feelings. First, *ganqing* (feelings) is an emotional bond that develops between people or groups who believe they have a personalistic relationship based to some degree on trust and understanding.[63] Thus, violating the trust, obligation, and loyalty that cement social interaction incurs hurt feelings. A second dimension focuses more on the emotional offense taken to the actions of others. This requires a belief that the critique is somehow personal, directed perhaps at the cherished identity myths of the valued in-group. In the Chinese case, one of these myths is the notion that, as an ancient civilization, criticisms from the United States are not appropriate given China's status. As one of Chen's interviewees put it, "The United States is always hoping to lead the world on questions such as human rights, and so forth. But our China has 5,000 years of history as a civilization; the United States only has 200 plus years of history—there's no way we can obey it."[64]

So when Chinese discourse about some U.S. action refers to hurting the feelings of the Chinese people, this suggests that the United States has not only violated agreements that undergird the entire normalization of the relationship but has also violated a social relationship based on an obligation and/or done something that implies a challenge to a core component of collective self-valuation. A 2000 survey asked people in an open-ended question what American actions "hurt their feelings": the two main ones were the embassy bombing of 1999 and U.S. policy toward Taiwan.[65]

The "century of humiliation" discourse takes China's negative experiences with Western imperialism from the 1840s through the 1940s and stresses in particular how political, economic, and military weakness in the face of Western great powers and Japan led to China's semi-colonization and its loss of control of strategically important parts of its territory. The loss of Taiwan to Japan after China's defeat in 1895, for instance, was blamed, in part, on the squandering of financial resources by a corrupt semifeudal government. Taiwan was restored to China (the Republic of) after 1945. When the Nationalist Party lost the civil war, the island became the refuge for the government of the Republic of China. When the PRC was on the verge of taking control of the island in 1950, the Korean War began. China was forced to shift military resources to Korea, and the United States announced it would defend Taiwan against its liberation by the CCP. Thus the fact that Taiwan has never been controlled by the PRC is blamed on internal backwardness, military weakness, and

---

63. We benefited from the insights into *ganqing* provided by Don Keyser and Chas Freeman (personal e-mails, May 20, 2005). See also Chen and Chen 2004, 305–24.

64. Chen 2002b, 6. The phrase "hurting Chinese feelings" also reflects a tendency toward the anthropomorphization of the group in the face of sharp in-group–out-group differences. Anthropomorphization is a key feature of nationalism (Wendt 1999, 195, 219; O'Neill 1999, 11–16). Attacks on the state are personalized and emotionalized. This effect could be reinforced by the relationship between self-esteem and perceived esteem bestowed on the social group, a relationship at the heart of social identity theory. See Druckman 1994, 48–49.

65. Zhao 2001, 8.

Japanese and American imperialism. It symbolizes the PRC's incomplete sovereignty.[66]

Chinese officials give a number of reasons why the CCP considers Taiwan's formal independence to be an existential threat. One is that independence would be a strategic threat to China (an independent Taiwan will likely become a formal ally of the United States). This is a historical concern that predates CCP rule.[67] Another reason is that independence is a threat to CCP legitimacy—the Chinese population will blame the CCP leadership for selling out the country. This could possibly lead to the collapse of the party; most certainly the leadership that "lost Taiwan" would be removed. A third reason is that Taiwan's independence could encourage a domestic domino effect, strengthening the determination of Tibetan, Uighur, and Mongolian separatists.

Given this discourse, it is not surprising that the mainstream view in China sees any U.S. policies that enhance Taiwan's capacity to pursue formal independence as a challenge to China's most fundamental interests. Here the hegemony discourse is invoked to explain how the United States could possibly maintain and deepen a military and political relationship with one part of China against the rest of China. One of the general claims of the hegemony discourse is that after the collapse of the USSR the United States has worried that a rising China will challenge U.S. hegemony, and thus that China is the major obstacle to the consolidation of this U.S.-centered international system.[68] The United States hopes, therefore, to keep China weak and divided. In this context, Taiwan is an "unsinkable aircraft carrier," meaning that Taiwan could serve as a useful outpost of U.S. power to contain China within a ring of formal and informal alliances from Northeast Asia through Southeast Asia and, after 9/11, through to Central Asia. For this reason U.S. strategy is aimed at preventing unification. Thus, in this view, the U.S. and Chinese positions on an ideal solution to the Taiwan issue are essentially zero sum.

Opinion polls suggest that ordinary urban Chinese share political leaders' views about U.S. policy toward Taiwan. According to one study conducted in 2000, most respondents believed that the United States is an obstacle to unification.[69] In the Beijing Area Study we asked respondents for three years running (2001–3) which issue constituted the main threat to China's national security.[70] In 2002 and 2003 Taiwan's independence was the choice of the largest portion of respondents, and the percentage choosing this answer has increased over time (see figure 20). It is not surprising that the Chinese government routinely refers to the Taiwan issue as the most important and most sensitive in Sino-U.S. relations.

66. Huang 2003, 74. For discussions of the century of humiliation, national humiliation, and victimization discourses in China see Callahan 2005 and Gries 2004, 43–53, 69–85. Of course, humiliation and victimization discourses are central components in other nationalisms as well. See Ashley 2001.

67. Wachman 2005.

68. See Zhang and Xu 2003, 263.

69. The study combined a multicity random sample survey with a focus group–type workshop of reporters and students. See Zhao 2001, 8, 10.

70. For question wording see Johnston and Stockmann 2005.

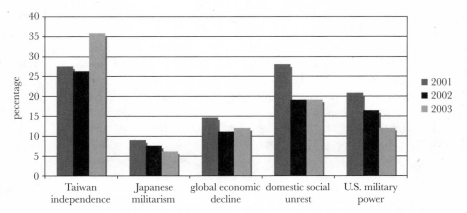

Figure 20. Main threat to Chinese national security. The increase in perceived threat from Taiwan's potential independence in 2003 is interesting because in both 2002 and 2003 BAS respondents were given two additional choices for threats to national security, Russian military power and transnational problems (e.g., AIDS and pollution). *Source:* Beijing Area Study 2000–2003.

Terrorism

As with the Taiwan question, Chinese discourses about the war on terror start with the critique of U.S. hegemony. But there is one difference: the critique of U.S. hegemonic motives behind its war on terror is tempered by the belief that terrorism is a real problem that sovereign states, including China, all face.

In the view of many, the broader strategic purpose of the U.S. war on terror is to strengthen its military relationships with other countries, to interfere in the internal affairs of other nations,[71] to spread American values, and to consolidate its dominant position in the international system. The war on terror is characterized by military preemption, violation of sovereign boundaries, unilateralism, the pursuit of "absolute security," and a lowering of the threshold of force against other sovereign states.[72] These are all the characteristics of hegemonism.[73] Yet the effect of these policies is to exacerbate extreme nationalism and to challenge local social and cultural beliefs. One result is the emergence of large-scale organized terrorism.[74] Thus there is a symbiotic relationship between modern terrorism and the militaristic U.S.

71. Chinese commentators suspect a double standard when the United States criticizes China for using counterterrorism as the justification for cracking down on minorities (e.g., the United States downplays the seriousness of separatist terror to China's integrity relative to the Islamic terrorist threat to the United States).

72. For an ideological explanation of these features that stresses U.S. exceptionalism and messianism see Tang 2004, 13–14. For a historical-materialist explanation (mainly coming from neo-left nationalists) see Fang 2003, 7–16. And for a traditional realpolitik explanation that stresses the U.S. use of the war on terror to consolidate its military dominance of international relations, see Wang 2002b, 136.

73. Indeed, according to military analysts, the main threat to global peace is not terrorism but hegemonism. See Ba 2002, 38–39.

74. Shen 2002, 154–55.

response. These are not necessarily mutually constitutive—they each have other origins—but their development is interactive. The United States is paying for its violent history of intervention, sanctions, and coercion in the Middle East, its dependence on Middle East oil, its rigid support of Israel's policies toward the Palestinians, and its almost exclusive reliance on national military power to fight terrorism.[75]

Cutting across much of the Chinese commentary on the war on terror, however, is a notion that the war is not wholly a bad thing. There are two basic arguments here. One is that terrorism poses a real threat to sovereign states, including China, and the fight against terrorism is generally a just one.[76] This has meant, in the view of a respected expert on U.S. foreign policy in a government think tank, that the Chinese are generally less critical or less vocal about U.S. interventionism in the war on terror than about humanitarian interventions such as Kosovo.[77] Another analyst implied—almost reminiscent of the line that "we are all Americans"—that the United States and China share a common danger, although Americans face even greater challenges.[78] At the highest levels of the Chinese leadership there was also genuine shock and horror at the 9/11 attack.[79]

A second argument about why China should support the war on terror concerns the implications for Sino-U.S. relations. Since 9/11 President Bush has sought China's cooperation in the war on terror, and he has declared that China is not an enemy. Although 9/11 and the subsequent increase in leader-to-leader contacts between China and the United States did not lead to a complete transformation of Bush's view of China as a potential competitor, it did lead to a more well-rounded one. Basically, 9/11 created an opportunity in the relationship for dialogue and improved understanding.[80]

This is certainly not to say that all Chinese were or are sympathetic to the American predicament. There was a fair amount of schadenfreude expressed after 9/11, particularly by urban youth.[81] The state evidently determined that this attitude was not constructive and tried to some degree to replace it with a more sympathetic view. Universities were required to show a movie that portrayed the Americans in a more sympathetic light.[82]

In sum, the discourse about terrorism is infused by a critique of hegemonism. But unlike the Taiwan issue, the Chinese accept the legitimacy of some U.S. actions. There is a degree of empathy and shared fate as sovereign states facing a common enemy. In the Taiwan case Chinese often lament that if only the United States correctly understood its broader strategic interests (cooperation with China), it would see that its Taiwan policy is counterproductive. In the terrorism case, Chinese

75. Wang 2002a.
76. See Zhang 2004, 48. See also Ba 2002, 37.
77. See Yuan 2001, 19–20.
78. See Wang 2002a, 1–2.
79. Conversation with senior Foreign Ministry official, October 2003.
80. See Yuan 2001, 20–21.
81. Chen 2004.
82. Ibid.

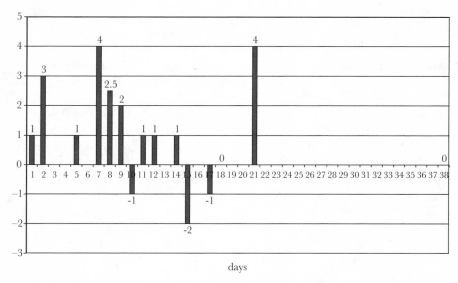

Figure 21. Trends in positive to negative terms referring to the United States in articles on tsunami assistance. *Source: China Daily*, December 28, 2004–February 3, 2005.

recognize that to a certain degree—at least in most of its interactions with the Chinese—the United States understands its strategic interests.[83]

Tsunami Assistance

The South Asian tsunami disaster of December 2004, while horrific, did not involve issues central to the Sino-U.S. relationship. Thus, we are interested in whether coverage of the United States exhibited any systematic negativity on an issue that, in principle, might be seen as distinct from China's concerns about U.S. hegemony. We are also interested in how much of an altruism gap there was in Chinese coverage: To what degree was China's contribution portrayed as selfless in *explicit* contrast to the American contribution?

To answer these questions we conducted a quantitative content analysis of tsunami stories in the *China Daily*. We used a computer program that isolates positively and negatively valenced words within a certain distance (thirty characters) of words referring to the United States.[84] The intuition is that the relative frequency of positive and negative terms provides a reasonable indication of positive or negative

83. For more details see Johnston and Stockmann 2005.

84. We examined the *China Daily* for three main reasons: (1) the computer program (Yoshikoder) at the time of writing could not analyze Chinese-language articles; (2) the *China Daily* is published in English for both foreign *and* domestic audiences; (3) the search engine provided us with articles published in the print version, not articles that appeared online only. To check whether our results were biased due to newspaper selection, we also observed Chinese media sources that publish and broadcast in Chinese. For further information on software and newspaper selection, the sampling method, data manipulation, and measurement see Johnston and Stockmann 2005.

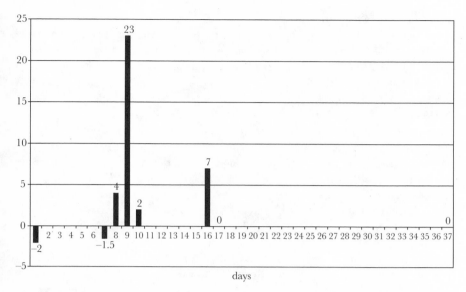

Figure 22. Trends in the difference of reporting about China and the United States in articles on tsunami assistance (China-United States). *Source: China Daily*, December 28, 2004–February 3, 2005.

valuation of the United States. The results show that, on average, the wording before and after references to the United States was slightly positive (+–0.95) (see figure 21). Only one article (January 6, 2005) was explicitly biased against the U.S. contribution—in the sense that the claims reflected a worst-case inference about American intentions. But in this case the bias came in a quote from the leader of the Tamil Tigers, in which he charged that the U.S. military's relief operations in the region might be used as a cover to spy on the rebels and assist the counterinsurgency in Sri Lanka. The article alluded to the stereotype of the United States pursuing a one-sided, self-serving, and hegemonistic foreign policy. There was no counterbalancing statement in the article. But as one of eighteen articles, this kind of story was the exception.

Other media occasionally put U.S. assistance in a hegemonistic light. One newspaper article argued that U.S. naval deployments were designed to change of the poor image of the United States in the region as part of an "investment" in improving its national security.[85] It featured an imposing picture of a U.S. aircraft carrier. Another short article in the same paper covered the criticisms of the expense of the Bush inauguration in light of the disaster in South Asia.[86] Still, television coverage tended to avoid any all-out criticisms of the U.S. effort.

As for an "altruism gap," reporting about the United States was, on average, about 1.5 words less positive than reporting about China (figure 22).[87] This is not surprising

85. See *Nanfang Ribao* (January 12, 2005), A9.
86. Ibid. (January 9, 2005), 5.
87. Average reporting on the United States was +0.96, on China +2.4. For explanation of measurement see Johnston and Stockmann 2005.

since work in social identity theory has established that people generally are inclined to feel sympathetic toward groups to which they belong, because they are motivated to retain a positive self-image. Reporting started off with a couple of articles about American assistance that tended to be slightly more positive than those about reports mentioning the PRC. But after the first week of January the tone changed; from then on the gap between reporting about Chinese and American aid widened.

Although U.S. assistance was not especially singled out as stingy, China's was singled out as altruistic. Television coverage, for instance, featured Chinese executives talking about what their businesses had contributed to relief funds. There were lots of images of citizens or employees lining up to put donations in boxes and stories of children donating money after seeing pictures of Southeast Asian students who had lost their schools. There were frequent broadcasts of a Chinese version of "We Are the World" sung by Chinese pop stars.[88] One station broadcast a show with songs and entertainment to raise money and to show the world China's "love."[89] The evening news on CCTV 9 on January 9, 2005, noted that the Chinese people had donated 100 million renminbi, and that China's Red Cross had been singled out by the International Committee of the Red Cross in East Asia for the speed with which it sent cash to the region.

In principle, noncoverage of an action can be as important a signal as extensive coverage. Given the relative size of different countries' contributions, Chinese coverage of U.S. and Japanese efforts could have been extensive. It was not. But the fact that the Chinese media did not go out of its way to critique U.S. assistance is at least some indication of a firewall between the hegemonism discourse and this particular international issue.

Images of the United States and Consumer Behavior

Do negative attitudes toward the United States negatively affect consumer choices about buying American brands, eating American fast food, or watching American movies? If there is an effect, this would be evidence that negative images and attitudes spill over into day-to-day activities, an indicator of bias in the sense developed in chapter 1. In addition, analyzing various areas of consumer behavior will give us some clue about how "active" anti-American sentiments are.[90]

Consumer Products   American consumer products are well-known, highly respected, very popular, and considered very influential in China.[91] In macrohistorical terms

88. CCTV 4, January 6, 2005.

89. CCTV 9 (English), January 9, 2005.

90. It is hard to get systematic time-series data on consumer behavior in China. Ideally one might look for changes in the sales volumes of particular products as the state of Sino-U.S. relations changes. Unfortunately, acquiring these data is very difficult because most major companies consider this confidential information. In lieu of such data, we rely on three kinds of evidence: interviews with U.S. businesspeople in Beijing, a small case study of McDonald's, and data on the consumption of McDonald's food and American movies.

91. Liu et al. 2004; Horizon 1997, 669–86.

this is quite a change. In the past, as one scholar remarked, "the idea was that China should be independent and self-reliant. It was politically incorrect to be *chong yang mei wai* ('worship foreign things'). Now people appear to be less and less concerned about this. To Chinese state and consumers alike, the main criterion is whether the product is a good buy."[92] This standard applies to American products as well.[93]

Survey results show that American computers, beauty products, and food products are doing quite well.[94] According to a 2001 Chinese Academy of Social Science study, cars, cosmetics, and computers were perceived as cutting edge (*ganjue gaodang*), well designed, and of good quality.[95] Our semistructured interviews with American business and marketing specialists in China confirmed those results.[96] As one interviewee from the American Chamber of Commerce pointed out: "Despite the problems in Sino-U.S. relations, [American products are perceived] overwhelmingly positively. I am always amazed. American products are highly favored in the market, they are perceived as being of high quality, the best technology, new, cutting-edge stuff."[97] Overall, when looking at the image of American products in China, we find little evidence of systematically negative views.

Does negativity toward other aspects of the United States influence consumer behavior? After all, China has a history of boycotting foreign products during periods of international conflict.[98] In 1999, after the bombing of the Chinese embassy in Belgrade, demonstrators threw garbage in front of American fast food chains in order to prevent people from entering. Some nationalists called for boycotting McDonald's and KFC.[99] If active anti-Americanism exists in China, we would expect lower sales volumes of American products when Sino-U.S. relations are tense. It is possible that those who hold radical views opposing the United States might permanently avoid purchasing U.S. products. However, during periods of political conflict, we would expect that some consumers would respond to a U.S. action by boycotting American products.

92. Jia 2005, 16.

93. See Johnston and Stockman 2005 for more details.

94. For example, in an Internet study conducted by Horizon in 2004, American-made computers were most often ranked the favorite (see Horizon 2005). Middle-income respondents in the 2001 CASS survey most often named American brands when asked which cosmetic and food products they liked: 43% named Olay as a cosmetic product, while 44% named Pepsi and 42% Coca-Cola.

95. According to a personal interview with one of the researchers, the survey was based on personal interviews with urban residents in Beijing, Shanghai, and Guangzhou (n = 1,500) by trained interviewers. Sampling was done according to probability proportional to size (PPS), a form of stratified random sampling. See also Liu et al. 2003.

96. Interviews were conducted between April 14 and May 19, 2005. Respondents were asked about the most popular American-identified products in China, what American images were used to sell products, whether international events influence sales in a positive or negative way, and whether the marketing strategies change due to sensitivity to perceived popular attitudes toward the United States (for example, after the bombing of the Belgrade embassy in 1999). Three interviews were face-to-face, two were by phone, and one was by e-mail.

97. Interview in Beijing, May 19, 2005.

98. See Gerth 2003. Slogans similar to those from the early twentieth century were shouted during the 2005 anti-Japanese demonstrations in Beijing (interview with participant, Beijing, May 14, 2005).

99. Interview with a bystander in Beijing, April 8, 2005.

To test this hypothesis we asked our interviewees about whether and how international events have influenced sales volumes of U.S. firms in China since 1998.[100] The responses differed somewhat. One interviewee from the American Chamber of Commerce pointed out that, based on talking to representatives of U.S. firms in China, there was no correlation between political events and sales volumes among the general population. A second interviewee confirmed that 9/11, the war on Iraq, and Jiang Zemin's visit to the United States had no impact on sales of American products. However, visits of U.S. presidents to China influenced sales slightly in a positive way. Both the bombing of the Chinese embassy in Belgrade and the EP-3 incident had negative effects on sales, but the impact of the embassy bombing was larger, taking about two weeks to wear off.[101] Overall, international events that caused changes in the public's view of the United States were not strongly related to consumption of American products. If there was any impact at all, it was small and short term.[102]

The perceptions of our interviewees that negative images of the United States rarely intrude in consumers' decisions is consistent with Global Market Insite's Internet surveys in late 2004 and early 2005. Internet users are wealthier, younger, more connected to the global economy, and more computer literate than most urban Chinese, let alone rural Chinese. But these are individuals who are also quite critical of U.S. domestic politics and foreign policy. In GMI wave 5 (October 2004) respondents were asked whether the U.S. war on terror had made them less willing to fly on an American airline. A small majority said yes, but when asked why, the main reason was fear of a terrorist attack (89.9 percent), not a desire to boycott the United States (13.5 percent). In wave 6 (November 2004) when asked "Has your willingness to purchase American products changed as a result of recent American foreign policy and military action?" 69.6 percent answered "no change." When asked whether they might change their purchasing habits for specific products, about 10 percent said they absolutely would avoid McDonald's, but 60 percent said they would not change their buying habits, and 12 percent said they would increase their purchases somewhat. Results for Microsoft software were essentially the same. In short, the effects of negative views of U.S. foreign policy on self-reported consumer behavior were relatively small.

Finally, it appears that efforts to mobilize boycotts of American products are minimal and unsuccessful. A Google search of the slogan "boycott American goods" (*dikang meihuo*) produced only six hits. In comparison, searching for the same keywords with respect to Japan had more than eighty-five thousand hits.[103] Overall, our

---

100. Interviewees were presented with a timetable of major events related to Sino-U.S. relations since 1998: President Clinton's visit (1998), the embassy bombing in Belgrade (1999), the EP-3 incident (2001), 9/11 (2001), President Bush's first and second visits (2001 and 2002), Jiang Zemin's visit to the United States (2002), and the war on Iraq (2003).

101. Interviews May 19, 2005, and April 28, 2005, respectively.

102. One reason might be that the quality of the product is more influential when consumers make up their mind about which product to buy. Interview with an advertising company executive in Beijing, May 25, 2005.

103. Accessed May 25, 2005. Results are similar when using different search engines (Sohu and Baidu).

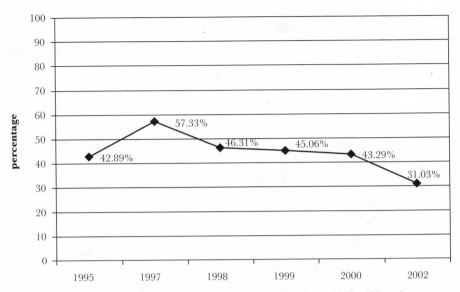

Figure 23. Percentage of Beijing respondents who self-report eating at McDonald's at least once a year. *Note:* Data is based on (PPS) random samples conducted in eight to ten districts of Beijing between 1995 and 2002. For more details on survey methodology and question wording, see Johnston and Stockmann 2005. *Source:* IMI Information Market Research Institute.

analysis suggests that the link between negative views of the United States and consumer behavior is weak.

Fast Food   McDonald's ought to be an obvious symbol of the United States in China, as many think it has become around the world. According to GMI Internet polls in late 2004 and early 2005, as many as 64.4 percent of Chinese respondents viewed McDonald's as an "extremely" or "very" American product. Thus attitudes toward, or purchases at, McDonald's might be a good test of whether images of the United States have an impact on consumer behavior. Unfortunately, we do not have access to the kind of data—monthly or yearly time-series sales volumes per store— that might allow us to test this relationship fairly efficiently. In lieu of this we look at two types of information: annual time-series data on the percentage of Beijing residents who self-reported eating at McDonald's in each year; and information on how McDonald's has fared in general in the China market, what kind of image it uses to attract customers, and how its relationship with its customers has evolved over time.

The percentage of those surveyed who report going to McDonald's at least once a year has declined somewhat over time, particularly between 2000 and 2002 (see figure 23). Although this may have been due to an intervening event such as the EP-3 incident of April 2001, the Belgrade bombing of May 1999, an event of far more

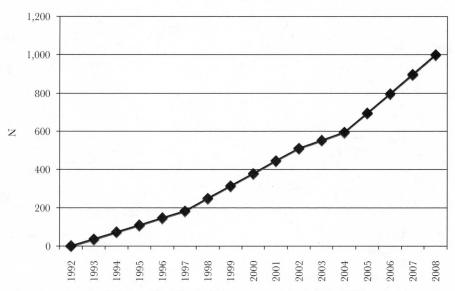

Figure 24. Growth of McDonald's outlets in China, 1992–2008 (projected). *Note*: Based on data points for 1992, 1997, 2002, and 2004, and on company projections for 2008. *Sources:* Reuters, September 25, 2002, and August 13, 2004; Bloomberg News, September 23, 2004; *China Daily*, January 15, 2004; Dow Jones Newswire, December 10, 2004.

emotional impact on Chinese citizens, appears to have had no effect. We suspect, then, that this overall decline in self-reporting about eating at McDonald's could simply reflect a growth in fast food alternatives in Beijing.

McDonald's has not yet been the target of a serious boycott. For a short time after the embassy bombing in 1999 some students and even families stopped eating there, but this did not last, and it appears not to have had much impact on the growth of the chain in China. Indeed, based on news reporting, the interpolated growth of McDonald's stores across China has been, and is planned to be, fairly steady (see figure 24).

The marketing of McDonald's in China does not hide its American connection. But neither does it go out of its way to identify itself as an American product. The ads include wholesome Asian hip-hop imagery, with images of young men (and some women), often on skateboards. The most recent ad campaign, "Wo jiu xihuan," is essentially a Chinese version of the U.S. campaign "I'm lovin' it."[104]

McDonald's appeals to a wide range of consumers. It is a favorite of young, educated, computer-literate males. Of the 1,000 respondents to a GMI Internet survey conducted in 2004, 583 listed their top choices for fast food, and McDonald's was

104. For more images of an urban hip-hop motif see also McDonald's China 2005.

the second most popular destination (31%).[105] Despite the comparatively high prices, McDonald's also attracts urban families and older people. It is a place where families can eat in relatively clean and bright conditions. By far the largest portion of McDonald's customers eat there with family or relatives.[106] It is used for hosting children's birthday parties. It is a place for retired people to gather and chat or take their grandchildren.

McDonald's has become localized.[107] It is a social space or experience rather than just an American product. It contrasts with the foreign products—everyday goods such as clothes, cigarettes, makeup, and personal hygiene products—that were boycotted in the first half of the twentieth century.[108] In those days foreign goods were daily evidence of China's "sick man of Asia" status. Today, however, the McDonald's phenomenon occurs at a time when Chinese leaders believe national greatness is linked to integration with the global economy. In short, at this moment in history there appears to be very little portending the successful use of McDonald's as a target of anti-American sentiment.

Movies   We use two sets of data about moviegoing in Beijing to judge the effects of images of the United States. The first is time-series data from the IMI Information Market Research Institute. It randomly sampled Beijing residents in five years, from 1998 to 2003, asking respondents to choose their favorite movies by country of origin. A plurality of respondents consistently selected American movies as one of their favorites (see figure 25).[109] Until recently, the slight downward trend in the level of liking appeared to have benefited mainland movies.[110] But most recently the competition U.S. films face is from other foreign films, not Chinese ones.[111] The important point is that the decline does not appear to be a function of specific shocks to Sino-U.S. relations—for instance, there was no apparent effect from the Belgrade bombing.

Disaggregating these data, certain socioeconomic factors appear to have important effects. U.S. movies are especially popular among people younger than thirty-five (the targets of the patriotic education campaigns after Tiananmen!) and those with high school and university educations.

The second set of data comes from the BAS 2004 survey in which we asked how much respondents like to watch American movies. This provides a bit more detail about the attitude strength of U.S. movie liking. The average Beijinger did not like

---

105. KFC (Kentucky Fried Chicken) was the most popular (49.3%). This is not surprising since there are many more KFC stores in China.

106. According to IMI Information Market Research Institute data, from 1995 to 2003, anywhere from 55 to 65% of those respondents who went to McDonald's went with family or relatives.

107. Watson 1997, 1–38; Yan 1997, 39–76; Yan 2000, 201–25.

108. Gerth 2003, 58–63.

109. Respondents could select more than one answer category. For more details on question wording see Johnston and Stockmann 2005.

110. Changes in percentages might also be related to changes in survey methodology. For more details on survey techniques see Johnston and Stockmann 2005.

111. For further discussion of the development of the Chinese film market see Rosen 2002.

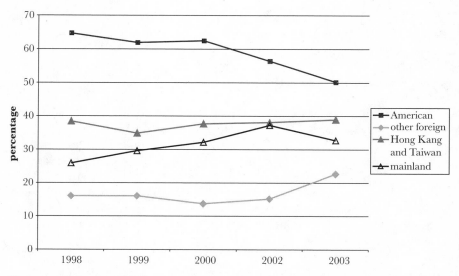

Figure 25. Percentage of Beijing respondents who like (*xihuan*) films from their own and other countries. *Source:* IMI Information Market Research Institute.

to watch them all that much (figure 26). Only 43.3 percent liked to watch American movies at least a bit (see the left three categories in figure 26) and only about 4 percent were fans. We speculate that those who said American movies were one of their favorites for the most part did *not* have strong preferences for U.S. movies.[112]

The data suggest that those who are better off and more educated, as well as those who have studied English and those who surf the Internet, tend to like American movies more. However, we did not find significant relationships between amity, identity difference, or perceived cultural threat and American movie liking.[113] Overall, our analysis of the BAS and IMI data suggests that the downward trend in American movie liking over time is not primarily related to political events and changes in attitudes toward the United States.

To summarize, when it comes to consumption of American products, food, and movies, negative images of the United States do not appear to affect overt behavior much.[114] People might, for example, perceive U.S. culture as a threat to Chinese

112. Differences in question wording between IMI and BAS make it difficult to link the results of the two surveys. In contrast to the BAS, the IMI question refers to watching movies at the movie theater, thus excluding VCDs and DVDs (both very popular in China). Differences in survey results might also be caused by differences in sampling techniques. See Johnston and Stockmann 2005 for more details.

113. We analyzed average levels of movie liking by amity, identity difference, and perceived cultural threat. Amity was slightly positively related to movie liking. See also Johnston and Stockmann 2005.

114. It might affect attitudes toward the political system and other types of political activism. Although we do not have data to observe political behavior, much of the literature on political participation suggests that most of the time attitudes do not affect political behavior much. See, for example, Verba, Schlozman, and Brady 1995.

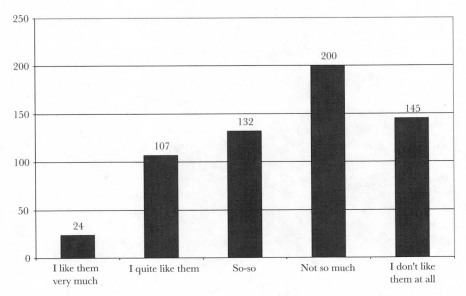

Figure 26. Frequency distribution of American movie liking. *Source:* Beijing Area Study 2004.

cultural values while at the same time they do not believe a burger from McDonald's is part of that threat. There is considerable distance between the population's consumption of U.S. cultural products and what authoritative government voices think the United States is trying to do with these products. Wang Hunning, later a close adviser to Jiang Zemin, wrote in 1994 that U.S. hegemony was being consolidated through the export of values.[115] This Gramscian-type argument resonates with cultural cadres, officials in the propaganda system, and cultural nationalists. Indeed, one of the more prominent critiques of globalization in China is that it constitutes an attack on Chinese cultural values and "ways of doing things," including forms of consumption and daily lifestyles. The blunter claim—heard more immediately after the Tiananmen crackdown, but still part of contemporary discourse—is that American culture, including consumer culture, is part of a peaceful evolution strategy aimed at undermining socialism in China. To some degree this claim is still a driver behind government policies to control information and cultural flows across China's borders.

Directions for Future Research and Implications of Findings

All the information about Chinese attitudes toward the United States—whether the anecdotal impressions of U.S. pundits and politicians or more systematic qualitative

115. Fewsmith 2001, 146.

and quantitative data—comes from urban China. Moreover, while we have used multicity studies data from other surveys and studies, most of the information we used in this chapter comes from Beijing, or Beijing-based scholars, analysts, officials, and interviewees. Many foreigners come to Beijing for work or travel. Beijingers thus are more familiar with Americans and the United States than those living in more remote parts of the country. So we are reluctant to generalize too much about "Chinese" views of the United States.

With that caveat in mind our analysis suggests the following. First, at all levels—official, media, intellectual, and mass—attitudes toward U.S. foreign policy are substantially negative, particularly so on the Taiwan issue. The default position on U.S. foreign policy is that it is hegemonic, arrogant, and, in China's case, aimed at preventing China's legitimate rise as an economically developed major power. Although there is debate at the margins about how proactive the United States is in trying to contain China's power or keep Taiwan permanently separate, the hegemony frame is hegemonic.

Second, this baseline suspicion of and hostility toward U.S. foreign policy bleeds into domains that are closer in some sense to traditional realpolitik security interests. So, for instance, U.S. counterterrorism policy is seen as an extension of U.S. hegemonic strategy, a neoimperialism that relies even more blatantly on military power to impose U.S. interests. But even in this domain there are some limits to this critique in that there is some empathy with the U.S. fight against violent nonstate actors. In domains even further removed from security issues—tsunami relief and American consumer products—there is no strong evidence that baseline negative beliefs about U.S. motives or American characteristics are the main driver of attitudes or behavior. We did not find an anti-American bias—a "pervasive condescension and denigration"[116] of all aspects of American political, ideological, and cultural identity traits—cutting across all domains. However, we realize that attitudes toward the United States and Americans are dynamic (the former less stable than the latter for the moment). As we suggested earlier, it would be a worthwhile project to continually monitor the strength of these firewalls between domains.

Third, there has been a substantial decline in the overall amity toward the United States as expressed by ordinary Chinese citizens (from Beijing). The main drivers of this decline are not clear. Up until the past couple of years it appeared to be a function of high-profile shocks to the U.S.-China relationship (the 1999 embassy bombing, the 2001 EP-3 incident). In the last couple of years there have not been these kinds of crises. Instead, from the Chinese perspective there has been a major U.S. war against Iraq in which the UN Security Council was essentially circumvented. There has also been a symbolic U.S.-Japanese affirmation of a joint interest in a peaceful solution to the Taiwan issue (read in Beijing as an affirmation that both would defend Taiwan if the PRC attacked). There is more acute awareness of the current U.S. leadership's efforts to consolidate American primacy, and there is more concern about deeper and wider U.S.-Taiwanese military cooperation, among other

116. Katzenstein and Keohane, chapter 10.

trends. Together these might be having a cumulative effect on attitudes toward the United States. Amity toward the United States is reaching levels as low as those for Japan a few years ago, and the degree of identity difference between Chinese and Americans may be increasing. Although attitudes toward the United States and Americans are substantially more positive than those toward Japan and the Japanese, we think we have established a rough baseline for attitudes toward the United States and a reasonable early warning indicator to watch, namely, the trends in difference between attitudes toward the United States and toward Japan. More research is also needed to examine why amity toward the United States is declining.

In some contrast to all this bad news for the United States, there is some not-so-bad news. First, levels of amity and identity difference generally vary in ways we might expect. Those who are wealthier, better educated, better traveled, and interested in information about the outside world have tended to like the United States more than poorer and not as well educated Chinese, and they have tended to perceive lower identity differences as well. These relationships do not hold in every year of our time series. But they are generally what one might expect as a result of China's increasing engagement in global economic and political institutions over the past twenty-five years. Second, Chinese do not seem to hold the actively radical anti-American attitudes that, as Keohane and Katzenstein posit, are a product of high degrees of identity difference and perceived U.S. cultural threat. Our findings suggest that Chinese attitudes are not at this point yet, although they might move toward it if the declining trend in sentiments continues. Rather, most respondents perceive moderate levels of cultural threat and moderate to high levels of identity difference. Unfortunately, we do not have any data that would allow us to examine the behavioral preferences vis-à-vis the United States that respondents who hold these views might have.

How, then, might one summarize attitudes toward the United States using the (modified) categories from the introductory chapter? In our view there is a substantial amount of distrust, even anger (an issue of what people do), but these attitudes are still quite distant from the level of hatred and bias (an issue of who people are) that is directed at Japan and the Japanese. Some of this distrust is based on perceptions of American dispositions, for example, hegemony rooted in American exceptionalism and the arrogance of the American creed. Some is based on situational assessments of U.S. behavior, for example, U.S. violations of its agreements with China on Taiwan. The anger manifests itself in perceptions that the United States is bullying China, is trying to keep China weak, and employs double standards in its policies toward China. The "century of humiliation" historical memory appears to be the prism through which this behavior is refracted and bestowed with more emotional content.

What are some of the implications of these characteristics in attitudes toward the United States for Chinese foreign policy in practice and in theory? First, contrary to the conventional wisdom we did not find that the regime is proactively timing the production of negative images of the United States to prime attitudes among the population for discrete policy initiatives. Rather, when exogenous shocks occur or when it is anticipating negative signals from the United States, the regime responds with messages to guide and constrain popular reactions. The regime believes it faces a legitimacy problem. Thus it has to walk a fine line between allowing public expressions of negativity (thereby boosting its nationalist credentials but risking large-scale protests that might turn against the regime and harm its international image) and constraining popular anger (thereby maintaining public order and protecting its external image but threatening the regime's internal legitimacy). Call this a legitimacy dilemma. This reactive legitimacy dilemma is evident in the regime's management of some anti-American and anti-Japanese demonstrations in 1999 and in 2005, respectively.[117] It is also evident from the predictability of the upticks in negative comments about the United States. For instance, criticisms of alleged U.S. double standards almost always peak in anticipation of or reaction to the annual U.S. human rights report.

Second, and relatedly, there is some degree of interactivity between the decline in amity toward the United States and perceptions of U.S. actions. The Chinese are responding to U.S. behavior and to the instability in the U.S.-China relationship. To the degree that the United States and China are increasingly locked in an unstable security dilemma, one should expect trends in perceptions of the United States to continue, and perhaps begin to seep into a wider range of domains of popular attitude and behavior.[118] But the China case suggests that there are three interactive variables that affect the speed and stability of security dilemmas: (self-perceived) legitimacy problems, historical memory, and popular perceptions of the other. Security dilemmas will evolve faster as the regime's internal legitimacy dilemma sharpens, when historical memory is primed for zero-sum interpretations of the other's behavior, and when identity difference is increasingly stark.[119] The intensification of security dilemmas, in turn, can increase the legitimacy dilemma, the prominence of zero-sum memories, and identity differences. One thing to look for is the degree to which Chinese officials and the population come to believe that an international power transition is actively desirable (and achievable). This will signal a change from the more status quo–oriented worldview of the last decade or so back to a more revisionist one in China. Barring an unpredictably radical change of regime in China, if such a reorientation occurs it will likely be a result of security dilemma dynamics. The dilemma might become acute enough for the Chinese to decide that U.S. power and hegemony is a fundamental threat to China's existence.

Finally, our findings have some implications for thinking about democratization and democratic peace. Much of the writing speculating about how democratization will affect China's foreign policy draws (often inaccurately) from Mansfield and Snyder,[120] and concludes that democratization promises to lead to more anti-Americanism and hypernationalism in Chinese foreign policy. The implications of

---

117. On the interaction between state censorship and media content see Stockmann forthcoming.

118. On the emerging U.S.-China security dilemma, see Johnston 2004a.

119. For important insights into how identity construction can sharpen security dilemmas, see Lyall 2005.

120. Mansfield and Snyder 1995.

our findings are somewhat less pessimistic. They suggest that the process of democratization may be critical to the outcome in foreign policy. If the process is one in which the preferences of educated urban middle classes with reasonably strong connections or access to the outside world are articulated in the policy process, we would expect to see foreign policy outcomes that are relatively less anti-American and hypernationalist than if these socioeconomic groups are shut out of the process. This is why we find the data on attitudes toward the United States in the last couple of years worrying. It is also why, to repeat, we believe a continuous comparison of the nature and intensity of attitudes toward the United States and Japan is needed. If the difference between views of the United States and of Japan continues, then an urban middle-class–centered democratization process ought to dampen the security dilemma dynamics in Sino-U.S. relations, while not changing domestic constraints on policy toward Japan all that much. If, on the other hand, the differences across socioeconomic groups in amity and perceptions of identity difference toward the United States fade, then we would have to revise our cautiously optimistic prediction about democratization.

7

Anti-Americanisms in the Arab World

MARC LYNCH

The findings of the 2003 Pew Global Attitudes Project survey that the bottom had fallen out of support for the United States in the Muslim world galvanized official and popular attention around the threat to national security posed by rampant anti-Americanism in the Arab world. Does this crisis of anti-Americanism really exist? As Timothy Mitchell puts it, most analysis of anti-Americanism in the region portrays it as "something elusive and yet ubiquitous . . . elusive because we are given no concrete evidence of it."[1] Marching crowds of protestors burning American flags tell us little about their motivations or the real depth of anger (protests could be manufactured by regimes for their own purposes, or they might be veiled protests against the regime itself using the only publicly permissible language). Public opinion surveys in authoritarian societies are fraught with methodological difficulties, ranging from the natural suspicion of strangers asking sensitive political questions to the conflation of different sources of anger. Editorials in most Arab newspapers are shaped by particular political interests and restrictions, in such a way that anti-Americanism in the Egyptian press could reflect an official regime strategy as easily as a genuine popular outrage. Complicating this further is an American tendency to interpret all political activity through an American lens, so that everything—Lebanese protests against Syria, Egyptian protests against Egyptian president Hosni Mubarak, Islamist railing against sexual imagery on television—must somehow be *about* America.

Analyses of Arab anti-Americanism have long been trapped in an unproductive standoff between explanations that consider it essentially a rational response to U.S.

For helpful comments, I thank Dale Eickelman, John Bowen, Charles Hirschkind, Shibley Telhami, the participants in workshops at Cornell University and Stanford University, and especially Peter Katzenstein and Bob Keohane.

1. Mitchell 2004, 88.

policies and those that consider it essentially irrational, explainable by some cultural, political, or civilizational pathology. Barry Rubin suggests that the disconnect between Arab perceptions of U.S. policies and American self-conceptions can only be explained by some pathology of Arab political culture. Fouad Ajami argues that anti-Americanism in the region stems from a cultural backlash against the modernity embodied by the United States, driven by the resentments engendered by civilizational failure ("the envy of the failed for the successful") and the stifling realities of domestic economic and political stagnation.[2] On the other side, many analysts argue that Arab anti-Americanism is a rational response to specific U.S. policies and that changing those policies would fairly quickly burst the anti-American bubble. Both views are unsatisfying. If policies have nothing to do with anti-Americanism, then why did such sentiments spike in 2002, in direct response to U.S. policies such as support for the Israeli reoccupation of the West Bank, President Bush's "Axis of Evil" speech, and the U.S. invasion of Iraq? If U.S. policies alone explain anti-Americanism, then how do we explain its persistence (among at least some sectors) across different administrations with what appear to be very different policies (Clinton's honest brokering of Israeli-Palestinian peace negotiations versus George W. Bush's vocal support for Ariel Sharon)?

The two might be reconciled by considering the role of the *schemas* through which Arabs interpret political developments. Arab public discourse is dominated by a well-entrenched narrative identifying America as generally hostile, aggressive, and untrustworthy. It is grounded in historical memories of specific U.S. policies and fueled by ongoing grievances with those policies. The deeply rooted *distrust* of American intentions is nicely captured by the opening words of one February 2003 al-Jazeera television program: "Who believes America?"[3] This distrust is not a permanent and unchangeable feature of Arab culture. Arab attitudes toward the United States were quite positive in earlier eras, especially after the Suez crisis when the United States was seen as a powerful force against European colonialism. It has, however, become increasingly entrenched in recent years, spilling over into almost every domain. Even more crucially, fear of American power is increasingly embedded within a deeply ingrained narrative at the heart of Arab identity.

Anti-American attitudes are therefore more than simply "political opinion," which could be expected to change relatively fluidly with political events. But these attitudes also demonstrate sensitivity to changes in U.S. foreign policy that would not be expected if there were a fully ingrained "bias." A very strong distrust characterizes Arab attitudes toward America, but this distrust is not yet so deeply entrenched that it resists change, and—crucially—it is most often articulated in the idiom of *hypocrisy* (failure to live up to professed values) than in a comprehensive rejection of professed American values. In contrast to anti-Israeli attitudes, which are far more fixed, intense, and deeply rooted in the core of Arab identity, attitudes toward America are

---

2. Rubin 2002, 54; Ajami 2003.

3. *The Opposite Direction*, February 18, 2003. All quotes from al-Jazeera, unless otherwise noted, are the author's translation of the official transcripts as published on http://www.aljazeera.net.

still openly contested. One of the most striking features of Arab politics in 2004–05 was an intense debate, in public and private, over U.S. intentions and credibility in promoting democracy in the region. As a recent Center for Strategic and International Studies report concluded, "There is remarkable dynamism in Arab attitudes toward the United States. Over a relatively short period they have shifted markedly, and we are confident that they can shift again."[4] At the same time, the fluidity of Arab attitudes toward the United States should not be exaggerated: in a Pew Global Attitudes report released in July 2005, support for the United States in Jordan—the only core Arab state included in the sample—did increase from 1 to 21 percent in two years, but it still had the lowest approval rating for the United States of any country in the survey, and was one of the few Muslim-population countries in which confidence in Osama bin Laden had actually increased (to 60%, from 55% in 2003) and in which support for suicide bombings had increased (to 57%, from 43% in 2002).

In my review of the evidence I have found little support for the thesis that anti-Americanism is rooted in essentialist cultural conflicts or a clash of civilizations. With some important exceptions, Arab anti-Americanism is almost entirely political. Even today, American culture and economy are widely admired.[5] In the 2004 Zogby poll, for example, 83 percent of Jordanians said they admired American technology; 57 percent admired American freedoms; and 56 percent liked American television, even as only 8 percent approved of U.S. policy toward Arabs and 2 percent supported U.S. policy toward Iraq. A very important subset of Islamists does comprehensively reject American culture and values, however, while many other Arabs fear for their cultural identity in the face of what they see as an American cultural onslaught. Like France, the Arab world is thus home to a variety of anti-Americanisms: the holistic anti-Americanism of the jihadis is entirely different from the politically motivated resentment that dominates al-Jazeera, just as the cultural anti-Americanism of conservatives obsessed with sexual imagery has little to do with the political complaints expressed by cosmopolitan Arab businessmen. The most virulent form of anti-Americanism, and the one that should most concern U.S. policymakers and theoretical analysts alike, comes when radical views break out into the wider population, or when anti-Americanism comes to resonate with the more intimate politics of identity and culture—both of which became increasingly prevalent after September 11.

Does anti-Americanism—whether a passing rage or an entrenched disposition—matter? Under certain conditions, it can lead to direct action against the United States—whether in the form of participation in or support for armed violence against U.S. interests, participation in economic boycotts, or marching in rallies and burning American flags. But, as Robert Keohane and Peter Katzenstein note in chapter 10, these effects tend to be indirect and difficult to demonstrate empirically. Making Arabs angry does not alone turn them into terrorists, nor does fierce anti-American public opinion necessarily change Arab state behavior. An entrenched anti-American disposition can shape the political arena in ways that make some political

---

4. Center for Strategic and International Studies 2005, 13.
5. Zogby 2002.

outcomes more or less likely, as when U.S. democratic reform proposals, which roughly accord with what majorities of Arabs say they want, meet fierce opposition. It can make it difficult for Arab leaders to publicly cooperate with the United States on controversial policies such as the invasion of Iraq, and make it easier for them to resist U.S. pressures. Most generally, it greatly hinders the emergence of a consensual, legitimate regional or international order.

First I examine Arab attitudes toward the United States, emphasizing two factors highlighted in chapter 1 and throughout this book: the normative evaluation of the United States and its perceived impact. Then I examine evidence for the existence of an anti-American dispositional bias, in part by looking at three key domains: the South Asian tsunami of 2005, the 2004 U.S. presidential elections, and the response to American democracy promotion efforts in 2004–05. Finally, I use analysis of talk shows on the leading Arabic satellite television station, al-Jazeera, as a window on the dynamics of Arab political arguments about America.

Arab Anti-Americanisms

Anti-Americanism in the Arab world, as in the other regions explored in this book, comes in a wide variety of political and cultural forms. What potentially unites them is a common narrative disseminated and developed in a shared transnational media in which America occupies a distinctive, and unflattering, place. This drives a strong tendency to view virtually all American actions as potentially threatening. Arab anti-Americanism has become far more intense and widespread in response to the increasing fear of U.S. power, driven by the combination of an increasingly present United States and a negative normative evaluation of American intentions.

Distrust and Presence: Ingredients for Anti-Americanism

In the 1950s and 1960s, when the United States was powerful but relatively remote, anti-American attitudes tended to be transient and superficial. These anti-Americanisms were rooted in the twin dynamics of the cold war and an intra-Arab ideological struggle, and were punctuated by periods of pro-Americanism (after the Suez crisis, for example) and by an enthusiasm for economic modernization. Arab anti-Americanism only began to take on its distinctive colorations after the 1967 Arab-Israeli War, when U.S. support for Israel reshaped a relatively fluid Arab political opinion into a more pervasive distrust. When Egypt made peace with Israel under U.S. auspices in the late 1970s, Egyptian civil society mobilized itself to enforce a "cold peace." This linked political anti-Americanism with hostility toward both Israel and pro-American Arab regimes. Even as this political anti-American trend grew in the 1970s, so did a parallel socio-cultural Islamist project. These political and cultural anti-Americanisms remained relatively latent and rhetorical, with their relative insignificance seen in the confidence with which beleaguered pro-American regimes permitted anti-American rhetoric in the media.

Since the end of the cold war, U.S. presence in the Arab region has steadily and inexorably increased. The 1991 Gulf War brought large numbers of U.S. troops into the region, involved the U.S. military directly in a war against an Arab state (Iraq), and put in place an intense sanctions and containment regime that remained in the headlines for the following twelve years. The Madrid peace conference and subsequent Arab-Israeli negotiations placed the United States at the center of a process that touched the core of Arab political concerns. Globalization, often equated with "Americanization" by Arab and Muslim intellectuals, decreased the perceived distance separating the United States and the region. American economic and military assistance to the Arab states of the region increased from $4.4 billion between 1950 and 1970 to over $66 billion between 1971 and 2000, and averaged around $4 billion (not counting Iraq) between 2001 and 2006.[6] Finally, the post-9/11 war on terror, the invasion and occupation of Iraq, and the George W. Bush administration's rhetorical push for Arab reform has brought the United States overwhelmingly into the region, physically and politically. The transnational satellite television stations that transformed the region in the late 1990s allowed Arabs to experience this American presence more viscerally and intensely, while uniting the disparate politics of local anti-Americanisms into a single, overarching anti-American frame.

All of this has increased the presence of the United States within Arab politics, and it has also increased the extent to which Arabs feel threatened by American power. Research surveys, like countless op-ed pieces, television programs, mosque sermons, and widely distributed booklets, express a deep fear of the American impact on Arab and Muslim identity. For example, in one opinion survey the sociologist Mansour Moaddel (2003) found that 64 percent of Egyptians believe that "Western cultural invasion is a very important problem." The influential Egyptian Islamist moderate Tareq al-Bishri captured this Arab sense of besiegement well in the title of his 2002 book: *The Arabs in the Face of Aggression.*

This increased U.S. impact manifests itself in an intense interest in American intentions: "It is impossible for the observer to miss the rising prominence of a new phenomenon in our Arab world, which is interest in American political discourse."[7] Whatever the distribution of opinions *about* America in these debates, it is clear that the United States had become more present *in* the political debate. For example, compare two al-Jazeera talk shows about political reform.[8] The first, in March 1999, ranged widely across the conflict between generations, the absence of democracy, the problem of hereditary rule, and the absence of effective opposition movements, with hardly a single reference to the United States. The second, in December 2003, focused almost entirely on the question of whether reformers should welcome U.S. support in their struggles for change. Table 7.1 shows the increasing incidence of al-Jazeera programs about the United States, with 10.1 percent of programs focusing on it in 1999 and rising to over 26 percent in 2003 (19% of all programs in this period).

6. Sharp 2005.
7. Abd al-Aziz al-Khadhar, *al-Sharq al-Awsat,* January 24, 2005.
8. *More Than One Opinion*, March 5, 1999, and *Open Dialogue*, December 6, 2003.

Table 7.1. Talk shows about America on al-Jazeera

Year	"America" programs	Total programs	Percent
1999	14	138	10.1
2000	12	142	8.5
2001	37	157	23.6
2002	38	170	22.4
2003	49	184	26.6
Total	150	791	19.0

Note: "America" programs are those in which "America," "United States," or some obvious referent appears in the *title* of one the five main general-interest programs. Because almost every program about Iraq could be considered "about America" this method undercounts American presence but has the benefit of avoiding interpretive decisions.

The intense U.S. presence has been matched, oddly, with a relative American absence from the most important sites of public political debate.[9] While the United States was well represented in the palaces and halls of power, its public presence sharply declined in the late 1990s with the restructuring of the U.S. Information Agency and declining spending for public diplomacy. Angry over al-Jazeera's coverage of Afghanistan, the Bush administration began boycotting (that is, refusing to send officials to appear on) the most widely watched Arab television station in late 2001. As the 2003 U.S. Advisory Commission on Public Diplomacy reported, "Often, we are simply not present to explain the context and content of our national policies and values. . . . The United States has deprived itself of the means to respond effectively—or even to be a significant part of the conversation."[10] This creates a curious, and troublesome, dynamic: even as the salience of the American presence has increased, America remained aloof from the public debates through which this presence has been interpreted and defined. This disregard for Arab public debate not only has fueled perceptions of the United States as arrogant and unilateralist but it also has meant that negative images and false information often have gone unchallenged, allowing for the consolidation of a hostile consensus bothered by little discordant information.

Whether increased presence translates into anti-Americanism—rather than into pro-Americanism or indifference (pragmatic adaptation to the American presence)—depends on the preexisting narrative frame through which it is interpreted. America invokes decidedly ambivalent feelings among Arabs. On the one hand, there is a long tradition of deep admiration for American values in Arab political culture. For example, Hussein Kana'an begins a book-length analysis of U.S.-Arab relations with deep praise for the ideals embodied by Lincoln, such as equality and liberty.[11] The ideals of national independence and freedom resonate well with many Arabs, while

9. Lynch 2003.
10. Advisory Commission for Public Diplomacy 2003, 16.
11. Kana'an 2005, 13.

democratic reforms and American economic vitality are prime concerns of much of the Arab public.[12] In a book-length study of U.S.-Arab relations, Ahmed Yusuf Ahmed claims that "deep-rooted Arab confidence" in the United States, dating back to the struggles against European colonialism, has been shaken by the policies of successive American administrations.[13] Salah al-Din al-Hafez, an Egyptian columnist and secretary-general of the Association of Arab Journalists, bemoans that the United States has been captured by "extremists" who drown out the many reasonable and attractive voices in American society.[14] Numerous opinion surveys have found very different attitudes toward the United States and other, equally "Western," countries such as France. In a five-country survey conducted by the University of Jordan's Center for Strategic Studies (2005), only 25 percent approved of the United States, but 57 percent felt positively toward France.

At the same time, a wide range of negative images have been increasingly attached to America. The Arab media routinely frames U.S. actions and policies in ways that cast doubt on U.S. intentions or present them as actively inimical. Editorial cartoons, which rely on instantly recognizable and resonant symbolism, constantly portray America as Zionist (a Star of David sewn on Uncle Sam's cloak), as aggressive and militant, and as the puppet master controlling Arab regimes. Hostility toward U.S. foreign policy has continued for so long, and has been so deeply entrenched, that it is difficult for nonpejorative descriptions of U.S. policy to gain any traction. Even defenders of the United States tend to argue pragmatically that the United States, like any country, is simply pursuing its self-interest. A wide range of hostile terms regularly attach to U.S. foreign policy: arrogant, destructive, indifferent, manipulative, biased.[15] Arabs express extremely high levels of mistrust of the United States and constantly complain of American hypocrisy and double standards. In March 2003, the *Washington Post* quoted a series of Egyptian university students, who said: "We don't know what to think. Should we love America or should we hate them now?"; "We were in awe of America, and now, we are bitter, confused. The admiration is gone."; "It's always been very easy to love the United States, now it's also easy to hate them."; "I used to say I would do anything to visit America. Now they won't even let me in, they would call me a terrorist."[16] In another article a student complained, "Americans think Arabs are animals, they think we don't think or know anything."[17]

Arabs themselves generally explain anti-Americanism as a rational response to U.S. policies. One recent survey found that Arabs saw U.S. policies as twice as important as American values in shaping their attitudes.[18] In the 2004 Zogby survey, roughly 80 percent of Arabs said that U.S. policies were more important than values

---

12. Zogby 2002, Tessler 2003.
13. Ahmed and Hamzah 2003, 14.
14. *Al-Ahram*, January 28, 2004.
15. Charney and Yakatan 2005.
16. *Washington Post*, March 24, 2003.
17. As quoted in the *Los Angeles Times*, March 29, 2003.
18. *From Conflict to Cooperation* 2005.

in explaining their attitudes. When posed questions about a dispositional bias, they tended to respond that the historical record renders skepticism about American intentions rational. The London-based Arabic daily *Al-Quds al-Arabi* explained:

> Arabs and Muslims do not hate the American people but rather American foreign policy, which relies on power and coercion, and imposes dictatorial and corrupt regimes upon them. . . . [Better public relations] will not persuade Arabs and Muslims that [American] support for Israeli aggression is a good thing, or that the occupation of Iraq is the ideal model for the Iraqi people or for the region.[19]

Jordanian columnist Fahd al-Fanik writes that "it would be a benefit to the entire world and for democracy and freedom if America used its power in the service of these goals. . . . The fault is not in the principles that America calls for but rather in the American practices that contradict them."[20] Many Arabs blame the United States for "a hostile campaign aimed at Islam and the Arabs, which tried to malign them and distort their image."[21] Crucially, these arguments hold out hope that U.S. policy could change, which points toward a nonessentialist view of the United States.

The two variables—presence and normative valence—come together in the concern that the United States seeks to use its power to fundamentally change Arab and Muslim identity in negative ways. Everything from educational reform initiatives to the promotion of democratic reforms to criticism of the Arab media to the war on terror has been open to interpretation as part of this campaign to target Arab identity. Many hear President Bush's rhetoric about "democracy" as a coded way of saying accept Israeli hegemony or of saying abandon Islamic values. American calls for a "war of ideas" becomes "an American war of ideas against Arabs."[22] Even the immense popularity of sexy Arabic music video clips is seen as an American plot to corrupt Arab youth.[23] Far from being seen as nonpolitical, U.S. proposals to governments for reforming educational systems or attempts to promote moderate Islam strike the most sensitive nerves.

There is one important additional point about Arab beliefs about American power: they represent frustrated expectations. Because of the widespread recognition of—and often overestimation of—American power, the failure of the United States to solve important problems is taken to be an intentional decision rather than as being beyond U.S. capabilities: "Why didn't America resolve the Middle East crisis in a fair and just fashion, when everyone knows that they are able to do so?."[24] In this line of argument, it is obvious that the United States could force Israel to retreat to its 1967 borders if it really wanted to do so: "Ninety-nine percent of the cards for resolving the Arab-Israeli conflict continue to be in the hands of the United States."[25]

19. *Al-Quds al-Arabi*, October 2, 2003
20. *Al-Rai*, March 9, 2005.
21. Jamal al-Shilbi, al-Jazeera, March 18, 2003; also see Ahmed and Hamzah 2003.
22. Fahmy Howeidy, *al-Sharq al-Awsat*, November 26, 2003.
23. Salim Azouz, on *The Opposite Direction*, al-Jazeera, June 23, 2005.
24. Kana'an 2005, 7.
25. *Open Dialogue*, al-Jazeera, April 28, 2001.

If America were serious in its calls for democratic reform, it should be able to force highly dependent Arab dictators to change. Similarly, many saw the U.S. failure to prevent the looting of Baghdad in April 2003, and its subsequent inability to control Iraq's borders, as evidence of an American conspiracy to generate conflict in Iraq, rather than the result of inadequate manpower or faulty decision making.

This argument about presence goes against a key tenet of the neoconservative analysis of anti-Americanism: that anti-Americanism is driven by contempt for an America deemed soft and weak.[26] In this view, when the United States demonstrates strength through successful military campaigns or demonstrations of resolve, Arabs will bandwagon with America, whether for realist reasons or out of a cultural predisposition to respect strength. If the argument about fear is correct, then it follows that because either military campaigns *or* democracy promotion would dramatically increase the American presence, either one would intensify rather than deflate the politics of anti-Americanism. Given the realities of globalization and U.S. interests, however, it does not follow that an American retreat from the region would necessarily reverse anti-Americanism. Even if such a withdrawal were possible, it would not satisfy radical anti-Americans who object to essential features of the United States, and it would likely only further frustrate those Arabs whose primary complaints are of a hypocritical America that misuses its power.

Concerns about American presence in the region therefore increasingly go deeper than simple opposition to particular foreign policies. It is fair to say that in virtually no cases does the United States get the benefit of the doubt, nor is there ever a presumption in its favor. This anti-American disposition has become increasingly entrenched and more widely distributed in the last five years. It is increasingly embedded within Arab identity, constantly reinforced in the narratives that dominate the Arab media. It interacts with cultural changes—from Americanization to Islamization—that might not be about the United States or the direct result of American policies but which are associated with the United States. The key question is whether this distrust has hardened into a bias that defies easy change or that bleeds into nonpolitical domains.

Sources of Anti-Americanisms

There are four specific factors that are often claimed to contribute to the distinctive politics of anti-Americanism: Israel, the Arab media, Islamism, and the configuration of distinctive national politics. Let us look at each in turn.

Israel   Although a discussion of Arab attitudes toward Israel is beyond the scope of this chapter, America's relationship with Israel does play a crucial role in the politics of Arab anti-Americanism. Intense identification with the suffering of the Palestinian people and a deep resentment of the injustice that they are believed to have suffered permeates Arab political identity. Since the outbreak of the Palestinian al-

26. Gerecht 2002.

Aqsa Intifada in September 2000 and the Bush administration's highly public support for Israeli prime minister Ariel Sharon's reoccupation of the West Bank in 2002, Arabs increasingly equate the United States with Israel. Arabs overwhelmingly believe that the United States is uncritically supportive of Israel and that the American failure to deliver Israeli concessions is prima facie evidence of hostile American intent. Perceptions of American bias toward Israel run so deep that even seemingly pro-Palestinian policies—Bush's endorsement of the idea of a Palestinian state, Clinton's frenetic peacemaking efforts—tend to be dismissed as serving Israeli goals. This has persisted for so long, and is felt so intensely at the core of Arab identity, that it complicates any "smooth change" political reading of Arab anti-Americanism. Arabs are so convinced of America's pro-Israel bias that most will interpret any U.S. policy as pro-Israel and anti-Palestinian. This is bias, extending from political difference into real anti-Semitism, in a way that more general Arab attitudes toward America are not. The most interesting question for this chapter is whether attitudes relating to U.S. policies toward Israel bleed into wider attitudes toward the United States. The evidence suggests that they do, especially since the collapse of the peace process. Quite simply, Israel enters into virtually every political conversation about the United States, as in the oft-heard "How can you talk about democracy when you support Ariel Sharon?"

Arab Media   The Arab media is often blamed for fanning Arab anti-Americanism. Such an analysis fails to account for the parallel rise of anti-Americanism in non-Arabic speaking Muslim countries such as Iran, Turkey, Pakistan, and Indonesia, to say nothing of Europe and Latin America. Numerous studies have failed to find significant correlation between watching Arab satellite television and anti-American attitudes,[27] although other studies suggest that watching al-Jazeera might intensify preexisting hostility to the United States.[28] Al-Jazeera viewers tend to be more supportive of values such as democracy and freedom, but also more hostile to U.S. foreign policy.[29] The absence of a direct relationship between media and attitudes does not mean that the unique qualities of the Arab media do not matter. Surveys have found significant differences in opinion about the United States between those with direct experience of the country and those whose primary source of information is the media.[30]

The existence of a transnational media enclave defined by an Arab identity arguably makes the Arab world genuinely unique as a region.[31] From the *Voice of the Arabs* radio broadcasts of the 1950s through the present day, there have been pan-Arab media outlets that address "Arabs" across state and geographic boundaries by appealing to certain key political issues. Since the mid-1990s, satellite television

27. Telhami 2005, Zogby International 2004, Center for Strategic Studies 2005.
28. Nisbet et al. 2004, Gentzkow and Shapiro 2004.
29. Tessler 2003.
30. Zogby International 2004, Center for Strategic and International Studies 2005, Pew Global Attitudes Project 2005e.
31. Lynch 2006.

directly and powerfully interprets political events through a lens of Arab identity. The emergence of a common Arab narrative, in which events throughout the Arab world have been linked together, therefore has facilitated increased focus on America by virtue of its being a common denominator in these otherwise perhaps tenuously related countries and issues.

The Arab media frames issues from within this narrative, clearly marking the normative valence of events and issues, while also conveying important information about the prevailing distribution of opinions about the issue. This raises an intriguing hypothesis: should the instance of pro-American voices in this media increase, it could send very different signals to mass audiences. Since February 2003, this proposition has been undergoing a direct test, as the rise of the more pro-American station al-Arabiya as the leading challenger to al-Jazeera has meant a significant increase in the range of pro-American voices available in this media enclave. This was also the logic behind the launch of the U.S. government funded Arabic satellite television station al-Hurra in February 2004. There is little evidence to date that this shift in the distribution of voices is producing a shift in public attitudes toward the United States, at least as measured in public opinion surveys, but this would certainly be a hypothesis to leave open for later testing.

Islamism   Islamist movements are playing a crucial role in creating a deeper form of anti-Americanism, one rooted not so much in politics as in a competing vision of universal principles governing all aspects of life. Social Islamist movements have concentrated on shaping basic worldviews and practices in order to create pious Muslims at the level of everyday life.[32] Islamists have cultivated a distinctive subpublic of mosques and cassette sermons and widely distributed books, offering a narrative and an identity quite different from that in the mainstream Arab media. This "pious" identity is constructed in clear contrast to the equally powerful forces of Americanization transforming Arab societies. Such movements do not have to manifest themselves in violent, jihadi political practices to contribute to the underlying foundations of an anti-American disposition. Their opposition to Western cultural influences prepares the groundwork for latent dispositions that might then be mobilized by strategic politicians in response to particular U.S. policies. The "Muslim" identity cultivated by these movements lavishes attention on struggles of Muslims around the globe, from Bosnia to Chechnya to Kashmir, which highlights the role of the United States as a common denominator.

There is great variation even within Islamism, however. Al-Qaida has made anti-Americanism the heart of its political identity, with a coherent narrative attributing Arab and Muslim woes to the United States. Osama bin Laden identifies the United States as the primary enemy of the Islamic *umma* (community of believers), and calls for a defensive jihad against "the new crusade against the Islamic umma led by America and its allies." This anti-American hard core advocates a "total resistance" to the United States that is substantively different from mainstream opposition to

---

32. Hirschkind 2001.

American policies or culture. For this small subset with intense preferences, America presents a virtual ideal type of *jahiliyya* ("age of ignorance," which the Egyptian radical Islamist Sayid Qutb famously used to describe the modern age). Its seductions must be resisted, its power checked, in a zero-sum war between Islam and evil.

Yusuf al-Qaradawi, the dominant Islamist voice on al-Jazeera and one of the most influential Sunni clerics in the world, is also deeply critical of U.S. foreign policy, but actively calls for democracy and civilizational dialogues. Qaradawi is a moderate Islamist and a fierce critic of bin Laden's brand of extremist Islamism. He has in the past made common cause with American religious conservatives, most notably during the 1994 UN International Conference on Population and Development in Cairo, where he grouped with Christian activists to oppose abortion. At the same time, he has equated globalization with Americanization, and in 2002 he blamed America for seeking "to destroy Arab and Islamic civilization," to keep the Islamic world living in fear of its power, and "to manufacture a generation with a new mentality which serves their interests."[33] In this one influential individual, then, support for important American values (pluralism, democracy) sits alongside fiercely anti-American political positions and a defensive rejection of cultural Americanization.

Not all Islamism should be seen as a hothouse for anti-Americanism. The Center for Strategic Studies reported in 2005 that "strong adherence to the precepts of Islam was not found to necessarily equate with hostility or negativity toward the West."[34] Moderate Islamists today represent one of the strongest social forces demanding democratic reforms, for example, and many urge peaceful coexistence with the West. To the extent that they have fundamentally reshaped deeply held belief structures and have transformed the language and symbolism of the public arena, however, even apolitical forms of Islamism are significant for understanding the politics of anti-Americanism.

National Political Configurations   While the Arab political arena is increasingly interlinked, bound by a common media and a common political agenda, local context still determines the resonance and the impact of anti-American politics. It matters greatly whether a government is allied with the United States, and whether that government is widely popular: an unpopular regime allied with the United States might seem conducive to a politics of anti-Americanism, for example, while an unpopular regime opposed to the United States might lead to a politics of pro-Americanism. Egypt's combination of an unpopular, authoritarian regime with a close alliance with the United States produces a very different anti-American politics than that in a Syria or (prewar) Iraq. In countries allied with the United States, anti-Americanism is often both a proxy for criticizing the regimes and, paradoxically, encouraged by those very regimes.

Egypt, for example, combines extremely close relations with the U.S. government with among the highest levels of expressed anti-Americanism. Egypt is one of the

33. Al-Qaradawi 2002.
34. "Revisiting the Arab Street" 2005.

largest single recipients of U.S. foreign assistance: $1.2 billion a year in military aid and more than $25 billion from the U.S. Agency for International Development since 1975, leading the Egyptian leftist Galal Amin to ask pointedly, "How did Egypt become an American colony?"[35] Despite these close relations, the Egyptian government both tolerates and encourages anti-Americanism, especially in the press and state-run media. Whenever the United States criticizes Egypt for human rights violations, the state-owned media erupts in a predictable frenzy of denunciations of foreign interference. When U.S. investigators blamed the 1999 crash of Egypt Air Flight 990 on a Muslim pilot, the Egyptian media was filled with exceptionally vicious anti-American rhetoric. In March 2003, the regime even offered official sanction for a massive anti-U.S. protest.[36]

Perhaps as a result, levels of expressed anti-Americanism are very high: "The Egyptian government criticizes American policies in the Middle East, but popular feelings go beyond that; these feelings are no longer limited to religious fundamentalists or armed leftist groups, but have found their way into popular culture."[37] Council on Foreign Relations focus groups in December 2004 found that "spontaneous criticism of the U.S. was particularly intense and angry in Egypt,"[38] with "aggressive images" dominating Egyptian associations with the United States. In the June 2004 Zogby survey, only 2 percent of Egyptians had favorable views of the United States, with 98 percent unfavorable.

Cultivating anti-Americanism puts the regime at risk of being tarred by association, however, and of ultimately eating away at its own freedom to maneuver and even legitimacy. During April 2002 protests over the Israeli reoccupation of the West Bank, protestors explicitly equated the United States with Israel, burning American flags, boycotting American products, and smashing up at least one Kentucky Fried Chicken franchise. In March 2004, denunciations of the U.S. occupation of Iraq quickly gave way to angry chants about the economic situation and scathing criticism of the Mubarak regime.[39] The impact of anti-Americanism can be seen in the attitudes expressed by the pathbreaking democratic movement Kefaya, whose rallies proliferated in 2004 and 2005. Kefaya activists vocally rejected any U.S. assistance, both because any association with the United States would discredit the movement in Egyptian eyes and because of opposition to U.S. foreign policies. One leader criticized "decades of 'hypocritical' U.S. policy in the Middle East," declaring that "we are strongly against U.S. influence." Another said bluntly, "We want a transformation against America and all its projects in the region."[40]

In Jordan, another close U.S. ally, expressed anti-Americanism is also exceptionally high. Favorable views of the United States in the Pew Global Attitudes surveys ranged dropped from 25 percent in 2002 to 1 percent in 2003, before rebounding to

35. Amin 2002, 23.
36. Schemm 2003.
37. *Financial Times*, September 28, 2004.
38. Council on Foreign Relations 2004, 45.
39. Moustafa 2004.
40. Both quotes from *Christian Science Monitor*, March 29, 2005.

21 percent in 2005. The Jordanian media is less vitriolic toward America than is the Egyptian media, suggesting the limits of that explanatory factor. Jordanian anti-Americanism is closely tied to intense public identification with both the Palestinian issue (half or more of Jordanians are of Palestinian origin) and Iraq (long a major Jordanian trading partner). It also is prevalent among a strong underground Salafi Islamist movement, from which Iraqi insurgency leader Abu Musab al-Zarqawi emerged. Jordanian public opinion overwhelmingly targeted the United States as a villain on both issues, putting the Hashemite monarchy in a perennially uncomfortable position. As passionately as Jordanians have about felt the Palestinian and Iraqi issues, anti-Americanism also has served as a proxy for criticizing the regime, solidifying an otherwise unlikely coalition of leftist, Arab nationalist, liberal, and Islamist opposition forces.

In Syria, anti-Americanism came from the top down, encouraged by a regime that has considered itself targeted by U.S. foreign policy. Large protests against the United States, including at one point the sacking of the ambassador's residence, were far from spontaneous. The official media has relentlessly highlighted U.S. perfidy, equated it with Israel, and warned against the American threat. Even if such rhetoric was only loosely believed by Syrians, this should not be taken to mean that anti-American feelings are not real or politically potent. Although it is difficult to rigorously measure opinion in Syria, most indicators suggest that most Syrians feel threatened by the United States and Israel. As Americans who expected to be received with hugs and flowers by grateful Iraqis in 2003 have so painfully learned, an unpopular anti-American dictator is no guarantee of pro-American popular views.

In Saudi Arabia the hostility toward the United States has far more of a cultural dimension than in the other Arab cases. Although Saudi Arabia, like Egypt and Jordan, is closely allied with the United States, it has made great efforts to insulate Saudi society from contact with the U.S. presence. Osama bin Laden, of course, emerged from this Saudi environment, with the presence of the U.S. military in the kingdom one of his primary political complaints. In contrast to the disconnection between admiration for American culture and hostility to American policies seen in most other Arab countries, Saudis express distaste for both. In the 2004 Zogby survey, 51 percent of Saudis disapproved of American technology, 60 percent disapproved of American freedoms and democracy, and 64 percent disliked Americans as a people (4% approved of U.S. policy toward Arabs, and 1% approved of U.S. Iraq policy). This represents a far deeper, more culturally embedded form of anti-Americanism than in the other Arab countries. Its roots lie in the powerful religious establishment and the educational system, which together cultivate a xenophobic, insular worldview. This form of anti-Americanism has spread through the Arab world through the Salafi networks associated with the Saudi-backed mosques that became increasingly widespread beginning in the 1980s.

Finally, examining the primary areas of traditional pro-Americanism in the region (Kuwait, Lebanon, Morocco) can offer vital perspective. Kuwait, especially since its liberation from Iraq by U.S. forces in 1991, has had consistently pro-American views.

Even in Kuwait, however, resurgent Islamist movements have expressed hostility to the United States. During the run-up to the 2003 invasion of Iraq, many Kuwaitis expressed hostility to the United States and suspicion of its intentions, with a 2002 Gallup poll finding 72 percent of Kuwaitis expressing disapproval of the United States. In line with this book's argument, this change in Kuwaiti attitudes might be explained by the dramatic increase in the presence of U.S. troops (Kuwait was a primary basing point for operations in Iraq) combined with the rise of Islamist movements and widespread anger over the Palestinian issue.

Lebanon offers a clear case in which attitudes toward America are filtered through domestic politics and identity: Lebanese Christians tend to have overwhelmingly positive views of America, while Lebanese Muslims—especially Shia—express profound distrust.

Finally, Moroccans have traditionally expressed great admiration for the United States, perhaps because of a relatively more intense interaction with France and Europe (77% approved of the United States in a 1999–2000 State Department survey).[41] Morocco was also the site of some of the largest public protests against the invasion of Iraq, however, reinforcing the point that cultural or general admiration does not prevent political disagreement.

Is There an Arab Anti-American Disposition?

Katzenstein and Keohane in chapter 1 suggest that whether a public has a dispositional bias (positive or negative) toward the United States could be best explored with reference to issues not closely connected to U.S. policy, since attitudes toward the latter could be explained by disagreement. In addition to tsunami relief, I examine two other issues that offer windows into the comparative dynamics of anti-Americanism. The 2004 U.S. presidential election offers a good opportunity to see how Arabs talk about the United States itself. American reform promotion efforts in the Middle East, where the United States supported goals that many Arabs claim to want, allows assessment of whether anti-American attitudes prevent cooperation. In each case, a hostile disposition toward the United States would be observed when opposition to U.S. foreign policy "bleeds in" to evaluation of less political issues, and when such a hostile view becomes locked in, so that it is relatively impervious to new information.

A powerful anti-American schema, observable in a wide range of domains, clearly now dominates Arab political rhetoric, even if it has not completely hardened into a relatively unchangeable bias. The argument that really matters now is not between pro-Americans and anti-Americans: it is between a political anti-Americanism that believes that U.S. policy could change for the better, and a radical anti-Americanism that either rejects U.S. values (Islamists) or views America as irredeemably corrupt.

---

41. Pew Global Attitudes Project 2005e. This support for America collapsed in the years after 9/11, according to the Pew surveys, but later rebounded slightly.

Revelations of prisoner abuse at Abu Ghraib and Guantánamo mattered because the powerful images reinforced the existing schema, discrediting pro-American voices in the region and confirming the anti-American narrative. But when the Bush administration offered some rhetorical support for democracy movements in the region in a speech in November 2003, it might have had the potential to win over these mainstream political anti-Americans.

The evidence confirms both that a strong anti-American schema exists in Arab political discourse and that the mainstream public remains open to argument. First, the anti-American schema: America rarely gets the benefit of the doubt with Arab audiences, and Arabs generally assume some ulterior, self-interested (or pro-Israel) motivation underlying any U.S. policy, no matter how appealing on its surface. Word choices, images, and symbols all reflect, and continually reconstitute, a deep distrust of the United States. Persistent refusal to accept al-Qaida's responsibility for 9/11 even in the face of overwhelming evidence to the contrary, for example, shows such an anti-American disposition. So do poll findings that only 35 percent of Jordanians considered the 9/11 attacks to be "terrorism," while 86 percent considered U.S.-led military activities in Iraq to be so.[42] In a survey conducted in late February 2003 in six Arab countries, virtually no respondents believed that the United States was motivated by a desire to promote democracy; more than 80 percent said oil was an important motivation and more than 70 percent also said support for Israel was important.[43] When the United States government and American nongovernmental organizations began to raise concerns about the massacres in the Darfur region of the Sudan, many Arabs immediately worried about another American intervention in a Muslim country.

On the other hand, the generally positive reception of the American relief efforts in response to the South Asian tsunami in January 2005 and the generally enthusiastic welcome for American criticisms of the Mubarak regime later that spring suggest that this disposition is neither fixed nor all-pervasive. Indeed, many Arab commentators seemed almost desperately eager to find evidence that the United States was serious about pushing for democratic reform—if only because of an overestimation of American power. Relations with the United States are openly, intensely debated—which means that they have not yet hardened into a rigid, taken-for-granted consensus.

Tsunami Relief

Arab media coverage was generally either favorable or indifferent on the subject of U.S. relief efforts after the 2005 tsunami. There was far less criticism of the United States for its initial response than might have been expected, and indeed little focus on the United States at all. In contrast to the findings reported by Katzenstein and Keohane that most people value their own country's performance most highly, the Arab media turned the tsunami into an opportunity to criticize the

42. CSS 2005, 72.
43. Shibley Telhami, "Arab Public Opinion," *San Jose Mercury News*, March 16, 2003.

inadequacy of the Arab world's response to an event that harmed large numbers of Muslims.

Al-Quds al-Arabi, the Arab daily most hostile to U.S. policies, almost completely ignored the opportunity to score points against the United States for its early failure to respond to the tsunami. Its prominent editorial response came from editor Abd al-Bari Atwan's front-page January 5 essay, "The Humiliating Arab Humanitarian Collapse." Rather than attack the United States, Atwan wrote: "Arab sympathy, official and popular, toward the earthquake disaster that struck the states of South Asia came as a great frustration of hopes, on all levels, which filled me with humiliation. The assistance was puny, the popular response and governmental action were pitiful." The editor of the most anti-American newspaper in the Arab world made Arab failures his primary target rather than those of the United States.

Al-Sharq al-Awsat, the most pro-American of the major Arab dailies, ran four op-eds about the tsunami in the first two weeks. Several discussed the human or environmental issues and said nothing about America. Mona Eltahawi, on January 2, asked, "Where is the jihad against the tsunami?" She wondered why, after seeing footage of this horrible natural disaster that killed over 125,000 people, she had not seen a videotape from Osama bin Laden appealing for help for the Muslims devastated by the tsunami. The United States came off well in contrast. Only one columnist (January 6) questioned the U.S. response, writing that the United States had only increased the size of its contribution out of concern for its image abroad and that its original contribution had been puny in comparison to what it spends on the war on terror or the war in Iraq.

Arab satellite television stations covered the tsunami heavily, with an emphasis on human suffering and its own highly publicized fund-raising campaign for relief operations. Coverage of the relief efforts tended to highlight the UN and NGO activities, but it did not ignore American contributions. When U.S. secretary of state Colin Powell arrived, the coverage was respectful but not overwhelmingly positive; the January 6 story on al-Jazeera prominently mentioned the $350 million in U.S. aid. The most prominent al-Jazeera talk show dealing with the tsunami focused on the weak response by Arab and Islamic NGOs, asking whether the U.S. crackdown on those NGOs as part of the war on terror had weakened them. But in the accompanying online poll asking whether "the global response to the Asian tsunami disaster was sufficient" (76.8% said no), the United States was not singled out as might have been expected had there been an anti-American agenda.

There were some more critical responses, such as a January 3 report aired on al-Jazeera titled, "The Emaciated American Role in Confronting the Tsunami Tragedy." It argued that the United States is determined to constantly affirm its leadership of a unipolar world and as the greatest defender of humanity all over the world but that the U.S. response to the tsunami was very disappointing. Even when the United States increased its aid, it did so only in response to the criticism it received. Another clearly anti-American contribution on al-Arabiya explored the "question" of what it would mean if the U.S. Navy had advance warning of the tsunami. But such views were outliers in relation to the overall coverage. The Arab media coverage of the tsunami suggests far less overt anti-Americanism than would have been predicted given a strongly anti-American bias. The more dominant themes were the failures of Arab governments, not American shortcomings.

The U.S. Presidential Election

Arab coverage of the 2004 U.S. presidential election offers another domain in which to search for a dispositional bias. More interesting than the question of whether Arabs preferred Kerry or Bush (given the evidence of overwhelming Arab antipathy toward Bush) is the more fundamental question of whether Arabs thought the elections mattered. If the race were covered as not being genuinely democratic, this might suggest a corrosive disregard for U.S. institutions. If the race were covered as if there were no real difference between the candidates, this might suggest a fatalistic determination that U.S. foreign policy was beyond repair. The evidence suggests that Arab attitudes oscillated in important ways between the idea that the outcome did not matter (which would suggest a dispositional bias) and the idea that a victory by one or the other would be better for Arab interests (which would suggest that anti-Americanism represents an opinion rather than a bias). Of course, radical anti-Americanism went beyond indifference to the outcome: one Egyptian explained that he supported Bush because "I want him to ruin the United States by applying his stupid policies."[44]

Live, unscripted call-in shows that aired in the days immediately before the election on the two most popular Arab satellite television stations offer one window into Arab attitudes: *Istifta ala al-Hiwa* (Survey on the Air) (al-Arabiya, October 30) and *Minbar al-Jazeera* (al-Jazeera, November 1). Of the thirty callers to al-Arabiya, fourteen expressed a preference: seven favored Kerry and seven favored Bush. Thirteen said that they would not support either candidate, with the most common explanation being that "they are two faces of the same Zionist coin." And four callers said that they would vote for Bush because, as one put it, "he is the only man in the world who can destroy America." Of the twenty-two calls to al-Jazeera, only seven expressed a preference (four for Kerry, three for Bush) while the other fifteen refused to support either for reasons ranging from "no difference between them" to "both candidates compete over who can kill the most Muslims." In an accompanying online poll, 61 percent said that there was no difference between the two candidates (11.4% supported Bush, while 27% supported Kerry). These discussions show a significant but not universal level of essentialist anti-Americanism: fifty-three percent of the al-Arabiya callers and 68 percent of the al-Jazeera callers felt that elections would make no difference to the U.S. policies that they detested.

This should not obscure the equally important prominence of nuanced interpretations of the elections. One typical article cited U.S. public opinion polls and the closeness of the race to argue that "half of America is with us"—breaking down

44. http://weekly.ahram.org.eg/2004/714/eg1.htm.

stereotypes of a monolithic America.[45] Guests on talk shows and editorialists frequently observed that the United States was deeply divided, while others urged Arab leaders to pay attention to the U.S. elections to see what real democracy looked like.

Perhaps the most important point here is that the Arab media coverage of the election was exceptionally intense, with regular programs on the satellite television stations and heavy news coverage of the campaign.[46] Al-Jazeera ran a popular weekly program about the election campaign, a step imitated by many of its competitors in the last weeks of the campaign. Abd al-Monim al-Said, director of Egypt's Al-Ahram Foundation's Center for Political and Strategic Studies, marveled at "the intense Arab scrutiny over a period of a full year [of the presidential campaign] . . . No other issue has so attracted the interest of Arab viewers."[47] If Arabs really believed that "Bush and Kerry, in their essence, did not differ much from one another," why was there such unprecedented interest in the campaign?[48]

Reactions to Bush's victory tended to interpret it as a confirmation of the anti-American position: "Bush wins, America loses."[49] One columnist cheerfully congratulated the American people for embracing Abu Ghraib.[50] While many writers complained that "Bush's victory threatens global stability" and others groused that "Bush's victory comes at the same time as the deterioration of the health of Yasser Arafat, and Israeli Prime Minister Sharon is celebrating both events as personal victories," at least some argued that a reelected Bush might in fact be the one president able to deliver on the promise of a Palestinian state.[51]

Arab media coverage emphasized how close the race had been, cutting against the urge toward an essentialist view of America, even as Bush's reelection strengthened such views. In short, the Arab response shows ambivalence, intense attention, and real disagreement. One undercurrent bears attention: Arab leaders did not share the popular hostility to Bush, which demonstrated their corruption and isolation from their publics.[52] The simple fact that many Arabs believed that the U.S. election could make a difference is an important indicator that Arab hostility toward Bush's foreign policy had not yet fully hardened into a systemic condemnation of the United States.

U.S.-Backed Reform Initiatives

Debates about U.S. reform initiatives in the Arab world get to the heart of the political importance of anti-Americanism. The democratic reform agenda pushed by the Bush administration clearly increased the salience of the United States in the

45. *al-Sharq al-Awsat*, August 15, 2004.

46. Najeeb and Wise 2004.

47. Abd al-Monim al-Said, *al-Sharq al-Awsat*, November 3, 2004.

48. Ibid. For a dissenting view, see Rami Khouri, *Daily Star*, October 2, 2004.

49. al-Jazeera, November 4, 2004.

50. Subhi Hadidi, *Al-Quds al-Arabi*, November 5, 2004.

51. Quotes from, in order, Abd al-Bari Atwan, *Al-Quds al-Arabi*, November 4, 2004; Mahmoud Athman, *al-Hayat*, November 5, 2004; Abd al-Rahman al-Rashed, *al-Sharq al-Awsat*, November 6, 2004.

52. Walid Shaqir, *al-Hayat*, November 5, 2004.

Arab world, but in a way that aligned it with rather than against Arab public opinion. The Bush administration began advocating Arab reform as a major foreign policy goal with a highly publicized presidential speech to the National Endowment for Democracy in November 2003, announcing an end to past U.S. practices of fore-going democracy in the name of stability in the Arab world. On February 13, 2004, a leaked draft of the U.S. Greater Middle East Initiative was published in the London-based Arab newspaper *al-Hayat*, triggering an intense public debate over both the need for reform and the acceptability of a U.S. role in promoting such reform.

The initial responses generally rejected U.S. support and complained that associ-ation with the United States was the kiss of death for their efforts. In the immediate aftermath of the invasion of Iraq, U.S. credibility was exceptionally low. In the early press commentary "none of the writers entertained the possibility that the Bush administration might actually be committed to democracy for its own sake."[53] As one report concluded:

> Mistrust of U.S. policy and concern at Egypt's dependence reached a peak during the post-war month. A culture conference, educational curricula reforms, calls for modernising religious discourse, and TV shows all became occasions for debating the so-called Americanization of Egyptian culture and society. U.S. decisions and statements were almost invariably interpreted negatively through the prism of growing distrust.[54]

By 2004, with the U.S. invasion of Iraq past and passions having somewhat cooled, a wider range of views could be seen.[55]

Some critics did reject U.S. promotion of democracy in principle, insisting that reform must be generated from within. Egypt's semiofficial *Al-Ahram*, for example, missed no opportunity to declare that "imposing democracy from abroad will not succeed"—a view widely echoed within other official media as well as within the Arab League.[56] Another trend criticized the process more than the substance. In this view, the United States had generated its reform proposals without consulting with Arabs and with no public dialogue, which exemplified American arrogance and dis-regard for Arab minds. Nader Fergany, lead author of the UN's *Arab Human Devel-opment Report* (AHDR), bitterly criticized the U.S. Greater Middle East Initiative and argued that "Arabs sorely need to refuse reform from abroad."[57] A final group crit-icized the emptiness of the U.S. reform promotion effort, highlighting the small amounts of money proposed for it ($250 million) and U.S. unwillingness to challenge friendly regimes—Syria was targeted, but not Jordan; Iran, but not Saudi Arabia.

---

53. Ottoway 2003, 8.
54. International Crisis Group 2003, 8–9.
55. Hawthorne 2004.
56. *Al-Ahram*, November 10, 2003.
57. *al-Hayat*, February 19, 2004. Fergany also criticized the U.S.'s alleged blocking of the 2004 edition of the *AHDR* for its criticism of U.S. policies in Iraq.

Finally, a significant portion welcomed European assistance, or United Nations action, but rejected American involvement. Such critics complained "not only because it is 'foreign' but also and more specifically because of its sponsorship by the United States . . . What such leaders object to is not so much the content of the U.S. reform initiative as the ulterior motives alleged to lie behind it."[58]

There were also arguments in favor of accepting American assistance in the pursuit of reform, as well as reasonably significant numbers of groups and individuals willing to quietly work with the United States on reform initiatives. The first argued for harnessing U.S. power for their own ends, on the grounds that no change would ever be possible without external help, given the realities of state power. The second group urged indifference to the United States, focusing on the demands of the reform movement without regard to what America did or did not do: "Reform is good thing even if America supports it." Finally, some argued for a positive identification with America, often in the context of harsh and comprehensive critiques of the pathologies of Arab political culture, although these Arab neoconservatives tended to be marginal figures.

American credibility and sincerity is perhaps the single most crucial theme running through these debates. There is a deep desire for the United States to be sincere in its democracy promotion, a desire that cuts against the "bias" hypothesis, but there are enormous doubts that this is the case. When George W. Bush issued a mild condemnation of regime-backed violence against Egyptian protestors in late May 2005, for example, every major regional Arab media outlet ran lead stories celebrating his statement. They did the same when Secretary of State Rice canceled a meeting with Egyptian officials over the arrest of a prominent liberal politician. But, at the same time, many Arabs feared that American democracy promotion veiled some inimical interest, whether the promotion of U.S. hegemony or the protection of Israeli interests. Trust, long lost, was not easily regained.

Anti-Americanism on al-Jazeera

The Arabic satellite television station al-Jazeera can be used as a window on Arab political attitudes. With some fifty million viewers, al-Jazeera is the most influential and widely viewed mass media in the Arab world. To assess the dynamics of anti-Americanism on al-Jazeera, I concentrate on talk shows rather than the news in order to get at the features of Arab political argument. I use al-Jazeera here as a rough proxy for wider Arab public opinion; indeed, since its populist politics push toward anti-American expressions, this should be an easy case for finding an anti-American disposition. The relationship between mass media and wider attitudes is of course complex, but examining the discourse on al-Jazeera at least provides evidence about the nature of public arguments.

58. Wickham 2004, 1.

Table 7.2. Selected al-Jazeera programs about America

A1 American policy in the Middle East (1/15/1999)
A2 Future of American policy toward the Middle East (1/17/2001)
A3 American disregard for Arabs and their issues (3/20/2001)
A4 Current Arab-American relations (4/28/2001)
A5 American presence in the Gulf (12/12/2000)
B1 Relations between Americans and Arabs (1/26/2002)
B2 Is the present century American? (2/19/2002)
B3 Arabs and America (2/22/2002)
B4 America and its contempt for the minds of the world (7/2/2002)
B5 Arab-American relations after 9/11 (9/3/2002)
B6 The future of American hegemony over the world after 9/11 (9/18/2002)
B7 American presence in the Arab region (2/4/2003)
C1 Political reform in the Arab world (12/6/2003)
C2 The Greater Middle East Project (2/20/2004)
C3 Calls for change in the Arab world (2/28/2004)
C4 Middle East Project (3/16/2004)
C5 Future of reform projects (5/25/2004)
C6 American intervention to overthrow governments (6/4/2004)
C7 American demands on Arab states (9/29/2004)
D1 America and the Middle East in the coming phase (11/5/2004)
D2 Arab future and the reform issue (1/1/2005)
D3 Freedom in the Middle East between inside and outside (3/11/2005)
D4 American invasion of Iraq and its effect on reforms (3/29/2005)
D5 American role in moving Arab politics (4/2/2005)

Of the 150 talk shows coded as "about America" in table 7.1, I selected a sample of twenty-four shows about the United States for closer analysis, divided into four periods (table 7.2): (A) from 1999 to before September 11, 2001; (B) early 2002 to early 2003, before the invasion of Iraq; (C) late 2003 to 2004, before the U.S. presidential election; (D) early 2005, during the so-called Arab spring of reform movements. This sample is not representative in the sense of being chosen randomly; instead, I chose programs that gave a representative sense of the station's discussions about the United States. I avoided the most directly contentious periods, such as during the invasion of Iraq, to better measure the indirect manifestations of anti-Americanism: Does the anger generated by the U.S. invasion of Iraq, or its support of Sharon, translate into anti-Americanism in other issue areas and time periods?

Following John Bowen's argument in chapter 8 about the importance of framing for establishing the terms of debate and bringing forward certain kinds of issues and evidence rather than others, I looked at how the hosts of the programs framed discussions about the United States. To determine the framing, I looked at the introductory remarks made by the host, the identity of the guests chosen for the program, and the narrative of each program as revealed in the editorially inserted section breaks. I then examined the major kinds of arguments made about the United States in the course of the program. The goal is not statistical content analysis; instead, I viewed these talk shows as a kind of focus group, each a case of public Arab political argument.

Overall, negative images of the United States clearly predominated over positive images. The most common themes and descriptions had to do with American power and arrogance, with far more reference to hypocrisy than to intrinsic evil. The dominant frames are a juxtaposition of American hostility with the complicity of Arab regimes, with arguments revolving around which party is more to blame for negative outcomes in Palestine, Iraq, or domestic repression; resentment of American "contempt" for Arab issues; and consistent discussion of how U.S. policies might be changed in a more positive direction. The most negative distribution of arguments (i.e., the most anti-American) came between early 2002 (after the "Axis of Evil" speech and during the Israeli reoccupation of the West Bank) and spring 2003 (the invasion of Iraq).

The high salience of U.S. presence ensures much discussion of and perhaps disproportionate focus on the United States (see table 7.1). In the early period (A), the United States generally showed up only as an aspect of other issues—a program on Palestine that included discussion of U.S. negotiating positions, for example, or a program on the sanctions on Iraq. In the latter three periods, after 9/11, direct discussions about the United States became far more common. "American hegemony" and "possibilities of resisting it" were topics of particular concern (A1, B2, B6). In February 2002, one program (B2) discussed the topic "Is the present century American?" The general question of "the American presence in the region" was a perennial theme (A5, B7). Complaints about irrational, unjustified U.S. hostility to Islam or to Arabs were common. One of the first programs al-Jazeera broadcast after 9/11 asked whether the terrorist attacks would lead the United States to initiate a clash of civilizations, which, according to most of the guests on the show, Arabs and Muslims desperately hoped to avoid. Numerous programs explored "the negative images of Islam in the West" or "the American media campaign against Islam," feeding into a sense of defensiveness and besiegement. As early as June 2001, a program took on the question of "the American enemy," while numerous programs had begun asking, even before the conclusion of the war in Afghanistan in late 2001, whether the United States would go to war with Iraq.

For all the negativity and fear expressed on these programs, there continued to be a remarkable amount of continuing hope that America would live up to its professed ideals and use its vast power to intervene on the Arab side (whether against Israel or against autocratic regimes). Some programs did indeed seem to show a distorted view of U.S. political life. A 2002 program revolved around the corruption of Congress and who really rules America (answer: Jews) and the American threat to the Islamic umma. Others featured ex-Nazi David Duke explaining how America was "exploiting 9/11," former U.S. attorney general Ramsey Clark excoriating alleged American war crimes in Afghanistan, and Georgia congressional representative Cynthia McKinney describing Zionist power in Washington. Other programs, especially the program *From Washington* and *Race for the Presidency*, consciously worked to give Arab viewers an accurate sense of American politics. All of the discussions of U.S. reform efforts (especially in periods C and D) began from the premise of great distrust of the United States and the kiss of death attached to overt cooperation with it. The strong presence of liberal anti-Americanism—criticism of the United States for failing to live up to its own rhetoric, rather than existential criticisms of those values themselves—is an extremely important finding.

Programs aired just after the fall of Baghdad demonstrate this range of confusion, anger, and hope. On the very first live call-in program broadcast after the fall of Baghdad (April 13), host Jumana al-Nimour challenged her guest's use of the term "occupation," pointing out that "the Americans present themselves as a liberating power which will surrender authority very quickly, giving authority to Iraqis." The first caller "celebrated the fall of the tyranny" but had "a message from the Iraqi people, with all frankness . . . : We will not be satisfied with an American occupation." The second caller declared that he was trapped between joy at being released from the tyranny and dictatorship of Saddam Hussein and fear that the Americans would remain in Iraq. A Palestinian caller yelled that "the issue is not the future of Iraq . . . it is the slaughter of Muslims and Arabs at the walls of Damascus, at the walls of Beirut, at the walls of Jerusalem, and now the slaughter of Muslims and Arabs at the walls of Baghdad." A Tunisian caller urged Arabs not to think of the Americans as enemies or friends but to think in terms of interests and power.

In a program the next day, host Faisal al-Qassem began with this question: "Have the Americans carried the project of democracy to the Arabs as they did to the Germans and Japanese after the Second World War?" One caller was dismissive: "Do you know the first thing the Americans did when they conquered Umm Qasr? They established an occupation of the oil installations, made them secure . . . fine. Are oil refineries more valuable than the Iraqi people?" Most callers were skeptical of American intentions, frightened of the chaos and anarchy unleashed by the fall of the regime, but suspecting that this must somehow have been by American design—how could a country able to defeat Saddam Hussein's army be unable to police the streets of Baghdad? One caller bluntly said that "those who dream or imagine that the Americans will bring democracy to Iraq or to the Arab world . . . are deluded." But when a caller doubted that the United States would ever really support democratization, the host challenged him: "If you ask people in Latin America, they might say yes."

An anti-American bias is not clearly seen in the distribution of guests invited to participate in the programs. Before 9/11, American guests included former ambassadors David Mack and Edward Walker. In the two middle periods (2001–4), programs more often featured guests from the extremes of American politics. This choice could be defended as dictated by the reality of a conservative Bush administration, but it nevertheless established a frame that arguably exaggerated the conservative or pro-Israeli profile of Americans. Partly, it reflects a policy choice by the Bush administration, which stopped sending representatives to appear on the station's programs due to anger over its coverage of Afghanistan.

As the figures in table 7.3 suggest, in this selection of programs, by far the strongest represented group was "political anti-Americanism," figures who articulated

Table 7.3. Guests

	1	2	3	4	5	6	Total
A (1/99–9/01)	0	1	3	5	0	2	11
B (1/02–3/03)	0	1	3	4	0	4	12
C (10/03–9/04)	1	0	5	6	0	4	16
D (1/05–5/05)	1	0	3	10	0	1	15
Total	2	2	14	25	0	11	54

Note: 1: American conservative; 2: American official; 3: Arab pro-American; 4: Arab political anti-American (critical of specific U.S. policies); 5: Arab "social anti-American" (critical of U.S. culture); 6: Arab "radical anti-American" (essentialist, calls for violent resistance).

criticism (often very sharply) of U.S. foreign policy but who refrained from voicing essentialist condemnations of the United States and remained open to the possibility that American policies might change.[59] Islamist "social anti-Americanism" was entirely absent from these programs, giving the lie to the notion that al-Jazeera actively promoted such radical Islamism. American voices were only lightly represented and came almost entirely from a spectrum ranging from government officials to conservatives. Arab pro-American voices were represented frequently, usually in debate shows pitting them against radical anti-American voices.

Many guests on these programs have complained that the way the programs were structured biased the argument against the American or pro-American interlocutor—the anti-American speaker got to go first, the host agreed with him or her, the questions were stacked against the United States. While this has sometimes been the case, it is not consistently so. In eight of the nine programs with multiple guests in the first two periods, the political or radical anti-American guest spoke first. But in period C, four out of the six programs had the pro-American guest speak first, while in the final period it was evenly balanced. In a November 2001 program about "American media freedoms," for example, the eloquent U.S. diplomat Christopher Ross was given the chance to speak first and was treated with respect. The other guest, Ibrahim Alloush, was hostile and aggressive, pressing Ross over whether the United States had intentionally targeted the al-Jazeera office in Kabul and denouncing the intentions of the "Zionist dominated" American media to destroy any media rival and to preserve the media hegemony of the American empire. But Ross held his own and was given every chance to respond. Other American guests, relying on simultaneous translation and unfamiliar with the nuances of Arab political discourse,

59. The coding of guests as "political" or "radical" anti-Americans is a charged and difficult process. I restrict the label "radical" to individuals who either attributed essential evils to the United States, such that its policies were intrinsically bad with no hope of change, or who advocated violence against the United States. The slope between "political" and "radical" is slippery, however: a political anti-American could sound like a radical on a particularly bad day. The sharp decline in "radical anti-Americans" from period C to period D is not simply an artifact of coding, however: the change in what people said is real, whatever inferences might be drawn.

did less well, but they did at least have the opportunity to inject American rhetoric and assumptions into the debate.

What about the content? The main themes and frames in the programs about the United States demonstrate significant changes over time. In period A topics tended to be general discussions of U.S. policy and the possibility of changing it. A2 (on the 2000 elections) held out the hope of a more pro-Arab policy under Bush, while A4 was entirely devoted to the question of how to achieve rapprochement between Arabs and Americans. Identification of the United States with Arab regimes was the main frame of three of the five programs. In period B (early 2002 to early 2003), almost all the programs focused on "American hegemony" and opportunities to challenge it, with focus as well on the complicity and weakness of Arab regimes. The tone and framing of these programs was markedly more negative than in the earlier period, with less optimism that U.S. policy could be effectively influenced. In period C (late 2003 to mid-2004), every single program revolved around American intentions in promoting democratic reform in the region, with the main axis of debate being whether the United States could be trusted. Skepticism was very high, but defenders could be heard and there was a tangible hope that it might be possible.

Detailed description of several typical programs about the United States from different time periods help illustrate how these dynamics have changed. An April 2001 program from Cairo (A4) explored what policy the Arab world should now take toward the United States, in the context of the new Republican administration. The show host posed these possibilities: "First, sever relations no matter the cost; second, correct the relations by using whatever means of influence are available; third, continue on the current, well-known path." When the host asked whether it was in the Arab countries' interest for the United States to be actively involved in the peace process, one guest responded that it would be far better to work within the UN, which the United States consistently wanted to push to the sidelines, while another guest responded that the United States was openly committed to putting Israeli security first and could never therefore really be an honest broker. Guests criticized American double standards (favoring of Israel) and its "attitude of supremacy," but they were willing to explain this as "America pursues its self-interest, like any state." One guest argued that even though it is biased toward Israel, the United States could be helpful on other issues, and argued against boycotting American products even as he suggested finding better ways of putting pressure on the United States. A Lebanese journalist complained in response that "we face a situation of complete bias . . . toward the Zionist entity" and that this spilled over into all issues. Another caller complained that the United States was so powerful that it was impossible for Arabs to engage in a dialogue with it. The host and some guests expressed hope that the new Bush administration would prove more pro-Arab, since it had fewer Jews in high positions than the Clinton administration did, and because they had positive memories of the first Bush administration, which had confronted Israel over its expansion of settlements in the West Bank.

A July 2, 2002, episode of *The Opposite Direction* (B4) focused on whether it was rational to doubt U.S. intentions and credibility. One guest, Jamal al-Tamimi, argued that the evidence of American dishonesty was so overwhelming that prior skepticism about any American claim was warranted. The other guest, Muwafic Harb, countered that it was unfair to criticize the United States for pursuing its interests like any other nation-state. He reminded listeners that had the United States claimed on September 10 that it had information of an impending terrorist attack it would likely not have been believed. Tamimi responded that he had initially believed American claims, but that they repeatedly had turned out to be lies—and how else could he rationally respond than to become skeptical?

Three programs with a similar theme of "relations between Americans and Arabs" offer a useful snapshot of the changing terms of debate. In a January 2002 program (B1), the section headings included "The image of Arabs that Americans hold after 9/11"; "The image of America that Arabs hold"; "The American media and its role in distorting the image of Arabs"; and "What is the route to rapprochement between the Arab and American peoples?" The summary headings of a similarly themed show in September 2002 (B5) suggest a palpable decline in belief in the possibility of cooperation and mutual understanding: "Arab-American relations between cooperation and dependency"; "The reality of the American turn against Arab states"; and "Arab states between submission to America and the possibility of confrontation." Another program on a similar theme in September 2004 (C7) featured these headings: "The secret behind American interest in the Middle East"; "Arab oil and economic hegemony"; "Imposing American values on the Middle East"; "The invasion of Iraq and serving Israeli interests"; and "Destroying the power of Arab states."

In period A, discussion of America revolved almost entirely around high politics—Iraq, Israel and the Palestinians, support for autocratic Arab regimes. In one (A5), the U.S. presence in the Gulf was likened by the host to a military occupation, as U.S. troops defended unpopular Arab regimes from their own people. Another (A3) framed the debate as a choice between "American contempt for Arabs" or "the Arabs themselves are contemptible" because of the failure to effectively bring about democratic changes or a more popular foreign policy. In period B, discussion largely revolved around questions of American power and hegemony and its increased presence in the region. Despite the greater urgency and greater pessimism, the terms of debate resembled those in period A: Arab weakness, American contempt for Arab concerns, and how the United States might be influenced or resisted. Period C, however, shows a dramatic change. Al-Jazeera programs featured enormous amounts of discussion and debate about Bush's calls for democratic reform: whether U.S. power might help the Arab people in their own struggles (C1), or worrying about the threat of U.S. power (C6). By period D, the United States had become more of a background feature in the reform debates, which tended to focus more on specific countries or on internal Arab concerns. An April 2005 program on "The American Role in the Movements of the Arab Peoples" (D5) offered this narrative progression: "American reforms between reality and deception"; "Truth of the failure of oppositions to confront regimes"; "The possibility of making national choices apart from external pressure." Liberal Arab politicians continued to struggle to reconcile accepting financial or other support from America with their opposition to U.S. foreign policy.

The Arab Politics of Anti-Americanism

Arab anti-Americanism is neither purely political nor completely detached from American policies. Expressions of anti-American sentiment do seem to fluctuate in response to unpopular—and intrusive—U.S. policies. But this does not mean that changed U.S. policies alone would easily erase an entrenched schema governing the evaluation of America. The deep distrust of America, which has hardened and deepened in the last few years, means that any American initiative will be greeted with suspicion, and will not likely quickly win goodwill. Nor would an American withdrawal from the region—even if this were possible in an age of globalization—assuage anti-Americanism: many liberal and political anti-Americans would view this as a calculated decision to abandon Arabs to Israeli designs and leave Iraq in chaos, while radical anti-Americans would claim victory and likely press even harder. Responding to Arab anti-Americanism will require real changes in policies, especially in the area of promoting democratic reform, an area in which many Arabs share America's expressed goals. It will also require a much greater effort to engage constructively with the ongoing Arab arguments about America.

What I have found supports some of the key contentions of this book. In the period between 1999 and 2004, the American presence in the Arab world measurably increased. The normative valence attached to this increased impact was overwhelmingly negative, in large part because of U.S. policies toward Israel and Iraq. But the continued centrality of the issue of U.S. hypocrisy to the Arab critique suggests that there is a reservoir of hope that the United States could live up to its rhetoric, particularly on issues related to democratic and economic reform. Were the United States to adopt appropriate policies (such as genuinely promoting democratic reform arranging an equitable settlement between Israel and the Palestinians) Arab attitudes might change. That U.S. criticism of Hosni Mubarak's regime has been well received is one example of an Arab willingness, even eagerness, to see the United States live up to its own democracy-promoting rhetoric.

Addressing political anti-Americanism is worth doing, particularly since the salience of the United States in Arab politics is likely to increase rather than decrease in coming years. Against Michael Doran, who argues that "anti-Americanism is a clever alibi, but hardly a unifying force across the great divides of a society,"[60] I suggest that anti-Americanism could become such a unifying force due to the increasingly commonly understood salience and valence of America's presence in the region, the presence of important actors interested in making it so, and the

60. Doran 2004.

increasing importance of a shared satellite television media. No single policy will satisfy all anti-Americanisms, nor should the United States try to do that. The radical, essentialist anti-Americanism of al-Qaida offers no room for dialogue or changed minds. But the vast mainstream of Arab politics remains open to persuasion, even if the burden is very much on the United States to prove its critics wrong. Should the United States respond effectively to the specific complaints of this political mainstream, it is far less likely that the cultural and radical anti-Americanisms in the Arab world will cohere into a master frame capable of sustaining a politically relevant anti-Americanism.

IV

DYNAMICS OF ANTI-AMERICANISM

8

Anti-Americanism as Schemas and Diacritics in France and Indonesia

JOHN R. BOWEN

The phrase "anti-Americanism" suggests a set of individual, irrational attitudes toward Americans, U.S. society, or the U.S. government. We can view the matter in a slightly different way, however: in terms of the ideas, images, and theories (or "schemas," a concept I develop below) held concerning the United States. These ideas might be negative, positive, or relatively neutral. People often hold a number of such ideas. They may be in tension with, or even contradict, one another. Some of these ideas will be more salient at some times rather than others, possibly because of current events. People also may deploy them in strategic fashion to justify their own policies, to formulate a sense of their national identity vis-à-vis features of the United States, or to criticize more general features of today's world, such as globalization or neoliberalism.

In some parts of the world, people may hold a set of ideas about the United States that have long historical depth and that they consider to have been confirmed by past events. In these cases they may not look for much new information before interpreting an event in terms of their preexisting understandings. In other countries (and the units need not be countries) people may not have such a set of well-formed ideas about the United States, or they may be less accustomed to drawing on such ideas. In these cases they may be more likely to radically revise their ideas in the face of new events.

In this chapter, I explore two cases that differ in the way just described: the long-term images and ideas found in France and the shallower and intermittent

I thank the continuing direction and friendly criticisms offered by the skillful organizers of this project, Bob Keohane and Peter Katzenstein, as well as the comments provided by other readers of earlier drafts of this chapter, and in particular David Laitin, Charles Hirschkind, and Sophie Meunier.

anti-Americanism found in Indonesia. These two cases are perhaps extreme versions of a broader contrast between Europe, where greater time and more contact have fashioned specific and deeply rooted schemas about the United States, and Asia, where contact has been intermittent, knowledge more often indirect, and schemas therefore less well-developed and more subject to sharp shifts. I pay special attention to the ideas and attitudes of Muslims in France and Indonesia. Because France has been given special attention both in this book (Sophie Meunier, chapter 5) and in books that she cites, I devote more of this chapter to Indonesia.

As an anthropologist I look for the particular ways in which people combine and change their ideas about the world in specific settings or events. This general orientation leads me to look to the ways in which actors develop schemas and theories about the United States and to the forms that these schemas take, particularly narrative forms that explain how the world works. This approach leads me to talk less about attitudes and more about positions, concepts, and strategic uses of both. It is largely a rationalist position but one that emphasizes the particular and the shifting natures of these ideas.

Concepts and Evidence

The very topic of "anti-Americanism" challenges my emphasis on the rational and the particular. Looking for common dimensions of statements by people throughout the world inevitably tends to depict anti-Americanism as a coherent and globally distributed phenomenon, as something that is "out there" and that can be measured across countries and followed over time. Adding credibility to this assumption are the strong resemblances across countries in ideas held about the United States. In all world regions one hears similar criticisms of the United States as imperialistic, hedonistic, and insufficiently concerned with the welfare of its own citizens. (One might argue, in accord with pragmatic theories of truth, that these convergences indicate the criticisms' plausibility.) The typology proposed by Peter Katzenstein and Robert Keohane in chapter 1 elegantly captures those resemblances.

Yet precisely because anti-Americanism consists of negative images and ideas, it often also serves as an alter image of one's own country or tradition, and thus retains a diacritic particularism. Actions, values, or institutions imagined as characteristic of the United States can become a convenient or psychologically satisfying object against which public leaders or intellectuals can fashion ideas of how *their* society ought to look. These processes of negative self-definition invoke anxieties, self-images, and political experiences that are quite specific to each country, and that often form part of broader political or social strategies. Thus we have on the one hand a single, broadly shared set of ideas, images, and complaints—about a materialistic society, imperialistic policies, hypocritical leaders—and on the other hand multiple sets of particular emotions and theories. This dual nature of anti-Americanism permits local actors to develop and draw on this general repertoire of ideas and images in culturally specific and strategically motivated ways.

Types of Evidence

The gap between the global and the particular dimensions of anti-Americanism is widened by a methodological division of labor between multiple-country surveys and single-country histories: the poll and the genealogy. The former add to the sense that there is a social phenomenon "out there" that rises and falls in intensity; the latter underscores the particularistic nature of conceptions of the United States.

Each approach has its strengths. Attitude surveys can track rises and falls in answers to survey questions; if the questions and methods remain constant, they can suggest hypotheses about causal relations between particular events and levels of anti-Americanism sentiment (see Pierangelo Isernia, chapter 3). The Pew Global Attitudes Project studies are good examples of this research. Pew researchers are able to pose interesting questions of their data (for example, between attitudes toward American policies and attitudes toward Americans), and they can track changes over time. However, what they capture is the result of a process whereby a respondent aggregates many different and sometimes conflicting beliefs at the moment a survey taker poses a question—but not how the respondent sorts through his or her ideas (Giacomo Chiozza, chapter 4).

Furthermore, survey research tells us little about the interplay among institutions, broad cultural orientations, and ideas about the United States. We may learn that Muslims in Indonesia and Muslims in Jordan view U.S. gender relations in very different ways, but we cannot go much further than that. What is it about Islamic teachings in the two countries that produce these differences? Are the respondents thinking of different things when they answer? We learn that French and Germans have differing forms and levels of anti-American sentiment but do not learn much more than that. Why does French anti-Americanism seem so stubborn and the German variant less so? Surveys are not really designed to answer such questions; they must be supplemented by other types of study.

We usually turn to studies of specific countries or traditions for answers to those questions. A genealogy (in Michel Foucault's sense) of anti-Americanism traces links, processes of transmission, and abrupt changes in the objects of study, as in Philippe Roger's *The American Enemy* (2005), a study of anti-Americanism in France during the eighteenth and nineteenth centuries. This literary approach traces topoi in French travel literature, essays, fiction, and political analysis, identifying the specific lines of transmission from one author to another. It has the virtue of focusing on specific ways of writing about the United States, making few assumptions about the content of anti-Americanism, and indeed allowing for sharp breaks in the main ideas and the emotional content of those ideas. If we had a dozen studies similar to Roger's, we could begin to undertake historical comparative work on ways of expressing ideas about the United States and processes by which those ideas are transmitted and changed.

The Pew surveys and Roger's genealogy concern very different objects. How could one translate between the history of a specific image—the barren landscape of New York City in twentieth-century literature, for example—and answers to a survey question about the dangers posed by the United States? Furthermore, the anti-American images themselves often are ambivalent: the urban landscape has power but is culture-free; America may be godless but it offers great economic opportunity. How and why do these images take on a specific value? Why do particular people evoke them in specific circumstances and to what ends?

These questions take us back to the concerns that motivate survey research: given a repertoire of negative images, what leads some people to adopt them and others not? But we wish to add: How do these images cohere, how are they deployed? We need to be able to break down broad attitudes into the specific ideas, images, and theories they contain, and the way these ideas are used.

Schemas and Narratives

The notion of a "schema" that Katzenstein and Keohane develop in chapter 1 has been adopted by many in psychology and anthropology as a way to study how people move through the world by drawing on categories. Schemas are sets of representations that process information and guide action.[1] They contain both relatively fixed ideas and ideas that depend on contextual cues. A schema followed by American students in a classroom would contain concepts of teacher and examination and "scripts" for answering questions, but these would be modified in interaction sequences. First-year law students famously must relearn the scripts for questions and answers that they had mastered in college, but this is true for anyone who moves from one institution to another, even within a single society.

In the social sciences, cross-cultural comparative research projects have developed schema-oriented approaches to variation. For example, Michèle Lamont and her colleagues have highlighted differences in ideas about worth across countries, across regions within countries, and across social-class lines.[2] In all these cases, differences among individuals are best captured as different weightings of the same bundle of normative qualifiers. All workers value work, for example, but they differ from one place to another in the weightings they give to income, task mastery, and consumption patterns. It is the particular weightings that define that which we often less precisely call "the culture."

These comparative sociological studies also point to the ways in which schemas are deployed to define one's identity negatively with respect to some other category of people. The "diacritic" use of schemas about kinds of people draws on the intrinsically negative nature of social schemas. One cannot have a social category schema without distinguishing it from other social categories: my notions of what "upper-class people" are like inevitably involve contrasts, positive or negative, with people of other classes.

How does this approach benefit the study of anti-Americanism? One frequent finding from attitude surveys is that people often hold multiple, conflicting views

---

1. In psychology, see Rumelhart 1980; in cultural anthropology, see Strauss and Quinn 1997.
2. See especially the collaborative French-American work, Lamont and Thévenot 2000.

about the United States, some positive and some negative (Chiozza, chapter 4). What we take to be overall levels of anti-American sentiment at any one moment is the result of a particular weighting of disparate, sometimes contradictory, schemas. This set may include schemas about American society, about Americans, or about particular policies or public officials. For example, in the eight Muslim-majority countries surveyed before the Iraq invasion, 47 percent of all respondents held positive attitudes toward American ideas of freedom and democracy. Country-specific studies allow us to further disentangle the elements combined in these responses; they include anger at hypocrisy (dragging the overall positive ratings down) and respect for the ideal of rule of law and voting (bringing the ratings up).[3]

These schemas coexist over time: they do not appear or disappear but rise or fall in salience relative to each other and relative to other concerns. For example, despite overall low approval for the United States, survey respondents continue to mention their admiration for the strength of the rule of law in the United States. This schema forms part of the phenomenon that Katzenstein and Keohane (chapter 1) call "liberal anti-Americanism." I would analyze this orientation not as a stable type of anti-Americanism but as a combination of several distinct schemas: positive ones, such as that about the rule of law in the United States, and negative ones, such as that about American disrespect for international law. Both schemas can be grounded in extensive knowledge of U.S. policies. I see this sort of complex combining of schemas not as evidence of "ambivalence" but as evidence of the awareness by some people of inconsistencies in U.S. policies and institutions.

Examining anti-Americanism in terms of schemas thus allows us to disaggregate "attitudes" into multiple ideas whose relative degrees of salience shift over time. A second benefit from this approach is that it corrects a tendency to think of these attitudes as irrational. If we analyze anti-Americanism into interconnected images and ideas, we continue to see it as involving biases and stereotypes, but not uniquely so. From a cognitive perspective, at least, anti-Americanism may not be any more irrational than pro-Americanism, liberalism, or a preference for German cinema. All these dispositions can bias our perceptions, and they may short-circuit our calling for more information before making a judgment. But they are not necessarily irrational: they may be the product of well-developed analyses of politics, history, or art.

Schema research also suggests some specific avenues for research into anti-Americanism. Some cognitive researchers argue that certain kinds of categories (e.g., race, ethnicity) are easier to conceptualize than others (e.g., class).[4] This finding is interesting for the study of anti-Americanism because researchers frequently note disclaimers among respondents that they object "to the policies not to the people." Such a distinction draws on two different types of representation, the essentialist (people) and the nonessentialist (policies). The cognitive findings could thus help explain survey and focus group findings. Yet we also note connections between anti-

3. See, for example, the focus group studies carried out by Charney Research in Morocco, Egypt, and Indonesia, December 1–14, 2004. Charney and Yakatan 2005.

4. For example, Hirschfeld 1996. It is interesting that much of this work has been done by social anthropologists who went to the psychological laboratory and brought their social concerns with them.

Americanism and anti-Semitism. Do we need to distinguish between more or less essentialist forms of anti-Americanism? Such a distinction could be important if it (a) allows us to better explore the implications of cognitive research for politics and (b) points to the different social consequences of racism-like forms of anti-Americanism and policy-focused forms of anti-Americanism.[5]

Cognitively, then, anti-Americanism might consist of two or more very different types of schemas. Some schemas would have to do with types of persons ("Americans"); these schemas are of the type that some cognitive psychologists believe are relatively easy to conceptualize. Others would have to do with systems, such as the image of the United States as hedonistic or overly multiculturalist, or with theories about the workings of an imperialistic economy. These schemas might exhibit distinct degrees of malleability, and they would not need to be consistent with one another.

Indeed, cognitive science suggests that the same bits of information might be integrated into two or more distinct schemas but that this "shared use of information" does not bring the schemas together.[6] So, the large number of eyewitnesses to the crash of an airplane into the Pentagon on 9/11 is consistent with and thus verifies the schema that terrorists were behind the attacks on that day. However, the same fact (as mentioned in the best-selling book by Thierry Meyssan, which I will explore later) is also consistent with an opposing schema in which the United States plotted the attacks and is so clever and powerful that it was able to get all those people to bear false witness!

Schemas also tend to be tightly organized internally, with an unchanging architecture. Occupants of positions will be more likely to change than will their relationships. For example, a French schema about authority, one that holds that elites do and should run the country, persists through the Revolution, across oscillations between empire and republic, and through the alternations of Left and Right governments. Its hold on people's imaginations makes it difficult for them to understand how other countries might be run. This finding suggests that any number of new "facts" about the United States can be assimilated into preexisting schemas, as when people take humanitarian aid to be evidence of designs on the assisted countries.

People often construct schemas in the form of narratives, where they may become cognitively more accessible to actors, and thus easier to transmit and to remember.[7] Sharing these narratives can then be said to constitute a community of narration, within which people can tell each other stories and expect to have their narratives ratified. Together, actors reinforce each other's sense that they have a good grasp of the world.

Narratives are thus both individual and collective.[8] We "know" things about the world because we read, or hear, or experience something that in most cases already

---

5. The research mentioned above would predict that anti-American sentiments that attempt to distinguish between policies and people would slide toward generalizing about people.

6. Pascal Boyer, personal communication.

7. Bruner 1986.

8. Wertsch 2002.

has been mediated or framed by producers of knowledge. We also bring to these acts of knowing templates or frameworks that we have derived from earlier instances of knowing. Knowledge is thus socially-mediated and iterative.

Research on memory shows that actors often construct memories out of what James Wertsch calls "schematic narrative templates": schemas that underlie narratives and that contain "implicit theories" about how the world works.[9] Narrative analysis involves discerning ways in which actors draw on schematic templates to produce a wide variety of surface-level narratives. Wertsch takes as an example the Russian template of "triumph-over-alien-forces," which has produced accounts of history from the Mongols to Hitler.[10] Wertsch emphasizes that this ubiquitous template does not lead Russians to deny "facts" but shapes the ways in which they view the motives of historical actors. Furthermore, the quite different stories of history written in the 1990s continue to be shaped by this template, only now the aliens are thought to be internal enemies of the society rather than external enemies.

These narrative templates may be superordinate or subordinate to schemas. They may regulate schematic variation by bringing together schemas from different domains, giving them an overall meaning and limiting the extent of their variation and recombination. Wertsch's Russian example shows this regulative function with respect to schemas, and it may be that stories of wars and revolutions may typically work in this way, as superordinate to schemas and thus both "regulative" of schemas and "constitutive" of historical understandings (see David Kennedy's chapter on European narratives about America, which serve to construct schemas). Alternatively, two or more distinct narratives may be constructed out of a single schema: in this case, the schema provides the common source of ideas and theories for alternative narratives.

French Anti-Americanism

These observations suggest that we should look for distinct schemas, possibly organized into narrative templates, that are shared by some number of actors in each country we study. In this chapter I consider anti-American schemas and their uses in France and Indonesia. France probably has the best-established repertoire of ideas and images about the United States, and we would expect that we would find this repertoire used to define and justify French institutions, ideas, and projects. Because Meunier (chapter 5) provides an extensive analysis of French anti-Americanism, I limit my discussion to several specific dimensions of the French case, and in particular the way that actors deploy schemas about the United States to comment on French society and politics.

At least some of the major French schemas about the United States may be inserted into more than one narrative and may be given positive or negative evalu-

9. Ibid., 59–60.
10. Ibid., 93–116.

ations. For example, the idea that the American economy and society are both based on a free-market ideology is not in itself positive or negative. Some writers present this schema in the form of a negative narrative, which brings together Tocqueville's warnings about excessive individualism, stories of late nineteenth-century robber barons, and contemporary data about the ragged American social safety net. Others present America's "liberalism" (in the European sense of free-market individualism) in a strongly positive way, as in the writings of Jean-François Revel[11] or the pro–free-market writings that came out of France during the 1980s, in the years after Mitterrand's policies had lost their luster.

The "liberal America" schema is thus neither pro- nor anti-American in itself but is a form of knowledge that is broadly distributed within France and that individual actors may view with enthusiasm, hatred, or, as I believe is the case with the vast majority of French people today, with a combination of positive and negative evaluations: positive with respect to low unemployment and high growth, negative with respect to the weak system of social support, and so forth. Many in France see with some regret that their society may move in a liberal direction. They may see that move as inevitable in order to counter the looming expenses of the safety net and the high rates of unemployment, but they may also fear the consequences for the sense of responsibility the French have for one another.

In these discussions, "liberal America" serves as a pole of reference for discussions about France. French evaluations of that schema vary across individuals and over time, and the schema may be internally dissected and parts of it assigned different evaluations, but the schema remains relatively stable. This example (and, indeed, the shift to "schemas" as an analytical tool) suggests the value of taking as our object the broad set of schemas about the United States, and not just schemas that have a negative value. Once we take that step, then "anti-Americanism" starts to look like a set of internally complex schemas.

We Are Not an "Anglo-Saxon" Society

Let us consider the "diacritic" use of schemas in more detail. In France, many studies of political theory and political institutions contrast France to "Anglo-Saxon societies." The negative features of the latter justify the contrasting features of French society. In these works, "Anglo-Saxon" means not common law and habeas corpus but a regrettable tendency toward multiculturalism or "communalism" (*communautarisme*) in both social life and political theory. In these strategic uses, the trope is less a theory about the United States and Britain than it is a shorthand way to refer to features that would be, or are, undesirable in France.

In my own interviews for a project on French ideas about religion and the state, intellectuals and public officials inevitably invoked "Anglo-Saxon societies" in this contrastive way, not with an elitist sneer but as a cool analytic attempt to point to a "French exception." (Generally, and intriguingly, references to legal or philosophical

11. See Revel 2003.

differences were to Britain, but references to the social and cultural consequences were to the United States.)

For example, in 2003, political philosopher Blandine Kriegel (who once ran a Maoist cell but now serves as an adviser to President Jacques Chirac on the integration of immigrants in France) explained to me the nature of the social contract in France by contrasting French *laïcité* (roughly, "secularity"). to the "Anglo-Saxon" idea of freedom of religion: "In Anglo-Saxon thinking, in Locke or Spinoza, it is the concrete individual who has rights; freedom of conscience is the foundation. In our tradition these liberties are guaranteed through political power, which guarantees a public space that is neutral with respect to religion." She went on to describe the importance of religious neutrality in the public sphere, and ended with the declaration that "there will never be Sikh civil servants in France!" Here she referred to the much-publicized British cases in which Sikhs, whose religious norms require them to keep their hair uncut and covered, had won the right to keep their turbans on even while working for the government.

This diacritical and negative reference to "Anglo-Saxon" thinking proved very useful for politicians in justifying the March 15, 2004 law against wearing religious signs in public schools. The law goes well beyond the 1905 law stipulating that the state would not favor or subsidize churches, and beyond the general political idea that political life should not be based on religious referents. The 1905 law and the relevant jurisprudence state that civil servants, including public school teachers, may not display their religious affiliations. The new law expands the obligation to include students. In the debates on the law at the National Assembly in February 2004, the deputies who favored the law had to find new grounds for this law. It was rhetorically important that they be able to point to mirror images of the French model in order to redefine the legal bases for that model. The most useful foil was the "Anglo-Saxon" model. They characterized this model as one in which society was a composite of distinct communities, with little or no obligation to work or live together, and where each community closed in on itself. This characterization was also applied to some Muslim communities in France. The United States, and certain communities within France, shared this feature of privileging narrow group interest over the general interest of society.[12]

More broadly, many French criticisms of U.S. ways of living, as opposed to policies, have to do with worries about French ways of living, and are really about broad challenges to sovereignty that have to do with globalization and Europeanization as much as with America. Current debates about whether the French should work more than they do often invoke the contrast with American work habits (as well as contrasts within Europe). The United States provides a particularly salient set of symbols for general social and economic processes. Choosing to attack an American symbol may also rally more people than would an attack on a French one. When José Bové and his followers tore down a partially built McDonald's restaurant in Millau in southern France, they were protesting broad economic processes that threatened

12. See the analysis of the law in Bowen 2006b.

small farmers and threatened an agriculture based on local products cultivated on local soil. They also were continuing in a long history of Larzac-area protests against actions by the French state that contradicted the interests of local farmers. The marketing policies of a large conglomerate such as Carrefour probably have a greater direct effect on these farmers and on French purchasing habits than does the presence and activities of the McDonald's chain. But attacking a salient symbol of American economic imperialism, culinary homogenization, and unhealthy food attracted more popular support than attacking a grocery store chain where many French people prefer to do their shopping.

The Real Causes of 9/11

Although one can find conspiracy theories almost anywhere, an interesting facet of French theories is the way in which they are given extensive and often uncritical media treatment. This treatment supports the idea that these theories about how the United States works show up because of a consistent anti-American bias for such theories. French television stations and newspapers are run by a tightly interlocking network of intellectuals and producers, a structural condition that promotes consistent media biases.[13]

Let me offer an especially striking example that nonetheless shows the general nature of the problem. In 2002, the French left-wing activist Thierry Meyssan wrote *L'effroyable imposture*, whose thesis was that the claim that Flight 77 crashed into the Pentagon on 9/11 was a fabrication by the U.S. government (which also had planted explosives in the base of the World Trade Center), designed to legitimate an invasion of Afghanistan for reasons of security, the control of oil pipelines, and domestic politics. The book quickly became the top nonfiction best seller and difficult to find. Throughout 2002 and 2003, French non-Muslim and Muslim friends of mine urged me to read it to discover the truth about 9/11.

The French media critic Daniel Schneiderman points to the television reception given this book as a prime example of the "media nightmares" increasingly characteristic of France. He singles out Thierry Ardisson of France 2 as "incarnating the infiltration of the logics of information marketing in public media, the channel France 2." Although all media compete desperately with each other for advertising dollars, the competition particularly affects France 2, a station that has a public mandate but must compete with totally private stations for its audience. Consequently, France 2 has not only to devote time to its mission of public service but also rather frantically looks for ways to attract viewers from the privatized TF1. France 2 thus has a very "bimodal" distribution of programs, including hours of Sunday morning programs on religions, on the one hand, and more exposé shows than any other station, on the other. Ardisson's show *Tout le monde en parle* (Everyone Is Talking about It) is frequently the first place where the latest accusations are aired. Such was the case for Thierry Meyssan's claims. Schneiderman shows how during the program

13. Halimi 1997.

Ardisson sometimes took Meyssan's side against detractors, working to keep the interest of the viewers, and failed to bring up the most telling set of facts others had cited against the conspiracy theory, namely, that many witnesses testified to seeing the plane crash.[14]

Although serious journalists eventually took on the claims, and rebuttal books were published by other French authors (followed by a second book by Meyssan), the argument's widespread appeal among ordinary French people needs to be explained. The book set out a logical argument that fit a schema about U.S. imperialist designs on the world. Many French writers and public intellectuals agree with one or more versions of this schema—Michael Moore is very popular in France. Some of these intellectuals have focused on the work of Leo Strauss as the key to a properly systematic and theoretical understanding of American neoconservatives, in particular those politicians and intellectuals associated with the Project for the New American Century. The Project's publications advocate a strong military presence in much of the world but particularly the Middle East.[15] Its founding members include William Kristol, Richard Cheney, Paul Wolfowitz, and Richard Perle. Some of those French intellectuals who read, or knew of, these publications took them to support the accusations made by Meyssan. Meyssan's book fits with this schema, even if it is not implied by it, nor sustainable on its own.

This example points up the difference between theories and biases. The theory that a combination of oil interests and neoconservative messianism lay behind the invasion of Iraq fits with quite a bit of evidence and thus is a theory well worth entertaining. Looking into or accepting such a theory is not a sign of anti-Americanism. Meyssan's claims, however, go well beyond this (or any other worthwhile) theory. A wide array of readers accepted claims that ignored the testimony of many onlookers only because they had taken on a degree of bias against American policies that obviated the need for strong evidence and well-reasoned arguments. In other words, the book was a best seller because it built both on reasonable theories about American policies and on strong biases among many French readers that led them to accept Meyssan's wild claims.

Other theories about 9/11 also circulated, although they would not have been aired in best sellers or on television. I heard theories that Jews were to blame for the attacks, either in the form of Israeli agents or through their control of the U.S. government. In the latter case, the Jewish conspiracy theories supplemented the Meyssan claims. Indeed, I heard considerable support for Meyssan's arguments by Muslim friends, who sometimes would add, briefly, a reference to the Jewish responsibility theories, usually the canard that "none of the Jewish workers showed up for work that day."

Muslim schemas about Jewish control of the media in France and the United States do not appear in surveys about French anti-Semitism, but they are deeply held.

14. Schneiderman 2003, 129.

15. Its September 2000 white paper on military strategy (Donnelly 2000) was very influential in shaping subsequent United States policy statements on military strategy.

Let me offer one example of how they surface. One Muslim teacher, a close acquaintance of mine, who has been especially vocal in denouncing anti-Semitism, was discussing why a certain television program portrayed Muslims in a bad light. He said that the producer's name was such-and-such, and then let his voice drop. I was supposed to perceive that it was a Jewish name and that this would explain the tone of the program. Nothing was "said," but the information that explained everything had been communicated.

These two schemas—American imperialism, Jewish media control—are distinct and not necessarily consistent with each other, but they can be and are held at the same time by a certain number of Muslims and by some non-Muslims in France. They also coexist with other schemas that are not at all anti-American, and these have to do with the "three-way" nature of references made to the United States by Muslims in Europe. Muslims in Europe deal most proximally with French or German or Italian governments, and their attitudes toward conditions of life in the United States, as distinct from U.S. foreign policy, are conditioned by those existentially prior encounters and struggles. Since 2002 public life in France has had an increasingly anti-Islamic flavor, occasioned by a government and media campaign to blame poor schools and a breakdown in social life on Islamic extremism, which supposedly infiltrates France by way of young Muslims in poor suburbs, and shows up when they force girls to wear head scarves. During the riots that swept French cities in fall 2005, some French politicians first blamed radical Muslims, before the secret police made it clear that there was no connection between Islamism and the riots.[16]

In this context the conditions of life for Muslims in the United States look pretty good to French Muslims. Many Muslim leaders in France have contacts with friends in the United States, and they are very aware of daily life there. They talk about the greater ease with which American Muslims organize, wear their head scarves, find ways to sacrifice on id al-Kabir, and so forth. One teacher in whose class on Islamic ethics I sat often strongly criticized the United States for its policies and in class would ask me to explain those policies, but in response to a student's use of "the West" (in October 2001, mind you) he said:

> I don't follow those who oppose "Islam" to "the West," who explain things by saying that "it is because we Muslims did such and such that the West did such and such" or vice versa. Things are all mixed together now, for example in the laboratories where they create airplanes and other things in the U.S., you have people from all over the world, a true mixing of all people from throughout the world.

For many Muslims in France, strong criticism of U.S. foreign policy, theories of Jewish influence on that policy, appreciation of religious freedom in the United States, and approval of international scientific and religious cooperation with the United States can all coexist. We learn more about these and other groups of people if we examine them as holding complex collections of schemas concerning the

16. See Bowen 2006a.

United States, only some of which exhibit the properties that would lead us to call them anti-American.

The French case thus points to ways in which broadly held and long-held schemas about the United States underlie ways of thinking about one's own society. These schemas are not all necessarily anti- or pro-American but serve to demarcate one way of life from another. They may be deployed in order to justify specific policies or to explain particular events in the world. In those actions of justification and explanation, they may be combined with other schemas. Public actors are able to use these schemas successfully precisely because many in France have made them part of their repertoires of concepts for understanding and evaluating what happens in the world around them.

Indonesian Anti-Americanism

Schemas about America are more central to French projects of self-definition and justification than to the corresponding Indonesian projects. I often hear Indonesians comment on individualism and violence in the United States in order to argue that Indonesian society is more humane. But these diacritic references to the United States are casual, often as part of a remark about a violent, imported television program. They are less important to Indonesian self-definition than are claims about the ability of Indonesians to live together without losing their cultural differences.

Related to this relatively shallow function of American schemas is the fact that Indonesia has shown the most extreme shifts in responses to questions about attitudes toward the United States of all Muslim countries. In 2002 61 percent of Indonesians surveyed in a Pew Global Attitudes Project study had "favorable" attitudes toward the United States, but one year later, after the invasion of Iraq, that number had dropped to 15 percent. After the American response to the tsunami in early 2005, sentiment changed sharply once again. A February 2005 survey found that negative opinion had dropped from 2003's 83 percent to 54 percent, and that the percentage expressing confidence in Osama bin Laden fell from 58 percent to 23 percent.[17]

We can think of a variety of explanations for the sharp nature of these swings relative to experiences in other countries. The Iraq invasion kicked off the rise and the tsunami explains the fall of anti-Americanism. But the amplitude of the swings requires other explanations. If it is simply the case that anti-Americanism is weak or superficial, could not one just as plausibly predict very mild responses to surveys, with lots of "don't knows"?

Direct and Indirect Anti-American Schemas

One starting point for an explanation may lie in making a new distinction, between schemas that are explicitly and solely about the United States and those that are, or

17. Lembaga Survey Indonesia results reported in *Singapore Straits Times*, March 7, 2005.

can be, seen as relevant to judging the United States but are directly about other issues. We can think of these two kinds of schemas as "direct" and "indirect" with respect to the United States.

Until recently, only indirect anti-American schemas have been widely diffused in Indonesia. These schemas concern Jewish plots, stories about forced Christianization, and narratives of the decline of the Muslim world. Obviously these three schemas can be linked to the United States, but often they exist on their own. Criticisms of U.S. one-sided policies in the Middle East also have a long life, but they have not been linked to everyday concerns in Indonesia. Only the interference by the CIA in Indonesian domestic affairs produced widely held directly anti-American sentiment, and it was perhaps balanced by knowledge of previous U.S. support for Indonesian independence.

In addition, many Indonesians have held positive views of the United States. A recent focus group study brought out the support for the greater role of the rule of law in the United States than in Indonesia. As one young Indonesian man said, "They obey the rules compared to our people, who usually ignore rules."[18] In studying Indonesian law, I have spoken with a great many Indonesian judges, lawyers, and clients, who invariably contrasted the corruption of the Indonesian legal system with the perceived transparency and fairness of the U.S. system.

Things have changed over the past eight to ten years, however. U.S. foreign policy has given credibility to new, *direct* anti-American views. These have to do with U.S. hostility toward Islam and Muslims, now functioning as schematic narrative templates that generate theories, often "conspiracy theories," and provide a negative spin to any event. For example, after the Bali bombing in October 2002, Indonesian vice president Hamzah Haz suggested that U.S. agents might have been responsible. Sidney Jones, head of the International Crisis Group's Indonesia project, reported that ordinary Indonesians, mostly mainstream Muslims, said the same, that the United States had engineered the blast to win sympathy for America. Many of these people were reacting against the pressure brought to bear by the United States on Indonesia and the Philippines to "step up" the war on terror and against the already looming invasion of Iraq.[19]

But what is interesting about these theories is that they are of a piece with other ideas that have nothing to do with Islam or Muslims. These ideas are generated by a schema in which the United States is assumed to always work for its own economic and political interests and against those of Indonesians. This schema knits together a number of otherwise unrelated claims, including, among others, (1) the notion that the United States, working with Australia, had brought about East Timor's independence, a loss deeply felt by many Indonesians; (2) the claim that the United States had somehow brought on the economic crisis of 1997; and (3) the opinion that although the United States did intervene to help Indonesians after the

18. Charney and Yakatan 2005.

19. Interview on Radio Free Europe, reported October 19, 2002, at http://www.rferi.org/nca/features/2002/10/17102002160603.asp (accessed June 1, 2005).

tsunami, Americans had known about the tidal wave in time to alert Indonesians but did nothing. This last argument is plausible (many Americans also have wondered why local authorities could not have been alerted) and fits the "imperialist schema."

In Indonesia, the more deeply anchored schemas are probably of the "indirect" sort, and in fact they could be considered to be "narrative templates" of the sort described by James Wertsch for Russia: those that have a long life and serve to regulate the content of new schemas.[20] Within Indonesian Muslim circles, two broadly distinguishable narrative templates vie for supremacy. One draws from the writings of the Muslim Brotherhood (Ikhwan ul-Muslimin) in Egypt and elsewhere and emphasizes the moral primacy of Islamic allegiances over particular nationalisms. A second narrative emphasizes broad processes of secularization and distinguishes the domain of religion from that of politics. The first can become anti-Semitic and anti-American; the second is strongly pluralistic and can be quite pro-Western.

These two templates coexist in the minds (and writings) of a number of Indonesian intellectuals and probably among many other Muslims in Indonesia. This commingling theory makes sense of polling and focus group data and of the statements of many "moderate" Muslim intellectuals over the years. It also helps explain why attitude surveys can exhibit such rapid rises and falls in levels of anti-Americanism.

These templates have their histories in the "intellectual pilgrimages" of Indonesian Muslims. Beginning in the late 1960s, Muslim leaders who had wished Indonesia to adopt Islamic law for Muslims (many of them associated with the political party Masjumi or the activist organization Dewan Dakwa Islamiyah Indonesia (DDII), under the leadership of Muhammad Natsir) moved close to the Muslim World League. The League provided funds for the DDII to sponsor students who wished to study in the Middle East. Natsir sent students to Saudi Arabia, where they learned the ideas and methods of the Ikhwan ul-Muslimin, especially the methods of neighborhood-based *dakwa* or "call" to Muslims to return to proper Islam. These methods were reproduced in Indonesia and influenced a new generation of dakwa activists. Intellectuals and activists returning from these DDII pilgrimages began to translate the works of Ikhwan founder Hassan al-Banna, as well as works by contemporary thinkers such as Yusuf al-Qaradawi.[21] During the 1980s, the number of Indonesian students in Saudi Arabia and Egypt rose sharply, nearing one thousand in each country, but these were mainly undergraduates; the Islam they returned with was learned in Brotherhood circles or discussion groups. It tended to include strong denunciations of Israel and of U.S. policy toward the Middle East.

In contrast with this Arabia-Cairo pole were the smaller numbers of more highly trained intellectuals sent to universities in North America from the late 1960s. Some, such as Amien Rais and Inaduddin Abdulrahim, were active in the dakwa movement. Others, such as Djalauddin Rahmat and the late Nurcholis Madjid, are better

---

20. See Wertsch 2002.
21. See Latif 2004 for an excellent discussion of these influences.

thought of as public intellectuals. The longer story of these intellectual pilgrimages includes the founding of the Islamic universities (IAINs), and the effect of the "liberal" orientation of Mukti Ali, minister of religious affairs in the 1970s, who sent students for postgraduate training in religious studies to North America, especially to McGill and the University of Chicago. These students were supposed to return with pragmatic ideas about Islam that could fit with technocratic ideas about society and development—and some did.

Some of these figures bridged these increasingly divergent communities and drew on both narrative templates. For example, Amien Rais and Syafi'i Ma'arif developed close ties with the DDII but then received their degrees under "liberal" teachers at Chicago. They kept both the Middle Eastern-Ikhwan schemas and the North American-liberal schemas at work in their minds. Amien Rais could preach a pluralist version of Islam consistent with his training at the University of Chicago. But on his return to Indonesia in 1978 he wrote in a mainstream reformist magazine that it was unfortunate that he had to study about Islam with Jews. He singled out his own dissertation supervisor.

The coexistence of these very different "schematic templates" about Islam, religion, and the United States show up in many different contexts. They are even more striking in neighboring Malaysia because of the higher income levels and long-term exposure to European and North American training. In the most sophisticated scholarly bookstores, the best-seller shelves look very much like those you would see in an American city, but next to the latest *New York Times* list and scholarly works in sociology and political science one discovers new editions of *The Protocols of the Elders of Zion*, Henry Ford's "The International Jew," and *Mein Kampf*—the last intended not for historical study but as a continuously relevant set of observations on how the world works.

Anti-American Narratives

As our concern here is primarily anti-American ideas, let me turn to two articles published in two Islamic magazines and on their respective Internet sites to illustrate how anti-American narratives draw on a wide variety of schemas. *Persatuan Islam* claims a heritage from the reformist writers and teachers of the 1920s and 1930s, in particular Ahmad Hassan, whose books explaining the reformist or modernist (*kaum muda*) approach, inspired by Muhammad 'Abduh, were distributed throughout Indonesia in the years before World War II and have continued to be reprinted and distributed. The movement and thus the publications have a broad following. *Sabili* is a more recent entry into Indonesia Islamic publishing. It takes a relatively hard line on international issues. *Sabili* translates Internet articles on foreign affairs and publishes them, or excerpts them with commentary by Indonesian Muslim writers and scholars. It is distributed outside mosques all over Indonesia and read by many Muslims.

In an article from September 2003, published first in *Sabili* and then reprinted in *Persatuan Islam*, a journalist analyzes the "Anti-American Tidal Wave" (the title of the article).[22] The rhetoric is one of a global surge in opposition to the United States in Europe, among Muslims, and by East Asians. The analysis is sophisticated: Korea opposes the U.S. crusade for free trade, Europeans resent American dominance, Muslims dislike the one-sided approach to the Middle East, and so forth. An editor of *Die Zeit* is quoted as saying that it was the Iraq invasion that started the "wave of hate" against the United States. The Pew Global Attitudes Project results are presented. A history of Middle East opposition is set out in which Osama bin Laden's "movement" appears among many others, most of longer duration.

A second *Sabili* article, from June 2003, analyzes the anti-Muslim prejudice of Americans, citing American journalists for its main points: Americans only know the rest of the world from films, they sent hate mail to Muslims after 9/11, and so forth.[23] The writer asks why those who write hatefully of Islam, from Samuel Huntington to Daniel Pipes, are listened to more than are writers such as John Esposito who urge cooperation with Islam. The answer, we learn, lies in the list of members of the Council for Foreign Relations, whose ranks include both Huntington and neoconservatives, many of whom are Zionists. From there the article slides into citations of *The Protocols of the Elders of Zion* as the plan that lies behind the writings of Paul Wolfowitz (who was U.S. ambassador to Indonesia before joining the Defense Department) and others. It closes with a long analysis by a "da'wa specialist," who reminds readers of the battle of Badr, when only 313 Muslims under Muhammad's leadership defeated far superior Meccan forces.

These articles are typical in the schemas they evoke: God's plan for Muslims' victory, the Jewish-Zionist conspiracy to dominate the world, in alliance with powerful Jewish and Christian Americans; Muslims' opposition to this domination through a number of convergent political movements; and the hatred created by the United States through its unilateral actions. Much of the analysis is sophisticated. Major political analysts in the United States and Europe are cited, and then their views are extended by Indonesian analysts, who add the bits about the *Protocols* and the Islamic historical parallels. Narratives familiar to the magazine's readers—the battle of Badr, the rise of Osama bin Laden in opposition to the U.S. presence in Saudi Arabia—are merely referred to, on the assumption that readers will fill in the details. This kind of writing potentially has a very broad appeal: more educated readers appreciate the wide reading behind the article; Muslims of all types respond to the linking of the battle of Badr, a key historical point of pride, to today's struggles.

"Jews" as an explanatory category is very much in the air, despite the absence of Jews from Indonesia and Indonesia's distance from the site of Jewish-Muslim conflicts. Focus groups held in Indonesia, Egypt, and Morocco elicited very similar comments, pointing up the degree to which the schema about Jewish control over U.S. affairs has spread:

22. Hardianto 2003.
23. Ridyasmara 2003.

Americans are mostly Jews. (older Indonesian man) Most Americans are Jewish. The richest person is Jewish. [America's] population, most are Jewish. Their religion is Jewish too. (young Indonesian woman) The real Americans are the Indians, but those who immigrated to the U.S. are Jewish. (older Moroccan woman) I think Christians and Jews are equal [in numbers in America but] Jews have wider influence. (older Indonesian woman)[24]

These statements might suggest a degree of ignorance on the part of these Muslims; a short piece by *New York Times* reporter Jane Perlez provides a very different idea. Perlez visited an Islamic school (*pesantren*) in Kalimantan (the island of Borneo), and quotes a student, called Muhammad in the article, as saying "I know from very deep in my heart, the United States is evil." His questions to Perlez revealed his relatively sophisticated schema for understanding the world: " 'Why is Milosevic a violator of human rights, but Ariel Sharon is not?' Sharon, he went on, 'killed a lot of people when he was head of the Israeli Army.' Why, asked Muhammad, was 'George Soros, the Hungarian Jew, such a rich man?' "[25]

Responses to 9/11 and the 2005 Tsunami Relief Effort

The aftermath of 9/11 provides important tests for the presence of anti-American bias, as does the American response to the 2004 tsunami. Gareth Barkin's analysis of Indonesian television coverage of the attacks of 9/11 concludes that (1) the major stations paid little attention to the evidentiary questions of who attacked and how, and that (2) they privileged coverage of anti-Muslim sentiment in the United States and ignored President Bush's and New York mayor Rudy Giuliani's admonitions to Americans to avoid anti-Muslim prejudice.[26]

Indonesian media responses thus fit the conditions outlined by Katzenstein and Keohane (chapter 1) for anti-American bias. Journalists reported different opinions about the causes of the attacks and did not try to sift out "the truth." Indonesian media also reminded viewers many times that Americans had wrongly accused Muslims of perpetrating the Oklahoma City bombing, reminders that, according to Barkin, may explain why in one magazine readers' poll, 46 percent of respondents claimed that the 9/11 attacks were done by Americans.

Anti-Semitic schemas were quickly activated after 9/11 in mainstream Islamic publications. *Republika* is a daily newspaper with high production values that developed as part of efforts in the late Suharto period to create a state-sponsored Muslim think tank. It takes self-consciously Islamic rather than more broadly Indonesian positions on issues but tries to attract and hold a broadly based Muslim readership. Right after 9/11, however, an editorial in the newspaper emphasized that the attacks were on "symbols of U.S. greatness [*kejayaan*]." The writer says that he will "put aside who

24. Charney and Yakatan 2005.
25. Perlez 2004.
26. Barkin 2001.

really masterminded the bombing" and instead focus on "New York as a city of Jews and a symbol of U.S. greatness." After describing the close relationship of Jews and the United States, the author predicts that the United States will attack a "scapegoat."[27]

Given this argument, it is not surprising that in a survey conducted for *Republika* between the attacks on the World Trade Center and the first attacks on Afghanistan, when asked who was responsible for the 9/11 attacks, 43 percent of the respondents said "anti-U.S. forces" but 34 percent said "radical Jews." In addition, 48 percent of respondents predicted that if the United States were to attack Afghanistan, U.S. forces would be wiped out. Barkin reminds readers that *Republika*'s positions and the opinions of its readers were more moderate than those of more extreme publications (such as *Sabili*).

Indeed, after the U.S. attacks on Afghanistan, it became difficult for Muslim groups to not support the call for jihad against the United States. The Majelis Ulama Indonesian, a national council of Muslim scholars drawn from the major, mainstream Muslim groups (mainly Muhammadiyah and Nahdlatul Ulama), called for jihad in late September 2001. When pressed, individual members of the organization fell back on the idea that jihad takes many forms, and condemned attempts to single out American tourists for violent action. Vice President Hamzah Haz, whose power base was with Muslim groups outside the two largest organizations, took on the mantle of defending Muslims, and opposed President Megawati Sukarnoputri support for the U.S.-led "war on terror."

"Moderate" Muslims, including many educated in the United States, subscribe to theories about the United States that we might wish to cite as evidence of anti-American attitudes. The quite "moderate" and English-language *Jakarta Post* (September 10, 2003) stated that "moderate" Indonesian Muslims "know very well" that the Afghanistan campaign was part of a long-standing "Bush and Co." plan to build an oil pipeline through Central Asia, and that oil also motivated the attack on Iraq.

The Indonesian response to the U.S. attack on Afghanistan also is supported by nationalism and resentment at outside meddling in Indonesian affairs. The arrest and trial of Abu Bakar Bashir, accused of heading Jemaah Islamiyah (labeled by the United States as a terrorist organization), was due to substantial U.S. pressure. It came not that long after (in Indonesian memories) the successful independence of East Timor, which was celebrated by most of the world but bitterly resented by most Indonesians as a loss of territory. The resentment was directed first and foremost at Australia, but the U.S. role in that conflict, in the 1965–66 massacres of "communists" (in which the role of the CIA was more fully revealed only recently), and in its post-9/11 pressures to arrest "fundamentalists," contributed to an overall picture of U.S. interference, now colored by a growing sense of U.S. opposition to Islam (a sense entirely absent in the 1980s, when I lived in Jakarta and Aceh).

27. quoted in Barkin 2001.

As recently as the middle of 2001 it would have been unthinkable for the leaders of Indonesia's two major Muslim organizations, the Nahdlatul Ulama and Muhammadiyah, to publicly decline invitations to come to Washington, as did those leaders in January 2003 on grounds that they were offended by the Bush policy on Iraq. The Muhammadiyah leader, A. Syafi'i Ma'arif, received his PhD from the University of Chicago; both are quite justly called "moderate" Muslim leaders in their efforts to develop pluralist forms of Islam in which Muslims of different schools can coexist, and to ensure that Indonesia remains a nonconfessional state in which Christians, Buddhists, and others can coexist with Muslims. That their refusal may have been mainly or even entirely required given the attitudes of their respective memberships only attests to a radical change in those attitudes. (That October they were able to tell President Bush in Bali that U.S. policies were a main cause of terror attacks.)

Indeed, our general sense that Indonesia stands for "moderate Islam" may need to be refined by looking at the dimension of receptivity to Western ideas. Here, Indonesians, perhaps because of less close interaction with European or American institutions, may be less receptive than other Muslim-majority countries. In the Pew survey, Indonesia was alone among the nine Muslim populations surveyed that had a (slim) majority, 53 percent, say that "democracy" would not work in their country because it was a Western way of doing things.

In the wake of the 2004 tsunami and the 2005 U.S. aid effort, Indonesian opinions shifted sharply once more. Most reporting on the effects of tsunami aid on world opinion has emphasized the rise in positive estimates of the role of the United States. In Indonesia as elsewhere (Katzenstein and Keohane, chapter 1), the aid given by the U.S. government to victims of the tsunami in Aceh met with widespread public approval.

However, writings about the aid have continued to be shaped by schemas about the negative role of the United States in the world. These negative shadings of stories show the continued presence of an anti-Americanism bias. *Persuatuan Islam*, on January 24, 2005, warned that foreign presence and foreign loans to Aceh for reconstruction might lead to foreign influence in what always had been known as the "Veranda of Mecca" for its strong commitment to Islam. But the article combines distinct, if not incompatible, evaluations of the United States. America is not giving enough aid compared to its earnings from Acehnese natural resources and should give more, says the author. But U.S. contributions are given in order to extract profit and make money through interest on loans. In any case, "foreign agents are running around" in Aceh, perhaps planting espionage devices.

The post-tsunami aid discussions have brought up not only anti-American biases but strategic uses of the idea of anti-Americanism by U.S. groups. This phenomenon exists whenever reasoned criticism of U.S. policies is dismissed as merely another instance of anti-Americanism. But in the U.S. Christian press, Indonesian resistance to U.S. tsunami aid itself was seen as anti-Americanism. Christian missionaries saw a duty and perhaps an opportunity after the tsunami to save lives and souls in Sri Lanka and Aceh. One of their ideas was to place orphans in Christian homes, an idea that ran against Indonesian ways of thinking for two reasons: a fear of Christian conversion through adoption (precisely what the missionaries intended) and a long-standing reliance in Indonesia on orphanages run by Muslim associations. The negative reaction led to a headline on an evangelical website, "Indonesia's Anti-American Stance Hinders Foreign Tsunami Aid."[28]

"Episodic" Anti-Americanism

Unlike the Russian one-size-fits-all narrative template of "triumph over alien forces" described by James Wertsch,[29] Indonesian schemas concerning the United States are varied and not necessarily consistent. U.S. actions are said to be motivated by the desire to secure oil revenues, to spread Christianity, or to work for the interests of Israel. The United States is seen as controlled by Jews or respectful of the rule of law and religious freedom. The two articles from *Sabili* I presented above do not neatly organize these various schemas into one consistent narrative. Indonesians do have such narratives—about the participation of all social groups in the struggle for independence, for example. President Suharto spent a lot of time and money trying to get Indonesians to internalize another narrative template, that the army saved Indonesia from the Communists by its slaughters in 1965–66.

Americans and America are not entirely absent from these narratives, but they do not play major roles. The salience of a schema about the United States is much more episodic, the result of specific events. After the Iranian Revolution one saw lots of anti-U.S. banners. These faded away but returned after the U.S. invasion of Iraq. It may be that the long-term fighting over Palestine has "ratcheted up" anti-American feeling such that it now has a somewhat higher floor than before, especially as those who adhere to the Muslim Brotherhood narrative have now become more active in schools and training institutes than was the case in the 1970s. But compared with the Middle East or France, anti-American schemas are of recent vintage and are not central to Indonesian narratives about their own past (on the Middle East, see Marc Lynch, chapter 7). They also tend to be accompanied by sentiments of anger and disillusionment rather than hatred.

Schemas about the United States may be more important as elements in episodes of political conflict. The sudden arrival of U.S. ships off the coast of Banda Aceh a relatively short time after the tsunami (and before any significant response by the Indonesian government) made salient a schema about a generous and powerful America, but even more dramatically it highlighted within Indonesia the Indonesian state's brutality toward the Acehnese. The event quickly raised levels of approval for the United States, in part because it placed into stark contrast the response of the two governments, a contrast frequently made by Acehnese in personal communications to me or in unguarded comments to journalists.

28. http://www.crosswalk.com/special/tsunami/1307891.html (accessed May 20, 2005).
29. Wertsch 2002.

The narrative templates followed by producers of television programs and editors of newspapers probably need to be analyzed in other terms, however: by their sense of their viewer or reader "base" and the limitations on how they are allowed by the state or by pressure groups in the society to depict events in the world. Television stations and newspaper offices were attacked in the early 2000s for stories said to be offensive to Muslims, events that partially explain the bias in coverage of 9/11 noted by Barkin. Unlike al-Jazeera (Lynch, chapter 7), Indonesian television stations and newspapers plot their production strategies with domestic consumers in mind and are less likely to take risks. It may be that an anti-American narrative template concerning the Middle East now has reached the point where it filters stories in at least some of these national news outlets.

Schemas, Diacritics, and Regions

Indonesian and French schemas about the United States share some elements, including a fear of imperialism and a dislike of arrogance, but overall they contrast strikingly in content and in function. Some of the differences are due to Indonesia's large Muslim majority, which shares with many other countries concerns about the oppression of Muslims and attacks on other Muslim-majority countries. But more important for comparative purposes is the different roles played by schemas about the United States in each country's public life, and the differences in the strategic deployment of anti-American schemas.

The United States and France each has a repertoire of schemas about the other that can be deployed for a range of purposes, from rallying against a cultural enemy to defining each country's own identity. Indonesia and the United States have no such reciprocal image repository to draw on. When Indonesian public figures do invoke images of the United States, those images have little to do with Indonesia. Conversely, when an Indonesian official strategically denounces U.S. interference in Indonesia's internal affairs in order to affirm Indonesian sovereignty, that denunciation does not invoke any particular features of the United States. Any country's interference would be denounced in much the same way—Indonesian attacks on Australia for the latter's involvement in East Timor are a case in point.

Indonesia and the United States are simply quite distant both from each other and from those current centers of conflict that generate many of the negative schemas about the United States, in particular the Palestine-Israel conflict. Of course, people can refer to historical frameworks that have their home elsewhere, as when Indonesian or American Muslims complain of U.S. Middle East policies, but these complaints do not have the same edge, rarely include personal knowledge, and do not relate to everyday life in a very pressing way. They are thus more likely to change quickly, or not to lead to action.

Consider how sheer distance or proximity makes a difference in these sentiments elsewhere. The relative proximity of Muslim-majority countries to France or Spain makes Muslim anti-Americanism in those counties very different from Muslim anti-

Americanism in the United States. The U.S. version is not fed by constant travel between regions, and the conflicts referred to in these schemas—in Palestine, Chechnya, or indeed against governments of Muslim-majority countries—are much farther away, subjectively as well as geographically.

Indonesians do have an inherited set of images about the Dutch and the Japanese that involve tangible memories or tales told by parents. During the Suharto years, the Japanese provided displaced targets for anti-Chinese sentiments (anti-Chinese demonstrations against Indonesion Chinese would have been severely repressed). Lingering anti-Japanese feelings could be mobilized for these demonstrations. Until recently, anti-Americanism has had very little such local historical purchase in Indonesia, CIA involvement in the 1965–66 massacres aside.

Nor is there deep anti-Americanism in neighboring Malaysia, despite former Prime Minister Mahathir's fulminations against George Soros. One anthropologist reported to me that anti-Americanism only concerns foreign policy, and even then has led to no graffiti or demonstrations: "It is all in thought and casual comments." Opinions are very policy-specific. For example, many on the faculty of the International Islamic University in Kuala Lumpur wanted George W. Bush to win the 2004 U.S. presidential election because they were afraid that if Kerry were president he would try to reverse the outsourcing of information technology work to Asia. On political issues, however, they all thought Bush was terrible, and these feelings were all about Iraq and not about American society: "They were not deep. People see CNN, and it shows the images that stoke these feelings—and it is CNN images and not those on al-Jazeera."[30]

Some regions may share internally more in the way of schemas about the United States than do others. It seems that there are more broadly shared negative attitudes toward America in the Arab world than in Europe, a difference that probably has most to do with (a) the importance of the Israeli-Palestine conflict for opinion in the Arabic-speaking Middle East, (b) the long history of anti-Americanism in certain European countries and consequently greater opportunity for the development of country-specific complaints and tropes, and (c) the sharp and equally long-term differences among European countries on issues that are also implicated in anti-Americanism, such as political philosophy and the role of religion.

The approach I have tried to illustrate here adds an ethnographic dimension to survey data on attitudes and genealogical accounts of tropes through time. It asks how people combine and deploy schemas in response to particular events. The three kinds of evidence—survey, genealogy, ethnography—allow us to "triangulate" on local understandings of global phenomena. Indonesians responded to 9/11 and the post-tsunami aid by acknowledging what happened but at the same time drawing on schemas about U.S. imperialism and Jewish control of foreign policy. These schemas have their own genealogies in the intellectual pilgrimages of Indonesian Muslim leaders. However, the sharp rises and falls in attitudes toward the United States

30. Shamsul, personal communication, December 2004.

suggest that most people either do not find these schemas deeply persuasive or that they also follow other, more positive schemas.

France shows similar filtering of accounts through the lens of a schema about U.S. imperialism, one that also assumes that Americans do everything nearly perfectly: How did they convince everyone to lie about the Pentagon crash? The schema of American technical perfection has a long French history, as Roger shows, and it facilitates conspiracy theories. The diacritic use of these schemas is particularly characteristic of France (and perhaps, conversely, of the use of anti-French images by Americans) and explains the attractiveness of schemas of disorderly "Anglo-Saxon societies" and greedy imperialistic ones to politicians and other public figures. They resonate because they are, in the end, more about France than about America.

9

Legacies of Anti-Americanism: A Sociological Perspective

DOUG MCADAM

Anti-Americanism is generally treated as yet another instance of American exceptionalism. Yet as the editors point out in the introduction, anti-imperial sentiments have a long history. The Roman Empire would surely have aroused fear, envy, and enmity among the peoples subject to or threatened by its rule. Even if we restrict ourselves to the contemporary world, anti-Americanism has been studied only rarely and then seemingly as a phenomenon unto itself. That is, it has not been seen as a specific, if extreme, example of any more generic social phenomenon. No doubt there are features of anti-Americanism that mark it as unique. At the same time, I think there are more general analytic lenses through which the phenomenon can be profitably observed. I will bring one such lens—the study of social movements or contentious politics—to bear on anti-Americanism in this chapter.

Scholars of nonroutine or contentious politics seek fundamentally to understand the development of conflict relations between groups and the dynamics of emergent mobilization that trigger specific episodes of contention motivated by these perceived cleavages.[1] From this perspective, it is useful to think of anti-Americanism as involving an "us/them" cleavage that, while variable across time and space, has the potential to set in motion specific episodes of reactive mobilization against the United States. When viewed in this light, anti-Americanism comes to resemble other political/cultural cleavages, such as those of race, ethnicity, class, and religion, that endure but only sporadically serve as the basis of widespread contention.

I am extremely grateful to Bob Keohane and Peter Katzenstein, not simply for their extraordinarily detailed and insightful comments on several drafts of this chapter but for inviting my participation in this book project. I am also indebted to David Laitin, Cynthia Brandt, Mary Katzenstein, Ruud Koopmans, Mayer Zald, John Bowen, and Giacomo Chiozza for their helpful comments on the chapter.
1. McAdam 1999; McAdam, Tarrow, and Tilly 2001.

Viewing mobilized anti-Americanism as a specific kind of social movement encourages comparing such instances to other forms of contentious politics. In this chapter, I first briefly apply one influential account of movement emergence to the onset of organized anti-Americanism to see whether the former provides a useful framework for studying the latter. But my real interest is in thinking about a question that has been neglected both by social movement scholars and by those concerned with anti-Americanism. Specifically, what factors shape the subjective legacy of any specific episode of contention? How episodes are remembered powerfully conditions the prospects for future conflict. From a practical political standpoint, we should be as concerned with understanding how and why cleavages endure as with how they emerge in the first place. If, for instance, the antipathy toward the United States expressed in these episodes is ephemeral, the implications are obviously going to be very different than if anti-Americanism becomes a more or less permanent ideational feature of the countries in question. But to offer educated guesses about this crucial issue, we have to begin to compare cases with an eye to better understanding the factors and processes that shape the enduring subjective legacies of political conflict.

Social Movement Theory and Anti-Americanism

Over the past thirty years, the literature on social movements has grown tremendously, with a wide range of specialized topics coming in for attention. Still, the causal origins of contention remain the centerpiece of social movement theory. Understanding how and why movements emerge has preoccupied scholars at least since the origins of the social sciences. Among the more influential contemporary perspectives on the topic is political process theory.[2] In its more static version, the theory stresses the importance of three broad sets of causal factors. The first is the level of organization within a given population; the second, the shared sense of grievance within that same population; and third, the objective shifts in the political opportunities or threats confronting the population. The first factor can be conceived of as the degree of "organizational readiness" within the group; the second as the level of "insurgent consciousness" among the movement's mass base; and the third as a shift in the broader political environment that motivates action. The conventional argument is that movements tend to develop during times of destabilizing change, as well-organized and politically conscious groups seek to mobilize in response to the new opportunities or threats posed by the changes.

Since the mid-1990s, however, proponents of this perspective have sought to replace this framework with a more dynamic model of the onset of contention.[3] In doing so, they have also urged analysts to focus not on single movements but on the broader "episodes of contention" in which they are typically embedded. The argument is that contention develops when at least one actor in a previously stable action

2. McAdam 1999, Tarrow 1998, Tilly 1978.
3. McAdam 1999; McAdam, Tarrow, and Tilly 2001.

field (a) defines the situation as posing an emergent threat to, or opportunity for, the realization of group interests, (b) creates or, more likely, appropriates a collective action vehicle, and (c) uses it to engage in innovative collective action vis-à-vis other actors in the field. Contention begins in earnest when at least one other group in the field then interprets the innovative action as posing a threat or opportunity to their interests and starts acting in innovative ways as well. The end result is a generalized sense of uncertainty within the field and a shared motivation to engage in innovative contentious action to advance or protect group interests. The episode is expected to last "as long as enough parties to the conflict continue to define the situation as one of significant environmental uncertainty requiring sustained mobilization to manage (in the case of threat) or exploit (in the case of opportunity)."[4]

This perspective takes broader "episodes of contention" as its analytic focus rather than the specific social movements that are often embedded in such episodes. In general terms an episode of contention can be defined as a period of emergent, sustained, contentious interaction between at least two collective actors utilizing new and innovative forms of action vis-à-vis one another. By "emergent" I mean to signal that episodes of contention are understood by the parties involved to represent some qualitative break from whatever relationship, if any, they shared in the past. Indeed, a shared sense of uncertainty about the nature of that relationship and the relative power enjoyed by the parties to the conflict is the hallmark and trigger of any episode of contention. When the precipitating sense of uncertainty that triggers an episode gives way to a resolution of the underlying conflict, the pace and innovative nature of the interaction are expected to subside, bringing the episode to a close.

Revisiting the Civil Rights Case

Substituting episodes for movements transforms our understanding of nonroutine or contentious politics. Consider the case of the civil rights movement. Conventional accounts of the struggle hold that the movement began with the onset of the bus boycott in Montgomery, Alabama, in December 1955. Catalyzed by Rosa Parks's arrest for refusing to surrender her seat in the "white" section of the bus, the boycott marked the onset of mass protest by African Americans against Jim Crow segregation in the United States. But, as important as this development was, the mass movement must be seen not as the trigger of the broader episode of contention over race that characterized the postwar United States but as a by-product and highly consequential phase of that larger struggle.

Without discounting the importance of certain domestic change processes, it was the dramatic restructuring of the international system in the wake of World War II that more than anything else "renationalized" the question of race in the United States and undermined the federal-Southern "understanding" that had held since the end of Reconstruction. Specifically, the onset of the cold war, the transformation of the United States from an isolationist nation to the policeman for

4. McAdam 1999, xxvii.

Democracy, and the founding of the United Nations with its emphasis on minority rights, quickly made racism at home a serious policy liability. The "Negro question" was no longer strictly a domestic issue but had become an important component of U.S. cold war foreign policy.

Three sets of actors read significant "threat" or "opportunity" into this fundamental shift and began, in the immediate postwar period, to interact with one another in new and innovative ways. First off the mark were certain federal officials who, in the context of the cold war, came to view American racism as a profound "threat" to the realization of the country's foreign policy aims. This view inspired calls for civil rights reforms to counter Soviet efforts to exploit Jim Crow for its obvious propaganda value.[5] President Truman's civil rights initiatives were one response to these pleas. Another was the series of briefs filed by the attorney general in support of a string of NAACP-initiated civil rights cases heard by the Supreme Court after 1948.

Established civil rights organizations clearly recognized and sought to exploit the leverage the cold war framing of race afforded them. By drawing a stark parallel between Jim Crow policies in the United States and the suppression of freedom in the Soviet bloc, these groups sought to pressure a reluctant federal establishment into action by framing civil rights reform as a tool in America's struggle against Communism. Finally, the increasing rhetorical support for civil rights reform among federal officials prompted the South's political elite to mobilize to counter the perceived threat "to the southern way of life." The first major instance of innovative mobilization came in 1948 when southern segregationists formed the States Rights Party to challenge Truman in that year's presidential election. In the end the Dixiecrats failed to defeat Truman, but the challenge clearly marked the onset of national contention over race and was a harbinger of even greater conflict to come.

The implication of this sketch is that the Montgomery bus boycott was not the beginning of an episode of contention. On the contrary, the broader episode of contention over race began very early in the postwar period and certainly by the time of the Dixiecrat revolt in 1948. Montgomery then represents a crucial escalation of the conflict (and the beginnings of the mass movement) but not its point of origin. Indeed, rather than Montgomery making the movement, the reverse is true. It was the prior "re-nationalization of race" that granted the local struggle in Montgomery so much significance.

Mobilized Anti-Americanism as Contentious Episodes

It may seem like a stretch to go from contention over race in the postwar United States to a contemporary episode of mobilized anti-Americanism. But, despite their apparent differences, I would argue that the framework sketched above aids in understanding both cases. Take, for example, the current insurgency in Iraq. A conven-

5. Dudziak 2000, Layton 2000, McAdam 1999, Plummer 1996, Skrentny 1998.

tional social movement approach to the case would focus almost exclusively on the insurgents: their identities, the organizations and/or networks through which they mobilize, their framing strategies, the evolution of tactics, and so forth. The origin of the insurgency would, of course, be seen as a response to the U.S.-led invasion of Iraq, but the actions of the United States would remain largely unanalyzed and unexplained.

Shifting the focus to the broader episode of contention within which the insurgency is embedded, however, brings U.S. actions and actors back to center stage. Indeed, as the clear catalyst for the insurgency, the invasion of Iraq becomes the central "innovative action" to be explained. This, in turn, pushes the analysis back to the "exogenous shock" of 9/11 and the critically important effort of the Bush administration to sell Congress, the American public, and the international community on the terrorist "threat" posed by Saddam Hussein. Though the administration ultimately failed to convince the international community of the salience of this threat, they were able to gain sufficient backing at home to launch and sustain the invasion. The invasion, in turn, has clearly been interpreted by many Islamists as a severe threat—indeed, as a call to jihad against the infidel. The resulting uncertainty spawned by the invasion—uncertainty about who will wield power in a post-Hussein Iraq, uncertainty about the "war on terror" going forward, uncertainty about how long the U.S. occupation will last, and so forth—is sure to sustain the episode for some time to come.

This same kind of framework would seem useful in explaining past instances of anti-Americanism as well. Consider the anti-American protests that erupted in China following the apparently inadvertent U.S. bombing of the Chinese embassy in Belgrade at the height of the war in Yugoslavia. The bombing was clearly the "exogenous shock" that led to the protests, but it did so not directly but through the intervening processes identified above. Student protesters—or party/state elites who may have urged them to protest—first had to define the bombing as a threat to China's interests and/or sovereignty and to then "appropriate" suitable action vehicles for mounting and sustaining the protests. In chapter 6 Alastair Iain Johnston and Daniela Stockmann use rich data and analysis to paint a stark picture of the deep-seated nationalism that no doubt informed the popular response to the embassy bombing and continues to shape how the Chinese interpret U.S. actions today.

I could apply this same analytic framework to other episodes of anti-Americanism, but I hope the point has been reasonably made. The same kind of explanatory perspective that social movement scholars have proposed to account for Western-style episodes of contention can be profitably adapted to an analysis of mobilized anti-Americanism.

Legacies of Episodes of Contention

But, as noted above, my central interest in this chapter is in exploring a question neglected by both movement analysts and scholars of anti-Americanism. How do the subjective legacies of earlier contentious episodes condition the likelihood of future conflict? In recent years, movement scholars have begun to redress their longstanding neglect of the all-important issue of movement outcomes. Accordingly, we are beginning to understand a good deal more about the conditions under which movements achieve effects and the mechanisms by which they do so.[6] But curiously the longer-term impact movements have on the likelihood of future conflict has not been a part of this systematic study of the outcomes of contention. I want to use the balance of the chapter to highlight the importance of the topic and to speculate a bit about the dynamic processes that determine whether specific episodes reduce or increase the prospects for recurrent conflict. As before I will do so by comparing the subjective legacy of the U.S. civil rights movement to various episodes of anti-Americanism.

What can we say about the legacies of American racial contention on black and white understandings of the racial cleavage in the United States? Sadly, like so many aspects of contemporary American life, whites and blacks tend to diverge sharply on these issues. Most whites tend to downplay the conflict and overstate the gains achieved by the civil rights movement. They also now embrace the fundamental goals and tactics of the movement and retain a positive view, not only of the civil rights movement but of the more integrated, color-blind society they believe the movement helped bring about. Large majorities of whites now firmly embrace a set of outcomes—including residential integration, intermarriage, and school integration—that were just as clearly opposed on the eve of the struggle.[7] Credit the struggle, then, with significantly reducing the aggregate level of white antipathy toward African Americans. To the extent that enduring social cleavages depend on deep-seated hostility between groups, we might be justified in concluding that this revolution in racial attitudes has reduced the overall salience of the cleavage for whites and, in doing so, lessened the threat of periodic episodes of sustained racial contention.

The problem with this conclusion is that it fails to take into account the attitudinal legacy of the struggle within the black community. And here the legacy appears to be quite different. To understand that legacy we need to reclaim that part of the history of the African American freedom struggle that has been conveniently elided from the canonical account summarized above. The conventional account only works if we discount the later black power–cultural nationalist movement as a relatively insignificant and ephemeral phenomenon that lasted but a few years and left no enduring legacy. But the available evidence does not support this conclusion.

Far from being a minor footnote to the struggle, this later movement ushered in a period of extraordinary political and cultural ferment within the African American community. William Van Deburg captures the essence and vitality of the movement as well as its enduring impact on the African American community:

6. Amenta, Carruthers, and Zylan 1992; Andrews 1997, 2001; Burstein 1979; Burstein and Freudenburg 1978; Gamson 1990; McAdam and Su 2002.

7. C.f. Schuman, Steeh, and Bobo 1988.

The Black Power movement was not exclusively cultural, but it was essentially cultural. It was a revolt in and of culture that was manifested in a variety of forms and intensities. In the course of the revolt, the existence of a semipermeable wall separating Euro and African-American cultural expression was revealed. The distance separating the two cultural spheres mirrored significant differences in the black and white world view and situation. Conceptualized in this manner, the Black Power movement does not appear, like it so often has, as a cacophony of voices and actions resulting in only miniscule gains for black people. Viewing the movement through the window of culture allows us to see that language, folk culture, religion, and literary and performing arts served to spread the militants' philosophy much farther than did mimeographed political broadsides.

When activists entered the cultural arena . . . they broadened their appeal and facilitated the acceptance of Black Power tenets. They thereby contributed importantly to making the movement a lasting influence in American culture.[8]

It is during this period of vibrant cultural struggle and creativity that many of the behavioral patterns and attitudes characteristic of contemporary African American life developed, born of a radical rejection of the integrationist worldview of the civil rights era. Separatism replaces integration as the cultural, if not political, coin of the realm. Underlying this separatist impulse is both a positive assertion of African American pride and cultural distinction *and* anger and frustration at the perceived limits of the gains of the civil rights era. White America, or so the view held, had once again shown its deep aversion to any meaningful vision of racial justice. Better then to give up on integration and focus on developing the distinctive cultural, political, and social character of the African American community.

Much has obviously changed since the Black Power era. There is, to be sure, little organized expression, within the black community, of the central tenets of Black Power or cultural nationalism. And yet, I would contend, the modal black understanding of race and, in particular, the black/white cleavage in the United States continue to bear the imprint of the separatist logic that marked the close of the contentious episode rather than the emphasis on integration that white America associates with the struggle. In contrast to white America, then, the postwar civil rights struggle left the African American community less optimistic about the prospects for racial change and no less antagonistic and distrustful of whites than before. From this perspective, the prospects for future racial contention have not diminished much if at all.[9]

8. Van Deburg 1992, 9–10.

9. An important question remains unanswered: Why did organized contention by African Americans shift its focus from politics to more cultural arenas? As a host of scholars including Van Deburg 1992, Kelly 1997, 2002, and Martin 2005 remind us, the line between political and cultural struggle is blurry at best. But to the extent that black activists began to eschew formal political targets in the late 1960s and early 1970s, it's worth asking ourselves why. My provisional answer is a straightforward extension of political process theory. Activists are strategically savvy, constantly assessing the leverage available in different arenas and at different jurisdictional levels within a federal system like that of the United States. As national political leverage declined in the late 1960s—as a result of détente with the Soviet Union, the collapse of the New Deal coalition, and so forth—black activists mobilized in venues that seemed more receptive or vulnerable to challenge. This included southern electoral politics (Andrews 1997), the American university system, *and* a wide range of cultural arenas.

Collective Memory and Legacy Anti-Americanism

The important implication of the previous section is that the way a group remembers an earlier episode of contention shapes their subsequent behavior. It is far more than a minor postscript to the struggle. Provided it is sustained in collective memory, the dominant, constructed account of that struggle will serve to either perpetuate or extinguish the antipathy that motivated the original episode. In turn, these shared feelings (and supporting perceptions) powerfully condition the likelihood of future conflict. All of this argues for close attention not only to manifest episodes of contention but to the processes of within-group (or within-society) contestation that such episodes invariably trigger. These processes simultaneously determine (1) which groups emerge as politically and culturally dominant in the wake of the episode; (2) how the episode comes to be understood going forward; and (3) the extent to which the cleavage expressed in the episode endures or diminishes in time.

This is all by way of encouraging scholars of anti-Americanism to look beyond the immediate episodes that typically command attention and analyze the ways in which the constructed legacies of these struggles increase or decrease the likelihood of later conflict. Fortunately, scholars are beginning to take up this important topic. In chapter 5, Sophie Meunier argues that the long history of French anti-Americanism has not only left a rich reservoir of negative images but has enabled French politicians to scapegoat the United States with little fear of incurring political costs as a result. In the spirit of encouraging more such explorations, rather than offering definitive historical sketches or interpretations, I will make a brief comparison of four cases of mobilized anti-Americanism, with an eye to understanding the longer term "legacies" of contention that followed—or are likely to follow—from these episodes.

Spain

Spain would appear to represent a case of linear anti-Americanism. In this sense, Spain stands in contrast to the rest of Europe (with the likely exception of Greece, which has also harbored strong anti-American sentiments for a long time). Comparing the 2002 and 2004 Pew Global Public Attitudes Project survey data suggests that the greatest increases in anti-American views have generally been recorded in Europe. But this says as much about the generally positive sentiments that have prevailed in Europe in the past as it does about the relatively high levels of expressed anti-Americanism in 2004. The former baseline leads most analysts to believe that contemporary European enmity toward the United States will not persist into the future. Shared values, cultural traditions, and interests, coupled with a lack of any enduring cognitive/affective legacy of contention, would seem to support this reassuring conclusion.

But Spain may well represent an exception to this rule. At least that is how I interpret the consistently less positive views of the United States provided by Spanish respondents on various surveys conducted since 1980 by the State Department's

Office of Research.[10] For example, in 1985 only 41 percent of Spanish respondents reported favorable attitudes toward the United States as compared to 80 percent of their Italian counterparts and 62 percent for the study as a whole. By 2001 the Spanish figure had dropped to some 30 percent as compared to a modal figure around 60 percent.

How can we explain the consistently more negative views of the United States in Spain? Two contentious chapters in the history of Spanish/U.S. relations come to mind. The first is the Spanish-American War of 1898 through which the United States took possession of Cuba and the Philippines, thereby stripping Spain of the last vestiges of its once expansive colonial empire. Consistent with my earlier speculation concerning "winners" and "losers," the war, to this day, remains a source of anti-Americanism in Spain. The second chapter is Francisco Franco's now widely discredited nearly forty-year reign in Spain. Although some Americans fought against Franco's forces in the Spanish Civil War of the late 1930s, strong U.S. support for Franco after World War II is also implicated in the widespread antipathy toward the United States that continues to inform popular opinion in Spain today. In turn, this enduring legacy of anti-Americanism probably helps to explain the extraordinarily high rates of expressed opposition to Spain's participation in the "coalition of the willing."

That participation, of course, motivated the horrific train bombings that occurred in March 2004 in Spain. In that incident, anger over the bombings came to be directed at the conservative government of José María Aznar after state officials clumsily tried to blame the attacks on the Basque separatist group ETA. In the end, that anger helped to bring the government down in elections held only days after the bombings. But that incident took place while the country was participating in the Iraq War. What if another series of attacks took place in Spain in the face of the current government's stated opposition to U.S. policy on Iraq? I could certainly imagine popular anger being directed in part at Muslims and/or Arabs living there. At the same time, it would not be far fetched to envision a deepening antipathy toward the United States as well. Since the United States is principally responsible for the Iraq invasion and the expanded war on terror, it might quite reasonably be blamed for inciting additional attacks elsewhere. The chances of blame being attributed to the United States would only increase were politicians to frame the attacks in this way to realize domestic political gain. German chancellor Gerhard Schröder successfully used this tactic to revive his flagging political fortunes and win reelection in the wake of the initial Iraq invasion. Given the significantly higher "baseline" of anti-American sentiment in Spain than in other European countries, the electoral incentives for engaging in U.S. bashing would seem, if anything, to be even greater there than elsewhere on the Continent. Properly mobilized, Spain's suspected "legacy anti-Americanism" would, under this scenario, yield yet another episode of contention whose effect would be to reinforce the enduring Spanish antipathy toward the United States.

10. Dean and Demeri 2002.

Philippines

Notwithstanding the case of Spain, my admittedly nonsystematic survey of other cases leads me to believe that discontinuity and sharp reversals frequently characterize the legacies of anti-Americanism. Consider the case of the Philippines. To say that the history of U.S.-Filipino relations is objectively pregnant with raw materials out of which an account of anti-Americanism might be constructed seems indisputable. The Filipino Left has long articulated just such a perspective on U.S. imperialism in relation to the Philippines.

This account is rooted first and foremost in America's history of neocolonial dominion over the Philippines, starting with its appropriation of the Philippines during the Spanish-American War of 1898 and continuing through its decades-long support of the corrupt form of "cacique democracy" that vested power in a small number of large landlords.[11] This system consigned the vast majority of Filipinos to poverty and political powerlessness, helping to fuel the rise of an embryonic Left in the 1930s.

But World War II and its aftermath helped to damp down the anti-American sentiments that four decades of neocolonial rule had encouraged. As bad as the Americans had been, the Japanese forces that occupied the Philippines during the war were seen as far worse. So "liberation" at the hands of the United States in 1945 fostered pro-American sentiments. So too did the granting of formal independence by the United States in 1946. The next two decades brought nominal democracy and considerable (if uneven) prosperity to the country *and* a generally favorable popular perception of the United States.

Ferdinand Marcos's ascension to the presidency in 1965 did not, initially, change the status quo. Indeed, his first six to seven years in office were more or less continuous with the immediate postwar period. But with Marcos's imposition of martial law in 1972 things began to change. Justified as necessary to counter a growing Communist insurgency, Marcos's action initially had strong popular backing. As Benedict Anderson explains:

> At its outset, the martial-law regime had a substantial . . . social base. Its anticommunist, "reformist," "modernizing," and "law and order" rhetoric attracted the support of frustrated would-be technocrats, much of the . . . urban middle-class, and even sectors of the peasantry and urban poor. . . . But as time passed, the greed and violence of the regime became ever more evident, and much of the support dried up. By the late 1970s the technocrats were a spent force, and the urban middle-class was increasingly aware of the decay of Manila, the devastation of the university system, the abject and ridiculous character of the monopolized mass media, and the country's economic decline.[12]

To this list of estranged former allies, I would add one other of at least equal importance: the official hierarchy of the Catholic Church of the Philippines and its

---

11. Anderson 1998.
12. Ibid., 215.

popular head, Cardinal Jaime Sin. Under the sway of liberation theology, many urban and rural priests had long ago abandoned Marcos for active roles in various wings of the mushrooming opposition movement. Sin and the rest of the official hierarchy had resisted doing so for most of Marcos's reign. But the growing disaffection of the middle class coupled with the regime's increasingly repressive response to Left-progressive elements within the Church forced Sin's hand.

By the early 1980s just about the only significant ally Marcos had left was the United States. Even the 1983 assassination of Marcos's longtime political rival, Benigno Aquino, failed to shake the Reagan administration's staunch and very public support of the regime. Indeed, Reagan himself held firm until the last hours of Marcos's rule, which ended February 25, 1986, as a result of the "people power" revolution. So intransigent was Reagan that he turned a deaf ear to the anti-Marcos views of both the U.S. ambassador to the Philippines and Richard Lugar, the most influential member of the election-watch team that Reagan had sent to the country to observe the "snap election" held in early February, an election marked by widespread fraud by Marcos's supporters.

This steadfast support for the by-now-hated Marcos fueled anti-American sentiment throughout the Philippines. But little of that intense antipathy toward the United States is in evidence today. In 2002 the Pew Global Attitudes Project carried out comparative surveys in forty-four countries around the world. Among the items on the survey were ones designed to measure attitudes toward the United States. In response to one such item, 90 percent of Filipinos expressed a favorable view of the United States, the largest such figure in the study.[13] What happened to the widespread anti-American feelings that characterized the Philippines in the last days of Marcos's rule? The answer reminds us again that the perpetuation or extinction of anti-American sentiment at the close of a contentious episode depends critically on which political faction(s) gain ascendance and what account of the United States they help encode in the collective memory.

In the case of the movement to oust Marcos that developed in the wake of the Aquino assassination—dubbed the "Yellow Revolution" after Aquino's favorite color—the opposition elements most invested in strident anti-Americanism were precisely those who were organized out of the political settlement that restored order to the Philippines. And in the case of the Communists they were those who oddly chose to remain on the sidelines during the escalating popular unrest of the early 1980s. The effect of this decision on the fate of the Communists is all too clear. On the eve of Marcos's ouster, "the NPA[New People's Army, the Communist guerrilla force] had between twenty and twenty-four thousand members and controlled an estimated 20 percent of the country's villages and urban neighborhoods. . . . But by the early 1990s, the movement's fortunes had declined sharply. The [movement's] . . . 'mass base' had diminished to 3 percent of the country's villages and neighborhoods."[14]

The sharp decline in the fortunes of the Communist insurgents dates to the Yellow Revolution and to the tactical choices made by movement leaders during the years

13. Pew Research Center 2002, 55.
14. Kerkvliet 1996, 9.

of that struggle and the early days of the Corazon Aquino regime. Though these choices were vigorously contested within the movement, the general decision to refrain from active engagement with the increasingly centrist anti-Marcos movement and later with the Aquino regime was reaffirmed at every critical juncture. In the end, this decision rendered the Communists a nonfactor in the post-Marcos Philippines. As Kathleen Weekley writes:

> While the Communists could neither have instigated nor prevented the 1986 revolt even if they had wanted, internal and external critics of the CPP [Communist Party of the Philippines] agree that the ... movement would have suffered less from this change in political regime had they been participants in the process. If they had not opted for boycott, but instead joined with the broad opposition to defeat Marcos first at the ballot and then on the streets, then the revolutionary movement would have been in a better position to influence the course of events that followed.[15]

And, to the extent that they had been a part of the new settlement, their strongly anti-American views would presumably have been incorporated into the dominant account of the episode and the legitimating frame of the new regime. Absent Communist participation, it was the views of the centrist coalition responsible for toppling Marcos—consisting primarily of the Church, moderate business elements, the middle class, and most of the military—that came to dominate public discourse about the event and the past and present image of the United States. The point is that none of the key coalition partners were invested in strong anti-American views. Moreover, they collectively viewed ongoing U.S. aid as critical to the restabilization of political life and the rebuilding of the Philippine economy. As a result, despite lots of antipathy toward the United States during the revolution, very little of it got carried forward into the post-Marcos period. The suppression of the Communists (and other radical elements) in the 1990s further weakened an important source of anti-U.S. sentiment in the country. The withdrawal of U.S. military bases in 1992 further strengthened pro-American feelings by eliminating a controversial issue that had frayed U.S.-Philippine relations. U.S. troops returned to the Philippines in 2002, but ironically, their renewed presence in the country also reinforced pro-American sentiments. The reason: U.S. troops were in the country to help fight Muslim separatists who were kidnapping and killing Catholic Filipinos.[16]

---

15. Weekley 1996, 29.

16. Nor should we assume that the Philippines is such an anomalous case. For instance, Japan in the 1960s appears broadly similar to the Philippines in the 1980s. In both cases there was a strong and virulently anti-American Left. In the Philippines that Left was associated primarily with the rural Communist insurgency. In Japan it was centered in a university-based student movement that was strongly supported by the powerful teacher's union and other social sectors. The Communists expanded significantly in the Philippines during the 1970s and 1980s; the Japanese student Left remained strong through the 1960s. But, as proved true in the Philippines, the views of the Japanese Left were never incorporated into the worldview of those who held power in Japan in the 1970s and 1980s. Without this kind of elite "sponsorship" the strident anti-Americanism that had been such a part of Japanese student discourse in the 1960s fell out of favor and enjoys little salience in the country today.

South Korea

In its history of anti-Americanism, South Korea affords another interesting case of sharp reversals. Its trajectory is, however, the mirror image of the Philippines. While the Philippines moved from high levels of anti-Americanism throughout most of the 1980s to relatively low levels today, South Korea has experienced the reverse. That is, the strongly pro-American sentiments that characterized South Korea in the 1945–80 period gave way in the 1980s and 1990s to high levels of antipathy toward the United States. The 2002 Pew Global Attitudes Project's data confirm that those sentiments remain very much in evidence today. Outside of the Middle East, only Bangladesh and Argentina had less favorable views of the United States than South Korea. The contrast with the Philippines is especially stark. Only 7 percent of the Filipino respondents reported unfavorable views of the United States as compared to 44 percent in South Korea.[17]

What accounts for the dramatic change in "legacy anti-Americanism" in South Korea over the past three decades? The contrast with the Philippines is again instructive. In the Philippines the moderate ruling coalition that took power in the wake of Marcos's ouster aggressively repressed the Communist insurgents and other leftist elements that were the principal "carriers" of doctrinaire Marxist anti-Americanism. The long-term economic needs and interests of the coalition required close ties with the United States, ties that would have been jeopardized had the new regime sought to sustain the anti-American feelings catalyzed by the anti-Marcos movement. In short, the sharp decline in anti-Americanism in the Philippines was due primarily to the strategic choices made by the post-Marcos leadership—choices that simultaneously silenced the leading voices of anti-Americanism within the country while strengthening its political and economic ties to the United States.

By contrast, the story in South Korea has more to do with the influence of popular movements than entrenched political elites. The explanation for the extraordinarily positive feelings toward the United States in Korea in the post–World War II period should be fairly obvious: "The legacy of anti-communism and memories of the Korean War [produced a] feeling of genuine warmth towards the U.S. for supporting South Korea with the sacrifice of thousands of young men and millions in dollars in aid."[18] As Shin Gi-Wook puts it: "It is no exaggeration to say that for many Koreans, the United States was more than a friend; it was a savior of their nation, first from Japanese colonial rule and then from communist aggression."[19] This view not only had great popular resonance but was encoded in the official ideology of the virulently anticommunist military regimes that ruled South Korea during this period.

U.S. popularity remained high even as opposition to these nondemocratic regimes began to develop in the 1970s. Indeed, so positive was the prevailing view of the United States that it was widely assumed that America's democratic ideals assured its strong backing of the burgeoning democracy movement. That all changed in the

17. Pew Research Center 2002, 55.
18. Shorrock 1986, 1198–99.
19. Shin 1996, 793.

sustained crisis of 1979–81. The crisis was set in motion by the October 26 assassination of South Korea's longtime autocratic strongman, Park Chung Hee. In the wake of the assassination, Prime Minister Choi Kyu Hah was named acting president, martial law was imposed, and a fairly minor figure, Maj. Gen. Chun Doo Hwan, was assigned to investigate the death of President Park.[20] Things seemed to be returning to normal when, quite unexpectedly in December, Chun roiled the South Korean power structure by staging a coup within the military. In the words of the U.S. ambassador William J. Gleysteen, the coup left Korea with "dual authority structures, the formal one headed by the president [Choi] and the effective one headed by General Chun."[21]

Still, 1980 opened on a hopeful note, with the release of political prisoners, the reopening of the universities, and President Choi's announcement of planned democratic reforms. Despite the dual power structure, it seemed as if both Choi and Chun were committed to a process of democratization that would lead, in timely fashion, to direct elections that would among other things reunify governmental authority in South Korea. It was not to be. Power was soon reunified, but by way not of elections but of a legalistic coup on May 17 that left Chun in total control of the country.

Opposition to the power seizure was immediate and widespread. Kwangju, a city in South Cholla Province, was among the first cities to erupt in anti-Chun protests. What started out as a peaceful student demonstration soon escalated into an uprising by several hundred thousand citizens opposed to the seizure of power. Chun responded with force of his own, sending in troops who, in the climactic battle of May 27, killed somewhere between two hundred and several thousand antigovernment protestors.[22]

Consistent with the prevailing popular view of the United States, it was widely believed that the United States would intervene to stop the armed confrontation. It did not. Indeed, whatever the prevailing view of the time, most Koreans came to believe that the United States was complicit in the massacre. President Chun's official state visit to the Reagan White House early in 1981 confirmed this suspicion for most Koreans. The die was cast. From then on, opposition to the military regime was informed by a strong and strident anti-Americanism. Nor did the collapse of the military government in 1987 and the gradual transition to democracy in the late 1980s and early 1990s undermine the prevailing antipathy to the United States. Why not? The answer speaks to the general dynamics I have touched on throughout this chapter. In contrast to the Philippines, where the anti-Marcos coalition effectively distanced itself from the popular anti-Americanism that informed the Yellow Revolution, the South Korean pro-democracy forces effectively incorporated the popular antipathy to the United States into their account of the transition and the legitimating frame for the new civilian government.

20. Drennan 2005.
21. Quoted ibid., 285.
22. Ibid., 288–89.

Nor are there any signs that this strong ideological link between civilian rule in South Korea and a resonant anti-Americanism is likely to disappear anytime soon. Indeed, the fact that many of the key figures in the current government of Roh Moo Hyun are veterans of the democracy movement virtually ensures that anti-American sentiments will remain strong within official government circles. Demographic data and current events also support the view that antipathy to the United States is likely to remain strong or increase in the near term. Demographically, the distribution of anti-American views is a generational phenomenon. It is hardly surprising that older South Koreans retain very positive views of the United States, while younger cohorts are far more anti-American in their attitudes. The distribution of favorable and unfavorable views of the United States is 49–15 percent among South Koreans fifty and over and 25–43 percent for those in their twenties.[23] Unless the distribution of these views changes, generational replacement portends a sharp increase in anti-American sentiment within South Korea.

As for current events, tensions with North Korea have exacerbated popular animosity toward the United States in South Korea. At the heart of the current antipathy to the United States is deep nationalist resentment at what is perceived to be the unequal nature of U.S.–South Korean relations. Democratization and rapid economic development have generated enormous pride among South Koreans, a pride that is deeply wounded by the apparent lack of political and economic respect accorded the country by the United States. Although he was writing about the nuclear negotiations between the United States and North Korea in the mid-1990s, Shin's cautionary remarks apply equally well to the current situation:

> Despite insistence by both Seoul and Washington that the South Korea–U.S. relationship is a partnership, many Koreans do not accept this claim. For them, the recent treatment of the North Korean nuclear issue by the United States demonstrated that Seoul is still largely left out of the decision-making process. Such a perception angered even the conservative right that would otherwise remain highly pro-American. The U.S. must take seriously the rising tide of Korean [anti-American] nationalism so as to work out a genuine partnership involving more consultation and decision making.[24]

This clearly has not happened in the years since Shin wrote his article. To the extent that nothing is done to redress this situation, increasing anti-American sentiments are likely to be the result.

Iraq

So far, I have chosen cases outside of the Middle East. I have done so primarily because the current attention being lavished on the region threatens to obscure what

23. Shin 1996, 796.
24. Ibid., 803.

I see as the more general dynamics of "legacy anti-Americanism" and, more important, the significant stakes that confront the United States elsewhere in the world in
regard to this issue. But let me close with some admittedly speculative remarks about
the preeminent case of mobilized contention against the United States in the world
today. I refer, of course, to the insurgency in Iraq.

To say that current Iraqi views of the United States are negative is to risk com-
mitting the mother of all understatements. The question is will these views endure
and become an ideological staple of Iraqi popular discourse and consciousness.
Clearly, the majority of speculation offered up since the onset of the invasion, and
especially since President Bush's declaration of the end of "major hostilities" in Iraq,
has tended to predict the long-term instantiation of anti-American views into Iraqi
culture and politics. Based on the theoretical framework sketched here and the set
of unexpected trajectories reflected in the aforementioned cases, I would resist any
simple answer to the question of what the future holds for Iraq. Two very different
trajectories seem plausible to me.

The first conforms closely to the negative predictions implicit in much contemporary speculation. In this view, the long-term impact of the invasion and subsequent insurgency on Iraqi-U.S. relations is, under almost any scenario, likely to be
overwhelmingly negative. A number of plausible scenarios are in accord with this
conclusion. Three, in particular, come to mind. The first is a state of sustained insurgency that effectively subverts efforts to reestablish a stable political and economic
order in Iraq. The second is civil war, with the current insurgency eventually devolv-
ing into generalized conflict involving two or more claimants to popular sovereignty.
In both of these cases, the expectation is that the United States would be blamed—
not unreasonably—for the ongoing conflict, chaos, and loss of life that would
inevitably follow. In short, the intense enmity sparked by the invasion and resulting
occupation would only be reinforced and sustained in either case.

The third scenario is entirely different, but also in accord with the image of intense
and enduring anti-American sentiment in Iraq. In this final case, the sustained animosity toward the United States results from regime stability, rather than instability.
As this was being written, Iraq was on the verge of forming a fundamentalist
Shiite–dominated government with strong ties to Iran. Given the enduring, mutual
enmity between Iran and the United States, such a scenario would likely lead to sustained anti-Americanism in Iraq as well.

But before we conclude that the future of U.S.–Iraq relations is set in stone, we
would do well to reflect on the surprising cases reviewed above. If nothing else, these
cases tell us that straight-line projections from some current baseline of anti-
American sentiment—no matter how negative—are not always reliable guides to the
future. The more important analytic insight is that to make intelligent guesses about
legacy anti-Americanism in a given country following a sustained contentious episode
we need to think long and hard about the strategic calculus of the political and cultural elites that emerge as dominant in the postconflict period. Given this perspective, one can plausibly imagine scenarios under which emerging coalitions in Iraq

would in time play down anti-American rhetoric and ideas in favor of other frames of reference. To illustrate the point, I offer one such scenario.

No one pretends that an Iraqi coalition government in which religious Shiites are numerically dominant will cause the insurgency to magically disappear. But what if as appears to be happening the insurgency comes, in time, to take on even more of an anti-Shiite character? Prominent Shiite government figures are killed or kidnapped. Shiite mosques and schools become the central targets of suicide bombers, as was the case with the February 22, 2006, bombing of the Askoriya shrine in Samaria. If this were to happen, much of the current enmity toward the United States by Shiites in Iraq might well be transferred to Sunni insurgents, or Sunnis in general. Imagine further that somewhere down the road two other important developments take place. The first is the withdrawal of the vast majority of U.S. troops. The second is the institution of a sustained and generous U.S. aid package to the new Shiite-dominated government. The first development would have the effect of removing a critically important visual catalyst of enduring anti-American sentiment. The second would provide the new government with a powerful set of incentives for de-emphasizing anti-American rhetoric and ideas in order to curry ongoing favor with the United States. Would I bet the farm on this scenario? No, but it *is* in keeping with the general analytic principles gleaned from the set of surprising cases reviewed earlier.

Understanding Legacies of Contention

Anti-Americanism is a form of contentious politics. We can gain some insights into its dynamics and effects by comparing it to well-studied instances of contentious politics, such as those revolving around race relations in the United States. In particular, an analysis of anti-Americanism calls attention to the long-term legacies of a period of intense mobilization. Since we have to take into account its somewhat unpredictable legacies, we can gauge the "effects" of anti-Americanism only with considerable difficulty.

In chapter 10, Robert Keohane and Peter Katzenstein seek to assess the consequences of contemporary anti-American sentiment. Their assessment of these effects is creative and systematic. To this point they find little evidence of significant negative consequences from contemporary anti-Americanism. The key phrase here is "to this point." I think, as they do, that it would be premature to draw firm conclusions from this preliminary evidence. For the effects they tend to focus on bear the imprint not of mobilized but of diffuse and unorganized anti-Americanism. The best example of this is consumer behavior where the authors show virtually no impact of rising levels of anti-American sentiment on spending on brand-name products of leading American firms.

But consumer behavior is notoriously hard to organize for political or economic effect. So long as anti-Americanism remains diffuse and unorganized, we have little to fear. Mobilized anti-Americanism is quite another matter, however. And that is where the study of social movements and/or contentious politics can be an invaluable aid to those seeking a more thorough understanding of the dynamics, and especially the longer-term impact, of anti-Americanism.

The most consequential of these impacts will come, I believe, either as a direct result of current instances of mobilized anti-Americanism or the longer-term outcome of legacy anti-Americanism. The mobilizing agents in the former cases can either be institutional political elites who see domestic advantage in activating and sustaining anti-U.S. views at home or noninstitutional terrorist or other movement groups intent on damaging U.S. interests wherever they can. In my view, it is still too early in the current wave of such mobilizations to reach a firm conclusion about their ultimate effect on the United States.

Scholars of contentious politics are well equipped to analyze and assess the outcomes of episodes of mobilized anti-Americanism. But they have paid far less attention to the longer-term legacies of such episodes. That is why I have chosen to focus most of my attention here on the dynamics of what the editors in chapter 1 call legacy anti-Americanism. In short, it is the different trajectories of legacy anti-Americanism that account for whatever the baseline view of the United States is at a given historical moment. In turn, this cognitive-affective baseline can be expected to powerfully condition the likelihood of future anti-U.S. mobilization. Although a full-blown theory of these trajectories is well beyond the scope of this chapter, the following propositions are offered as provisional steps in this direction.

First, winners tend to harbor far less enmity toward losers than the reverse. So to the extent that a prior contentious episode yields consensual "winners" and "losers," we can expect the latter to retain far more animus toward the former than vice versa. Winners can afford to be magnanimous, losers tend to invest in millennial visions of ultimate triumph. Consider the very different cases of virulent and enduring Southern anger over the "War of Northern Aggression" in the United States and the overwhelmingly positive contemporary view of the United States within Vietnam.[25]

Second, sustained episodes of contention generally devolve into polarized struggles between two large warring sides. But each of these sides—especially the "challenger"—is typically made up of a set of very strange bedfellows. More accurately these should be seen as unruly coalitions united only in their virulent opposition to the other side. The key implication is that how a particular episode is remembered will depend in large part on which faction(s) emerge as dominant in the wake of contention and what worldview or ideological resources they bring to the construction of "legacy." Had, for instance, secular reformers, rather than Islamic hardliners, gained power in post-Shah Iran, the current Iranian view of the United States would, no doubt, be very different. Or imagine the following counterfactual trajectory in the Philippines. What if, instead of remaining on the sidelines, the Communists had

---

25. Survey data from the 2002 Pew Global Attitudes Project confirm this conclusion. In the survey, 71% of Vietnamese respondents held a positive view of the United States, with just 26% responding negatively. Pew Research Center 2002, 55.

successfully inserted themselves into the anti-Marcos struggle and somehow managed to prevail in the political scrum that followed his ouster? Had that happened I cannot imagine we would today see the stunningly high levels of expressed pro-Americanism revealed by the 2002 Pew survey.

Finally, it is worth distinguishing between "legacies" that primarily reflect elite versus more popular understandings of a particular contentions episode. In general, we should expect elite-generated accounts to more often mute rather than exacerbate the divisions reflected in the original episode. The American and French Revolutions offer a sharp, if familiar, contrast in this regard. While the planter elite of the fledgling American republic remained firmly in control of the reins of power and the constructed legacy of the struggle, popular contestation over both was the order of the day in France. The result was a far more radical—floridly so—revolutionary legacy in France than in the United States, with profound cultural and political implications down to the present. In the cases reviewed here, the Philippines and South Korea offer the most instructive contrast in this regard. While a coalition of elite groups dominated the reestablishment of political and social order in the Philippines following the ouster of Marcos, South Korean democratization brought an entire generation of anti-American, pro-democracy activists into positions of institutional prominence. This elite–mass contrast helps account for the starkly different views of the United States in contemporary South Korea and the Philippines.

The final two factors focus on the outcome of internal power struggles within countries emerging from episodes of mobilized anti-Americanism. The objective policies that the United States adopts toward a given country at the close of such an episode are sure to influence, though hardly determine, the outcome of these "internal" processes. That said, I have chosen to focus far more on these internal dynamics than on the impact of objective policy outcomes. I have done so not because I believe the former is necessarily more important than the latter but because the tendency among American political analysts is to assume the unilateral power of the United States to affect events elsewhere. Too often this blinds us to the important consequences to the United States of decisions reached elsewhere. The point is, who emerges as politically and culturally dominant at the close of a contentious episode, and how they construct their interests going forward, will go a long way in determining whether an enduring legacy of anti-Americanism gets encoded in collective memory. The elite coalition that deposed Marcos in the Philippines sought to damp down the anti-American sentiments that were freely expressed during the Yellow Revolution. Khomeini and his political heirs have done the opposite in Iran, routinely exploiting enduring anti-American sentiments to bolster domestic support for an otherwise fragile regime. In short, quite apart from U.S. policy, the identity and strategic political calculus of domestic political actors regarding the potential domestic benefits of anti-American symbols and rhetoric is another key factor shaping the legacy of anti-Americanism elsewhere. Scholars and policymakers would do well to accord this topic more systematic attention.

V

CONSEQUENCES AND CONCLUSIONS

10

The Political Consequences of Anti-Americanism

ROBERT O. KEOHANE
and PETER J. KATZENSTEIN

When one of us recently told a U.S. passport control officer about having just given a lecture in Canada on anti-Americanism, the officer commented, "We could just say we don't care." When told that such an option had deficiencies, the officer replied, "It would send a wake-up call to the rest of the world."

Should we care about anti-Americanism? To persuade Americans that it should not be so easily shrugged off, one would have to provide evidence that anti-Americanism either has direct political effects that damage U.S. interests and values, or that its indirect effects would be harmful. This chapter reports on an effort by the authors to find such evidence.

We found, to our surprise, that direct and immediate consequences of anti-Americanism are surprisingly hard to identify. But we also develop a perspective on how to think about the longer-term consequences of anti-American attitudes. To understand the consequences of attitudes for policy and world politics, one has to trace their effects on social movements and especially on the nature of political regimes: that is, one needs to study not only opinion, bias, and distrust but their organization and institutionalization.

We presented earlier drafts of this chapter at two workshops on anti-Americanism held at the Center for Advanced Study in the Behavioral Sciences, January 21–22, April 8, and June 9–11, 2005, as well as at a seminar hosted by the Political Science Department of the University of California, Berkeley, on March 29, 2005, and a public lecture at the University of Southern California, April 28, 2005. Robert Keohane presented a version of this chapter to a seminar at the Center for International Security and Arms Control at Stanford University, May 26, 2005. We are grateful to all participants for their helpful comments, criticisms, and suggestions. We are particularly grateful to Naazneen Barma, Miles Kahler, Doug McAdam, Barak Mendelsohn, Joseph S. Nye Jr., and John Gerard Ruggie for their careful reading and trenchant comments on prior drafts, and to Susan Shirk for pointing out to us, early on, that our emperor was wearing no clothes.

In discussing the consequences of anti-Americanism, we need first to remind ourselves of three important distinctions made in the introduction and throughout this book. First, anti-Americanism needs to be sharply differentiated from opposition to U.S. policy. Sometimes observers refer to policy opinions that differ from those of the U.S. government, such as opposition to the war in Iraq or support for the International Criminal Court, as "anti-American." This is a big mistake. If it were anti-American to hold views different from those of the U.S. government, many loyal Americans would be "anti-American" and the Bill of Rights would be meaningless.

The second distinction that we need to recall is that among opinion, distrust, and bias. In chapter 1 (table 1.4) we introduced the idea of a continuum between unbiased opinion and systematic bias, with distrust as an intermediate category. The problem, as we noted there, is that most of our systematic information, from public opinion polls, is about opinion rather than bias. It is very difficult, as we argued, to distinguish opinion based on policy disagreements from opinion based on distrust or bias. Yet over time critical opinion can harden into distrust and distrust into bias. Critical opinion thus is politically consequential in the short term, and it is the ground from which can spring, over the longer term, distrust and bias. When we discuss the consequences of "anti-Americanism" in this chapter, we will mostly be commenting on the consequences of anti-American opinion.

The third major distinction to remember is that expressed in our typology of anti-Americanisms in chapter 1. We identified four major types of anti-Americanism: liberal, social, sovereign-nationalist, and radical. These types of anti-Americanism can be expected to matter more or less depending on the context, and to have different types of effects. Liberal and social forms of anti-Americanism are chiefly found in democratic societies and might affect cooperation with the United States by countries normally disposed to work closely with America. Sovereign-nationalist anti-Americanism is more prevalent outside than within Europe and can be found in authoritarian states, such as China, or democratic ones, such as Mexico. Radical anti-Americanism is now widespread only in the Middle East, although pockets of it can be found elsewhere. We will not belabor these distinctions in our discussion of the consequences of anti-Americanism below, but they should be kept in mind.

We investigate the possible consequences of anti-American opinion in three distinct political domains in which anti-American opinion could have political consequences for the United States. First we discuss the effects of anti-American opinion on the war on terror. Anti-Americanism could make it harder to fight terrorism. Such an impact could be exerted in one of two ways. Anti-Americanism could provide a "breeding ground for terrorism," by helping terrorist organizations recruit activists and by creating a pool of sympathizers and supporters of terrorism. Just as Communist guerillas were once said to move like a "fish in the friendly sea of the people," members of al-Qaida, for example, depend on help from sympathizers. Without food, shelter, money, logistical support, and a willingness to protect them, terrorists cannot operate effectively, either in rural or urban areas. Or anti-Americanism could hinder cooperation on counterterrorism between governments. Distrust of the United States, or bias against it, could conceivably lead other governments to refuse to participate in American-led efforts to track down and disrupt terrorist networks.

The discussion of terrorism raises one aspect of a broader issue we will then address: whether anti-Americanism will prevent the United States from achieving important political objectives that can only be attained through extensive international cooperation. In the election campaign of 2004, Senator John Kerry argued that the policies of the Bush administration had unnecessarily antagonized America's natural friends and allies, making it more difficult for the United States to attain its goals. Has the United States been hindered in its attempts to persuade other states to accede to its requests, on a variety of issues, without the interference of anti-American views? Anti-Americanism is often claimed to undercut American "soft power." Much of the influence of the United States in the world seems to depend on the power of its example and its ability to persuade others. One might therefore surmise that if the United States is viewed negatively rather than positively, its persuasive ability would diminish, requiring it to use more "hard power"—in the form of material resources—to obtain its objectives, if they can be obtained at all. If this effect is important, there should be a discernible impact of anti-Americanism on the ability of the United States to obtain its objectives through multilateral diplomacy. With respect to this set of questions, we must be careful not to confuse cause and effect. An observed association between anti-Americanism and opposition to U.S. policy does not necessarily imply that anti-Americanism caused the opposition. The reverse could equally well be the case. Indeed, American soft power could well be damaged by U.S. foreign policies, as a result of those policies' adverse effects on public opinion abroad, quite independently of these publics' prior views of the United States. In such a situation, it would not be anti-Americanism that led to a reduction in American soft power, but U.S. policy itself.

We then focus not on governments' behavior but on the actions of individuals and groups. Various journalistic reports have suggested that anti-Americanism has led to formal or informal boycotts of corporations identified with the United States. If many people are biased against the United States, as consumers they could have measurable, adverse effects on U.S. corporations. Furthermore, it seems plausible that anti-Americanism could have negative economic consequences through a reduction in U.S.-bound tourism. It is relatively easy for tourists to change their destinations, and it seems intuitively that those who are hostile to the United States would be less likely to visit, as tourists, than those who have favorable views toward it.

In view of the attention that anti-Americanism has received in the media and by politicians, it is surprising how little hard evidence can be found, in any of these three domains, that anti-American opinion has had serious direct and immediate consequences for the United States on issues affecting broad U.S. policy objectives. Cooperation between the United States and its allies, on issues such as terrorism and on more general issues of international diplomacy, has not been disrupted. Furthermore, we find little evidence of actions by individuals, motivated by anti-Americanism, to boycott American products or refuse to visit the United States. In the absence of stronger evidence, skepticism is justified about assertions that anti-Americanism has had major effects on the capacity of the United States to conduct a successful foreign policy.

Our failure to find strong evidence that anti-Americanism has specific and measurable effects supports the argument of Giacomo Chiozza in chapter 4 that, with the exception of the Arab Middle East, bias is not yet deeply embedded in global public opinion. In a sense, our null findings shift the burden of proof toward those who believe that anti-Americanism is having major effects. Yet our findings by no means prove that anti-Americanism is inconsequential. Anti-American views may have had an important impact at critical junctures—such as the March 2003 decision by the Turkish parliament not to permit an attack on Iraq from Turkish territory, or the September 2002 reelection campaign by Chancellor Schröder in Germany in which he committed himself to refuse participation in a possible invasion of Iraq under any circumstances even if the invasion were sanctioned by the UN Security Council. Furthermore, the tests that we employ below are quite stringent. We ask whether there is clear evidence that states, or members of the public, have acted on negative views of the United States despite interests that they may have to the contrary.[1] Yet, while policymakers' concern for their national or personal interests could lead them to avoid overtly anti-American actions, the initiatives they take or from which they refrain could be subtly affected by pervasive anti-American attitudes.[2] In regions of the world that this book does not cover, notably Latin America, distrust and bias have increased rapidly in recent years as left-wing governments are taking over in the wake of widespread disappointment with the effects of the neoliberal policies supported by the United States.[3] The large demonstrations against the United States that greeted President Bush in Mar del Plata, Argentina, in November 2005 illustrate the intensity of opposition to U.S. policy in large segments of Latin American publics.

We then shift our attention to the possible indirect and longer-term effects of anti-Americanism. Our analysis of these effects provides a counterbalance to the previous generally negative findings. The effects of anti-American sentiment could well be more subtle, and operate more indirectly, than our measures are capable of detecting. Widespread critical opinion can open the door in democratic polities for elites to use anti-Americanism as a way of mobilizing resources and support for their electoral campaigns and other favored causes. Furthermore, if anti-Americanism is widespread, and if a country does not depend for its protection or for other forms of support on the United States, politicians may have few incentives to defend the United States or criticize anti-American pronouncements. The eventual result can be the development of uncontested "background knowledge" that embodies a pervasive bias toward the United States and its policies. Sophie Meunier (chapter 5) and

1. This point has been made strongly to us by John Gerard Ruggie.

2. In personal communication (October 24, 2005) Andrei Markovits has emphasized his view that in Europe elites share an "acutely felt and openly articulated continentwide anti-Americanism," although he agrees with us that "antipathies, though substantial, will not be allowed to interfere with interests."

3. Sweig 2006. Kathryn Sikkink has also emphasized this point to us.

John Bowen (chapter 8) show that anti-Americanism is embedded deeply in the policy discourse of France. Marc Lynch (chapter 7) argues similarly that different forms of anti-Americanism also profoundly mark political discourse in the Arab world. And Alastair Iain Johnston and Daniela Stockmann (chapter 6) show how entrenched distrust of the United States is among the population of Beijing. Finally, Doug McAdam's chapter contains a subtle and wide-ranging analysis of how legacies of bad relations with the United States can either become entrenched over time or change dramatically with new events.

In view of recent highly unfavorable publicity about U.S. human rights practices at Guantánamo, Abu Ghraib, and elsewhere, there is reason for serious concern that even if anti-Americanism has not yet had dramatic foreign policy effects, it could become endemic and increasingly important in years to come. Our failure to identify immediate and specific consequences of anti-American opinion in recent years should not be read as dismissing the long-term importance of anti-Americanism. The continuing outrage, abroad and at home, over U.S. human rights practices, and the Bush administration's defense of both indefinite detention and measures that arguably constitute torture, offer, with respect to the longer-term effects of anti-Americanism, no grounds for complacency.

Anti-Americanism and the Struggle against Terrorism

When Americans think about the consequences of anti-Americanism for the struggle against terrorism, two ideas typically dominate the discussion. First, are anti-American views a fertile breeding ground for terrorism? Second, do anti-American views hinder the efforts of the U.S. government to organize joint actions with others to combat terrorism? We consider these two possible effects in turn.

Is Anti-Americanism a Breeding Ground for Terrorism?

One of the most frequently cited and dreaded effects of anti-Americanism is as a breeding ground for future generations of potential terrorists. In a 2004 poll conducted in Morocco, Saudi Arabia, Jordan, Lebanon, and the United Arab Emirates (UAE), respondents expressed more than twenty times as many unfavorable as favorable views of U.S. policy toward Arabs, the Palestinians, and the war in Iraq.[4] In a public opinion poll that the Pew Research Center conducted in 2004, pluralities of respondents in Pakistan, Jordan, and Morocco justified suicide bombings under some circumstances against Americans and other Westerners in Iraq.[5] The figures in Indonesia were much lower in 2003, when 27 percent thought that suicide bombings were often or sometimes justified.[6] Fears that anti-Americanism is a breeding ground

---

4. Zogby International 2004, 3.
5. Pew Research Center for the People and the Press 2004, 33–34 (questions 13, 15).
6. By 2005, that figure was only 9%, as noted in table 1.3. Terror Free Tomorrow 2005, 4.

for terrorism are thus most relevant in Muslim societies, particularly in the Middle East, and with respect to small groups of the Muslim diaspora in Europe and Canada.[7]

What we know about earlier formations of left-wing terrorist groups, such as the Red Army in Japan, the Red Army Faction in Germany, and the Red Brigades in Italy in the 1960s and 1970s, suggests that hatred of a regime and its policies is part of an exceedingly complex set of processes. Based in part on extended interviews with terrorists who had been incarcerated, scholars have reconstructed how social movement activists grew more radical over time and at a crucial moment decided to form clandestine terrorist cells.[8] Breakaway groups created networks, often only loosely linked if at all, that recruited activists, often accidentally, whose identities were then formed and reformed by peer group pressures among activists. Spirals of radicalization fed on social isolation and constricted political vocabulary and conceptions of political action. Violence was not calculated as a matter of individual choice but emerged from a set of group processes. Radicalization and escalation of violence accompanied a progressive militarization of the conflict, growing commitment to abstract and nonrealizable goals, intensified vilification of the other, and growing political isolation and the creation of a small community of the like minded. The search for revolutionary authenticity through violence was exceedingly complex.[9]

We do not know how much resemblance there is between the politics of fundamentalist Islamists committed to jihad and that of radical left-wing activists in Europe and Asia in the 1960s through the 1980s. However, they have some common elements. In both situations, hatred is a motivating factor. Islamic militants, like the earlier European radicals, seek empowerment through violence.[10] And both cohorts of terrorists are organized in cells, loosely linked in networks. But it seems likely that the nature of terrorist politics differs between societies in which there is widespread sympathy for their goals, such as Pakistan and Saudi Arabia, and those in which they are no more than a tiny, if feared, minority, as was true in Europe and Japan in the 1970s and 1980s. In the case of contemporary jihadis, recruitment in Europe and Canada focuses on men who have emigrated from their native countries and have weak links to the societies in which they live.[11]

In recent decades, jihadi movement politics has gone through three historical stages. The first stage was the war in Afghanistan in the 1980s. One of the war's main effects was to revive the notion of jihad as a collective duty. Equally important, the war against the Soviet Union helped forge strong personal links among the many

---

7. See especially Sageman 2004, 25–59, and Stern 2003, 3–137. Data on Canada are sketchy. We do know, however, that terror-related money laundering in Canada in fiscal year 2004–5 was estimated to be double the previous year at $140 million, according to Horst Intscher, director of Canada's Financial Transactions and Report Analysis Centre (Fintrac); http://cnews.canoe.ca/CNEWS/World/WarOn Terrorism/2004/11/04/700533-cp.html (accessed March 23, 2005).

8. Zwerman, Steinhoff, and della Porta 2000.

9. Katzenstein 1997, 13–21.

10. Juergensmeyer 2000, 214.

11. Sageman 2004, Stern 2003.

volunteers who came from many different countries and learned how to fight side by side. The contribution of Arabs in the war was small in numbers, but the impact of Muslim NGOs and activists was a major one. The states that supported the mujahideen (the United States, Saudi Arabia, and Pakistan) lost control over the radicals who were intent on exporting jihad beyond Afghanistan, based on the strong interpersonal links that had been forged and the extremist ideology that they had come to adopt during the war.

The second phase occurred in the 1990s. The veterans of the war in Afghanistan tried, and failed, to win their separate struggles against their home governments, for example, in Algeria and Egypt. Other jihadi struggles in the periphery of the Muslim world—in Kashmir, Bosnia, and Chechnya—also brought little success. Al-Qaida under Osama bin Laden's leadership then emerged as a regional—and eventually global—network that provided organizational and ideological support for local jihadi movements. This was the political context for bin Laden's strategy of attacking the United States in order to eventually eliminate the Saudi regime. Afghanistan and later western Pakistan became training grounds for a new phase of the struggle.

The 9/11 attacks on the United States and the American response initiated the third phase. The conflict between radical Islam and the United States has become global. Radical Islam can be found in the Islamic diaspora that is rapidly growing in democratic, postmodern Europe, in the modernizing, authoritarian states that dominate the Middle East, and embryonically perhaps in Southeast Asia. Even the outbreak of strictly local violence is now framed by both sides as evidence of the existence of a global struggle. This change in perception rescued the movement from the problems of collective action that came with the elimination of its territorial sanctuary in Afghanistan. It also made up for resource scarcities and factional infighting. Various groups can operate locally or globally, although most of them continue to operate with greatest ease in the Middle East. The Iraqi insurgency is currently the central stage for jihadi politics. Al-Qaida hopes to draw the United States deep into a protracted conflict that bin Laden had vainly hoped for in Afghanistan. U.S. allies fear that the return of fighters to the Middle East and Europe who have been trained in the Iraq insurgency will eventually shift the sites of violence while spreading the anti-American and anti-Western thrust of jihadi movement politics.

The U.S. occupation of Iraq, by most accounts, has attracted hundreds of Muslim militants from Europe to fight the Americans. In the words of one high-ranking German police official, "The war in Iraq has somehow mobilized this scene so that people who before just had some sort of contact or sympathies with extremist groups now think they have to do something."[12] Although this exodus to Iraq has been much smaller than the departure from Europe of thousands of Muslims in the 1980s to fight in Afghanistan,[13] it poses a serious threat. France's top antiterrorism judge, Jean-Louis Bruguiere, reflected a broad view among European counterterrorism experts

12. Rising 2005.
13. Ibid., Haahr-Escolano 2005, Sciolino 2005b, 2005c.

when he warned publicly that a more fragmented al-Qaida has become a bigger threat than before.[14] The war in Iraq has created a new and more dangerous generation of younger, more radical groups of Islamic extremists, many of whom have been trained and battle-hardened through their participation in the insurgency against the U.S. occupation of Iraq. According to Balthazar Garzon, Spain's leading magistrate prosecuting Islamic terrorists, this "second generation" has in many cases no history of affiliation with al-Qaida or other established terrorist organizations. Terror cells recruit over the Internet or in jails, primarily among second-generation immigrants with dim life chances at the periphery of European society. Holding European passports, these recruits have ready access to North America. They organize around loose constellations of personal relationships rather than cells linked in a network structure: for them, al-Qaida is an ideological reference point rather than an organizational structure. Lacking any contacts with extremist groups, these constellations are very difficult for intelligence and law-enforcement agencies to track. Roger Cressey, the White House deputy counterterrorism coordinator between 2001 and 2004 concedes that the creation of a new cadre of hardened Islamic terrorists was "one of the biggest unintended consequences of the war in Iraq. The administration had no appreciation of the danger of creating a new cadre of jihadis."[15]

The number of fighters who left their home countries in the Middle East or Afghanistan after the fall of the Taliban to fight in Iraq appears to be much larger than those leaving Europe. The threat they pose to the Gulf states is considerably greater than the threat to Europe. One study shows that 60 percent of foreign fighters killed in Iraq were from Saudi Arabia, compared to only a handful from Europe.[16] In contrast to Europe or the United States the effects of Iraq as a regional training ground for terrorists are already very much in evidence in bloody gun battles and bombing attacks in the small Gulf states and Saudi Arabia.[17] The primary target of al-Qaida has not been the United States. For many years al-Qaida has sought chiefly to destroy the political regimes in Saudi Arabia and the other Gulf states; more recently, it has focused much of its attention and resources on Iraq. And while anti-Americanism is surely a very important part of the insurgency, so is the fear of Shiite ascendancy that is mobilizing Sunnis and Salafis. The fear of Shiite influence emanating from Iran and now Iraq is deeply disruptive of a region in which before March 2003 eighteen of twenty-one countries were ruled by Sunnis.[18]

As was true of West European terrorists a couple of decades ago, anti-Americanism interacts with a host of other factors. In the squalid housing projects in the suburbs of Europe's major cities, with unemployment rampant and channels

14. BBC News, http://news.bbc.co.uk/go/pr/fr/-/2/hi/europe/4595313.stm (accessed May 31, 2005).

15. Cofer Black, the State Department's chief counterterrorism expert between 2002 and 2005, predicts "that the quality of all our lives will change . . . as measures previously considered needed (only) in forward areas will increasingly be . . . adopted in our home countries." Both quotations are in Waterman 2005. It remains to be seen whether the Iraq War is transforming al-Qaida from a network of cells into a regional or global jihad, as a highly placed CIA operative argues. See Anonymous 2001, 2004.

16. Waterman 2005.

17. Ambah 2005, Watkins 2005, Moamen 2005.

18. Aslan 2005, Smith 2005. Barak Mendelsohn, personal communication, March 23, 2005.

for upward social mobility all but closed, different branches of Islam offer political options that are attractive to more than a few. In France alone the number of converts to Islam numbers in the tens of thousands in recent years. The Islam they choose is not a uniform set of doctrines and practices. The small number of adherents of jihad, for example, are in constant rivalry with the much larger number of explicitly nonviolent and pietistic followers of Islam who are intent on total separation from secular Europe and the West. The clashes within and between these different groupings are intense and are played out in European chat rooms on the Internet. Anti-Americanism plays a role in these political debates and struggles, but since the setting for these trends is Europe, the salience of anti-Americanism is smaller than, for example, in the Middle East.[19]

We lack reliable information about the precise effects of anti-Americanism as a breeding ground of militant Islamists. With due caution we conclude that among a complex set of factors, anti-American attitudes most probably have a mobilizing effect that is motivating individuals and small groups to act violently against Americans, and that this effect is much stronger in the Middle East than in Europe or North America. It seems quite plausible, considering the dynamic changes from the first to successive generations of extremists, that the enhanced recruitment of younger cohorts of extremists will pose serious security risks for Europe and North America in the future.

Counterterrorist Government Policies

What are the effects of anti-Americanism on governments that are participating in the war on terror or that are potential targets of jihadi attacks? Is widespread anti-Americanism reflected in the initial reaction of the European allies of the United States and the subsequent evolution of the deployment of NATO forces in Afghanistan? Have anti-American views encouraged greater military cooperation among European NATO members that are growing distrustful of U.S. policies? Are such views reflected in the debates occurring in and decisions taken by various multilateral fora, such as the UN or the G8 summit meetings? And, finally, can we track the effects of anti-American views in the policies of democratic or authoritarian governments in Europe, the Middle East, and Asia? Generally speaking, the data suggest negative answers to most of these questions. If we can trust the public record, despite the spread of anti-American views, military, diplomatic, police, and intelligence cooperation have intensified greatly since 9/11.

NATO and Afghanistan   Right after 9/11 European publics reacted with a heartfelt outpouring of sympathy for Americans, with hundreds of thousands marching in the streets in a massive display of public support for the United States. Contrary to the widely reported claim of Robert Kagan, furthermore, public, as opposed to elite and government opinion, on both sides of the Atlantic was largely similar in its

19. Kepel 2004, 241–87; Stern 1999, 69–86, and 2003; Sageman 2004; Burdman 2003.

reaction.[20] And government policy mirrored public views. In reaction to the attacks and against the initial opposition of the United States, NATO invoked the collective defense provision in Article 5 of the NATO treaty.[21]

Even though anti-Americanism increased sharply in late 2002, NATO began at precisely that time to plan, in response to U.S. demands, for its first-ever out-of-area deployment—in Afghanistan. As the war in Iraq began to loom larger and larger in 2002, fierce opponents of the war, such as Germany, Canada, and Turkey, and reluctant supporters, like the Netherlands, agreed that NATO should take over the command of the peacekeeping operations in Afghanistan. For Germany, this agreement reflected a fundamental change in policy. In fact all twenty-six NATO members contributed to the NATO contingent, deployed initially under German-Dutch command in early 2003 until NATO stepped in formally in August 2003 to assume full command. At the time of the October 2003 Afghan election, 95 percent of the 5,500 peacekeepers serving in Afghanistan were NATO troops. Troop deployments have subsequently expanded, and many troops have moved out of Kabul into other provincial capitals. These NATO troops are complementing about eighteen thousand U.S. troops still hunting al-Qaida and Taliban fighters in Afghanistan.

NATO's deployment in Afghanistan, which took place quietly as the largest-ever, worldwide antiwar demonstrations were held in February 2003, is proof of the insulation of the war on terror from the strong anti-American views of mass publics. Of about 7,800 German troops stationed abroad in June 2004, some 40 percent were directly engaged in counterterror missions, including 2,300 soldiers stationed in Afghanistan, and Germany has also hosted two international conferences addressing Afghanistan.[22] There is nothing surprising about any of this. German and European mass publics and governments see an effective war on terror and a lasting reconstruction of Afghanistan to be very much in their interest. What they oppose strongly is the U.S. penchant for militarizing the war, for expanding the war's aims to include unrelated objectives such as the spread of democracy, and for acting unilaterally in the pursuit of U.S. interests. The fact that anti-American views did not undermine close cooperation in Afghanistan as the core of the war on terror is a first indication of their limited effect, also readily observable in other multilateral settings.

The American War in Iraq and European Defense Cooperation   What has been the effect of the unilateral turn in U.S. foreign policy and the war it is waging in Iraq on the military cooperation among its European allies? European commitment to an institutionalization of defense cooperation has grown gradually, especially in the 1990s. The war in Bosnia gave European governments conclusive proof that they lacked the necessary military capabilities to act effectively even in Europe. Prime Minister Tony Blair altered long-standing British defense policy when he agreed in Decem-

---

20. Isernia and Everts 2004, Kagan 2003.
21. Lansford 2002, 60–83; Tuschhoff 2002, 2003.
22. Congressional Research Service 2004, 9–11.

ber 1998 with French president Jacques Chirac that the European Union needed to acquire operational military capabilities. At a subsequent July 1999 summit the European Union agreed to take over the crisis management tasks of the European Union and signed up for a common European security and defense policy. By the end of 1999 the European Union had committed itself to create a military force of sixty thousand ready to be mobilized in sixty days and equipped for a deployment of up to one year.[23] Chirac argued repeatedly that "the multipolar world France is seeking will provide balance and harmony. But it will not be feasible unless Europe is organized and able to play its role on the international stage."[24] This shift in European policy and perspective occurred before the contested election of George W. Bush as U.S. president in November 2000.

U.S. reaction to the gradual emergence of a more autonomous European military capability has varied among ambivalence, skepticism, and hostility. During the brief war in Afghanistan the Europeans took issue with the U.S. preference for a purely military response. European reaction to the new national security strategy of the United States, which was announced in September 2002, was largely critical, especially to the doctrine's emphasis on unilateralism or merely ad hoc multilateral arrangements. The war in Iraq, waged only with the support of Britain and the nominal support of a "coalition of the willing," deepened the transatlantic rift. Nevertheless, the German government, publicly very critical of the Iraq War, provided important intelligence information to the United States in March 2003.[25]

Significantly, the tensions between Britain, France, and Germany over the Iraq War did not interfere with the new EU defense dialogue. In September 2003, at a meeting requested by the British government, Europe's "big three" agreed to establish a strategic and operational military planning body inside the European Security and Defense Policy, outside of NATO. In December 2003 the European Union adopted its security strategy paper, "A Secure Europe in a Better World." The following year EU governments agreed to a European armaments agency, the creation of a civil-military planning body within the EU military staff, development of a European airlift command, and to ready, by 2008, an aircraft carrier with air wing and escort.

The emergence of a European defense initiative predates the wave of anti-Americanism that swept Europe in 2002 and 2003. But distrust of the U.S. approach to the war on terror has propelled a series of European defense initiatives, with the full support of the British government.

Multilateral Fora   Since the early 1960s the United Nations has set up a number of specialized agencies that address issues of terrorism, including a counterterrorism office located in Vienna. Although the General Assembly has not yet arrived at a consensual definition of the term "terrorism," over the decades a norm against

23. Katzenstein 2005, 130–32.
24. Chirac 2000.
25. Gordon 2006.

terrorism has spread.[26] The United Nations has adopted twelve international counterterrorism conventions, open to signature and ratification by all UN members. After seven years of negotiations, in April 2005 the General Assembly passed unanimously a nuclear terrorism treaty that requires states to prosecute or extradite individuals found in possession of atomic devices or radioactive materials. "By its action," U.S. deputy ambassador Stuart Holliday said, "the General Assembly has shown that it can, when it has the political will, play an important role in the global fight against terrorism."[27] Between 1996 and 2004 the UN Security Council passed twenty-five resolutions condemning acts of terrorism.[28] By spring 2004 all 191 UN members had filed first-round implementation reports with the Counter-Terrorism Committee established by UN Security Council Resolution 1373, passed on September 28, 2001, which called on members to become party to the twelve UN conventions and various regional documents that condemn terrorism.[29]

Unusually, this resolution imposes uniform requirements on all UN member states and thus has been highly effective in pressuring third world countries to comply. In addition, as of May 2005 twelve third world states had passed domestic antiterror legislation with minimal delay; seven states passed such legislation after extensive debate; and in another five states such debate was continuing in 2005. In general, more authoritarian governments were much more ready to constrain domestic freedom than less authoritarian or democratic ones. On this issue multilateralism is widely perceived as a screen for U.S. pressure, and complying is widely interpreted as a way of currying favor with the United States. The perceived heavy-handedness of the United States has fostered distrust in countries such as Kenya and South Africa, and may fuel further distrust, especially in countries such as Morocco and Tunisia that are just beginning to move toward liberalization and democratization.[30]

Starting in 2002 the G8 leaders launched a global partnership based on six principles that were designed to further collaborative action to prevent terrorists and those who harbor them from acquiring weapons of mass destruction as well as missile and related technologies. Subsequent meetings reinforced that commitment by creating a counterterrorism action group that is cooperating closely with the United Nations and regional organizations and undertaking other counterterrorism initiatives. These measures build on thirty-one similar declarations that the G8 issued between 1975 and 2001.[31] The G8 summits thus express a long-standing and widely shared consensus by heads of states to combat terrorism. Furthermore, compliance with resolutions against terrorism passed by the G8 is twice as high as for other issues.

26. In 2004 a UN panel proposed a definition of terrorism, but it was not approved by the UN Summit of September 2005. For the definition, see High-Level Panel 2004, paragraph 164, and Annan 2005, paragraph 91. For the 2005 World Summit outcome, see United Nations, General Assembly, 2005.

27. Quoted in *New York Times* 2005 (April 14), A6.

28. We would like to thank Barak Medelsohn for sharing these data with us.

29. Council on Foreign Relations 2004, 9. Three committees of the UN Security Council coordinate a global sanctions regime against al-Qaida and the Taliban, counterterrorism activities, and the tracking of weapons of mass destruction.

30. Whitaker 2005, 6, 10–14.

31. Belelieu 2002, 20.

Only eight days after 9/11 the G8 leaders reiterated their renewed commitment to jointly fight terrorism.[32]

When the United States demanded action, its international partners were eager to respond. For example, military planners from sixty-eight states met in Bucharest in May 2005 to plan cooperation in the war on terror, ten more than attended the Warsaw meeting in October 2004.[33] Furthermore, legislation passed by the U.S. Congress at the end of 2002 required that by July 2004 all ports in the world have in place counterterrorism systems. The legislation permits the United States to deny entry to any ship should any of the last ten ports at which it has taken cargo or passengers on board not meet new U.S. standards. Pressured by the U.S. government, the International Maritime Organization adopted the International Ship and Port Facility Security Code in December 2002, to be enforced by July 2004, which, in the words of Elizabeth DeSombre, "greatly increase[s] the transparency of most ships flying flags of convenience."[34] Within eighteen months the International Maritime Organization reported that worldwide 86 percent of the ships and 69 percent of the ports met the new requirements.[35] The new measures were intrusive and costly, yet states were eager to comply in record time.

The summit machinery involves not only the heads of states but also ministers of finance, foreign affairs, interior, and justice as well as G8 experts, such as the Counter-Terrorist group. As early as October 2001 the finance ministers of the G8 submitted an action plan designed to combat the financing of terrorist activities. The 12th UN Counter-Terrorism Convention on the Suppression of Terrorist Financing and the Financial Action Task Force's Eight Special Recommendations on Terrorist Financing also focused on these issues.[36] National legislation in the United States, Britain, the European continent, the Middle East, and southwest Asia (Iran, Iraq, and the Arabian Peninsula) has complemented these international actions. Significantly, although unresolved issues remain, a series of bombing attacks in 2003 and 2004 on targets in Saudi Arabia has moved the policy of the Saudi government closer to the international norm.[37] In September 2001 only four states had ratified the International Convention for the Suppression of the Financing of Terrorism. By June 2005 that number had increased to 117.[38]

A final example of multilateral cooperation is the Proliferation Security Initiative (PSI), which the U.S. government launched in May 2003. Its aim is to prevent the spread of weapons of mass destruction to nonnuclear states and terrorist groups. The PSI is an instance of creating a coalition of states willing to support the United States in its effort to plug the evident holes in the Treaty on the Non-Proliferation

32. Ibid., 15, 21.

33. osint@yahoogroups.com (accessed May 25, 2005).

34. DeSombre 2006, 177. We are grateful to Professor DeSombre for sharing with us portions of her book.

35. Ibid.

36. Winer and Roule 2002; Belelieu 2002, 15. The Financial Action Task Force is a twenty-nine-member intergovernmental organization established by the G7 in 1989 to set international anti–money laundering standards.

37. Council on Foreign Relations 2004, 3–5, 11–25, 27–29.

38. http://untreaty.un.org/ENGLISH/status/chapter_xviii/treaty11. asp (accessed June 14, 2005).

of Nuclear Weapons (NPT) that now make it possible for nonnuclear states, such as Iran, to move toward nuclear status. Such moves to nuclear status were facilitated enormously in the 1990s by Pakistan's chief nuclear engineer, Abdul Qadeer Khan. His network of scientists, engineers, and traders spread nuclear technology and the capacity to enrich uranium to countries such as Iran, North Korea, and Libya. Because, for a variety of reasons, the NPT looks like an ineffective instrument for addressing proliferation, the Bush administration has relied on a more selective approach with which it hopes to isolate potentially threatening states bent on the acquisition of nuclear weapons. Estimates of the number of states participating vary widely. The original eleven founding members have grown to around sixty and perhaps as many as sixty-six, according to various government statements and publications which, it should be noted, do not provide a list of countries in any publicly available documentation.[39] Joseph Cirincione, a knowledgeable observer of nuclear proliferation, reportedly speaks of only twenty-one actively participating states.[40] The discrepancy is likely due to a U.S. policy that simply asks for minimal levels of cooperation to create the appearance of a large multilateral effort, when intensive cooperation actually involves many fewer states. Such cooperation can be effective; the interception of a freighter carrying nuclear components in October 2003 is widely credited to have led to Libya's abandonment of its nuclear program. But the lack of near-universal membership is also a serious liability. Pakistan has refused to join the PSI and has cooperated only in part in the effort to track down the global network that Khan had built. And without China's participation there is scant hope of enforcing an effective embargo on North Korea. The shift from a large multilateral forum, the NPT, to a much smaller one, the PSI, is in line with the general strategy of the Bush administration.

With this one caveat, we conclude that anti-Americanism has not had a major impact on the numerous deliberations on counterterrorism in various multilateral fora since 9/11. What mattered much more were the interests of all governments in jointly promoting effective counterterrorist policies. As documented above, coordination of policy is reflected in numerous issues.[41] Although policy coordination has been far from perfect, at least in the short-term, the effects of anti-Americanism seem to have posed no major obstacles to the war on terror that the United States has waged in global as well as regional organizations.

Anti-Americanism and "Soft Power"

Joseph S. Nye defines "soft power" as being able to get others to want the outcomes you want and devotes a section of his book to the subject of anti-Americanism. Three major potential power resources may contribute to soft power: convergence

---

39. Sanger 2005a, 2005b; Baker and Meese 2005, Bureau of Nonproliferation 2005, Rice 2005.
40. Fidler 2005.
41. See also Mendelsohn 2005. This conclusion is not to deny the obvious counterfactual point that in the absence of anti-American views government policy coordination might have been even greater.

of political values, an attractive culture, and policies that seem benign to others. Without stating so explicitly, Nye implies that anti-Americanism adversely affects American soft power.[42] It certainly seems plausible that if others dislike the United States, they will be less willing to defer to U.S. wishes and support U.S. policy.

However, it is remarkably difficult empirically to establish the specific proposition that anti-Americanism has systematically hindered the successful conduct of American diplomacy, as Senator John Kerry claimed in his campaign for the presidency in 2004. In this section, we explore the hypothesis that anti-Americanism since 2001 has adversely affected one dimension of the soft power of the United States: the ability of the United States to achieve its objectives through diplomatic means. We probe here whether anti-American sentiments in other societies created resistance to supporting U.S. policy in general—quite apart from opposition to specific U.S. policies. Empirically, it is often difficult to tell what is driving opposition or support for the United States, but conceptually it is crucial to keep in mind the difference between what we called in chapter 1 "what we do" and "what we are."

Leaders of states devise strategies in a forward-looking way, hoping to achieve the best results that serve both their interests and values. A long tradition of political realism emphasizes that in the effort to be successful leaders need to subordinate their emotional reactions and ideological predispositions to strategic calculations. Such calculation should preclude the direct translation of anti-American views into policy. Instead, leaders should act as filters, ensuring that damaging actions are not taken on the basis of envy or resentment. These filters should be especially strong in nondemocratic societies, but they should also operate in democracies. Certainly the effect of anti-Americanism on policy will not be as direct and simple as the effect of dislike on a personal relationship between two individuals.

We therefore should expect that when governmental elites have strong interests, and when the details of their actions are largely hidden from public view, these interests may take precedence over public views, even in democracies. Indeed, members of the public may not want to know too many of the details, since they wish for problems such as terrorism to be dealt with effectively, without engaging their moral scruples. The controversy over the possible complicity of European intelligence services, perhaps even European governments, with the growing practice of rendition, transferring suspects held in the war on terror to third countries for interrogation, is a telling example. We should therefore not be too surprised to find that public opinion that is unfavorable toward the United States has not significantly affected cooperation against terrorism. However, in more public areas of diplomacy, where the stakes tend to be lower, one might well expect anti-American views to be more important.

Impacts on American Diplomacy in General

How can we test the hypothesis that anti-Americanism, as distinguished from mere opposition to U.S. foreign policy, hinders the exercise of soft power by the United

42. Nye 2004a, 44.

States? The most general and strongest form of this claim holds that anti-American views deeply affect relationships on issues not directly related to major political conflicts such as the war on terror or the 2003 invasion of Iraq by the United States and members of its coalition. At its most intense, anti-Americanism would be so pervasive that the United States would have difficulty persuading other states to support it on a whole range of issues in world politics.

Such across-the-board effects, at a global level, are not observed. We have reviewed a number of issue areas in which the United States interacts regularly with other countries, and we have consulted experts with deep knowledge of these areas. There is little evidence that anti-American opinion matters very much. All of the people we consulted indicated that in their own areas of expertise, it was not an important factor. For instance, in George W. Bush's first term as president, the United States and Europe avoided serious trade wars, showing the ability to reach compromises on a variety of intrinsically contentious issues, from trade in genetically modified organisms to tax policy and subsidies for aircraft manufacturers Boeing and Airbus. If European anti-Americanism had affected trade policy, one would have expected much more bitterness and even deadlock, rather than the usual contentious politics driven by competing economic interests. Likewise, bilateral controversies on free trade agreements with such disparate countries as Australia and Morocco do not seem, from the standpoint of informed observers, to have been affected by anti-American views.[43]

In other areas, also, the effects of anti-Americanism on U.S. diplomacy seem slight. There seems to be no indication that European-American cooperation in organizations such as the IMF or World Bank, or on development issues more generally, has been stymied by European anti-Americanism. Indeed, European governments not only declined to block the nomination of Paul Wolfowitz (often referred to as the architect of the Iraq War) but expressed considerable support for him after he discussed his views with them before his official selection as president of the World Bank.[44] Even negative decisions that might seem to have been motivated by anti-Americanism turn out, in the view of people with different political views who understand their complexities, to have been determined by other factors.

This null finding is not entirely surprising. Sometimes, governments' assessments of their interests are deeply affected by mass opinions; often, however, governments have strong ideas about interests, and publics defer to their judgment as long as the results seem acceptable. For leaders to let anti-American views change their political positions would require sacrificing some interests in order to indulge in the expression of strongly held opinions or negative predispositions, or to punish the United States for its behavior on issues such as the war in Iraq. Representatives of these interests, inside and outside the government, would strenuously resist such a course of action. Unless the issues are salient and there is a particular domestic political

43. Communications from Linda Weiss (on Australia) and Rob Satloff (on Morocco), April 2005.
44. See *New York Times* 2005 (April 3), 11.

reason to make an anti-American appeal, the costs to policymakers of letting one's policies be affected by anti-American views will often outweigh the benefits.

A particularly surprising situation in which anti-American opinion does not seem to have had strong effects on American diplomacy involves the International Criminal Court (ICC). Beginning in 2001, the Bush Administration asked a large number of countries to sign agreements stipulating that they would not surrender U.S. servicemen or officials to the ICC. Judith Kelley has studied the factors leading states to sign, or not sign, such agreements in response to U.S. requests. She argues convincingly that this situation "provides a terrific quasi-experiment," because the United States "sought an agreement with almost all states within a relatively short period of time" and because states did not anticipate such demands from the United States when they decided to ratify the ICC treaty.[45]

Kelley's main purpose is to explain decisions to sign or not sign nonsurrender agreements—that is, acceding to American demands. Her analysis shows that refusals to sign nonsurrender agreements are explained by the level of a state's commitment to the rule of law, conditional on ratification of the ICC treaty. None of the twenty-seven states that had ratified the treaty and had a strong commitment to the rule of law signed nonsurrender agreements. In contrast, almost half of the states with low rule-of-law scores that had ratified the treaty, and well over half of states that had not ratified the treaty, signed such agreements.[46]

Kelley did a further, more detailed analysis to discover whether her results could be affected by anti-Americanism.[47] She found that publics in the seven countries that had both ratified the ICC treaty and signed nonsurrender agreements viewed the United States more favorably than those that had refused to do so. However, the states that cooperated with the United States also had lower democracy scores than those that refused to sign nonsurrender agreements, suggesting that it was their lower commitment to the rule of law, rather than greater pro-American sentiment, that may have led them to accede to U.S. requests. Kelley concludes that there is no convincing evidence of a relationship between public attitudes toward the United States, as measured in the 2002 Pew poll, and the signing of nonsurrender agreements.[48] Her analysis, therefore, does not support the hypothesis that anti-Americanism had a significant impact in this policy domain.[49]

---

45. Kelley 2005, 3.

46. Six of ten states not party to the treaty with high rule-of-law scores and twenty of twenty-three nonmembers with low rule-of-law scores signed nonsurrender agreements, compared to twenty-one of forty-four state parties with low rule-of-law scores and zero of twenty-seven state parties with high rule-of-law scores. Kelley 2005, 22 (table 3). Beth Elise Whitaker (2005, 6) arrives at an analogous conclusion in her analysis of the adoption of antiterror legislation in the third world after 9/11. Authoritarian regimes were the quickest ones to comply with U.S. pressure to change their laws.

47. Personal communication, March 15, 2005.

48. The figures in the 2002 Pew poll are 73.4% vs. 62.2%.

49. Logit analyses, using Kelley's entire data set, do not yield significant coefficients for the variable of "U.S. image" under a variety of specifications: a basic logit equation, or equations that control for ratification, the rule of law, or simultaneously for the rule of law and democracy. Since the number of states for which data are available is relatively small (thirty-six), these results need to be interpreted with caution. We are very grateful to Kelley for doing this analysis and sharing her findings with us.

Even if U.S. requests are not rejected, there could be another, subtler result of anti-American views. The U.S. government could craft requests depending on its estimate of the likelihood of acceptance. Sometimes governments make requests that they know will be rejected, particularly if they want to make a symbolic point or demonstrate their commitment to a policy. But often, when potential requesters anticipate rejection, they will not ask in the first place. Put differently, there can be selection effects resulting from requests not being independent of anticipated responses.[50] Some well-informed observers of the U.S. government think that beginning in the 1990s U.S. policymakers became more reluctant to make general requests, particularly after most American allies rejected the pleas of the U.S. government not to conclude the land mines treaty. In this view, the reflection of greater anti-Americanism would not be rejection of American requests but the absence of such requests.[51]

The Impact of Anti-Americanism on Iraq-Related Diplomacy

It seems that pervasive anti-Americanism should most strongly affect responses to highly controversial American policies, such as U.S. policy in Iraq. What, for example, happened when the U.S. government requested others to participate in the invasion and occupation of Iraq?[52] Was anti-Americanism related to decisions not to send troops, trainers, or election monitors, or to join the "coalition of the willing," when the United States sent a general appeal to friendly states to join its coalition in March 2003? A United States Senate resolution on March 27, 2003, listed forty-nine countries as members of the coalition.[53] Prior to the war, the Pew Research Center for People and the Press conducted a poll in July–October 2002 asking a question about favorable/unfavorable views of the United States in forty-two countries.[54] What can we learn from bringing these two sets of data together?

50. Both the endogeneity effect and the selection effect would introduce systematic bias into our test. Endogeneity will inflate the magnitude of any correlation. Selection reduces variation in observed outcomes.

51. Personal communication from Richard Steinberg, UCLA law school, March 2005, on the basis of conversations in Washington, D.C. However, one problem with this argument is that, as we have seen, public opinion in most countries was pro-American as late as 2002. In view of this, the inability of the United States to get agreement with its views on such subjects as the land mines treaty and the International Criminal Court was likely less an effect of general anti-American sentiment than of deep policy disagreements between the United States and its allies, and strong issue-specific public opinion (on issues such as land mines and the ICC) in allied countries.

52. In thirty-eight countries, on average, 53% of the population opposed the war under all circumstances, 30% would have supported it if it were sanctioned by the United Nations, and 8% supported unilateral action by the United States and its allies. In the United States corresponding figures were 21, 34, and 33 percent. http://www.gallup-international.com (accessed November 1, 2004).

53. See http://www.usiraqprocon.org (accessed May 2, 2005). The Heritage Foundation listed fifty-six countries and the Institute for Policy Studies listed forty-six. See also the website of Perspectives on World History and Current Events at http://www.pwhce.org (accessed March 15, 2005). The White House website contains a press release from March 21, 2003, listing forty-eight members. See http://www.whitehouse.gov (accessed March 15, 2005).

54. See Pew Global Attitudes Project 2002, at http://www.people-press.org (accessed May 2, 2005). It is essential to examine public opinion data *prior* to the war, since we wish to test the inference that general public sentiment shaped policy toward the Iraq war, rather than vice versa.

Before trying to answer this question, we should recognize that such an analysis would be subject to bias in favor of the hypothesis that attitudes toward the United States affected decisions on war-related issues. Strong opposition to U.S. policy can generate anti-American attitudes as well as vice versa, or both opposition and anti-American views can be explained, as in Chiozza's analysis in chapter 4, by other factors such as the percentage of the population that is Muslim. Therefore, there exists a strong *ex ante* bias in favor of the proposition that pro-American attitudes will predict membership in the coalition.

The relationship between attitudes toward the United States in 2002 and membership in the coalition of the willing in 2003, as listed in the Senate resolution, is displayed in table 10.1a, which also categorizes states by whether they had democratic or nondemocratic polities in 2003.[55] Among democratic states there is at most only a slight relationship between public attitudes toward the United States in 2002 and subsequent coalition membership. The median favorability score toward the United States for democracies not members of the coalition of the willing is sixty-three percent, only nine points lower than the median score for members of the coalition. Among nondemocratic states the difference between favorability scores of members and nonmembers is much wider. Table 10.1b summarizes the same evidence, which does not support the view that mass opinion toward the United States in democratic countries affected decisions on whether to join the coalition.

Evidence with respect to economic support from other countries for reconstruction in Iraq is more ambiguous. In October 2003 representatives from over seventy states and a number of multilateral organizations pledged about $32 billion for an "International Reconstruction Fund Facility for Iraq," with components administered by the World Bank and the United Nations. However, not much more than $1 billion of that sum had actually been deposited with the fund, as of the most recent reports available in early 2006. Of the sums deposited, about three-quarters came from Japan, the European Commission, and the United Kingdom. France and Germany did not contribute independently, and no European country other than the UK contributed more than $20 million.[56] In November 2004 the "Paris Club" of creditors to Iraq agreed on what the club estimated to be an 80 percent reduction in Iraqi debt. The participants included countries with widely varying levels of public anti-Americanism, although the countries involved had many pragmatic

---

55. The Senate resolution (and the White House) listed Turkey as a member of the coalition of the willing, which seems controversial given the Turkish parliament's refusal to permit an attack on Iraq from Turkey. Table 10.1a, however, accepts the Senate's statement of coalition membership. (Turkey's parliament voted in October 2003 to offer to send troops to Iraq, but this offer was rejected by Iraq.)

56. See U.S. State Department 2005 and the website of the International Reconstruction Trust Fund for Iraq: http://www.irffi.org (accessed March 15, 2006). The materials cited below are all available on that website. Data on the pledges are in World Bank Report No. P7615, January 14, 2004, p. 2. Data for deposits to the World Bank–administered fund can be found in "World Bank Iraq Data Sheet," as of January 1, 2006. Data for deposits to the UN-administered fund can be found in Annex 2 of the "Second Six Month Report on Activities implemented under the UNDG Iraq Trust Fund of the International Reconstruction Fund Facility for Iraq," United Nations Development Programme, 30 November 2005, part 1.

Table 10.1a. Pew "Favorable to U.S. Scores" (Pew 2002) by polity type

Type of Polity	Member of coalition of the willing	Nonmember	N
Democratic	[11]	[20]	31
	Philippines (90)	Ghana (83)	
	Honduras (80)	Guatemala (82)	
	Ukraine (80)	Venezuela (82)	
	Poland (79)	Kenya (80)	
	United Kingdom (75)	Mali (75)	
	Bulgaria (72)	Canada (72)	
	Japan (72)	Czech Rep. (71)	
	Italy (70)	Peru (67)	
	Slovakia (60)	South Africa (65)	
	South Korea (53)	Mexico (64)	
	Turkey (30)	France (63)	
		Germany (61)	
		Indonesia (61)	
		Russia (61)	
		Senegal (61)	
		Bolivia (57)	
		India (54)	
		Brazil (52)	
		Bangladesh (45)	
		Argentina (34)	
	Median: 72	*Median: 63*	
Nondemocratic	[3]	[6]	9
	Uzbekistan (85)	Ivory Coast (84)	
	Uganda (74)	Vietnam (71)	
	Angola (54)	Lebanon (35)	
		Jordan (25)	
		Pakistan (10)	
		Egypt (6)	
	Median: 74	*Median: 30*	
N	14	26	40

Note: Table 10.1a lists all forty countries polled by Pew in 2002 that had Polity IV scores for 2003 either −2 or below (clearly nondemocratic) or +6 and above (clearly democratic). Two countries were omitted because their categorization would be ambiguous: Tanzania (with a score of 2) and Nigeria (with a score of 4). Polity scores (2003) are drawn from: http://www.cidcm.umd.edu/inscr/polity (accessed May 26, 2005). Coalition of the willing membership is taken from a March 27, 2003, Senate resolution: http://www.usiraqprocon.org (accessed May 26, 2005).

reasons to go along with the debt reduction. This pattern of accommodating, at least nominally, to U.S. policy is consistent with the UN Security Council's unanimous vote on May 22, 2003, confirming the status of the United States and United Kingdom as occupying powers in Iraq.[57]

57. See American Society of International Law, *Insights*, May 2003, by Frederick L. Kirgis: http://www.asil.org/insights/insigh107.htm (accessed March 14, 2006). See also http://www.clubde-paris.org/en/news/page_detail_news.php?FICHIER=com11011125170, November 21, 2004 (accessed March 15, 2005).

Table 10.1b. Associations among public attitudes, democracy, and membership in the coalition of the willing

Democratic countries			
Pew favorability	Member	Nonmember	N
Pro-United States (over 50%)	10	18	28
Anti-United States (under 50%)	1	2	3
N	11	20	31

Nondemocratic countries			
Pew favorability	Member	Nonmember	N
Pro-United States (over 50%)	3	2	5
Anti-United States (under 50%)	0	4	4
N	3	6	9

Source: Table 10.1a.

Regional and Conjunctural Effects of Anti-Americanism on U.S. Diplomacy

The apparent absence of strong global effects of anti-Americanism on U.S. diplomacy does not mean that the impact of anti-Americanism is small. Its effects could be more specifically regional. Alternatively, such effects could exist at specific conjunctures when decisions that would be close on other grounds were tilted against the United States by anti-American views.

Latin America offers a telling example of regional anti-Americanism. During the spring of 2005, for the first time ever, the Organization of American States (OAS) chose a candidate for secretary-general, José Miguel Insulza of Chile, whom the United States had opposed. A United States proposal, evidently directed against Venezuela, aimed at creating a committee of the OAS to monitor democracy within countries, was facing serious opposition. At the time, President Hugo Chávez of Venezuela was being lionized by Latin American masses and elites alike as a symbol of opposition to the United States and the market-oriented reforms it had promoted.[58]

Anti-Americanism can also be consequential at specific conjunctures. Often cited in this context is the decision by the Turkish parliament on March 1, 2003 not to let U.S. forces attack Iraq from Turkish territory. Knowledgeable commentators on this topic have attributed this decision to a variety of factors, including divisions within the Justice and Development Party (AKP), lack of explicit support by the Turkish military, and widespread opposition to the American invasion of Iraq. Such opposition was apparently motivated in part by feelings of solidarity with other Muslims and by fear that the American invasion would lead eventually to an independent Kurdistan.[59]

58. Brinkley 2005a, 2005b; Forero 2005.
59. Gordon and Shapiro 2004, 161–62; U.S. Congress 2003.

We do not know of any systematic analysis investigating the impact of widespread anti-Americanism in Turkey on this decision. In March 2003 polls showed that 90 to 95 percent of Turks opposed Turkey's involvement in the Iraq War.[60] A 2003 Pew poll showed that only 12 percent of Turks had a favorable view of the United States, as compared with 30 percent a year earlier.[61] It is a reasonable inference that opposition to the Iraq War was a significant factor in the sharp decline in favorable views of the United States over the previous year. A keen observer of Turkish society has argued that the self-perceived vulnerability of all sectors of that society to American pressure has generated distrust of the United States and that when U.S. policy seemed to threaten Turkish interests in 2003, public views turned negative.[62] Anti-Americanism may well have been a factor in parliament's refusal to agree to the U.S. request, although it is impossible to disentangle its effects from those of opposition to the war itself.[63]

Shortly after the March 1 vote, a new government was formed under Prime Minister Racep Erdogan, the leader of the Justice and Development Party. In early October 2003, his government managed to reverse the March 1 decision, authorizing the sending of Turkish troops to Iraq, although Iraq rejected Turkish participation. At this point, a strong majority of Turks still opposed Turkish involvement in the war, although the intensity of opposition had decreased. By March 2004, the level of favorable views of the United States was back at 30 percent, where it had been in 2002.[64]

Another crucial juncture where anti-Americanism, one might think, had an effect, occurred in March 2005. The minority government in Canada, led by Prime Minister Paul Martin, decided not to commit Canada to an integrated North American ballistic missile defense (BMD), despite pressure by the United States. Prime Minister Martin later emphasized criticism of the United States in his unsuccessful campaign for reelection, which he lost to a markedly pro-American conservative, Stephen Harper. If anti-Americanism had effects in Canada, they were ambiguous.[65]

Germany offers the most often-cited example of the effects that anti-Americanism can have at specific historical junctures. In July 2002 Chancellor Schröder's reelection chances looked dim. Two-thirds of the electorate viewed the Red-Green coalition negatively, and while the chancellor was leading the rival candidate of the conservative CDU-CSU in the polls, his party was lagging behind the opposition, and the gap was widening. In launching his reelection campaign on August 5, 2002 the chancellor warned the United States against possible "adventurism" in Iraq, and

60. Heath Lowry, Princeton University, interviewed on *The NewsHour with Jim Lehrer*, October 7, 2003. http://www.pbs.org/newshour/bb/middle_east/july-deco3/turkey_10-07.html (accessed March 15, 2005).

61. http://people-press.org/reports/print.php3?PageID=683 (accessed March 15, 2005).

62. See Barkey 2005.

63. Personal communication from Bruce Kuniholm, Duke University, March 2005.

64. http://people-press.org/commentary/pdf/104.pdf (accessed March 15, 2005).

65. Communications from Michael Byers (University of British Columbia) and Louis Pauly (University of Toronto), March 2005; discussions in Canada with Canadian academic experts, February and March 2006.

he criticized American economic conditions while defending the German social market economy. From the very beginning of the campaign, and before Vice President Cheney's bellicose speech later that month, Schröder was running as a peace candidate, a position that had the support of over 70 percent of the German public. Aided by effective crisis management in the floods of the Danube, Elbe, and Oder valleys in the middle of August, Schröder's resolve not to support a possible invasion of Iraq stiffened as his party began to close the gap with the opposition. Alone among the European states at this time, the chancellor ruled out German participation in a military intervention even if that intervention were backed by the United Nations. His position may have helped his campaign in 2002, but he was defeated for reelection in the fall of 2005 by the CDU, whose leader, Angela Merkel, was pro-American.

Evidence from these cases of a systematic anti-American bias is slight. Yet it is quite often possible, even plausible, to argue that anti-American views can matter greatly at specific conjunctures. In addition to the cases of Germany, Turkey, and Canada, it could well be that other decisions—such as that of Mexican president Vicente Fox not to support the U.S. resolution on Iraq in the Security Council in March 2003—were influenced by anti-American sentiment as well as specific opposition to the U.S. policy at issue.

This survey of the possible effects of anti-Americanism on soft power suggests that, at specific conjunctures, anti-Americanism may have exerted significant effects on state policies that were important to the United States. Yet in each case, refusal to support the United States could be as well explained by opposition to U.S. policy as by anti-Americanism. As noted earlier, it is crucial to make a clear distinction between opposition to U.S. policy and anti-Americanism, in order to avoid attributing to anti-Americanism what should be attributed instead to responses to specific U.S. policies.

Overall, our survey provides little reason to expect that a more systematic analysis would identify general short-term policy effects. Even on issues such as ICC non-surrender agreements and the coalition of the willing, where significant correlations could be expected (whether reflecting causality or not), such correlations are either not found or extremely weak. In the absence of compelling evidence to the contrary, we cannot reject the null hypothesis—that anti-Americanism has failed to have measurable, direct effects on the ability of the United States to attain its diplomatic objectives. Yet the caveats that we introduced at the beginning of this chapter must be kept in mind. A continuation of policies such as those at Abu Ghraib, Guantánamo, and apparently at secret CIA sites around the world could undermine the sense among America's potential friends that the United States exemplifies the values of a liberal democracy. That sentiments of anti-Americanism as expressed to pollsters do not correlate strongly with policy does not preclude the possibility that American soft power is being undermined through a gradual process of erosion.[66] Our finding does,

---

66. We are grateful to Joseph S. Nye Jr. for written comments on an earlier draft of this chapter, which have helped us to clarify this point.

however, make us reluctant to embrace the common conclusion that deeply ingrained anti-Americanism—as distinct from opposition to the policies of the Bush administration—has dramatically undermined or reversed the soft power of the United States.

Direct Action by Individuals and Groups

Two possible ways for individuals or groups to express their anti-American views would be to boycott brand-name products associated with the United States and to refuse to travel as tourists to the United States. We consider both domains in turn.

Boycotts of Brand-Name Products

Is anti-Americanism consequential for corporations that sell American products abroad? It is plausible that people hostile to the United States would be reluctant to purchase products from American firms, especially those products associated strongly with the United States.[67] A priori, corporations that are closely identified with the United States seem quite vulnerable to boycotts because these corporations are often perceived to be part of an American "power structure." Trust in major U.S. corporations (such as Coca-Cola, McDonald's, Burger King, United Parcel Service, Kraft Foods, Procter & Gamble, and Johnson & Johnson) was recently reported as running at about 40 percent in Europe compared to 70 percent in the United States.[68]

Some recent survey evidence suggests that anti-Americanism in Europe is affecting consumer behavior toward American firms. In a December 2004 poll, conducted by Global Market Insite,[69] one thousand consumers in each of eight countries (Canada, China, France, Germany, Japan, Russia, Great Britain, the United States) were asked two questions about fifty-three American companies: would they avoid American products because of recent American foreign policy and military action; and to what extent did they regard particular companies as "extremely American." Overall, 20 percent of European and Canadian consumers reported that they were consciously avoiding American products. Firms perceived by respondents as most subject to consumer boycotts included American Airlines, United Airlines, General Motors, Wal-Mart, CNN, American Express, McDonald's, Coca-Cola, Pepsi, and Marlboro, with firms such as Nike not far behind. Not surprisingly, there is a strong correlation between firms perceived as closely identified with the United States and firms that consumers reported that they had decided to boycott.

---

67. We have done some exploratory work on nonprofit organizations, conducting two interviews with high officials of environmental organizations that operate on a global basis. Neither official indicated that the organization had encountered any significant obstacles in their work due to anti-Americanism, including in Muslim societies such as Indonesia. For a description of one NGO's battle with Coca-Cola, see Stecklow 2005.

68. Edelman 2005, 2, 5.

69. http://www.worldpoll.com.

Anecdotal reports in the press also suggest that sales of U.S. firms have been affected. For example, in March and April of 2003 several news stories trumpeted boycotts against American firms such as McDonald's and Coca-Cola. Will Hutton asserted that the center of the boycott movement was in Germany and that "the boycotts and the surrounding avalanche of negative publicity are a storm warning of what may lie ahead."[70] A German restaurant boycott of American products was reported by Reuters to have spread rapidly in the days after the war in Iraq began:

Diners at the Osteria Restaurant in Berlin are finding that "things go better without Coke" and are ordering Germany's long overshadowed imitation of "the real thing"— the slightly sweeter Afri-Cola—to express their outrage. "We wanted to do something to express our annoyance," Osteria owner Fabrio Angile told Reuters. "We want to hit America where it hurts—in their wallets."[71]

Looking back on more than a year and a half of experience since the Iraq War began, the *Financial Times* reported:

Coca-Cola, which makes 80 percent of its profits outside North America, sold 16 percent less beverage to Germans in the third quarter of 2004 than a year previously. McDonald's blamed falling German sales for virtually eliminating growth across Europe. Altria sold 24.5 percent fewer Marlboro cigarettes in France and 18.7 percent fewer in Germany during the third quarter [of 2004].[72]

The sharp fall in Coca-Cola's beverage sales in Germany in the third quarter of 2004 coincided with market shifts resulting from a new law that required deposits on nonreturnable bottles. Since anti-Americanism seems to have peaked in Europe in 2003, it would have been very strange indeed to observe a sharp decline in sales in 2004.

Tables 10.2a and 10.2b offer more systematic data. We examined the European revenues of three major U.S.-based consumer products firms and three European competitors between 2000 and 2004. These firms include three American firms often mentioned as potential targets of anti-American boycotts: Coca-Cola, McDonald's, and Nike. We chose these firms since they are likely targets of a consumer boycott motivated by anti-American views, have substantial European sales, and information was available on their sales by world region.[73] We included three European firms— Adidas-Solomon, Cadbury Schweppes, and Nestlé—as controls. They compete with the American firms and are similarly multinational.

---

70. "Goodbye, Coke. Hello, Mecca Cola," *Washington Post*, April 18, 2003.

71. Erik Kirschbaum, "EU Consumers Boycotting Starbucks, McDonald's, and Coca-Cola in War Protest," Reuters, March 25, 2003; http://www.organicconsumers.org/Starbucks/boycott032703.cfm (accessed March 3, 2005).

72. *Financial Times* (December 30, 2004), 7.

73. We originally sought to include Pepsi-Co also, but its reports do not break out sales by region in a sufficiently disaggregated way to permit meaningful comparisons. Had we included figures for Pepsi-Co non–North American sales, our overall conclusions would have been unchanged.

Table 10.2a. Sales of selected American and European firms (with percentages of total firm sales in Europe)

	2000–2001 average	2002	2003	2004	2003–4 average
U.S. firms					
Coca-Cola[a]	3,945 (23)	5,262 (27)	6,556 (31)	7,195 (33)	6,875 (32)
McDonald's	4,753 (33)	5,136 (33)	5,875 (34)	6,737 (35)	6,105 (35)
Nike[b]	2,496 (27)	2,731 (28)	3,242 (30)	3,834 (31)	3,538 (31)
European firms					
Adidas-Solomon	2,962 (50)	3,200 (49)	3,365 (54)	3,470 (54)	3,418 (54)
Cadbury Schweppes	1,883 (41)	2,263 (43)	2,809 (44)	2,899 (43)	2,854 (43)
Nestlé	26,513 (32)	28,068 (31)	28,574 (32)	28,563 (33)	28,569 (33)

Note: Figures for U.S. firms are in millions of dollars for the European market. Figures for Adidas-Solomon are in euros, Cadbury Schweppes in pounds sterling, Nestlé in Swiss francs. Figures are derived from SEC annual report filings.
  [a] European figures include Euroasia and Middle East.
  [b] European figures include Middle East and Africa.

Table 10.2b. Sales as percentages of 2000–2001 average sales

	2000–2001 average	2002	2003	2004	2003–4 average
U.S. firms					
Coca-Cola[a]	100	133	166	182	174
McDonald's	100	108	123	141	128
Nike[b]	100	109	130	154	142
U.S. firm average	100	117	140	159	149
European firms					
Adidas-Solomon	100	108	114	117	115
Cadbury Schweppes	100	120	149	154	152
Nestlé	100	106	108	108	108
European firm average	100	109	124	126	125

Note: The percentages in this table are based on the figures reported in table 10.2a.
  [a] European figures include Euroasia and Middle East.
  [b] European figures include Middle East and Africa.

If anti-Americanism had a significant impact on sales, one should find U.S.-based firms' sales falling in 2003–4 as compared to earlier years, since anti-American views rose sharply in Europe between 2001–2 and 2003–4. This fall in the sales of American firms should have occurred both in absolute terms and relative to the performance of European firms.

Tables 10.2a and 10.2b demonstrate that American firms in Europe did not suffer in the aftermath of the Iraq War. Between 2000–2001 and 2003–4 all six firms increased their European sales. Furthermore, all three American firms increased the *share* of revenues that they derived from Europe. Between 2000–2001 and 2003–4 the average sales gain for the three American firms was over one-third, compared to about one-quarter for the three European firms.[74] Details aside, it is safe to say that during this period the American firms did not suffer, in their European sales, compared to the European firms. Our research shows that American corporations have performed strongly in Europe, compared to large European firms operating in similar markets.

This evidence is consistent with statements by business leaders. Keith Reinhard, president of Business for Diplomatic Action, declares that "research across much of the globe shows that consumers are cooling toward American culture and American brands, but there is still no hard evidence showing direct impact on bottom lines."[75] Ronald DeFeo, chief executive of the Terex Corporation, argues that "the multinationals that focus on customers, not politics, can still do business. If we go back on our heels and think about world politics, we should go back to the university."[76] Informally, business leaders report that although anti-Americanism makes business harder to conduct, there are ways to alleviate it, whether through brand names that do not suggest American ownership or by putting Palestinian employees rather than Americans on al-Jazeera.[77] We conclude that reports of consumer anti-Americanism damaging sales of U.S.-based firms in Europe are highly exaggerated. If anti-Americanism ever posed a serious threat to American business in Europe, corporate strategies have been able to avert dramatic negative effects.

Effects of Anti-Americanism on Tourism to the United States

Worldwide, tourism fell after 9/11, then recovered strongly. Tourism to the United States, however, fell more sharply. Between 2000 and 2003, tourism to the United States fell 20 percent, twice as much as tourism to Mexico and Canada. On average, the other top seven tourism destinations (six European countries and China) experienced a slight increase in tourist arrivals during that time.[78] These aggregate data are no more than suggestive. Apart from anti-Americanism there exist numerous plausible explanations for this pattern. They include fear of travel to the United States and real or anticipated difficulties in obtaining visas due to stricter U.S. controls.[79] To test whether it is plausible to associate the decline in tourist travel to the United States with anti-Americanism, we need to establish whether these declines were particularly sharp from those countries in which anti-American views were running especially high.

74. Precise comparison is not possible here, since Coca-Cola's figures include Asia and the firm's reported gains between 2000–2001 and 2003–4 are probably inflated as a result.

75. Interview reported in *Corporate Citizen* (September–October 2005), quoted in Meunier, chapter 5. Mr. Reinhard goes on to warn that "in marketing, we know that attitude precedes behavior, and the warning signs are there."

76. Quoted in Holstein 2005.

77. This statement is based on conversations that we, and colleagues of ours, have had with business leaders in charge of firms operating in the Middle East. In particular, we are indebted to John Gerard Ruggie for information provided to us on October 30, 2005, on this subject.

78. World Tourism Organization 2003.

79. The fall in the value of the dollar over this period should enhance tourism to the United States since it made visiting America cheaper from both Europe and Japan.

Table 10.3. 2004 opinion toward the United States compared with 2001–2003 changes in tourist travel to the United States

Country	Percentage favorable to United States, 2004	Rank, unfavorable (most "anti-American") first	Change in tourism to United States 2001–3, in percent	Rank, largest decline first
France	31	1	−21.3	3
Germany	39	2	−10.1	5
Netherlands	44	3	−9.2	6
United Kingdom	46	4	−3.9	7
Japan	47	5	−22.4	2
China	53	6	−33.3	1
Italy	58	7	−13.3	4
Denmark	65	8	−0.8	8
India	68	9	+1.0	9

Sources: Opinion data: GMI 2004. Tourism data: World Tourism Organization 2004.

Note: Between July 1, 2001 and July 1, 2003 the euro appreciated 37% against the dollar, the Danish krone 26.9%, the British pound 17%, the yen 4%, and the rupee 1.1%. The value of the Chinese yuan remained constant. See http://www.imf.org, and click on "exchange rate archives." Accessed March 5, 2005. If exchange rates were determining tourism, countries with the greatest currency appreciation during the 2001–03 period should show the largest declines in tourism. The rank order of decline would be France/Germany/Netherlands/Italy, Denmark, Britain, Japan, India, China. These do not match well with the results. China and Japan experienced the largest declines in tourism, although their currencies appreciated not at all or very little against the dollar.

We offer a crude test with the data in table 10.3. We have selected nine countries for which data are available on changes in tourism to the United States, between 2001 and 2003, and on general levels (among urban populations) of pro- or anti-American views. Since we are trying to make inferences about foreigners' decisions to visit the United States, not about American measures to restrict such visits, we have excluded countries that were particular objects of U.S. border security measures and visa restrictions. Table 10.3 shows that there is not a strong correlation between anti-Americanism and changes in tourism.

Table 10.3 is deficient in two ways: we do not have data on changes in levels of anti-American opinion between 2001 and 2003 for all of these countries, and the exchange rates of various currencies vis-à-vis the dollar fluctuated differentially. Although there is no correlation between exchange-rate fluctuations and tourism, this does constitute a complicating factor. Furthermore, visa requirements could have been tightened differentially. In table 10.4 we therefore focus only on the three states in the euro zone—France, Germany, and Italy—for which we have data on changes in levels of anti-Americanism between 2001 and 2003. The most we can say on the basis of table 10.4 is that there exists no strong linear relationship between declines in favorable views of the United States and changes in tourism.

The negative findings on consumer boycotts are stronger than on tourism. On balance the available evidence, spotty as it is, does not support the widespread conjecture that anti-Americanism has had a major effect on the economic choices of individuals and groups.

Table 10.4. Changes in tourism and changes in anti-Americanism: Eurozone

Country	Anti-Americanism: % decline in favorable views of United States, 2002–4	Rank, strongest shift toward anti-Americanism	Tourism to United States, change, 2001–3	Rank, from largest to smallest decline
France	51	1	−21.3	1
Germany	34	2	−10.1	3
Italy	12	3	−13.3	2

Sources: Opinion data: Pew 2004 and GMI 2004. Tourism data: World Tourism Organization 2004.

Long-Term and Indirect Effects

At first glance it may be surprising that we could not find strong evidence tracking the effects of anti-Americanism for United States diplomacy or individual actions toward America and firms identified with America. Yet since the measure of anti-Americanism on which we have primarily relied in this chapter is public opinion, this finding may be less surprising than it seems. For half a century, studies of public opinion have pointed out that the effect of mass opinion on foreign policy is quite diffuse.[80] As we have emphasized throughout this book, many aspects of anti-Americanism cannot be captured by public opinion data.[81]

Stopping our analysis of the effects of anti-Americanism at this point would leave it incomplete. Persistently critical opinion creates conditions that in the longer term can yield unforeseen anti-American effects. The connection between opinion (or distrust and bias) on the one hand and international·cooperation on the other is mediated by domestic politics, such as through social movements or political institutions, which shape the political options that are available to decision makers seeking to fashion international strategies. We need to understand these intervening links in order to come to a reasoned assessment of the longer-term and indirect effects of anti-Americanism.

McAdam's chapter analyzes how movement leaders and politicians sought to mobilize and gain advantage during the civil rights movement in the United States during the 1960s, and how the events of the 1960s are now interpreted very differently by black and white Americans. McAdam argues analogously that the ebb and flow of diffuse anti-American views provides a ground on which political elites can mobilize movements and organize groups during episodes of contention. When anti-American movements get institutionalized and seize power at the national level, the room for cooperation with the United States shrinks, perhaps drastically, as the domestic constituency of the government prohibits adoption of policies that appear to be too favorable or accommodating to the demands of the U.S. government. For example, after two decades of neoliberal reform policies informed by the

---

80. A classic early work is Almond 1950.
81. Comments by Kenneth Schultz and Page Fortna helped us clarify the points in this paragraph.

"Washington consensus" of the U.S. Treasury and the IMF that have had very disappointing results, many Latin American governments have now adopted a left-wing complexion and are feeling strong domestic pressures to resist U.S. political initiatives. The longer-term consequences of anti-Americanism are therefore complex and difficult to predict.

The linkages between opinion, distrust, and bias, on the one hand, and international policy cooperation, on the other, differ under different types of political systems and in the context of different historical experiences. French anti-Americanism is so deeply institutionalized that, in contrast to Germany, politicians do not pay a price for invoking it. At times the same is also true of China where politicians and intellectuals must watch carefully the policy line of the government in order to fit into the prevailing tone of anti- or pro-Americanism. (In contrast, no member of the Chinese elite can expect to avoid paying a high price for articulating pro-Japanese views.) Since the legitimation needs of the Chinese government are variable, so is the usefulness of anti-Americanism. While French anti-Americanism is deeply institutionalized and moves from the top down toward a generally receptive mass public, China's anti-Americanism is both directed by the elites and resonant with the grass roots. Elites react to events and seek to mold the anti-Americanism that presents them with both challenges to the regime's stability and opportunities for reaffirming its shaky legitimacy. In both cases, it is not merely public opinion but a conjunction of public attitudes and elite interests that activates anti-Americanism and makes it consequential.

In Indonesia, as Bowen demonstrates in chapter 8, anti-Americanism has less traction and is less deeply institutionalized than in France, so it tends to be more sporadic. Furthermore, the impact of anti-Americanism on policy seems to have been affected by the transition from authoritarianism to democracy. Under Suharto anti-Americanism was anathema to the regime, and oppositional groups paid a high price for being perceived as "anti-American." After Suharto's fall, under the conditions of a fledging democracy, shifting political circumstances and coalitions are conditioning the political use of anti-Americanism and therefore its consequences. Yet, as in France and China, for anti-American attitudes to become significant for policy, political entrepreneurs need to have interests in using rather than suppressing them.

Unlike Indonesia, Germany did not experience a change in political regime in recent decades. Yet, even within a given regime type, anti-Americanism can take surprisingly complex twists and turns over time, with consequences for policy. The anti-Americanism of Germany's "1968 generation," which had protested against the Vietnam War, turned into surprising support of U.S. policy in the war in Kosovo by the Green Party and its leader, Joschka Fischer, who later was named Germany's foreign minister. As in the other cases the existence of diffuse anti-American views provides leaders with the material from which to fashion coalitions and strategies.

Whether and how attitudes, coalitions, and strategies congeal into more enduring institutional patterns is central to our assessment of the long-term political effects of the current, unprecedented wave of anti-Americanism. Such coalescence has occurred in France, where anti-Americanism is deeply ingrained.[82] But it is not yet evident in Germany, Indonesia, or even China. Local circumstances involving the legitimacy of established political elites and the opportunities available to challengers are likely to be important, in the long run, in shaping whether anti-American attitudes become embedded in social movements and political organizations in these countries. The fact that accurate predictions about the long-term, indirect effects of anti-Americanism are difficult in no way undermines their substantive importance for U.S. foreign policy and world politics.

Decoupling Attitudes from Action

Our analysis suggests that even high levels of expressed anti-Americanism do not translate readily into government or individual action. Even when anti-American sentiments could be largely a result of recent U.S. foreign policy, their effects are often less strong than one might have expected. Consumers do not boycott the products of American corporations even when they say they do. International travel shows no more than a faint correspondence to variations in anti-American views. Governments cooperate with the United States on counterterrorism in various ways, and, despite upsurges in anti-American views at home, they are maintaining ordinary diplomatic relations across a variety of policy domains. When we attempt more carefully to examine the effects of prior anti-Americanism on responses to the United States, doubts about the effects of anti-Americanism are reinforced. We find a remarkably weak association between popular views toward the United States in mid-2002 (before issues involving a possible invasion of Iraq became salient) and decisions by governments to join the American war in Iraq through participation in the coalition of the willing. We also find no significant correlation between anti-American views in 2002 and refusal to sign nonsurrender agreements with the United States under Article 98 of the treaty establishing the ICC. (A major albeit regional rather than global exception to this null finding is the recent and growing resistance in Latin America to the exercise of U.S. influence.)

To conclude from this evidence that anti-Americanism does not matter, however, would be to miss the forest for the trees. Some big decisions, such as the Turkish decision on whether to support the Iraq War and the German elections of 2002, almost certainly have been affected by negative views of the United States, although in these cases it is difficult to distinguish the effects of anti-Americanism from the effects of opposition to the U.S. effort to persuade other countries to join its attack on Iraq. Over the longer term, disagreement with U.S. policy could lead other publics and elites to be more negatively predisposed toward the United States—and more unwilling, therefore, to be persuaded by the United States of the existence of common interests. Guantánamo, Abu Ghraib, and other prisons where suspects in the war on terror are being held have become symbols of American arrogance and hypocrisy.

82. Roger 2005.

When an American weekly reported, and subsequently retracted, that a copy of the Koran had been flushed down a toilet so as to degrade and humiliate Muslims held captive in Guantánamo, deadly riots broke out in several Arab countries. The retraction of the story by *Newsweek* magazine under intense pressure from the White House was overshadowed by the subsequent release of numerous reports of desecration of the Koran in 2002–3 by U.S. military interrogators or guards.[83] Over the medium and long term such events could easily harden anti-American views by consolidating distrust and bias.

Despite ominous trends, especially in the Middle East, the effects of anti-American public opinion on governmental or individual behavior toward the United States seem to have been relatively weak, at least so far. The burden of proof is on those who claim that anti-American opinion, as distinguished from opposition to particular U.S. foreign policies, has had significant policy effects.

To us there are three plausible explanations for this finding. First, as Chiozza demonstrates in chapter 4, views of the United States in 2002 were largely positive. Second, even when (after 2003) attitudes toward the United States became more negative, their expression in terms of policy was inhibited by the fact that individuals and states have interests—in purchasing desirable products, traveling to interesting places, and in benefiting from cooperation with the world's preeminent power, or at least in not antagonizing it. Although some of those perceptions of interest may be affected by American words and actions—and therefore subject to variation depending on predispositions toward the United States—many of them are likely to be based on other values. Third, the potential targets of anti-Americanism—businesses, nonprofit organizations, or the U.S. government itself—may devise effective strategies to combat it or mitigate its effects. As a result, if anti-Americanism has significant direct effects on the influence of the United States in world politics, they are not general and across the board but more regional and specific to particular situations.

The weakness of the identifiable effects of anti-Americanism sheds some light on the question raised in chapter 1: Does anti-Americanism reflect opinion or bias? Some groups, such as parts of the French elite or small segments of Islamic movements, hold to anti-American attitudes that reflect deep distrust and systematic bias. Firmly held, such attitudes discourage cooperation with the United States and are not susceptible to change on the basis of new information. The relatively scattered and specific effects that we have discovered, however, suggest that opinions about the United States are more mixed than one would expect were deep distrust and bias widespread. They therefore tend to reinforce the conclusion of Chiozza in chapter 4: consistently strong and negative attitudes toward the United States, across many dimensions, are rare. If anti-American attitudes were principally fueled by distrust or bias, they should be more persistent and exert more clearly identifiable effects than in fact they do.

What then accounts for the persistence of heterogeneous anti-American attitudes that appear to have relatively small and specific effects? In the concluding chapter

---

83. Sengupta and Masood 2005, Lewis 2005, Shanker 2005, Schmitt 2005.

we will explore one possible answer: that American symbols are polyvalent. They embody a variety of values with different meanings to different people and indeed even to the same individual. We examine whether America's polyvalence helps us understand the odd mixture that we have observed—strongly expressed negative views coupled with few changes in behavior. The disjunction we have uncovered between anti-American attitudes and actions prompts us to analyze America's symbolic projection abroad.

Conclusion: Anti-Americanisms and the Polyvalence of America

PETER J. KATZENSTEIN
and ROBERT O. KEOHANE

When we think about the varieties of anti-Americanism, two puzzles are readily apparent. First, why does such a rich variety of anti-American views persist? Second, why do persistent and adaptable anti-American views have so little direct impact on policy and political practice? Anti-Americanism reflects opinion and distrust, and sometimes bias. Often it generates expressive activity: demonstrating, marching, waving banners, even symbolically smashing the windows of a McDonald's restaurant in France. But it is not a political force that frequently overturns governments, leads American multinational firms to disguise their origins, or propels the U.S. government to make major policy changes.

We suggest a single answer to both puzzles. In a phrase, the symbolism generated by America is so *polyvalent* that it continually creates a diversity of material on which to construct anti-Americanism. The polyvalence of America embodies a rich variety of values: secular science and religious fundamentalism, moralism and sexual permissiveness, rigorous science and a rich popular culture. The values associated with America resonate differently with the various cognitive schemas held by individuals and reinforced by groups—schemas that vary greatly cross-nationally. Furthermore, these schemas are internally complex and may contain elements that are in tension or contradiction with one another. When polyvalent American symbols connect with varied, shifting, and complex cognitive schemas, the resulting reactions refract like a prism in sunlight. Many colors appear in the prism, just as America elicits many different reactions around the world. Often, different components of what is refracted will simultaneously attract and repel.

Our emphasis on the polyvalence of American society is quite different from three popular explanations for anti-Americanism, all of which we took seriously in our inquiry: power imbalances, a backlash against globalization, and conflicting identities. Although all three arguments seem to resonate with expressions of anti-Americanism in some parts of the world at some times, they are insufficient to understand anti-Americanism in other places and at other times. This book amply documents that anti-American views are simply too heterogeneous to be explained by one or a few broad factors. We begin this chapter with these popular explanations, then turn to our own interpretation, centered on polyvalence.

Three Perspectives on Anti-Americanism

The study of anti-Americanism is a specific application of the analysis of different types of beliefs in world politics.[1] One could imagine a world in which only material resources count. Stalin once famously asked, "How many divisions has the pope?" In such an imaginary world, national interests would be assessed by elites who calculate only on the basis of material interests. Influence would be exerted only through the use or threat of force and material resources. Since states and the elites who control them use their material resources to achieve their preferred outcomes, positive or negative attitudes toward or beliefs about the United States would have no impact either on policies or on outcomes. But the Catholic Church is still around, while Soviet Communism can be found only in the dustbin of history. The premise of Stalin's rhetorical question was plainly wrong: attitudes and beliefs matter greatly in world politics.

In our analysis of anti-Americanism we assume that different analytical traditions can be complementary and compatible.[2] Rationalism focuses our attention on how interests can affect attitudes and beliefs and their strategic use in politics. It emphasizes that anti-American schemas often persist because they serve the political interests of elites as well as the psychological needs of mass publics. Constructivism highlights the importance of identities and the social and subjective processes by which they are created. Finally, both rationalism and constructivism contribute much to our understanding of norms. Anti-American attitudes and beliefs, expressing schemas, identities, and norms, are always contested or at least contestable. They are objects of political struggle. Our analysis of anti-Americanism thus is fundamentally about politics.

Political observers typically frame their understanding of anti-Americanism in three explanatory sketches that focus on power imbalances, a backlash against globalization, or conflicting identities. Although these sketches cannot be applied easily to specific instances of anti-Americanism, they often seem to be useful starting points as one thinks about the sources of anti-Americanism in world politics.

Generations of balance of power theorists have argued that imbalances of power lead to the formation of balancing coalitions: "Secondary states, if they are free to choose, flock to the weaker side."[3] These arguments suggest that we may now simply

1. Goldstein and Keohane 1993, Katzenstein 1996.
2. Katzenstein, Keohane, and Krasner 1999; Fearon and Wendt 2002.
3. Waltz 1979, 127.

be observing the predictable effects of extraordinary U.S. dominance. Conservative analysts point out that "Mr. Big" is never liked.[4] Their critics stress the lack of subtlety or restraint in the exercise of power by the United States. Both views provide a basis for understanding why traditionally powerful and respected states such as China, France, and Russia feel offended or threatened by U.S. power and its exercise.

Since the end of the cold war the United States has been by far the most powerful state in the world system, without any serious rivals. The collapse of the Soviet bloc means that countries that formerly required U.S. protection from the Soviet Union no longer need such support. This change may have enabled leaders and publics in countries such as Germany to be more critical of the United States. Furthermore, U.S. political hegemony makes the United States a focal point for opposition. U.S. political hegemony is not a necessary condition for anti-Americanism—anti-Americanism in Europe dates back further than the American Revolution in the late eighteenth century—but it may be conducive to it. Acting in its own interest, or in accordance with its own values, the United States can have enormous impacts on other societies. When it fails, the costs of failure are often imposed on others more than on itself: one aspect of power is that the costs of adjustment are forced onto the relatively powerless. In this view, it is no accident that U.S. political power is at its zenith while American standing is at its nadir. Resentment at the negative effects of others' exercise of power is hardly surprising.

A second overarching explanation focuses on the *backlash against globalization*. The expansion of capitalism—often labeled globalization—generates what Joseph Schumpeter called "creative destruction." Those adversely affected can be expected to resist such change. The classic statement of this argument is by Karl Polanyi, who claimed that networks of social support in precapitalist societies were destroyed by the effects of the market: "A civilization was being disrupted by the blind action of soulless institutions the only purpose of which was the automatic increase of material welfare."[5] Polanyi argued that the unregulated market violates deep-seated social values and thus supports political movements, such as fascism in the 1920s and 1930s, that demanded state control and protectionism. In Benjamin Barber's catchy phrase, the spread of American practices and popular culture creates "McWorld," which is widely resented even by people who find some aspects of it very attractive.[6] The anti-Americanism generated by McWorld is diffuse and widely distributed in world politics. It does not generate suicide bombings or demands for the overthrow of capitalism. José Bové may wield an axe against a McDonald's restaurant for the sake of the television cameras, but he does not drive a truck loaded with explosives into a restaurant full of people. Applied to contemporary globalization, Polanyi's argument has implications that could be empirically observed. Hostility toward the United States should follow in the wake of market changes that displace people from their locales and livelihoods, as was true in East Asia in 1997–98. In this view, rapid eco-

4. Joffe 2001.
5. Polanyi 1957, 219.
6. Barber 1995.

nomic change and the uncertainty deriving from dependence on distant markets and sources of capital would generate resentment at the United States, the center of pressures for such changes. Hostility in this view should therefore emanate from those areas of the world. An influx of capital and the opening of markets to the world should be associated with anti-Americanism.

A third argument ascribes anti-Americanism to *conflicting identities* in the United States and elsewhere.[7] In this view, anti-Americanism is generated by cultural and religious identities that are antithetical to the values being generated and exported by American culture—from Christianity to the commercialization of sex. The globalization of the media has made sexual images not only available to but also unavoidable for people around the world. One reaction is admiration and emulation, captured by the concept of soft power. But another reaction is antipathy and resistance. The products of secular mass culture, as Seyla Benhabib notes, are a source of international conflict between competing values. They are bringing images of sexual freedom and decadence, female emancipation, and equality between the sexes into the homes of patriarchal and authoritarian communities, Muslim and otherwise.[8]

Yet at the same time, religion has become a "very important" fact in the lives of 59 percent of Americans, about twice as many as in Britain and Canada and about five times as many as in France and Japan. In the words of Andrew Kohut, director of the Pew Research Center for the People and the Press, American religiosity "represents an important divide between the United States and our traditional allies" on issues such as abortion, the death penalty, and the use of new biological technologies.[9] Christian missionaries are deeply grating to Leninist capitalism in China, to Hindu radicalism in South Asia, and to Muslim fundamentalism throughout the Islamic world. Americans export sex and the Gospel, both of which are resented by many people abroad. Secular polities, as in western Europe or East Asia, will object more to the rise of religiosity in American life and foreign policy, and less to the effects of the spread of American popular culture. Religious polities in the Middle East and South Asia will object to their exposure to the products of American popular culture and, in the case of Christian missionaries, to the rise of American religiosity.

Although each of the three macroperspectives contributes some insights, the taxonomy of different types of anti-American views that we developed in chapter 1 suggest that anti-Americanism is not well explained by any of them. The richly documented case studies by Sophie Meunier, Marc Lynch, and Iain Johnston and Daniela Stockmann in part 3 of this book support that conclusion. Sovereign-nationalist anti-Americanism could be activated by power imbalances; social anti-Americanism may be heightened by the contrasts between European and American values highlighted by the incursions of McWorld; and radical anti-Americanism can

---

7. Nau 2002, Lieven 2004, Huntington 2004.

8. Benhabib 2002, 251–52.

9. Pew Research Center poll, December 2002, as quoted in the *Ithaca Journal* 2002 (December 20), 2A; Norris and Inglehart 2004, 83–110.

be generated by clashes of identity. However, liberal, legacy, and elitist anti-American views do not fit well within any of these broad themes.

The Chinese case study, by Johnston and Stockmann, provides the best illustration of the impact of power imbalances. Johnston and Stockmann show that contemporary Chinese discussions of the United States revolve around what they call a "hegemony discourse," which implies that the United States is not only powerful but also overbearing, unjust, hypocritical, and illegitimate. It is supplemented by a "century of humiliation" discourse, which reflects China's terrible experiences with Western and Japanese imperialism. The combination of these discourses with American power—and support for Taiwan—helps to explain both the deep Chinese distrust of the United States that Johnston and Stockmann found in the Beijing public and the periodic outbursts of at times violent anti-American demonstrations in response to perceived threats, such as the bombing of China's embassy in Belgrade or the flight of a spy plane over or near Chinese territory.

Meunier's analysis of French distrust of the United States shows the value of the globalization explanation. The French public, Meunier argues, reacts particularly strongly against the Americanization of globalization—whether by Google or as expressed in the Bush administration's disdain for multilateral regulations of globalization. The French do not boycott McDonald's, but the golden arches are a ready symbol of what many people in France dislike about globalization. It is striking that French attitudes toward the United States started declining during the 1990s, the "decade of globalization," whereas attitudes of publics in other major European countries remained very favorably disposed toward the United States until the run-up to the war in Iraq.

France and China are in this respect a study in contrasts. Both publics distrust the United States. The French public does not worry much about U.S. propensity to use military force—France has been quite ready to use military force itself—but rather about American-led globalization. The Chinese, in contrast, are in favor of those aspects of globalization that make them richer. The government, however, fears the global spread of democratic ideas, and Chinese nationalists fear American hegemony. Chinese students thus can throw rocks at the American embassy and then repair to McDonald's for refreshments and to discuss strategy.

The conflicting identities argument may have some purchase in both China and France, but the contrasts are muted by perceived similarities between these publics and the Americans. Indeed, Meunier argues that the French distrust America partly because the societies—carriers of universalistic democratic ideologies—are so similar. In contrast, Chinese differentiate themselves quite sharply from Americans, but even more sharply from Japanese, contradicting those who believe in the existence of a global "clash of civilizations." In the Middle East, however, the conflicting identities argument, in a moderate form, may offer more explanatory power. In chapter 7 Lynch holds that Arab anti-Americanism is not driven by an essentialist, civilizational conflict; he does, however, argue that there is widespread concern and fear that the United States is seeking to use its power fundamentally to alter Arab and Muslim identity. Insecurity about Arab identity combines with assertive American power to make a potent brew.

These illustrations suggest that in many instances distinctive combinations of different explanatory factors will help us best in accounting for varieties of anti-Americanisms.[10] These varieties do not so much compete with one another as interact, picking up on different aspects of American society that are resented by different people outside of the United States, or by the same people at different times. Each form of anti-Americanism waxes and wanes in response to changing situations. Table 1.7 in chapter 1 tried to capture this flux by distinguishing between latent and intense anti-Americanism, depending on the degree of perceived threat that the United States poses.

Furthermore, anti-Americanism can take different forms, depending on the climate of opinions and ideological sentiments as well as on power politics. Radical anti-Americanism took a largely Marxist-Leninist form between 1918 and the 1980s. As the Soviet Union weakened and collapsed, Islam and its radical fringes grew. Marxist-Leninist anti-Americanism unquestionably was the most prominent form of radical anti-Americanism in the third world in the early 1980s; by 2005 it had been eclipsed by radical Islamic anti-Americanism. To complicate matters further, the four scaled types of anti-Americanism—from liberal to radical—do not exhaust our typology of anti-American views. Those views are further enriched by elitist and legacy anti-Americanism. As Meunier shows in chapter 5, French elitism is both deeply embedded and remarkably flexible, adapting its forever skeptical view to the dynamic changes in American society. John Bowen writes in chapter 8 about the "diacritical" function that anti-Americanism plays for French but not Indonesian elites. This enables French elites to identify and justify desirable features of their own society by contrasting them with the "Anglo-Saxons." In April 2005, for instance, French president Jacques Chirac defended the proposed European constitution treaty by declaring, "What is the interest of the Anglo-Saxon countries and particularly the US? It is naturally to stop Europe's construction, which risks creating a much stronger Europe tomorrow."[11] McAdam demonstrates in chapter 9 that legacy anti-Americanism can become more strongly institutionalized as part of a discourse, as in Spain or Greece, but that it can also reverse itself, as in the Philippines and Japan. Much depends on who wins the political struggle not only to control state institutions but also to frame the dominant political discourse in society. Focusing closely on only one of the three explanatory conjectures—power imbalances, globalization backlash, and conflicting identities—is unlikely to advance our understanding much when confronting the complex array of anti-American views in contemporary world politics.

Polyvalent America and Anti-Americanism

What accounts for the persistence of heterogeneous anti-American views, which appear to have relatively small effects on government policy? This conundrum, we

10. Katzenstein and Sil 2004.
11. Hollinger, Minder, and Thornhill 2005.

argue here, becomes less puzzling in light of the fact that American symbols are polyvalent. They embody a variety of values with different meanings to different people and indeed even to the same individual. Elites and ordinary folks abroad, in the words of Mark Hertsgaard, "feel both admiring and uneasy about America, envious and appalled, enchanted but dismissive. It is this complex catalogue of impressions—good, bad, but never indifferent—that Americans must confront."[12] As David Laitin has noted, the World Trade Center was a symbol not only of capitalism and America but of New York's cosmopolitan culture, so often scorned by middle America.[13] The Statue of Liberty not only symbolizes America's conception of freedom but has also become America's symbol of welcome to the world's "huddled masses." The potential stream of immigrants into the United States is unending. And as we have documented in the introductory chapter, many people who hold very negative views about the United States also have very positive assessments of the lives that people who leave their countries can make in the United States. Here we follow up on David Kennedy's discussion in chapter 2 and explore further the proposition that the often-conflicting values of contemporary America generate multidimensional attitudes toward the United States, both pro- and anti-American.

The United States has a vigorous and expressive popular culture, which is enormously appealing both to Americans and to many people elsewhere in the world. This popular culture is quite hedonistic, oriented toward material possessions and sensual pleasure. At the same time, however, the United States is today much more religious than most other societies and, in the words of two well-informed observers, "has a much more traditional value system than any other advanced industrial society."[14] One important root of America's polyvalence is the tension between these two characteristics. Furthermore, both American popular culture and religious practices are subject to rapid change, expanding further the varieties of expression in the society, and continually opening new options. The dynamism and heterogeneity of American society create a vast set of choices: of values, institutions, and practices.

Part of the dynamism of American culture results from its openness to the rest of the world. The American fast-food industry has imported its products from France (fries), Germany (hamburgers and frankfurters), Italy (pizza), and more recently Mexico (tacos and burritos). What it added was brilliant marketing and efficient distribution. In many ways the same is true also for the American movie industry, especially in the last two decades. Hollywood is a brand name held by Americans and non-Americans alike. In the 1990s only three of the seven major Hollywood studios were controlled by U.S. corporations. Many of Hollywood's most celebrated directors and actors are non-American. And many of Hollywood's movies about America, both admiring and critical, are made by non-Americans. Like the United Nations,

---

12. Hertsgaard 2002, 8.

13. We are extremely grateful for David Laitin's trenchant and helpful comments at a conference on anti-Americanism, Center for Advanced Study in the Behavioral Sciences, Stanford, April 8, 2005.

14. Inglehart and Baker 2001, 20.

Hollywood is both in America and of the world. And so is America itself—a product of the rest of the world as well as of its own internal characteristics.

"Americanization" in world politics, therefore, does not describe a simple extension of American products and processes to other parts of the world. On the contrary, it refers to the selective appropriation of American symbols and values by individuals and groups in other societies—symbols and values that may well have had their origins elsewhere. Americanization thus is a profoundly interactive process between America and all parts of the world. And, we argue here, it is deeply intertwined with anti-American views.[15]

Americanization and anti-Americanism interact and occur through a variety of venues.[16] Through its distinctive combination of territorial and nonterritorial power, the United States has affected most corners of the world since 1945. The Middle East, Latin America, and East and Southeast Asia have experienced U.S. military might firsthand. By contrast, western Europe has been exposed only to the peaceful, emporium face of American hegemony, from shopping malls to artistic and intellectual trends.[17] Indeed, European avant-garde and American popular culture often coexist in a complicated symbiosis. On questions of popular culture, for example, cross-fertilization of different innovations bypasses most politics as conventionally understood. American popular culture is sometimes viewed as undermining local cultures, a charge that nationalist political entrepreneurs often seek to exploit to create a political backlash against processes of Americanization. However, just as often Americanization reinvigorates and enriches local cultures, as has been true of reggae as a Caribbean musical import into the United States, that eventually was reexported to other societies, such as France. It has provided France's African immigrants with a new cultural medium with which to write and sing in French, and thus to become part of France in ways that previously were simply not available.

The interactions that generate Americanization may involve markets, informal networks, or the exercise of corporate or governmental power—often in various combinations. They reflect and reinforce the polyvalent nature of American society, as expressed in the activities of Americans, who freely export and import products and practices.[18] But they also reflect the variations in attitudes and interests of people in other societies, seeking to use, resist, and recast symbols that are associated with the United States. Similar patterns of interaction generate pro-Americanism and anti-Americanism, since both pro- and anti-Americanism provide an idiom to connect concerns about America with local issues. Where that idiom is exceptionally well developed, it can crystallize into a diacritical form that makes sense of the "self" in juxtaposition to the "other." Such diacritics are characteristic, according to Bowen's argument in chapter 8, of France but not of Indonesia. In any event, the receptiv-

---

15. The close coupling of anti-Americanism and Americanization in the case of Germany is analyzed in Stephan 2005.

16. Stephan 2005, Nolan 2005.

17. Hari 2005, Grazia 2005.

18. See Katzenstein 2005, 198–207.

ity of other societies to American culture varies greatly, as these societies interact with a complex, diverse, and dynamic America.

The open and interactive character of American society is also much in evidence on questions of technology. In the second half of the twentieth century the United States has been in a position of technological leadership not rivaled by any other polity. In particular decades and for specific product ranges, some countries, such as Japan or Germany, have been able to hold their own when put in direct competition with the United States. But across the full range of technologies, the United States has not relinquished the lead that it has held for more than half a century. The annual parade of American Nobel Prize winners in various fields of basic scientific research gives testimony to the international strength of American research universities and research institutes. American higher education attracts outstanding foreign students and scholars in the early stages of their careers, and many of them decide to make a life in the United States rather than returning home. Furthermore, American corporations are especially apt in transforming basic advances in science and technology into marketable products.

Yet Americanization does not create a norm of best practice to which others simply adjust. Rather, as Jonathan Zeitlin and Gary Herrigel and their colleagues have discovered, more typical are innovative hybrids that incorporate piecemeal borrowing and selective adaptation.[19] Americanization is as much about the learning capacity of local actors as about the diffusion of standardized American practices. The global automobile industry was revolutionized by Henry Ford in the first third of the twentieth century, just as Detroit was remade by the Japanese automobile industry in the last third. And the growing complexity of modern weapon systems means that the center of the U.S. military-industrial complex, like Hollywood, is both in the United States and of the world. Stephen Brooks has documented the deep inroads that sourcing with foreign suppliers has made in a policy domain strongly geared to U.S. national autarky.[20] With technological insularity no longer an option even on matters of national security, the transnational extension of American technology has only increased.

Anti- and pro-Americanism have as much to do with the conceptual lenses through which individuals living in very different societies view America as with America itself. Johnston and Stockmann report that when residents of Beijing in 1999 were asked simply to compare on an identity difference scale their perceptions of Americans with their views of Chinese, they placed them very far apart. But when, in the following year, the Japanese, the antithesis of the Chinese, were added to the comparison, respondents reduced the perceived identity difference between Americans and Chinese.[21] In other parts of the world, bilateral perceptions of regional enemies can also displace, to some extent, negative evaluations of the United States. For instance, in sharp contrast to the European continent the British press and public

19. Zeitlin and Herrigel 2000.
20. Brooks 2005.
21. Comment at a workshop on anti-Americanism, Center for Advanced Study in the Behavioral Sciences, June 11, 2005.

continue to view Germany and Germans primarily through the lens of German militarism, Nazi Germany, and World War II.[22]

Because there is so much in America to dislike as well as to admire, polyvalence makes anti-Americanism persistent. American society is both extremely secular and deeply religious. Its complexity is played out in the tensions between blue "metro" and red "retro" America and the strong overtones of self-righteousness and moralism that conflict helps generate. If a society veers toward secularism, as much of Europe has, American religiosity is likely to become salient—odd, disturbing, and, due to American power, vaguely threatening. How can a people who believe more strongly in the Virgin Birth than in the theory of evolution be trusted to lead an alliance of liberal societies? If a society adopts more fervent Islamic religious doctrine and practices, as has occurred throughout much of the Islamic world during the past quarter century, the prominence of women in American society and the vulgarity and emphasis on sexuality that pervades much of American popular culture are likely to evoke loathing, even fear. Thus anti-Americanism is closely linked to the polyvalence of American society.

Polyvalent Anti-Americanisms

Kennedy in his historical survey of "imagined America" in chapter 2 and Chiozza in his analysis of the individual attitudes of anti-Americanism in chapter 4 approach their material with very different methods. Yet both highlight the importance of multidimensionality, heterogeneity, and polyvalence in all manifestations of anti-Americanism. So did Hannah Arendt when she wrote in 1954 that "America has been both the dream and the nightmare of Europe."[23] The tropes of anti-Americanism, Kennedy argues, date back to a dialogue about the American character that started in the aftermath of Columbus's discovery and Thomas More's invention of America in the fifteenth and sixteenth centuries.[24] That dialogue is structured by two images. Are Americans natural men in a Garden of Eden, operating in an imaginary space not bounded by geography or time? Or are they barbarians, uncivilized, and unrestrained in appetites and aspirations that both repudiate and challenge human reason and experience? Tocqueville and those who have followed his trail have vacillated between hope and fear. A constant theme, Kennedy argues, is that America is seen as an unconstrained place, with great potential for both good and ill.

Kennedy's argument raises a more general theme that runs through this book. Societies often have constitutive narratives, which explain their history to themselves. For the United States, Kennedy argues, the narrative revolves around breaking new ground by going beyond the frontier: it is a story of human progress. Meunier

22. Negative evaluations of one society may, however, reinforce negative evaluations of another. French anti-Americanism, with deep historical roots, has contributed to negative American attitudes toward France. See Roger 2005.

23. Arendt 1994, 410.

24. O'Gorman 1961, Gerbi 1973.

discusses the conceptions that define France's distinctive culture, embedded in a historical narrative of intellectual and aesthetic accomplishment. Lynch argues that the emergence of a common Arab narrative has focused attention on the United States as a common denominator in the experiences of highly varied Arab societies. Johnston and Stockmann emphasize the Chinese narrative of the century of humiliation as a way in which Chinese organize their views toward the United States and Japan in particular. And Bowen stresses that Indonesian narratives that connect to the United States are much thinner than French narratives about America.

We began this book by citing Henry Luce's prescient statement about the American Century, made during World War II. We return to Luce at the end. The second half of the twentieth century indeed inaugurated the American Century, which still continues today. In 1941 the United States was about to step onto center stage in world politics, sometimes acting multilaterally, sometimes unilaterally, always powerfully. During the next sixty-five years the United States profoundly shaped the world. Others, wherever they were, had to react, positively or negatively, to America's impact. Yet during this time the United States itself changed fundamentally. In 1941, exports and imports were both near all-time lows. For twenty years its borders had been virtually closed to immigration, except from Europe. The South was legally segregated, with African Americans in an inferior position, and the North was in fact segregated in many respects. Racism was widespread in both North and South. Hence, American soft power was slight—but so was its salience to most potentially hostile groups and governments abroad. By 2006 both American soft power and hard power had expanded enormously, and so had its salience to publics around the world. The American Century created enormous changes, some sought by the United States and others unsought and unanticipated. Resentment, and anti-Americanism, were among the undesired results of American power and engagement with the world. Anti-Americanism is as important for what it tells us about America as for its impact on world politics and American foreign policy. It poses a threat to America's collective self-esteem. This is no small matter, as Tocqueville observed in the remark we quoted in our introduction to this book: Americans "appear impatient of the smallest censure, and insatiable of praise."

The United States is both an open and a critical society. It is also deeply divided. Our own cacophony projects itself onto others and can be amplified as it reverberates, via other societies, around the world. When Americans are polled, they express high levels of dissatisfaction with many aspects of American society and government policy. But these expressions of unfavorable opinion are typically not interpreted as anti-American. When non-Americans are polled, similar views are interpreted as anti-American. We will not understand anti-Americanism by asking "Why do they hate us?" We will only be able to understand anti-Americanism if we shine a search light into all corners of the world while also holding up a mirror to ourselves.

References

Abdelal, Rawi. 2006. "Writing the Rules of Global Finance: France, Europe, and Capital Liberalization." *Review of International Political Economy* 13, no. 1 (February): 1–27.

Abrams, Dominic, and Michael Hogg, eds. 1990. *Social Identity Theory.* New York: Harvester Wheatsheaf.

Abravanel, Martin, and Barry Hughes. 1973. "The Relationship between Public Opinion and Governmental Foreign Policy: A Cross-National Study." In *International Yearbook of Foreign Policy Studies*, vol. 1, edited by Patrick J. McGowan, 107–34. Beverly Hills, Calif.: Sage.

Agence France Presse. 2005a. "La lenteur de la réponse américaine aux tsunamis critiquée par deux journaux." January 2. LexisNexis [last accessed December 6, 2005].

———. 2005b. "Rapport annuel: Amnesty critique Washington, notamment sur la torture." May 25. LexisNexis [last accessed December 6, 2005].

———. 2005c. "Three French Militants Held by US in Iraq: Newspaper Report." February 4. LexisNexis [last accessed December 6, 2005].

Ahmed, Ahmed Yusef, and Mamduh Hamzah, eds. 2003. *Sana'a al-Karahiya fi al-Aliqat al-Arabiya al Amrikiya* [Manufacturing Hatreds in Arab-American Relations]. Beirut: Center for Arab Unity Studies.

Ajami, Fouad. 2003. "The Falseness of Anti-Americanism." *Foreign Policy* 138 (September–October): 52–61.

Al-Bishri, Tareq. 2002. *Al-Arab fo Muwajiha al Udwan* [*Arabs in the Face of Aggression*]. Cairo: Dar al Shuruq.

Alesina, Alberto, Rafael Di Tella, and Robert MacCulloch. 2004. "Inequality and Happiness: Are Europeans and Americans Different?" *Journal of Public Economics* 88, nos. 5–6: 2009–42.

Almond, Gabriel A. 1950. *The American People and Foreign Policy.* New York: Harcourt, Brace.

Al-Qaradawi, Yusuf. 2002. *Muslims and the West: Dialogue or Clash?* Available from http://www.qaradawi.net.

Alvarez, R. Michael, and John Brehm. 2002. *Hard Choices, Easy Answers: Values, Information, and American Public Opinion.* Princeton: Princeton University Press.

Amalric, Jacques. 2005a. "Du bon usage des catastrophes." *Libération,* January 6. LexisNexis [last accessed December 6, 2005].

———. 2005b. "Tsunami et faux-amis." *Libération*, January 20, 37.

Ambah, Faiza Saleh. 2005. "Iraq: Spinning Off Arab Terrorists?" *Christian Science Monitor*, February 8.

Amenta, Edwin, Bruce G. Carruthers, and Yvonne Zylan. 1992. "A Hero for the Aged? The Townsend Movement, the Political Mediation Model, and U.S. Old-Age Policy, 1934–1950." *American Journal of Sociology* 98: 308–39.

Amin, Galal. 2002. *Ulema al-Qahar*. [The Globalization of Conquest]. Cairo: Dar al Shuruq.

Anderson, Benedict. 1998. *The Specter of Comparison*. New York: Monthly Review.

Andrews, Kenneth T. 1997. "The Impact of Social Movements on the Political Process: The Civil Rights Movement and Black Election Politics in Mississippi." *American Sociological Review* 62: 800–819.

———. 2001. "Social Movements and Policy Implementation: The Mississippi Civil Rights Movement and the War on Poverty, 1965–1971." *American Sociological Review* 66: 71–95.

Annan, Kofi. 2005. *In Larger Freedom: Towards Development, Security and Human Rights for All*. United Nations General Assembly, Report of the Secretary-General. Document A/59/2005, March 21.

Anonymous. 2001. *Through Our Enemies' Eyes: Osama bin Laden, Radical Islam, and the Future of America*. Washington, D.C.: Brassey's.

———. 2004. *Imperial Hubris: Why the West Is Losing the War on Terror*. Washington, D.C.: Brassey's.

Arendt, Hannah. 1994. *Essays in Understanding, 1930–1954*. New York: Harcourt, Brace.

Armstrong, Charles K., ed. 2002. *Korean Society: Civil Society, Democracy, and the State*. London: Routledge.

Ashley, Mark. 2001. "Nations as Victims: Nationalist Politics and the Framing of Identity." Paper presented at the annual meeting of the American Political Science Association, San Francisco, August 29–September 2.

Aslan, Reza. 2005. *No God but God: The Origins, Evolution, and Future of Islam*. New York: Random House.

Azar, Edward A., R. A. Brody, and C. A. McClelland. 1972. *International Events Interaction Analysis*. Beverly Hills, Calif.: Sage.

Ba Zhongtan, ed. 2002. *Zhongguo Guojia Anquan Zhanlue Wenti Yanjiu* [Research on the Question of China's National Security Strategy]. Beijing: Academy of Military Sciences Press.

Bailey, Thomas A. 1980. *A Diplomatic History of the American People*. 10th ed. Englewood Cliffs, N.J.: Prentice-Hall.

Baker, James A., III, and Edwin Meese III. 2005. "The Best Man for the Job." *New York Times*, May 11, A21.

Barber, Benjamin. 1995. *Jihad vs. McWorld*. New York: Random House.

Barkey, Henri J. 2005. "The State of U.S.-Turkish Relations." Testimony before the House Committee on International Relations, May 11. http://wwwc.house.gov/international_relations/euhear.htm.

Barkin, Gareth. 2001. "Indonesian Media Reaction to Terrorist Attacks in the United States." *Reconstructions*, September 19. http://web.mit.edu/cms/reconstructions/communications/indonesia.html.

Barnett, Michael. 1999. "Culture, Strategy and Foreign Policy Change: Israel's Road to Oslo." *European Journal of International Relations* 5, no. 1: 5–36.

Behrens, Jan C., Árpád von Klimó, and Patrice G. Poutrus, eds. 2005. *Antiamerikanismus im 20. Jahrhundert: Studien zu Ost- und Westeuropa*. Bonn: J. W. W. Dietz.

Beleliu, Andrew. 2002. "The G8 and Terrorism: What Role Can the G8 Play in the 21st Century?" *G8 Governance*, no. 8. http://www.g7.utoronto.ca/governance/beleliu2002gov8.pdf.

Benhabib, Seyla. 2002. "Unholy Wars: Reclaiming Democratic Virtues after September 11." In *Understanding September 11*, edited by Craig Calhoun, Paul Price, and Ashley Timmer, 241–53. New York: New Press.

Berinsky, Adam J. 2004. *Silent Voices: Public Opinion and Political Participation in America.* Princeton: Princeton University Press.

Berman, Russell A. 2004. *Anti-Americanism in Europe: A Cultural Problem.* Stanford: Hoover Institution Press.

Bernstein, Richard. 2005. "Europe Urges Linking Lifting of Chinese Arms Ban to Rights." *New York Times,* April 15, A9.

Bourdieu, Pierre. 1992. "Deux impérialismes de l'universel." In *L'Amérique des Français,* edited by Christine Fauré and Tom Bishop, 149–55. Paris: Editions F. Bourin.

Bowen, John R. 2006a. "France's Revolt: Can the Republic Live Up to Its Ideals?" *Boston Review,* January/February, 29–32.

———. 2006b. *Why the French Don't Like Headscarves.* Princeton: Princeton University Press.

Boyles, Denis. 2005. *Vile France: Fear, Duplicity, Cowardice, and Cheese.* San Francisco: Encounter Books.

Brady, Henry E., and Paul M. Sniderman. 1985. "Attitude Attribution: A Group Basis for Political Reasoning." *American Political Science Review* 79, no. 4: 1061–78.

Brewer, Marilyn, and Robert J. Brown. 1998. "Intergroup Relations." In *Handbook of Social Psychology,* ed. Daniel T. Gilbert, Susan T. Fiske, and Gardner Lindzey, 4th ed., 2:554–94. Boston: McGraw-Hill.

Brinkley, Joel. 2005a. "Latin States Shun U.S. Plan to Watch Over Democracy." *New York Times,* June 9, A10.

———. 2005b. "U.S. Proposal in the OAS Draws Fire as an Attack on Venezuela." *New York Times,* May 22, 10.

Brooks, Stephen G. 2005. *Producing Security: Multinational Corporations, Globalization, and the Changing Calculus of Conflict.* Princeton: Princeton University Press.

Brown, Roger. 1986. *Social Psychology: The Second Edition.* New York: Free Press.

Brubaker, Rogers. 2004. *Ethnicity without Groups.* Cambridge: Harvard University Press.

Bruguière, Jean-Louis. 2003. *Terrorism after the War in Iraq: U.S.-France Analysis Series.* Washington, D.C.: Brookings Institution.

Bruner, Jerome S. 1996. *The Culture of Education.* Cambridge: Harvard University Press.

Buchanan, William, and Hadley Cantril. 1953. *How Nations See Each Other.* Urbana: University of Illinois Press.

Bueno de Mesquita, Ethan. 2005. "The Quality of Terror." *American Journal of Political Science* 49, no. 3: 515–30.

Burdman, Daphne. 2003. "Education, Indoctrination, and Incitement: Palestinian Children on Their Way to Martyrdom." *Terrorism and Political Violence* 15, no. 1 (Spring): 96–123.

Bureau of Nonproliferation. 2005. "The Proliferation Security Initiative (PSI)." May 26. http://www/state.gov/t/np/rls/other/46858.htm [last accessed June 1, 2005].

Burstein, Paul. 1979. "Public Opinion, Demonstrations, and the Passage of Antidiscrimination Legislation." *Public Opinion Quarterly* 43: 157–72.

Burstein, Paul, and William Freudenburg. 1978. "Changing Public Policy: The Impact of Public Opinion, Antiwar Demonstrations, and War Costs on Senate Voting on Vietnam War Motions." *American Journal of Sociology* 84: 99–122.

Buruma, Ian, and Avishai Margalit. 2004. *Occidentalism: The West in the Eyes of Its Enemies.* New York: Penguin.

Cai Cuihong. 2004. "Kongbuzhuyi—Xin Diguozhuyi: Wu Fa Zhengmian Jiaofeng de Maodun" [Terrorism and Neoimperialism: The Contradiction That Can't Have a Frontal Clash]. In *Zhong Mei Guojia Liyi Bijiao* [Comparison of Sino-U.S. National Interests], edited by Ni Shixiong and Wang Yiwei, 216–32. Beijing: Current Events Press.

Callahan, William A. 2005. "History, Identity, and Security: Producing and Consuming Chinese Nationalism in International Space." Paper presented at the workshop "Identity, Nationalism, and Chinese Foreign Policy," Fairbank Center for East Asian Research, Harvard University, March.

Casey, Michael. 2005. "French Tsunami Relief Effort Shows Small Force—with Its Wine and Painter—Can Make Difference." Associated Press, January 29. LexisNexis [last accessed December 6, 2005].

Castle, Stephen. 2005. "Google Book Project Angers France." *Independent*, May 6, 33.

Ceaser, James W. 1997. *Reconstructing America: The Symbol of America in Modern Thought*. New Haven: Yale University Press.

———. 2003. "A Genealogy of Anti-Americanism." *Public Interest* 152: 3–18.

———. 2004. "The Philosophical Origins of Anti-Americanism in Europe." In *Understanding Anti-Americanism: Its Origins and Impact at Home and Abroad*, edited by Paul Hollander, 45–64. Chicago: Ivan R. Dee.

Changing Minds, Winning Peace. 2003. Report of the Advisory Group on Public Diplomacy for the Arab and Muslim World. October 1.

Charney, Craig, and Nicole Yakatan. 2005. *A New Beginning: Strategies for a More Fruitful Dialogue with the Muslim World*. Council on Foreign Relations Special Report No. 7, May. New York: Council on Foreign Relations.

Chazelle, Bernard. 2004. "Anti-Americanism: A Clinical Study." *Counterpunch* Online. http://www.businessfordiplomaticaction.org/news/articles/0409cccnewsletter.pdf [last accessed December 6, 2005].

Checkel, Jeffrey T. 2001. "Why Comply? Social Learning and European Identity Change." *International Organization* 55, no. 3 (Summer): 553–88.

Chen Shengluo. 2002a. "Liangge Meiguo: Zhongguo Daxuezheng de Meiguo Guan" [Two Americas: Chinese University Students' Views of the United States]. *Qingnian Yanjiu* [Youth Studies] 6: 1–8.

———. 2002b. "Zhongguo Daxuesheng dui Meiguo Duiwai Zhengce de Kanfa" [The Views of Chinese University Students toward American Foreign Policy]. *Zhongguo Qingnian Zhengzhixue Yuan Xuebao* [Journal of the China Youth Politics University] 21, no. 5: 5–10.

———. 2004. "The Events of September 11 and Chinese College Students' Images of the United States." Paper prepared for Center for Strategic and International Studies conference "Chinese Images of the United States," Washington D.C., April. http://www.csis.org/isp/chineseimages/cius_shengluo.pdf.

Chen Wenke. 2002. "Lun Zhongguo Jingji Zhuangui Zhong de Nandian yu Gongguan Tese" [On the Difficulties and Special Characteristics of the Attack Points on China's Economic Track]. *Zhuangui Tongxun* [Bulletin of the China Reform Forum] 6. http://www.chinareform.org.cn/cgi-bin/Library/Communication_Read.asp?text_id=133.

Chen Xiaoping and C. Chao Chen. 2004. "On the Intricacies of the Chinese Guangxi: A Process Model of Guanxi Development." *Asia-Pacific Journal of Management* 21: 305–24.

Chesnoff, Richard Z. 2005. *The Arrogance of the French: Why They Can't Stand Us—And Why the Feeling Is Mutual*. New York: Sentinel.

China Mainland Marketing Research Company. 1998. *Zhongguo Gongzhong dui Kelindun Zongtong Fanghua de Taidu ji dui Meiguo Liaojie* [Chinese Public's Attitude toward the Visit of President Clinton to China, and Their Understanding of the United States]. Beijing: CMMR.

China Statistical Yearbook. 2001. National Bureau of Statistics, People's Republic of China. Available from http://chinadatacenter.org/newcdc/.

Chinese Academy of Social Sciences. 2004. *Zhongguoren kan Zhong Mei Guanxi* [Chinese Look at Sino-U.S. Relations]. http://www.people.com.cn/GB/paper68/14196/1264756.html.

Chiozza, Giacomo. 2003. "Anti-Americanism: A Description of the Data." Unpublished paper, Duke University, June 14.

———. 2004a. "Love and Hate: Anti-Americanism in the Islamic World." Paper presented at the 2004 Midwest Political Science Association Conference, Chicago, April 15–18.

———. 2004b. "Love and Hate: Anti-Americanism and the American World Order." PhD diss., Duke University.

Chirac, Jacques. 2000. "Speech on European Security and Defence by Mr. Jacques Chirac, President of the French Republic, to the Presidential Committee of the WEU Assembly at the Elysée Palace, Paris, 30 May 2000." http://www.assembly-weu.org/en/documents/sessions_ordinaires/rpt/2000/1699.pdf [last accessed July 12, 2004].

Clymer, Adam. 2002. "World Survey Says Negative Views of U.S. Are Rising." *New York Times*, December 5, A22.

Congressional Research Service. 2004. *Germany's Role in Fighting Terrorism: Implications for U.S. Policy.* Congressional Research Report RL32710, December 27. Washington, D.C.: Library of Congress.

———. 2005. *U.S.-EU Cooperation against Terrorism.* Congressional Research Report RS22030, January 19. Washington, D.C.: Library of Congress.

Converse, Philip E. 1964. "The Nature of Belief Systems in Mass Publics." In *Ideology and Discontent*, edited by David E. Apter, 206–61. New York: Free Press.

Cook, Thomas D., and Donald T. Campbell. 1979. *Quasi-Experimentation.* Boston: Houghton Mifflin.

Corporate Citizen. 2004. "Interview with Keith Reinhard." September–October. http://www.businessfordiplomaticaction.org/news/articles/0409cccnewsletter.pdf [last accessed December 6, 2005].

Council on Foreign Relations. 2004. *Update on the Global Campaign against Terrorist Financing: Second Report of an Independent Task Force on Terrorist Financing.* New York: Council on Foreign Relations.

Crockatt, Richard. 2003. *America Embattled: 9/11, Anti-Americanism and the Global Order.* London: Routledge.

Cruz, Consuelo. 2000. "Identity and Persuasion: How Nations Remember Their Pasts and Make Their Futures." *World Politics* 52, no. 3 (April): 275–312.

Da Wei. 2005. "Guoji Guanxi Zhong de Shuangchong Biaozhun" [Double Standards in International Relations]. *Renmin Wang* [People's Net]. April 14. http://world.people.com.cn/GB/1030/3321111.html.

Dante, Alighieri. 1964. *The Comedy of Dante Alighieri, the Florentine.* Translated by Dorothy Sayers. London: Penguin.

D'Attorre, Pier Paolo. ed. 1991. *Nemici per la pelle: Sogno Americano e mito Sovietico nell'Italia contemporanea.* Milan: Angeli.

Davidson, Richard J. 1994. "On Emotion, Mood, and Related Affective Constructs." In *The Nature of Emotion: Fundamental Questions*, edited by Paul Ekman and Davidson, 51–55. New York: Oxford University Press.

Dean, Anna, and Mary Demeri. 2002. "Europeans and Anti-Americanism: Fact vs. Fiction." Unpublished manuscript. Office of Research, U.S. Department of State.

Deutsch, Karl W., and Richard L. Merritt. 1966. "Effects of Events on National and International Images." In *International Behavior: A Social-Psychological Analysis*, ed. Herbert C. Kelman. New York: Holt, Rinehart, and Winston.

Debouzy, Marianne. 1996. "L'antiamericanismo nella stampa di sinistra francese, 1946–1954." *Acoma: Rivista Internazionale di Studi Americani; Culture nella Guerra Fredda* 3, no. 7: 63–74.

Defleur, Melvin L., and Margaret H. Defleur. 2003. *Learning to Hate Americans: How U.S. Media Shape Negative Attitudes among Teenagers in Twelve Countries.* Spokane, Wash.: Marquette Books.

Delhommais, Pierre-Antoine, and Eric Le Boucher. 2005. "Asie du Sud: La générosité tombe dans l'excès." *Le Monde*, January 18. http://www.lemonde.fr [last accessed December 6, 2005].

Deng Bing. 2003. "Leng Zhan hou Meiguo dui Hua Zhanlue de Lilun he Xianshi Fenxi" [Theoretical and Realistic Analysis of Post–Cold War U.S. Strategy toward China]. *Shijie Jingji yu Zhengzhi Luntan* [World Economics and Politics Forum] 4: 75–77.

Deng Xiaoping. 1986. "Qizhi Xianming de Fandui Zichanjieji Ziyouhua" [Boldly and in a Clear-cut Fashion Oppose Bourgeois Liberalization]. *Deng Xiaoping Wenxuan* [Selected Works of Deng Xiaoping], vol. 3. English version at http://english.peopledaily.com.cn/dengxp/vol3/text/c1630.html.

Deng Yong. 2006. "Reputation and the Security Dilemma: China Reacts to the 'China Threat Theory.'" In *New Directions in the Study of China's Foreign Policy*, edited by Alastair Iain Johnston and Robert S. Ross, 186–216. Stanford: Stanford University Press.

Derrida, Jacques, and Jürgen Habermas. 2003. "Europe: Playdoyer pour une politique extérieure commune." *Libération*, May 31. LexisNexis [last accessed December 6, 2005].

DeSombre, Elizabeth R. 2006. *Flagging Standards: Globalization and Environmental, Safety, and Labor Regulations at Sea*. Cambridge: MIT Press.

Diner, Dan. 1996. *America in the Eyes of the Germans: An Essay on Anti-Americanism*. Princeton: Markus Wiener.

Donnelly, Thomas. 2000. "Rebuilding America's Defenses—Strategy, Forces and Resources for a New Century." Washington, D.C.: Project for the New American Century.

Doran, Michael. 2004. "The Iraq Effect?" *Wall Street Journal*, December 17, A14.

Drennan, William M. 2005. "The Tipping Point: Kwangju, May 1980." In *Korean Attitudes toward the United States*, edited by David I. Steinberg, 280–306. Armonk, N.Y.: M. E. Sharpe.

Druckman, Daniel. 1994. "Nationalism, Patriotism, and Group Loyalty: A Social Psychological Perspective." *Mershon International Studies Review* 38, no. 1: 48–68.

D'Souza, Dinesh. 2002. *What's So Great about America*. New York: Penguin.

Dudziak, Mary L. 2000. *Cold War Civil Rights*. Princeton: Princeton University Press.

Duhamel, Georges, and Charles M. Thompson. 1931. *America: The Menace; Scenes from the Life of the Future*. New York: Houghton Mifflin.

Duncan, J. Greg, and Graham Kalton. 1987. "Issues of Design and Analysis of Surveys across Time." *International Statistical Review* 55, no. 1: 97–117.

Dupont, Stéphane. 2005. "Aide à l'Asie du Sud: Les Etats-Unis montent en première ligne." *Les Echos*, January 4, 5.

Duroselle, Jean-Baptiste. 1978. *France and the United States from the Beginnings to the Present*. Chicago: University of Chicago Press.

Eagly, Alice H., and Shelly Chaiken. 1993. *The Psychology of Attitudes*. Fort Worth, Texas: Harcourt, Brace.

Economist. 2004. "Is It Rejection or Seduction: Both Anti-Americanism and the Opposite Have Deep Roots in Germany." July 31, 46.

———. 2005a. "Anti-Americanism: The View from Abroad." February 19–25, 24–26.

———. 2005b. "Anti-Americanism, the American Left and the American Right." February 19–25, 34.

———. 2005c. "Google à la française." April 2. LexisNexis [last accessed December 6, 2005].

———. 2005d. "Jacques Chirac, Socialist." March 19. LexisNexis [last accessed December 6, 2005].

———. 2005e. "More Generous Than Thou: The World's Response." January 8. LexisNexis [last accessed December 6, 2005].

Edelman Trust. 2005. *Sixth Annual Edelman Trust Barometer: A Global Study of Opinion Leaders*. January 24. http://www.edelman.com/image/insights/content/Edelman_Trust_Barometer2005_fina_final.pdf.

Efron, Sonni. 2004. "U.S. Aid Generous and Stingy: It Depends on How the Numbers Are Crunched." *Los Angeles Times*, December 31, A1.

Elias, Norbert. 1996. *The Germans: Power Struggles and the Development of Habitus in the Nineteenth and Twentieth Centuries*. New York: Columbia University Press.

Elliott, John. 1970. *The Old World and the New*. Cambridge: Cambridge University Press.

Ellwood, David W. 1999. *Anti-Americanism in Western Europe: A Comparative Perspective*. Occasional Paper Series, European Studies Seminar Series No. 3, November. Bologna: Johns Hopkins University Bologna Center.

Elster, Jon. 1999. *Alchemies of the Mind: Rationality and the Emotions*. Cambridge: Cambridge University Press.

Evans, J. Martin. 1976. *America: The View from Europe*. Stanford: Stanford Alumni Association.

Fang Ning. 2003. *Xin Diguozhuyi Shidai de Zhongguo Zhanlue* [China's Strategy in the Era of Neoimperalism]. Beijing: Beijing Press.

Fearon, James, and Alexander Wendt. 2002. "Rationalism v. Constructivism: A Skeptical View." In *Handbook of International Relations*, edited by Walter Carlsnaes, Thomas Risse, and Beth A. Simmons, 52–72. London: Sage.

Fewsmith, Joseph. 2001. *China since Tiananmen: The Politics of Transition*. Cambridge: Cambridge University Press.

Fewsmith, Joseph, and Stanley Rosen. 2001. "The Domestic Context of Chinese Foreign Policy." In *The Making of Chinese Foreign and Security Policy in the Era of Reform, 1978–2000*, edited by David Lampton, 151–87. Stanford: Stanford University Press.

Fidler, Stephen. 2005. "Testing Times: How the Grand Bargain of Nuclear Containment Is Breaking Down." *Financial Times*, May 23, 13.

Finkelstein, David. 2000. *China Reconsiders Its National Security: The Great Peace and Development Debate of 1999*. Alexandria, Va.: CNA Corporation.

Finnemore, Martha, and Kathryn Sikkink. 1999. "International Norm Dynamics and Political Change." In *Exploration and Contestation in World Politics*, edited by Peter J. Katzenstein, Robert O. Keohane, and Stephen D. Krasner, 247–77. Cambridge: MIT Press.

Firebaugh, Glenn. 1997. *Analyzing Repeated Surveys*. Sage University Paper Series on Quantitative Applications in the Social Sciences, No. 07-115. Thousand Oaks, Calif.: Sage.

Fish, M. Steven. 2002. "Islam and Authoritarianism." *World Politics* 55, no. 1: 4–37.

Fiske, Susan T., and Shelley E. Taylor. 1991. *Social Cognition*. New York: McGraw-Hill.

Flacks, Richard. 1988. *Making History*. New York: Columbia University Press.

Forero, Juan. 2005. "Opposition to U.S. Makes Chavez a Hero to Many." *New York Times*, June 1, A4.

Fourcade, Marion, and Evan Schofer. 2004. "The Multifaceted Nature of Civic Engagement: Forms of Political Activity in Comparative Perspective." Working Paper. Available from the author at http://sociology.berkeley.edu/faculty/FOURCADE-GOURINCHAS/publications.htm.

Free, Lloyd A. 1976. *How Others See Us: Critical Choices for Americans*. Vol. 3. Lexington, Mass.: D.C. Heath and Company.

Friedman, Thomas L. 2003a. "A Theory Of Everything." *New York Times*, June 1, D13.

———. 2003b. "Our War with France." *New York Times*, September 18, A31.

Friendly, Michael. 1999. "Visualizing Categorical Data." In *Cognition and Survey Research*, edited by Monroe G. Sirken et al. 319–348. New York: John Wiley and Sons.

From Conflict to Cooperation. 2005. Center for Strategic and International Studies Advisory Commission on U.S. Policy in the Arab World, March. Washington, D.C.: Center for Strategic and International Studies.

Gaddis, John Lewis. 2004. *Surprise, Security, and the American Experience*. New Haven: Yale University Press.

Gallie, W. B. 1956. "Essentially Contested Concepts." *Proceedings of the Aristotelian Society*, n.s., 41: 167–98.

Gallup, George H., ed. 1976. *The Gallup International Public Opinion Polls: Great Britain, 1937–1975.* Vol. 1, *1937–1964.* New York: Random House.

Gamson, William. 1990 [1975]. *The Strategy of Social Protest.* 2nd rev. ed. Belmont, Calif.: Wadsworth.

Gao Mobo Changfan. 2004. "The Rise of Neo-Nationalism and the New Left: A Postcolonial and Postmodern Perspective." In *Nationalism, Democracy and National Integration in China,* edited by Leong H. Liew and Shaoguang Wang, 44–62. New York: Routledge Curzon.

Gentzkow, Matthew A., and Jesse M. Shapiro. 2004. "Media, Education, and Anti-Americanism in the Muslim World." *Journal of Economic Perspectives* 18, no. 3: 117–33.

Gerbi, Antonello. 1973. *The Dispute of the New World: The History of a Polemic, 1750–1900.* Rev. ed., translated by Jeremy Moyle. Pittsburgh: University of Pittsburgh Press.

Gerecht, Reuel. 2002. "Better to Be Feared Than Loved, Cont." *Weekly Standard,* April 29.

German Marshall Fund. 2004. *Transatlantic Trends 2004 Top Line Data.* http://www. transatlantictrends.org/apps/gmf/ttweb2004.nsf/0/461EA7D25CC77DA185256F020059C7 6D/$file/Topline+with+logo+final.pdf [last accessed June 13, 2005].

Gerth, Karl. 2003. *China Made: Consumer Culture and the Creation of the Nation.* Cambridge: Harvard University, Asia Center.

Gilpin, Robert. 2005. "War Is Too Important to Be Left to Ideological Amateurs." *International Relations* 19, no. 1: 5–18.

Glaeser, Edward L. 2005. "The Political Economy of Hatred." *Quarterly Journal of Economics* 120, no. 1: 45–86.

GMI (Global Market Insite). 2004. Poll of Consumers in Eight Countries, December 10–12. http://www.worldpoll.com [last accessed January 5, 2005].

———. 2004. "Half of European Consumers Distrust American Companies." Press release, December 27. http://www.gmi-mr.com/gmipoll/release.php?p=20041227 [last accessed March 16, 2006].

———. 2005. "Global Backlash against U.S. Brands: Can Tsunami Relief Efforts Stem the Anti-American Tide?" Poll of consumers in twenty countries, January 8–16. http://www.worldpoll. com [last accessed March 17, 2005].

Goldstein, Judith, and Robert O. Keohane, eds. 1993. *Ideas and Foreign Policy: Beliefs, Institutions, and Political Change.* Ithaca: Cornell University Press.

Goodwin, Jeff, and James M. Jasper. 1999. "Caught in a Winding, Snarling Vine: The Structural Bias of Political Process Theory." *Sociological Forum* 14: 27–54.

Gopnik, Adam. 2003. "The Anti-Anti-Americans." *New Yorker,* September 1, 30.

Gordon, Philip. 2005. "The Dog That Has Not Barked." *E!Sharp,* May–June 2005. http://www.brookings.edu/views/articles/gordon/20050504.htm [last accessed December 6, 2005].

———. 2006. "The Struggle for Iraq: Intelligence; German Intelligence Gave U.S. Iraqi Defense Plan, Report Says." *New York Times,* February 27, 1.

Gordon, Philip, and Sophie Meunier. 2001. *The French Challenge: Adapting to Globalization.* Washington, D.C.: Brookings Institution.

Gordon, Philip, and Jeremy Shapiro. 2004. *Allies at War: America, Europe, and the Crisis over Iraq.* Washington, D.C.: Brookings Institution.

Granatstein, J. L. 1996. *Yankee Go Home? Canadians and Anti-Americanism.* Toronto: HarperCollins.

Grant, Ruth W. 1997. *Hypocrisy and Integrity: Machiavelli, Rousseau, and the Ethics of Politics.* Chicago: University of Chicago Press.

Grazia, Victoria De. 2005. *Irresistible Empire: America's Advance through Twentieth-Century Europe.* Cambridge: Belknap Press of Harvard University Press.

Greenblatt, Stephen, ed. 1993. *New World Encounters.* Berkeley: University of California Press.

Gries, Peter Hayes. 2004. *China's New Nationalism.* Berkeley: University of California Press.

Gries, Peter Hayes, and Kaiping Peng. 2002. "Culture Clash? Apologies East and West." *Journal of Contemporary China* 11, no. 30: 173–78.

Guo Yingjie. 2004. "Barking Up the Wrong Tree: The Liberal-Nationalist Debate on Democracy and Identity." In *Nationalism, Democracy and National Integration in China*, edited by Leong H. Liew and Shaoguang Wang, 23–43. New York: Routledge Curzon.

Gurrey, Béatrice. 2005. "On ne peut pas dire je suis européen et voter non." *Le Monde*, May 4. http://www.lemonde.fr [last accessed December 6, 2005].

Haahr-Escolano, Kathryn. 2005. "Italy: Europe's Emerging Platform for Islamic Extremism." *Terrorism Monitor* 3, no. 4. osint@yahoogroups.com [last accessed February 24, 2005].

Haas, Ernst B. 1993. "Nationalism: An Instrumental Social Construction." *Millennium* 22, no. 3 (Winter): 505–45.

Halimi, Serge. 1997. *Les nouveaux chiens de garde*. Paris: Liber.

Hardianto Dwi. 2003. "Gelombang Pasang Anti Amerika" [The Rising Anti-American Tide]. *Persatuan Islam*, September 27.

Hari, Johann. 2005. "McEurope: How American Capitalism Has Changed the Continent Forever." *New York Times* book review, May 8, 8.

Harris, John F., and Robin Wright. 2004. "Aid Grows amid Remarks about President's Absence." *Washington Post*, December 29, A1.

Hart, Stephen. 1996. "The Cultural Dimensions of Social Movements." *Sociology of Religion* 57: 87–100.

Haseler, Stephen. 1985. *The Varieties of Anti-Americanism: Reflex and Response*. Washington, D.C.: Ethics and Public Policy Center.

Hawthorne, Amy. 2004. *Political Reform in the Arab World: A New Ferment?* Middle East Series, Working Paper 52. Washington, D.C.: Carnegie Endowment for International Peace.

Hertsgaard, Mark. 2002. *The Eagle's Shadow: Why America Fascinates and Infuriates the World*. New York: Farrar, Strauss and Giroux.

High-Level Panel on Threats, Challenges and Change. 2004. *A More Secure World: Our Shared Responsibility*. United Nations General Assembly, A/59/565, November 29.

Hirschfeld, Lawrence A. 1996. *Race in the Making: Cognition, Culture, and the Child's Construction of Human Kinds*. Cambridge: MIT Press.

Hirschkind, Charles. 2001. "Civic Virtue and Religious Reason: An Islamic Counterpublic." *Cultural Anthropology* 16, no. 1: 3–34.

Hobsbawm, Eric. 1994. *The Age of Extremes: A History of the World, 1914–1991*. New York: Vintage.

Hoffmann, Stanley. 2000. "Deux universalismes en conflit." *Tocqueville Review* 21, no. 1: 65–71.

Hollander, Paul. 1992. *Anti-Americanism: Critiques at Home and Abroad, 1965–1990*. New York: Oxford University Press.

——. 1995. *Anti-Americanism: Irrational and Rational*. Somerset, N.J.: Transaction.

——. 2004a. "Introduction: The New Virulence and Popularity." In *Understanding Anti-Americanism*, edited by Hollander, 3–42. New York: Oxford University Press.

——, ed. 2004b. *Understanding Anti-Americanism: Its Origins and Impact at Home and Abroad*. New York: Oxford University Press.

Hollinger, Peggy, Raphael Minder, and John Thornhill. 2005. "Chirac Will Not Resign If Vote Lost EU Treaty." *Financial Times*, April 15, 8.

Holstein, William J. 2005. "The Multinational as Cultural Chameleon." *New York Times*, April 10, B9.

Holt, Douglas B., John A. Quelch, and Earl L. Taylor. 2004. "How Consumers Value Global Brands." *Harvard Business Review*, September 20. http://hbswk.hbs.edu/item.jhtml?id=4377&t=marketing [last accessed December 6, 2005].

Horizon. 1997. *Guancha Zhongguo* [Investigating China]. Beijing: Gongshangchubanshe.

———. 2003. "2003 Nian Zhongguoren Yan Zhong de Shijie Zhuanti Diaocha zhi 2—Zhong-guoren kan Meiguo" [2003 Special Survey on the World in the Eyes of Chinese People—Chinese Views of the United States]. http://www.horizonkey.com/showart.asp?art_id= 274&cat_id=6.

———. 2004. "Zhongguoren kan Meiguo de Ganshou hen Fuza" [Chinese Feelings toward the United States Are Very Complicated]. http://www.horizonkey.com/showart.asp?art_id= 418&cat_id=6.

———. 2005. "Kuaguo Qiye Ruhe Huode Yingxiangli" [How Multinational Corporations Obtain Influence]. *Di Yi Shou* [Firsthand]. Available from http://www.horizonkey.com [last accessed February 2005].

Howorth, Jolyon. 2003. "France and the Iraq War: An Initial Appraisal." Paper presented at the conference "The New Cleavages in France," Princeton University, October 9–12.

Huang Renwei. 2003. "Chuli hao Zhongguo Jueqi Zhong de Zhong Mei Guanxi he Taiwan Wenti" [Handling Well Sino-U.S. Relations and the Taiwan Issue during the Process of China's Rise]. *Mao Zedong Deng Xiaoping Lilun Yanjiu* [Studies in Mao Zedong and Deng Xiaoping Theory] 1: 74.

Huntington, Samuel P. 1996. *The Clash of Civilizations and the Remaking of World Order.* New York: Simon and Shuster.

———. 2004. *Who Are We? The Challenges to America's National Identity.* New York: Simon and Schuster.

Hutapea Rivai. 2005. "Aceh Harus Tetap Serambi Makkah" [Aceh Must Remain the Veranda of Mecca]. *Persatuan Islam,* January 24.

Inglehart, Ronald, and Wayne E. Baker. 2001. "Modernization's Challenge to Traditional Values: Who's Afraid of Ronald McDonald?" *Futurist* 35, no. 2: 16–21.

International Crisis Group. 2003. *The Challenge of Political Reform: Egypt after the Iraq War.* http://www.crisisgroup.org/home/index.cfm?id=2297&l=1 [last accessed September 30, 2005].

Isernia, Pierangelo, and Philip P. Everts. 2004. "Partners Apart? The Foreign Policy Attitudes of the American and European Publics." *Japanese Journal of Political Science* 5, no. 2 (November): 229–58.

Jasper, James. 1997. *The Art of Moral Protest.* Chicago: University of Chicago Press.

Jeanneney, Jean-Noel. 2005. "Quand Google défie l'Europe." *Le Monde,* January 24. http://www.lemonde.fr [last accessed December 6, 2005].

Jepperson, Ronald J., Alexander L. Wendt, and Peter J. Katzenstein. 1996. "Norms, Identity, and Culture in National Security." In *The Culture of National Security: Norms and Identity in World Politics,* edited by Peter J. Katzenstein, 33–75. New York: Columbia University Press.

Jia Qingguo. 2005. "Disrespect and Distrust: The External Origins of Contemporary Chinese Nationalism." *Journal of Contemporary China* 14, no. 42: 11–21.

Jiang Zemin. 2001. "Speech on the 80th Anniversary of the CCP." http://www2.scut.edu.cn/ party_sch/llyd/71jh/71jh6.htm.

Joffe, Josef. 2001. "Who's Afraid of Mr. Big?" *National Interest* (Summer): 43–52.

———. 2004. "The Demons of Europe." *Commentary* 17, no. 1: 29–34.

Johnston, Alastair Iain. 2004a. "Beijing's Security Behavior in the Asia-Pacific: Is China a Dis-satisfied Power?" In *Rethinking Security in East Asia: Identity, Power, and Efficiency,* edited by J. J. Suh, Peter Katzenstein, and Allen Carlson, 34–96. Stanford: Stanford University Press.

———. 2004b. "Chinese Middle Class Attitudes towards International Affairs: Nascent Liberaliza-tion?" *China Quarterly* (September): 603–28.

Johnston, Alastair Iain, and Daniela Stockmann. 2005. "Chinese Attitudes toward the United States and Americans." Paper presented at the Workshop on Anti-Americanism, Center for Advanced Studies in the Behavioral Sciences, Palo Alto, June. Available from http://www.

people.fas.harvard.edu/~johnston/johnstonstockmann.pdf and http://www.sitemaker.umich.edu/daniestockmann.

Johnston, Gregory, and Leonard Ray. 2004. "Balancing Act? Anti-Americanism and Support for a Common European Foreign and Security Policy." Paper presented at the annual meeting of the Southern Political Science Association, New Orleans, January 7–10.

Jonas, Klaus, Philip Broemer, and Michael Diehl. 2000. "Attitudinal Ambivalence." *European Review of Social Psychology* 11: 35–74.

Judt, Tony, and Denis Lacorne. 2005. *With Us or against Us: Studies in Global Anti-Americanism.* New York: Palgrave Macmillan.

Juergensmeyer, Mark. 2000. *Terror in the Mind of God: The Global Rise of Religious Violence.* Berkeley: University of California Press.

Kaase, Max, and Andrew Kohut, eds. 1996. *Estranged Friends? The Transatlantic Consequences of Societal Change.* Gütersloh: Bertelsmann Foundation.

Kagan, Robert. 2003. *Of Paradise and Power: America and Europe in the New World Order.* New York: Alfred A. Knopf.

Kahneman, Daniel, and Amos Tversky, eds. 2000. *Choices, Values, and Frames.* New York: Cambridge University Press.

Kana'an, Hussein. 2005. *Mustaqbal al-Aliqat al-Arabiya al-Amrikiya* [The Future of Arab American Relations]. Beirut: Dar al Khalil.

Kaplan, Edward H., and Charles A. Small. 2005. "Does Anti-Israel Sentiment Predict Anti-Semitism in Europe? A Statistical Study." Unpublished manuscript, Yale University, School of Management and School of Medicine.

Katzenstein, Peter J., ed. 1996. *The Culture of National Security: Norms and Identity in World Politics.* New York: Columbia University Press.

——. 1997. "Left-Wing Violence and State Response: United States, Germany, Italy, and Japan, 1960s–1990s." Unpublished paper, Cornell University, December.

——. 2005. *A World of Regions: Asia and Europe in the American Imperium.* Ithaca: Cornell University Press.

Katzenstein, Peter J., Robert O. Keohane, and Stephen D. Krasner. 1999. "*International Organization* and the Study of World Politics." In *Exploration and Contestation in the Study of World Politics*, edited by Katzenstein, Keohane, and Krasner, 5–45. Cambridge: MIT Press.

Katzenstein, Peter J., and Rudra Sil. 2004. "Rethinking Asian Security: A Case for Analytical Eclecticism." In *Rethinking Security in East Asia: Identity, Power, and Efficiency,* edited by J. J. Suh, Peter J. Katzenstein, and Allen Carlson, 1–33. Stanford: Stanford University Press.

Keck, Margaret E., and Kathryn Sikkink. 1998. *Activists beyond Borders: Advocacy Networks in International Politics.* Ithaca: Cornell University Press.

Kelley, Judith. 2005."Principles and Power in State Behavior: Bilateral Non-Surrender Agreements as a Quasi-Experiment." Terry Sanford Institute of Public Policy, Working Paper SAN04-05, Duke University.

Kelley, Robin D. G. 1997. *Yo' Mama's Disfunktional! Fighting the Culture Wars in America.* Boston: Beacon Press.

——. 2002. *The Black Radical Imagination.* Boston: Beacon Press.

Kelman, Herbert C. 1966. "Social-Psychological Approaches to the Study of International Relations: Definition of Scope." In *International Behavior: A Social-Psychological Analysis*, ed. Kelman. New York: Holt, Rinehart, and Winston.

Kennan, George F. 1951. *American Diplomacy, 1900–1950.* Chicago: University of Chicago Press.

Kepel, Gilles. 1997. *Allah in the West: Islamic Movements in America and Europe.* Stanford: Stanford University Press.

——. 2004. *The War for Muslim Minds: Islam and the West.* Cambridge: Belknap Press of Harvard University Press.

Kerkvliet, Benedict J. 1993. "Contested Meanings of Elections in the Philippines." Paper prepared for the conference "Elections in Southeast Asia: Meaning and Practice." Woodrow Wilson International Center, Washington, D.C., September 16–18.

Killion, M. Ulric. 2003. "China and Neoliberal Constitutionalism." *Global Jurist Frontiers* 3, no. 2: 11–12.

King, Gary, Robert O. Keohane, and Sidney Verba. 1994. *Designing Social Inquiry: Scientific Inference in Qualitative Research.* Princeton: Princeton University Press.

Kipling, Bogdan. 2005. "The French Have No Reason to Fear Google." *Ottawa Citizen*, April 15, A15.

Kiser, Edgar, and Michael Hechter. 1998. "The Debate on Historical Sociology: Rational Choice Theory and Its Critics." *American Journal of Sociology* 104: 785–816.

Kissinger, Henry. 1994. *Diplomacy.* New York: Simon and Schuster.

Klingberg, Frank L. 1983. *Cyclical Trends in American Foreign Policy Moods: The Unfolding of America's World Role.* Lanham, Md.: University Press of America.

Knowlton, Brian. 2005. "Tsunami Aid Joins Transatlantic Squabble." *International Herald Tribune*, January 5. LexisNexis [last accessed December 6, 2005].

Krauthammer, Charles. 2003. "To Hell with Sympathy." *Time*, November 17, 156.

Kroes, Rob, and Maarten van Rossem, eds. 1986. *Anti-Americanism in Europe.* Amsterdam: Free University Press.

Kronstadt, K. Alan. 2004. "Education Reform in Pakistan." Congressional Research Service RS22009, December 23.

Krueger, Alan B., and Jitka Malečková. 2003. "Education, Poverty and Terrorism: Is There a Causal Connection?" *Journal of Economic Perspectives* 17, no. 4: 119–44.

Kuisel, Richard F. 1993. *Seducing the French: The Dilemma of Americanization.* Berkeley: University of California Press.

———. 2004. "What Do the French Think of Us? The Deteriorating Image of the United States, 2000–2004." *French Politics, Culture and Society* 22, no. 3: 91–119.

Kunda, Ziva. 1999. *Social Cognition: Making Sense of People.* Cambridge: MIT Press.

Kuran, Timur. 1995. *Private Truths, Public Lies: The Social Consequences of Preference Falsification.* Cambridge: Harvard University Press.

Lacorne, Denis, et al. 1986. *L'Amérique dans les têtes: Un siècle de fascination et d'aversions.* Paris: Hachette.

Lacorne, Denis, Jacques Rupnik, and Marie-France Toinet. 1990. *The Rise and Fall of Anti-Americanism: A Century of French Perceptions.* Translated by Gerald Turner. London: Palgrave Macmillan.

Lamont, Michèle, and Laurent Thévenot. 2000. "Introduction: Toward a Renewed Comparative Cultural Sociology." In *Rethinking Comparative Cultural Sociology: Repertoires of Evaluation in France and the United States*, edited by Lamont and Thévenot, 1–22. Cambridge: Cambridge University Press.

Lansford, Tom. 2002. *All for One: Terrorism, NATO and the United States.* Aldershot: Ashgate.

Larson, Deborah Welch. 1985. *Origins of Containment: A Psychological Explanation.* Princeton: Princeton University Press.

Larson, Eric V., Norman D. Levin, Seonhae Bak, and Bogdan Savych. 2004. *Ambivalent Allies? A Study of South Korean Attitudes toward the U.S.* TR-141-SRF. Santa Monica: Rand Corporation.

Latif, Yudi. 2004. "The Muslim Intelligentsia of Indonesia." PhD diss., Australian National University, Canberra.

Layton, Azza Salama. 2000. *International Politics and Civil Rights Policies in the United States, 1941–1960.* New York: Cambridge University Press.

Lazarus, Richard. 1984. "On the Primacy of Cognition." *American Psychologist* 39: 124–29.

Lederer, William J., and Eugene R. Burdick. 1958. *The Ugly American.* New York: W. W. Norton.

Leicester, John. 2004. "France, in Generosity Contest with the United States, Doubles Aid for Asian Disaster." Associated Press, December 30. LexisNexis [last accessed December 6, 2005].

Le Monde. 2005a. "Les grandes entreprises multiplient les dons et les initiatives humanitaires." January 6. http://www.lemonde.fr [last accessed December 6, 2005].

———. 2005b. "McDonald's France." February 8. http://www.lemonde.fr [last accessed December 6, 2005].

Leser, Eric. 2005. "L'aide aux victimes dispensée par les Etats-Unis s'accompagne d'objectifs politiques." *Le Monde,* January 7. http://www.lemonde.fr [last accessed December 6, 2005].

Levy, Daniel, Max Pensky, and John Torpey, eds. 2005. *Old Europe, New Europe, Core Europe: Transatlantic Relations after the Iraq War.* London: Verso.

Lewis, Neil A. 2005. "Documents Say Detainees Cited Abuse of Koran: FBI Agents Received Repeated Complaints." *New York Times,* May 26, A1.

Libération. 2005. "L'Europe défie Google." May 3. LexisNexis [last accessed December 6, 2005].

Lichbach, Mark. 1995. *The Rebel's Dilemma.* Ann Arbor: University of Michigan Press.

———. 1997. "Contentious Maps of Contentious Politics." *Mobilization* 1: 87–98.

Lichtblau, Eric. 2004. "Airlines Ground 6 Flights to U.S. over Concerns about Terrorism." *New York Times,* February 1, A1.

Lieven, Anatol. 2004. *America Right or Wrong: An Anatomy of American Nationalism.* New York: HarperCollins.

Link, Arthur S., ed. 1989. *The Papers of Woodrow Wilson.* Princeton: Princeton University Press.

Liu Zhiming, Liu Xiaohong, Chen Yan, Li Weimin, Ding Xiaobing, and Peng Xie. 2004. "Meiti Baodao yu Qiye Xingxiang Yanjiu" [Research on Media Reporting and Company Images]. In *Zhongguo Xinwen Nianjian: Chuanmei Diaochajuan* [China Journalism Yearbook: Media Survey Volume], edited by Zhongguo Xinwen Kexue Xinwen yu Chuanbo Yanjiusuo [Chinese Academy of Social Sciences Journalism and Communications Research Institute], 288–332. Beijing: Zhongguo Xinwen Nianjianshe.

Locke, John. 1980. *Two Treatises on Government.* Edited by C. B. MacPherson. Indianapolis: Hackett Publishing.

Locy, Toni, Kevin Johnson, Mimi Hall, and John Diamond. 2004. "Source Gave U.S. Details of New Plot." *USA Today,* January 12, A1.

Lorentzsen, Erika. 2005. "Chirac Defends EU Constitution on TV." *Washington Post,* April 15, A19.

Luce, Henry R. 1941. "The American Century." *Life,* February 17, 61–65.

Lundestad, Leir. 1998. *"Empire" by Integration: The United States and European Integration, 1945–1997.* New York: Oxford University Press.

Luzzato Fegiz, Pierpaolo. 1956. *Il volto sconosciuto dell'Italia: Dieci anni di sondaggi in Italia.* Milan: Giuffrè.

Lyall, Jason M. K. 2005. "Great Games: Russia and the Emerging Security Dilemma in Central Asia." Paper presented at the International Relations Colloquium, Princeton University, February.

Lynch, Marc. 2003. "Taking Arabs Seriously." *Foreign Affairs* 82, no. 5: 81–94.

———. 2006. *Voices of a New Arab Public: Iraq, Al-Jazeera, and a Changing Middle East.* New York: Columbia University Press.

Machiavelli, Nicoló. 1999. *The Prince.* Translated by George Bull. London: Penguin.

MacMillan, Margaret. 2003. *Paris 1919: Six Months That Changed the World.* New York: Random House.

Mallet, Victor. 2005. "Outpouring of Cash Pledges Creates a Challenge for UN." *Financial Times,* January 7, 2.

Mansfield, Edward D., and Jack Snyder. 1995. "Democratization and the Dangers of War." *International Security* 20, no. 1 (Summer): 5–38.

March, James G., and Johan P. Olsen. 1989. *Rediscovering Institutions: The Organizational Basis of Politics*. New York: Free Press.

Marcus, George E. 1988. "The Structure of Emotional Response: 1984 Presidential Candidates." *American Political Science Review* 82, no. 3: 737–61.

———. 1991. "Emotion and Politics: Hot Cognition and the Rediscovery of Passions." *Social Science Information* 30, no. 2: 195–232.

———. 2002. *The Sentimental Citizen: Emotion in Democratic Politics*. University Park: Pennsylvania State University Press.

Marcus, George E., W. Russell Neuman, and Michael MacKuen. 2000. *Affective Intelligence and Political Judgment*. Chicago: University of Chicago Press.

Markovits, Andrei S. 2003. "European Anti-Americanism: Past and Present of a Pedigreed Prejudice." Inaugural Lecture of the Karl W. Deutsch College Professorship, University of Michigan, Ann Arbor, September 24.

———. 2004a. *Amerika, dich haßt sich's besser: Antiamerikanismus und Antisemitismus in Europa*. Hamburg: KKV Konkret.

———. 2004b. *European Anti-Americanism (and Anti-Semitism): Ever Present Though Always Denied*. Working Paper 108. Ann Arbor: University of Michigan, Center for European Studies.

———. 2006. *The Uncouth Nation: European Anti-Americanism from the American Revolution to George W. Bush*. Princeton: Princeton University Press.

Marquis, Christopher. 2003. "World's View of U.S. Sours after Iraq War, Poll Finds." *New York Times*, June 4, A19.

Martin, Waldo E., Jr. 2005. *No Coward Soldiers: Black Cultural Politics in Postwar America*. Cambridge: Harvard University Press.

Marx, Karl. 1995 [1867–94]. *Capital*. Edited and translated by David McLellan. Oxford: Oxford University Press.

Marx, Karl, and Friedrich Engels. 1953. *Letters to Americans, 1848–1895*. Edited by Alexander Trachtenberg, translated by Leonard E. Mins. New York: International Publishers.

———. 1992 [1848]. *The Communist Manifesto*. New York: Bantam.

Mathy, Jean-Philippe. 1993. *Extrême-Occident: French Intellectuals and America*. Chicago: University of Chicago Press.

May, Ernest. 1961. *Imperial Democracy*. New York: Harcourt, Brace & World.

McAdam, Doug. 1999 [1982]. *Political Process and the Development of Black Insurgency, 1930–1970*. Chicago: University of Chicago Press.

McAdam, Doug, John D. McCarthy, and Mayer N. Zald, eds. 1996. *Comparative Perspectives on Social Movements*. New York: Cambridge University Press.

McAdam, Doug, and Yang Su. 2002. "The War at Home: The Impact of Anti-War Protests, 1965–1973." *American Sociological Review* 67: 696–721.

McAdam, Doug, Sidney Tarrow, and Charles Tilly. 2001. *Dynamics of Contention*. New York: Cambridge University Press.

"McDonald's China." 2005. Available from http://www.wojiuxihuan.com [last accessed August 24, 2005].

McNeil, Genna Rae. 1983. *Groundwork: Charles Hamilton Houston and the Struggle for Civil Rights*. Philadelphia: University of Pennsylvania Press.

Mearsheimer, John J. 2002. "Hearts and Minds." *National Interest* 69: 13–16.

Mélandri, Pierre, and Justin Vaisse. 2001. *L'empire du milieu: Les Etats-Unis et le monde depuis la fin de la guerre froide*. Paris: Odile Jacob.

Mendelsohn, Barak. 2005. "Bringing the English School to America: Testing the Preservation-Seeking Quality of International Society." Paper prepared for the Forty-Sixth Annual Convention of the International Studies Association, Honolulu, March 1–5.

Merritt, Richard. 1995. *Democracy Imposed: U.S. Occupation Policy and the German Public, 1945–1949*. New Haven: Yale University Press.

Merritt, Richard, and Ann Merritt. 1980. *Public Opinion in Semisovereign Germany: The HICOG Surveys, 1949–1955*. Urbana: University of Illinois Press.

Meunier, Sophie. 2000. "The French Exception." *Foreign Affairs* 79, no. 4: 104–16.

———. 2003. "France's Double-Talk on Globalization." *French Politics, Culture and Society* 21, no. 1: 20–34.

Meyssan, Thierry. 2002. *L'effroyable imposture*. Paris: Carnot.

Miller, John J., and Mark Molesky. 2004. *Our Oldest Enemy: A History of America's Disastrous Relationship with France*. New York: Doubleday.

Mitchell, Timothy. 2004. "American Power and Anti-Americanism in the Middle East." In *Anti-Americanism*, edited by Andrew Ross and Kristin Ross, 87–105. New York: New York University Press.

Moaddel, Mansoor. 2003. "Public Opinion in Islamic Countries: Survey Results." *Footnotes* (American Sociological Association) 31, no. 1. Available from http://www. asanet.org/footnotes/jan03/indexthree.html.

Moamen, Al-Masri. 2005. "Web Threat: Jihad 'til Judgment Day: Got Most of Them . . . We'll Get the Rest." *Arab Times* online, February 3–4. osint@yahoogroups.com [last accessed February 3, 2005].

Moore, R. Laurence. 1970. *European Socialists and the American Promised Land*. New York: Oxford University Press.

More, Thomas. 1965. *Utopia*. Translated by Paul Turner. London: Penguin.

Moustafa, Tamir. 2004. "Protests Hint at New Chapter in Egyptian Politics." *Middle East Report* online. http://www.merip.org/mero/mero040904.html [last accessed April 9, 2005].

Mueller, John. 1994. *Policy and Opinion in the Gulf War*. Chicago: University of Chicago Press.

Najeeb, Usama, and Lindsey Wise. 2004. "Arab Satellite Coverage of U.S. Elections." *Transnational Broadcasting Studies Journal* 13. http://www.tbsjournal.com/Archives/Fall04/USelections.html.

Nathan, Hervé. 2004. "La concurrence entre les pays est très saine." *Libération*, December 31. LexisNexis [last accessed December 6, 2005].

Nau, Henry R. 2002. *At Home Abroad: Identity and Power in American Foreign Policy*. Ithaca: Cornell University Press.

New York Times. 2002. "French Leader Offers America Both Friendship and Criticism." September 8. LexisNexis [last accessed December 6, 2005].

———. 2004. "Are We Stingy? Yes." December 30, A22.

———. 2005. "Two Years Later." March 18, A20.

Nisbet, Erik C., Matthew C. Nisbet, Dietram A. Sheufle, and James E. Shanahan. 2004. "Public Diplomacy, Television News, and Muslim Opinion." *Press/Politics* 9, no. 2: 11–37.

Nolan, Mary. 2005. "Anti-Americanism and Americanization in Germany." *Politics & Society* 33, no. 1 (March): 88–122.

Nordholt, J. W. Schulte. 1986. "Anti-Americanism in European Culture: Its Early Manifestations." In *Anti-Americanism in Europe*, edited by Rob Kroes and Maarten van Rossem. Amsterdam: Free University Press.

Norris, Pippa, and Ronald Inglehart. 2004. *Sacred and Secular: Religion and Politics Worldwide*. New York: Cambridge University Press.

Nye, Joseph S., Jr. 2002. *The Paradox of American Power: Why the World's Only Superpower Can't Go It Alone*. New York: Oxford University Press.

———. 2004a. *Soft Power: The Means to Success in World Politics*. New York: Public Affairs.

———. 2004b. "You Can't Get Here from There." *New York Times*, November 29, A21.

O'Gorman, Edmundo. 1961. *The Invention of America: An Inquiry into the Historical Nature of the New World and the Meaning of Its History*. Westport, Conn.: Greenwood.

O'Neill, Barry. 1999. *Honor, Symbols, and War*. Ann Arbor: University of Michigan Press.

Ottoway, Marina. 2003. "Promoting Democracy in the Middle East: The Problem of U.S. Credibility." Middle East Series, Working Paper No. 35, March. Washington, D.C.: Carnegie Endowment for International Peace.

Palierse, Christophe. 2005. "McDonald's France table sur une 'croissance lente mais durable.'" *Les Echos*, February 8, 30.

Peel, Quentin. 2005. "Where Trade Comes before Politics." *Financial Times*, February 3, 17.

Pells, Richard. 1997. *Not Like Us: How Europeans Have Loved, Hated, and Transformed American Culture since World War II*. New York: Basic Books.

People's Daily. 2005a. "Meishi Minzhu Haishi Meishi Badao" [American-Style Democracy or American-Style Hegemonism?]. April 26. http://opinion.people.com.cn/GB/40604/3348745.html.

———. 2005b. "Tebie Cehua: Bushi Fang E Xu Duo Shi Shao Mei E Mao He Shen Li" [Special Scheme: Bush's Visit to Russia, Lots of Emptiness, Very Little Substance; U.S.-Russia Appear United, But in Essence Are Divided]. April 27. http://www.people.com.cn/GB/news/9719/9720/3351560.html.

Perlez, Jane. 2004. "The Impact Outside the Middle East." April 22. http://www.Bitterlemons-international.org.

Pew Global Attitudes Project. 2002. "What the World Thinks in 2002: How Global Publics View—Their Lives, Their Countries, the World, America." December. Washington, D.C.: Pew Research Center for the People and the Press.

———. 2003. "Views of a Changing World." June. Washington, D.C.: Pew Research Center for the People and the Press.

———. 2004. "A Year after Iraq War: Mistrust of America in Europe Ever Higher, Muslim Anger Persists." March 16. http://pewglobal.org/reports/display.php?PageID=796 [last accessed April 13, 2005].

———. 2005a. "American Character Gets Mixed Reviews." June 23. http://pewglobal.org/reports/display.php?ReportID=247 [last accessed December 6, 2005].

———. 2005b. "U.S. Image Up Slightly, But Still Negative: American Character Gets Mixed Reviews." Technical report of Pew Research Center for the People and the Press. http://pewglobal.org/reports/pdf/247.pdf [last accessed July 14, 2006].

———. 2005c. "Global Opinion 2005: The Spread of Anti-Americanism." Washington, D.C.: Pew Research Center for the People and the Press.

———. 2005d. "Global Opinion: The Spread of Anti-Americanism: A Review of Pew Global Attitudes Project Findings." http://people-press.org/commentary/display.php3?AnalysisID=104 [last accessed April 12, 2005].

———. 2005e. "Islamic Extremism: Common Concern for Muslim and Western Publics." July 14. http://pewglobal.org/reports/display.php?ReportID=248 [last accessed July 14, 2006].

Pew Research Center for the People and the Press. 2002. "What the World Thinks in 2002." http://people-press.org [last accessed May 3, 2005].

Pierson, Paul. 2000. "Increasing Returns, Path Dependence, and the Study of Politics." *American Political Science Review* 94, no. 2: 251–68.

PIPA (Program on International Policy Attitudes), University of Maryland, in conjunction with GlobeScan. 2005. "In 20 of 23 Countries Polled Citizens Want Europe to Be More Influential Than US." http://www.pipa.org/OnlineReports/EvalWorldPowers/LeadWorld_Apr05/LeadWorld_Apr05_rpt.pdf [last accessed April 4, 2005].

Pipes, Daniel. 2002. "A New Round of Anger and Humiliation: Islam after 9/11." In *Our Brave New World: Essays on the Impact of September 11*, edited by Wladyslaw Pleszczynski, 41–61. Stanford: Hoover Institution Press.

Plummer, Brenda Gayle. 1996. *Rising Winds: Black Americans and U.S. Foreign Affairs, 1935–1960*. Chapel Hill: University of North Carolina Press.

Polanyi, Karl. 1957 [1944]. *The Great Transformation: The Political and Economic Origins of Our Time.* Boston: Beacon Press.

Politi, James. 2003. "Perceptions of US Show Marked Decline." *Financial Times,* June 4, 2.

Polletta, Francesca. 2002. *Freedom Is an Endless Meeting.* Chicago: University of Chicago Press.

Pond, Elizabeth. 2004. *Friendly Fire: The Near-Death of the Transatlantic Alliance.* Washington, D.C.: European Union Studies Association/Brookings Institution Press.

PORI [Public Opinion Research Institute]. 1997. *Zhongguo Goutong: Zai Zhiliang Jiegou Zhong de Shenshi yu Sikao—Zhongguo Gongzhong Ribenguan Diaocha de Fenxi Baogao* [Chinese Communications: Study and Thought on the Structure of Quality—Research Report of Chinese Mass Opinions toward Japan]. Beijing: People's University of China Public Opinion Research Institute.

Priest, Dana. 2005. "Help from France in Covert Operations." *Washington Post,* July 3. LexisNexis [last accessed December 6, 2005].

Quatremer, Jean. 2005. "L'Europe promet une force de réaction rapide." *Libération,* January 11. LexisNexis [last accessed December 6, 2005].

Quinlan, Joseph, and Dan Hamilton. 2004. *Partners in Prosperity: The Changing Geography of the Transatlantic Economy.* Washington, D.C.: Brookings Institution.

Rabinovici, Doron, Ulrich Speck, and Natan Sznaider, eds. 2004. *Neuer Antisemitismus? Eine Globale Debatte.* Frankfurt: Suhrkamp.

Raynal, Abbé. 1813. *Philosophical and Political History of the Settlements and Trade of the Europeans in the East and West Indies.* Translated by J. O. Justamond. London: W. Baynes.

Renmin Wang [People's Net]. 2005a. "Lianheguo di 61 jie Renquan Huiyi zai Reneiwa Bimu" [The Closing of the 61st Meeting of the UN Human Rights Commission in Geneva]. April 22. http://world.people.com.cn/GB/1029/3343267.html.

———. 2005b. "Zhonguoren kan Zhong Mei Guanxi" [Chinese People See Sino-U.S. Relations]. March 2. http://www.people.com.cn/GB/paper68/14196/1264756.html.

Revel, Jean-François. 2003. *Anti-Americanism.* San Francisco: Encounter Books.

"Revisiting the Arab Street: Research from Within." 2005. Amman: Center for Strategic Studies, University of Jordan.

Rice, Condoleezza. 2005. "Remarks on the Second Anniversary of the Proliferation Security Initiative." May 31. http://www.state.gov/secretary/rm2005/46951.htm [last accessed June 1, 2005].

Riding, Alan. 2005. "France Detects a Cultural Threat in Google." *New York Times,* April 11, C4.

Ridyasmara, Rizki. 2003. "Intelektual dan Konsiprasi Perang Global" [Intellectuals and Global War Conspiracy]. *Majalah Sabili,* June 22.

Riker, William R. 1996. *The Strategy of Rhetoric: Campaigning for the American Constitution.* New Haven: Yale University Press.

Rising, David. 2005. "Groups Scour Europe for Iraq Fighters." osint@yahoogroups.com [last accessed March 5, 2005].

Roger, Philippe. 2005. *The American Enemy: The History of French Anti-Americanism.* Chicago: University of Chicago Press.

Rosen, Stanley. 2002. "The Wolf at the Door: Hollywood and the Film Market in China from 1994 to 2000." http://www.asianfilms.org/china/wolf.html [last accessed August 23, 2005].

———. 2004. "Chinese Media and Youth: Attitudes toward Nationalism and Internationalism." In *Chinese Media, Global Contexts,* edited by Chin-Chuan Lee, 97–118. New York: Routledge Curzon.

Rosenberg, Emily S. 1982. *Spreading the American Dream: American Economic and Cultural Expansion, 1890–1945.* New York: Hill and Wang.

Ross, Andrew, and Kristin Ross, eds. 2004. *Anti-Americanism.* New York: New York University Press.

Rousseau, Jean-Jacques. 1997. *The Social Contract.* Translated by Victor Gourevitch. Cambridge: Cambridge University Press.

Roussel, Frédérique. 2005. "Google, le nouvel ogre de la littérature." *Libération*, March 19. LexisNexis [last accessed December 6, 2005].

Roy, Olivier. 2004. *Globalized Islam: The Search for a New Ummah*. New York: Columbia University Press.

Ruan Zongze. 2002. "Xin Diguo lun yu Meiguo Zhenghe Waijiao" ["Neo-imperial Theory" and American "Integrated Foreign Relations"]. *Meiguo yanjiu* [American Studies] 3: 36–49.

Rubin, Barry. 2002. "The Real Roots of Arab Anti-Americanism." *Foreign Affairs* 81, no. 6: 73–79.

Rubin, Barry, and Judith Colp Rubin, eds. 2002. *Anti-American Terrorism and the Middle East: A Documentary Reader*. New York: Oxford University Press.

——. 2004. *Hating America: A History*. New York: Oxford University Press.

Rubinstein, Alvin Z., and Donald E. Smith, eds. 1985. *Anti-Americanism in the Third World: Implications for U.S. Foreign Policy*. New York: Praeger.

Rumelhart, David E. 1980. "Schemata: The Building Blocks of Cognition." In *Theoretical Issues in Reading Comprehension: Perspectives from Cognitive Psychology, Linguistics, Artificial Intelligence, and Education*, edited by R. J. Spiro, B. C. Bruce, and W. F. Brewer, 33–58. Hillsdale, N.J.: Erlbaum.

Russett, Bruce M. 1963. *Community and Contention: Britain and America in the Twentieth Century*. Cambridge: MIT Press.

Sabatier, Patrick. 2004. "Calculs." *Libération*, December 31. LexisNexis [last accessed December 6, 2005].

——. 2005. "Renforts." *Libération*, January 3. LexisNexis [last accessed December 6, 2005].

Sageman, Marc. 2004. *Understanding Terror Networks*. Philadelphia: University of Pennsylvania Press.

Saint-Martin, Emmanuel. 2005. "Google invente la bibliothèque universelle." *Le Point*, January 13. LexisNexis [last accessed December 6, 2005].

Sanger, David E. 2005a. "Month of Talks Fails to Bolster Nuclear Treaty: No Gain on Proliferation." *New York Times*, May 28, A1.

——. 2005b. "Rice to Discuss Antiproliferation Program." *New York Times*, May 31, A3.

Santayana, George. 1920. *Character and Opinion in the United States*. New York: Scribner's.

Sardar, Ziauddin, and Merry Wyn Davies. 2002. *Why Do People Hate America?* Cambridge, England: Icon Books.

Savage, Charlie. 2003. "Terror Inquiry Founders, No Arrest Made by French." *Boston Globe*, December 27, A2.

Schauer, Frederick. 2003. *Profiles, Probabilities, and Stereotypes*. Cambridge: Harvard University Press.

Schemm, Paul. 2003. "Egypt Struggles to Control Antiwar Protests." *Middle East Report* online. http://www.merip.org/mero/mero033103.html [last accessed March 31, 2005].

Schmidt, Vivien. 1996. *From State to Market? The Transformation of French Business and Government*. Cambridge: Cambridge University Press.

Schmitt, Eric. 2005. "Military Details Koran Incidents at Base in Cuba." *New York Times*, June 4, A1.

Schneiderman, Daniel. 2003. *Le cauchemar médiatique*. Paris: Éditions Denoël.

Schuman, Howard, Charlotte Steeh, and Lawrence Bobo. 1988. *Racial Attitudes in America*. Rev. ed. Cambridge: Harvard University Press.

Sciolino, Elaine. 2005a. "Europe Meets the New Face of Terrorism." *New York Times*, August 1, A1.

——. 2005b. "France Seizes 11 Accused of Plotting Iraq Attacks." *New York Times*, January 27, A8.

——. 2005c. "Spain Continues to Uncover Terrorist Plots, Officials Say." *New York Times*, March 13, A11.

Scott, William A. 1966. "Psychological and Social Correlates of International Images." In *International Behavior: A Social-Psychological Analysis*, ed. Herbert C. Kelman. New York: Holt, Rinehart, and Winston.

Seabrooke, Len. 2006. *The Social Sources of Financial Power: Domestic Legitimacy and International Financial Orders.* Ithaca: Cornell University Press.

Sengupta, Somini, and Salmon Masood. 2005. "Guantánamo Comes to Define U.S. to Muslims: A Champion of Rights Is Accused of Torture." *New York Times,* May 21, A1.

Shambaugh, David. 1991. *Beautiful Imperialist: China Perceives America, 1972–1990.* Princeton: Princeton University Press.

——. "Where Are U.S.-China Relations Headed?" Testimony to the Senate Foreign Relations Committee, East Asian and Pacific Affairs Subcommittee, May 1.

Shanker, Thom. 2005. "Inquiry by U.S. Finds 5 Cases of Koran Harm: No 'Credible Evidence' Tied to Toilet Claim." *New York Times,* May 27, A1.

Sharp, Jeremy. 2005. *U.S. Foreign Assistance to the Middle East.* Congressional Research Service Report for Congress RL32260, February 17.

Shen Jiru. 2002. "Guojia Zhanlue yu Kongbuzhuyi" [National Strategy and Terrorism]. In *Kongbuzhuyi Suyuan* [The Source of Terrorism], edited by Yizhou Wang, 152–81. Beijing: Social Science Documents Press.

Shin Gi-Wook. 1996. "South Korean Anti-Americanism: A Comparative Perspective." *Asian Survey* 36: 787–803.

Shiraev, Eric, and Vladislav Zubok. 2000. *Anti-Americanism in Russia: From Stalin to Putin.* New York: Palgrave.

Shklar, Judith N. 1984. *Ordinary Vices.* Cambridge: Harvard University Press.

Shorrock, Tim. 1986. "The Struggle for Democracy in South Korea in the 1980s and the Rise of Anti-Americanism." *Third World Quarterly* 8: 1195–1218.

Skrentny, John. 1998. "The Effect of the Cold War on African-American Civil Rights: America and the World Audience, 1945–1968." *Theory and Society* 27: 237–85.

Smelser, Neil J. 1998. "The Rational and the Ambivalent in the Social Sciences." *American Sociological Review* 63, no. 1: 1–16.

Smith, Adam. 1981 [1776]. *An Inquiry into the Nature and Causes of the Wealth of Nations.* Vol. 2. Edited by R. H. Campbell and A. S. Skinner. Indianapolis: Liberty Fund.

Smith, Craig S. 2005. "A Dutch Soccer Riddle: Jewish Regalia without Jews." *New York Times,* March 28, A4.

Smith, Lee. 2005. "Bush, the Great Shiite Liberator." *New York Times,* May 1, D1.

Smith, Steven K., and Douglas A. Wertman. 1992. *U.S.–West European Relations during the Reagan Years: The Perspective of West European Publics.* New York: St. Martin's.

Sniderman, Paul M., and Edward G. Carmines. 1997. *Reaching beyond Race.* Cambridge: Harvard University Press.

Sniderman, Paul M., Pierangelo Peri, Rui J. P. de Figueredo Jr., and Thomas Piazza. 2000. *The Outsider: Prejudice and Politics in Italy.* Princeton: Princeton University Press.

Sniderman, Paul M., and Thomas Piazza. 2002. *Black Pride and Black Prejudice.* Princeton: Princeton University Press.

Sombart, Werner. 1976 [1906]. *Why Is There No Socialism in the United States?* Translated by Patricia M. Hocking and C. T. Husbands. White Plains, N.Y.: International Arts and Sciences Press.

Spiro, Herbert J. 1988. "Anti-Americanism in Western Europe." *Annals of the American Academy of Political and Social Science* 497: 120–32.

Starobin, Paul. 2003. "The French Were Right." *National Journal,* November 7. http://nationaljournal.com/members/news/2003/11/1107nj1.htm [last accessed December 6, 2005].

Stecklow, Steve. 2005. "Virtual Battle: How a Global Web of Activists Gives Coke Problems in India." *Wall Street Journal,* June 7, A1.

Steinberg, David. 2005. *Korean Attitudes toward the United States: Changing Dynamics.* Armonk, N.Y.: M. E. Sharpe.

Stephan, Alexander, ed. 2005. *Americanization and Anti-Americanism: The German Encounter with American Culture after 1945*. New York: Berghahn Books.

Stern, Jessica. 1999. *The Ultimate Terrorists*. Cambridge: Harvard University Press.

———. 2003. *Terror in the Name of God: Why Religious Militants Kill*. New York: Ecco.

Stimson, James A. 1991. *Public Opinion in America: Moods, Cycles, and Swings*. Boulder: Westview.

Stockmann, Daniela. Forthcoming. "The Chinese News Media and Public Opinion: Adaptation of a Propaganda Machine or Instrument for Political Change?" PhD diss., University of Michigan.

Strauss, Claudia, and Naomi Quinn. 1997. *A Cognitive Theory of Cultural Meaning*. Cambridge: Cambridge University Press.

Strauss, David. 1978. *Menace in the West: The Rise of French Anti-Americanism in Modern Times*. Westport, Conn.: Greenwood Press.

Sweig, Julia E. 2006. *Friendly Fire: Losing Friends and Making Enemies in the Anti-American Century*. New York: Public Affairs.

Tai Chong-Soo, Erick J. Peterson, and Ted Robert Gurr. 1973. "Internal versus External Sources of Anti-Americanism: Two Comparative Studies." *Journal of Conflict Resolution* 17, no. 3: 455–88.

Tajfel, Henry. 1981. *Human Groups and Social Categories: Studies in Social Psychology*. Cambridge: Cambridge University Press.

———. 1982. *Social Identity and Intergroup Relations*. Cambridge: Cambridge University Press.

Tang Renmo. 2004. "Meiguo 'Xindiguo Zhanlue' de Youlai ji Tezheng" [The Origins and Characteristics of the U.S. "Neo-Imperial Strategy."] *Heping yu Fazhan* [Peace and Development] 1: 13–14.

Tarrow, Sidney. 1998. *Power in Movement*. New York: Cambridge University Press.

Taviani, Paolo Imelio, et al., eds. 1994. *Accounts and Letters of the Second, Third, and Fourth Voyages of Christopher Columbus*. Rome: Istituto Poligrafico e Zecca dello Stato.

Telhami, Shibley. 2005. *Reflections of Hearts and Minds*. Washington, D.C.: Brookings Institution.

Teodori, Massimo. 2002. *Maledetti Americani: Destra, sinistra e cattolici; Storia del pregiudizio antiamericano*. Milan: Mondadori.

———. 2003. *Benedetti Americani: Dall'alleanza Atlantica alla guerra al terrorismo*. Milan: Mondadori.

Terror Free Tomorrow. 2005. "A Major Change of Public Opinion in the Muslim World: Results from a New Poll of Indonesians." February. http://www.terrorfreetomorrow.org [last accessed April 12, 2005].

Tessler, Mark. 2003. "Arab and Muslim Political Attitudes: Stereotypes and Evidence from Survey Research." *International Studies Perspectives* 4, no. 2: 175–81.

Tiesenhausen Cave, Friederike. 2005. "Aux armes citoyens pour l'internet!" *Financial Times*, March 12. LexisNexis [last accessed December 6, 2005].

Tilly, Charles. 1978. *From Mobilization to Revolution*. Reading, Mass: Addison-Wesley.

Timmerman, Kenneth R. 2004. *The French Betrayal of America*. New York: Crown Forum.

Toinet, Marie-France. 1988. "French Pique and Piques French." *Annals of the American Academy of Political and Social Science* 497 (May): 133–41.

Tong-a Ilbo. 2000. "Multinational Citizens' Poll on Current States surrounding the Korean Peninsula." December 4.

Tocqueville, Alexis de. 1994 [1835]. *Democracy in America*. New York: Alfred A. Knopf.

Turner, John C. 1987. *Rediscovering the Social Group*. Oxford: Basil Blackwell.

Tuschhoff, Christian. 2002. "The Ties That Bind: Allied Commitment and NATO before and after September 11." *German Issues* 27: 71–95.

———. 2003. "Why NATO Is Still Relevant." *International Politics* 40, no. 1 (March): 101–20.

Tversky, Amos, and Daniel Kahneman. 1986. "Rational Choice and the Framing of Decisions." *Journal of Business* 59, no. 4: S251–78. Reprinted in Daniel Kahneman and Amos Tversky, eds. 2000. *Choices, Values and Frames*, 209–23. Cambridge: Cambridge University Press.

United Nations General Assembly. 2005. "Resolution Adopted by the General Assembly." United Nations Document A/RES/60/1, October 24.

University of Maryland. 2002. "Perspectives toward the United States in Selected Newspapers of the People's Republic of China." Report for the U.S. China Security Review Commission by the Institute for Global Chinese Affairs and the Department of Communication, University of Maryland. http://www.comm.umd.edu/news/publications/ChinaMediaReport.pdf.

U.S. Congress, House of Representatives, 2003. "Turkey's Future Direction and U.S.-Turkey Relations." Hearing of the Europe Subcommittee of the House International Relations Committee, October 1.

U.S. State Department. 2005. *Section 2207 Report on Iraq Relief and Reconstruction, Bureau of Resource Management*. January 5. http://www.state.gov/m/rm/rls/2207/jan2005/html [last accessed March 16, 2005].

Vaisse, Justin. 2003. "American Francophobia Takes a New Turn." *French Politics, Culture and Society* 21, no. 2 (Summer): 33–49.

Van Deburg, William L. 1992. *New Day in Babylon*. Chicago: University of Chicago Press.

Védrine, Hubert, and Dominique Moisi. 2001. *France in an Age of Globalization*. Washington, D.C.: Brookings Institution.

Verba, Sidney, Kay Lehman Schlozman, and Henry Brady. 1995. *Voice and Equality: Civic Voluntarism in American Politics*. Cambridge: Harvard University Press.

Vernet, Henri, and Thomas Cantaloube. 2004. *Chirac contre Bush: L'autre guerre*. Paris: Jean-Claude Lattès.

Vertzberger, Yaacov Y. I. 1990. *The World in Their Minds: Information Processing, Cognition, and Perception in Foreign Policy Decisionmaking*. Stanford: Stanford University Press.

Vielemeier, Ludger. 1991. "Part Three: The European Union in Public Opinion Polls, 1945–50." In *Documents on the History of European Integration*, ed. Walter Lipgens and Wilfried Loth, vol. 4, *Transnational Organization of Political Parties and Pressure Groups in the Struggle for European Union, 1945–50*, 574–626. New York: Walter de Gruyter.

Wachman, Alan. 2005. *Why Taiwan*. Unpublished manuscript, Fletcher School of Law and Diplomacy.

Waldron, Arthur. 2003. "The Chinese Sickness." *Commentary* 116, no. 1: (July–August): 36–42.

Wallerstein, Immanuel. 2003. *The Decline of American Power: The U.S. in a Chaotic World*. New York: New Press.

Waltz, Kenneth N. 1979. *Theory of International Politics*. Reading, Mass.: Addison-Wesley.

Wang Jincun. 2002. "Daguo Guanxi yu Kongbuzhuyi" [Great Power Relations and Terrorism]. In *Kongbuzhuyi Suyuan* [The Source of Terrorism], edited by Yizhou Wang, 110–51. Beijing: Social Science Documents Press.

Wang Jisi. 2003. "Meiguo Baquan de Luoji" [The Logic of American Hegemony]. *China Daily*, August 21. http://www.chinadaily.com.cn/gb/doc/2003-08/21/content_257020.htm.

———. 2004. "From a Paper Tiger to Real Leviathan: China's Contrasting Images of the United States since 1949." Paper prepared for Center for Strategic and International Studies conference "Chinese Images of the United States," Washington, D.C., April. http://www.csis.org/isp/chineseimages/cius_jisi.pdf.

Wang Yizhou. 2000. "Guanyu Duojihua de Ruogan Sikao" [A Few Thoughts concerning Multipolarity]. Unpublished paper, Institute of World Politics and Economics, Beijing.

———. 2002. "Anti-Terrorism Struggle Needs to Search for [Terrorism's] Basic Source." In *Kongbuzhuyi Suyuan* [The Source of Terrorism], edited by Yizhou Wang, 1–10. Beijing: Social Science Documents Press.

Waterman, Shaun. 2005. "Eurojihadis: A New Generation of Terror." http://www.upi.com/view.cfm?StoryID=20050601-072835-2550r [last accessed June 2, 2005].

Watkins, Eric. 2005. "Yemen's Innovative Approach to the War on Terror." *Terrorism Monitor* 3, no. 4. osint@yahoogroups.com [last accessed February 24, 2005].

Watson, James. 1997. "Transnationalism, Localization, and Fast Foods in East Asia." In *Golden Arches East: McDonald's in East Asia*, edited by James Watson, 1–38. Stanford: Stanford University Press.

Weekley, Kathleen. 1996. "From Vanguard to Rearguard: The Theoretical Roots of the Crisis of the Communist Party in the Philippines." In *The Revolution Falters: The Left in Philippine Politics after 1986*, edited by Patricio N. Abinales, 117–45. Ithaca: Cornell University Press.

Weisman, Steven. 2005. "Europeans Said to Keep Embargo on Arms to China." *New York Times*, March 22, A1.

Wendt, Alexander. 1999. *Social Theory of International Politics*. Cambridge: Cambridge University Press.

Wertsch, James V. 2002. *Voices of Collective Remembering*. Cambridge: Cambridge University Press.

Whitaker, Beth Elise. 2005. "Exporting the USA Patriot Act: Democracy and the War on Terror in the Third World." Paper delivered at the Forty-Sixth Annual Convention of the International Studies Association, Honolulu, March 1–5.

Wickham, Carrie Rosefsky. 2004. "The Problem with Coercive Democratization." *Muslim World Journal of Human Rights* 1, no. 1. http://www.bepress.com/mwjhr/vol1/iss1/art6/.

Wiktorowicz, Quintan, ed. 2004. *Islamic Activism: A Social Movement Theory Approach*. Bloomington: Indiana University Press.

Winer, Jonathan M., and Trifin J. Roule. 2002. "Fighting Terrorist Finance." *Survival* 44, no. 3 (Autumn): 87–104.

Wistrich, Robert S. 1992. *Anti-Semitism: The Longest Hatred*. New York: Pantheon.

———. 2003. "The Old-New Anti-Semitism." *National Interest* 72 (Summer): 59–71.

Woodnutt, Tom, and Greg Burnside. 2004. "Wake Up and Smell the Cynicism: Anti-Americanism and Its Implications." Paper 25, Green Light International. http//:www.greenlighresearch.com/press_media/paper-25.pdf [last accessed March 16, 2006].

World Tourism Organization. 2003. *Yearbook of Tourism Statistics*. Lisbon 2003.

———. 2004. *Tourism Market Trends*. http://www.world-tourism.org.

Wu Xianbin. 2004. "Bushi Zhengfu dui Tai Zhengce de Tedian ji qi Yuanyin" [Origins and Characteristics of the Bush Administration's Taiwan Policy]. *Dangdai Yatai* [Contemporary Asia-Pacific] 3: 16–23.

Xinhua Net. 2005. "ZhongGong Zhongyang Guanyu Jiaqiang he Gaijin Dang Feng Jianshe de Jueding" [The CCP Central Committee concerning the Decision to Strengthen and Improve the Construction of Party Practice]. August 25. http://news.xinhuanet.com/ziliao/2003-01/20/content_698248.htm [last accessed 25 August 2005].

Xu Guangqiu. 1997. "The Rise of Anti-Americanism in China." *Asian Thought and Society* 12, no. 66: 208–26.

———. 1998. "Anti-American Nationalism in China: Causes and Formation." In *Image, Perception, and the Making of US-China Relations*, edited by Hongshan Li and Zhaohui Hong, 233–56. Lanham, Md.: University Press of America.

Yan Yunxiang. 1997. "McDonald's in Beijing: The Localization of Americana." In *Golden Arches East: McDonald's in East Asia*, edited by James Watson, 39–76. Stanford: Stanford University Press.

———. 2000. "Of Hamburger and Social Space: Consuming McDonald's in Beijing." In *The Consumer Revolution in Urban China*, edited by Deborah Davis, 201–25. Berkeley: University of California Press.

Yang Yunzhong. 2001. "Dui 21 Shiji Chuye Meiguo dui Hua Zhanlue he Zhong Mei Guanxi Zhongda Wenti de Sikao" [Thoughts on U.S. China Strategy and Major Questions in Sino-

U.S. Relations at the Beginning of the 21st Century]. *Dangdai Yatai* [Contemporary Asia-Pacific] 5: 3–12.

Yang Yusheng. 1997. *Zhonguoren de Meiguo Guan—yi ge Lishi de Kaocha* [The Chinese People's View of the United States—a Historical Interpretation]. Shanghai: Fudan University Press.

Yuan Peng. 2001. "9.11 Shijian yu Zhong Mei Guanxi" [The 9/11 Incident and Sino-U.S. Relations]. *Xiandai Guoji Guanxi* [Contemporary International Relations] 11: 19–23.

Zajonc, R. B. 1982. "On the Primacy of Affect." *American Psychologist* 39: 117–23.

Zaller, John. 1992. *The Nature and Origins of Mass Opinion*. New York: Cambridge University Press.

Zeitlin, Jonathan, and Gary Herrigel, eds. 2000. *Americanization and Its Limits: Reworking U.S. Technology and Management in Post-War Europe and Japan*. Oxford: Oxford University Press.

Zhai Zheng. 2002. *Zhong Mei Liang Guo zai Duifang Zhuyao Meiti Zhong de Xiezhao—dui (Renmin Ribao) he (Niuyue Shibao) 1998 Nian Baodao de Duibi Fenxi* [The Mutual Portrayal of China and the United States in Important Media—Comparative Analysis of 1998 Reporting in the *People's Daily* and the *New York Times*]. http://www.edu.cn/20030728/3088768.shtml [last accessed August 24, 2005].

Zhang Hongyi. 1994. "Meiguo de Jiazhi Guan he Women de Jiazhi Guan de Quxiang" [Trends in the American Value System and in Our Value System]. *Zhenli de Zhuiqiu* [Pursuit of Truth] 3: 28–31.

Zhang Mingcang. 2004. "Meiguo 'Fankong Zhanzheng' Zhong de liu ge Beilun" [Six Paradoxes in the American "Anti-Terror War"]. *Fujian Luntan: Renwen yu Shehuikexue ban* [Fujian Forum: Humanities and Social Sciences Version] 5: 48–52.

Zhang Xueli and Xu Peide. 2003. "Meiguo dui Tai Junshi Zhanlue Geju he Zoushi" [The Situation and Direction of U.S. Military Strategy toward Taiwan]. In *The World, the United States, and China*, edited by Shulong Chu and Geng Qin, 261–70. Beijing: Qinghua University Press.

Zhao Dingxin. 2005. "Differential Participation and the Nature of the 1999 Anti-U.S. Beijing Student Demonstration." Paper presented at the workshop "Identity, Nationalism, and Chinese Foreign Policy," Fairbank Center for East Asian Research, Harvard University, March.

Zhao Min. 2001. "Zhonguoren kan Meiguo" [The Chinese People View America]. In *Zhong Mei Changqi Duihua* [China–United States Long-term Dialogue], edited by Tao Meixin and Zhao Min, 3–20. Beijing: China Academy of Social Sciences Press.

Zhao Suisheng. 1998. "A State-Led Nationalism: The Patriotic Education Campaign in Post-Tiananmen China." *Communist and Post-Communist Studies* 31, no. 3: 287–302.

Zick, Andreas, and Beate Küpper. 2005. "'Die sind doch selbst schuld, wenn man was gegen sie hat!'" In *Deutsche Zustände 3*, edited by Wilhelm Heitmeyer, 129–43. Frankfurt: Suhrkamp.

Zogby International. 2004. "Impressions of America 2004: How Arabs View America, How Arabs Learn about America." http://www.zogby.com [last accessed April 12, 2004].

Zogby, James. 2002. "What Arabs Think." http://www.zogby.com.

——. 2005. "Saudis Reject Bin Laden and Terrorism." http://www.mediamonitors.net/zogby99.html [last accessed May 3, 2005].

Zwerman, Gilda, Patricia G. Steinhoff, and Donatella della Porta. 2000. "Disappearing Social Movements: Clandestinity in the Cycle of New Left Protest in the U.S., Japan, Germany, and Italy." *Mobilization* 5, no. 1: 85–104.

Contributors

John R. Bowen is the Dunbar-Van Cleve Professor in Arts and Sciences at Washington University in St. Louis.

Giacomo Chiozza is an Assistant Professor in the Travers Department of Political Science at the University of California, Berkeley.

Pierangelo Isernia is a Professor of Political Science at the University of Siena.

Alastair Iain Johnston is the Governor James Albert Noe and Linda Noe Laine Professor of China in World Affairs in the Government Department at Harvard University.

Peter J. Katzenstein is the Walter S. Carpenter, Jr. Professor of International Studies at Cornell University.

David M. Kennedy is the Donald J. McLachlan Professor of History at Stanford University.

Robert O. Keohane is a Professor of International Affairs at the Woodrow Wilson School of Public and International Affairs at Princeton University.

Marc Lynch is an Associate Professor of Government at Williams College.

Doug McAdam is a Professor of Sociology at Stanford University.

Sophie Meunier is a Research Associate in Public and International Affairs at Princeton University.

Daniela Stockmann is a PhD candidate in the Department of Political Science at the University of Michigan.

Index

Page numbers with an *f* indicate figures; those with a *t* indicate tables.

343